Islands in Time

A Natural and Cultural History of the Islands of Maine

Philip Conkling

Photographs by Peter Ralston

Revised and Expanded Third Edition

ISLAND INSTITUTE
ROCKLAND, MAINE

To all the islanders who taught us about their islands,

and especially to Betsy Wyeth, Hoddy Hildreth, Louis Cabot and Polly Guth

who helped launch the Island Institute

Preface

Another World Apart

They say anything worth doing is worth overdoing, which is a thin excuse for another edition of a book originally published three decades ago. But in island communities, celebrated as places resistant to change, a lot *has* changed. In fact a lot has changed in island communities even during the past dozen years since publication of the second edition of *Islands in Time.*

For starters, island populations are growing. A new year-round island community—the archipelago's 15th—has emerged on Great Diamond Island in Casco Bay after decades of conflict between the redevelopment of the historic Fort McKinley complex and a traditional "cottage" community at the other end of the island. Both ends of the island now have year-round settlers, struggling to integrate with each other.

For another, the three largest island communities in Penobscot Bay—Islesboro, North Haven and Vinalhaven—islanders and their friends, including Maine's Department of Education, have invested over $30 million in new and renovated schools in recognition of the critical centrality of quality education to the viability of year-round island communities to attract new settlers. The eight one- and two-room schoolhouses among the smaller outer islands are now all connected via videoconferencing technology that allows them to share classes, course material and even students, to reduce the pressures on parents who might otherwise decide to leave the islands' smallest schools for opportunities elsewhere for their children.

Downeast, Frenchboro's long effort to attract young families to settle on this remote part of the coast has succeeded in filling an island school that earlier had been reduced to a single student. On the very much less remote island of Great Cranberry, the island school has been closed for almost a decade, threatening its viability as a year-round community, although a community discussion is underway among young parents with kids as to whether the town should reopen the school there or send the young students on the mailboat to neighboring Islesford.

Politically, islanders have overcome the fierce territoriality that is a defining feature of island culture, and have organized themselves into the Maine Islands Coalition. The coalition has successfully advocated for a constitutional referendum granting property-tax reduction to commercial fishing properties along the coast, the passage of three working waterfront bonds to permanently protect access for fishermen and a multimillion-dollar housing bond to help finance affordable properties in high-cost island communities. That's a pretty good track record of cooperation for a bunch of fiercely independent individualists.

Lobsters are still the main economic driver in island communities—roughly 20 times as many year-round island residents hold lobster licenses than Maine residents as a whole. A half-century of conservation efforts enforced by the lobstermen themselves continue to result in abundant harvests, although at lower prices since the Great Recession took hold. Salmon aquaculture, which looked like a promising economic opportunity for remote communities and was moving westward from its Washington County stronghold along Maine's chain of islands, was halted in its tracks by a combination of overseas competition and environmental lawsuits.

I am especially gratified to be working on this new edition with Peter Ralston, using his iconic images to illustrate a corner of the world we have spent three decades exploring together in annual issues of *Island Journal*—but for the first time now in *Islands in Time*.

The Island Institute, which he and I—a pair of transplanted outsiders—launched two years after the first edition of *Islands in Time* appeared, has also become an accepted partner in island and working waterfront communities, with a staff of 40 or so professionals and a substantial endowment to ensure it will be a permanent part of the Maine island world.

This edition of *Islands in Time* thus differs from previous ones, by including not only the history and natural history of the islands, but also their present circumstances and future prospects. I have chosen to weave more personal stories into the narrative, including how I came to learn about the islands' history and ecology, as well as how my experiences in island communities during the past three decades has influenced my worldview. Thus the opening chapter is new; the next eight chapters retain their original focus, but have been substantially rewritten, and the last five chapters are entirely new.

Islands make you both proud and humble. They require you to be careful, to be thoughtful about your neighbors—whom you cannot escape—and to understand the intimate interconnections of all parts of island life. As I wrote in the first edition, "Out there between the place where you take your last dry step on the mainland and the faint horizon of your mind's eye, lies another world apart."

Islands in Time

Publication of *Islands in Time* was made possible by generous and deeply appreciated support
from The Charles Engelhard Foundation and Sally Engelhard Pingree
special friends for many years

Island Institute
386 Main Street, Box 648, Rockland, Maine 04841
www.islandinstitute.org

Islands in Time © Philip Conkling, 2011
Photographs © Peter Ralston, 2011, unless otherwise noted
Book Design and Layout: Paige Garland Parker
Editors: Polly Saltonstall and David Platt
Copy Editors: Melissa Hayes and Joyce Houston
Editorial Assistant: Kathy Allen
Production Advisor: Bridget Leavitt
Scanning: Warner Graphics and Jim Nickelson
Printing: J.S. McCarthy Printers, Augusta, Maine

ISBN Number: 978-0-9835613-0-9

Islands in Time

A Natural and Cultural History of the Islands of Maine

CHAPTER 1

Islandness

Though I had lived by the shore all my life, I seemed never to have been near the sea till then.
The smell of tar and salt was something new. I saw many old sailors, with rings in their ears . . .
and if I had seen as many kings or archbishops I could not have been more delighted.
I was going to sea myself; to sea in a schooner . . . bound for an unknown island.

—Robert Louis Stevenson, *Treasure Island*

Washington County
shoreline, near Addison;
(Facing) Petit Manan
Point with Petit Manan
Island in distance

I came to the Maine islands not as a resident or tourist, but to collect baseline ecological information on a dozen islands in the summer of 1975. I was in graduate school in forestry and desperately hoped to work in the north Maine woods, but there was a serious housing recession at that time, reducing demand for logs and lumber, so instead I got a summer job working for the Maine Chapter of The Nature Conservancy.

The Nature Conservancy wanted to identify ecological resources on islands they owned but had never visited. They also wanted me to survey the ecological impact of the Hurricane Island Outward Bound School's programs, which put students on these islands with a jug of water and a sleeping bag and expected them to eat their way across the environments The Nature Conservancy volunteers were supposed to protect. The experiences of that summer changed not just the trajectory of my graduate studies, but the rest of my life.

I found a small house to rent on the coast of Washington County down on Petit Manan Point that pokes its ledgy fingernails out into the ocean more than 10 miles from Route 1. In between expeditions to the islands to conduct field work, I began to hang out with young fishermen of the Point who fished among the islands of Pigeon Hill Bay, and who knew the histories of the families who had once lived on the islands where I would be collecting data. One of those fishermen had recently rerigged his lobster boat and invited me to go tuna-fishing with him offshore. I jumped at the chance.

The Harpooner

JULY 9, 1975, 4 A.M.—In the first faint hint of dawn, we cross over the legendary shoals between Petit Manan Point and Petit Manan Island and lay a course 30 miles south-southwest, to begin searching for an abstract point on the chart where a school of giant bluefin tuna were last seen. Jim Salisbury has spent his spare time this past spring rigging his boat with a crow's nest and a bow pulpit. And with a pair of harpoons handcrafted from two ash trees from his woodlot, Salisbury has got it in his mind to throw an iron into a bluefin tuna.

The day breaks over an oily gray ocean swell 30 miles offshore as we round up under the furthermost rocky outpost off the Maine coast—lonely Mount Desert Rock. Salisbury scrambles aloft into the tuna tower and begins running hour-long transects away from the Rock, scanning the surface where the sky meets the sea. After hours of silent searching, Salisbury puts the helm over sharply.

Looking out in the direction of our new heading, Salisbury's mate, Al Richardson, and I are aware of the faint outlines of gray gulls darting and wheeling over the gray ocean surface. Jim quietly calls Al to the helm in the crow's nest while he moves quickly, cat-like, down to the deck to check the bronze-tipped harpoon and the 150 fathoms of line attached to the buoy that have been carefully

rigged and stowed aft. Al has slowly and steadily opened the throttle to run toward where the birds are hovering and dipping. Meanwhile, Jim has moved into the bow pulpit with the long harpoon and stands leaning slightly forward, arms raised, silhouetted with an ancient weapon for catching the largest fish in the sea.

Al has pushed the throttle up to its maximum and has closed with the flock of gulls 40 or 50 yards ahead. On the flat gray ocean surface you see only the slight ripple of a wake—the telltale sign that there are giant bluefin tuna here, six to eight feet below the surface. Where there is one bluefin, there is likely to be a school of anywhere between 15 and 50 individuals varying in size between 300 and perhaps 1,000 pounds, and the two fishermen must concentrate on a single thought without talking; two minds, one vision.

Jim is following a single bluefin, pointing the harpoon at its wake while Al tries to follow the giant slalom course of the school still traveling at a fraction of the speed of which they are capable. The fish nearest the surface are only a boat length or so away, and

even I can see in the green-gray depths the flashing silver sheen of their immense sides. It is rare that a harpooner gets a second shot.

In one graceful motion, Jim launches the harpoon and an instant later we know he's ironed a giant because the 3/8-inch line is disappearing overboard in a high-pitched whine as the tub of line uncoils like a shot spring. On deck Jim scrambles back aft to make sure the line does not foul. Within a very short period of time, all 150 fathoms of line ending in a keg buoy are making a broken field pattern across the water's surface.

After three hours of Jim's and Al's combined efforts, most of the 150 fathoms of line have been hauled back on deck and the darted bluefin is careening from port to starboard quarter in its last bursts of effort. After another quarter of an hour of skill versus instinct and muscle versus muscle, the bluefin is gaffed alongside. Jim deftly reaches in and cuts the gill artery, an important consideration for the highly discriminating Japanese palate, which can tell not only a well-bled fish, but also the fat content of its flesh. The iridescent sheen of this great creature alongside transfixes all of us in a moment of transcendent pride and humility as 600 pounds of the North Atlantic's evolutionary masterpiece is hauled aboard.

Islands of Solitude

Located east of Petit Manan Point, Flint Island is one of Maine's outermost islands where I planned to camp for three days as the first stop on my Nature Conservancy island surveys.

Jim Salisbury dropped me off on a small shingle beach and arranged to pick me up three days later. For two days, I collected botanical specimens, made wildlife observations, ran transects through the forest, collected rock samples and thought I had all the pieces I needed for a detailed ecological description.

The morning Salisbury and his boat the JESSE was to arrive to pick me up, I ate my last food for breakfast, struck the tent, and wrote up field notes while waiting for the lobster boat to emerge out of the dense fog. I did not at first dwell on the condition of the fog, its dungeon thickness, but slowly over the hours of waiting, a contingent reality crept into my consciousness: I was not going ashore and I had no food.

The days are long in June at this latitude, so I re-pitched my tent and tried not to think about eating. After a long, slow afternoon, I crawled into the tent early, counting on sleep to mask my hunger.

The following morning I awoke early, a little-light headed from not having eaten in a day, and walked down the shingled shore and up toward the outer cliffs, navigating around the craggy island edges over which spruce boughs were combing tiny droplets of water from the wet breath of fog. The sea hardly seemed to move; it just murmured on the beach at slack tide. At such times everything is very close. The universe is narrowed down to a few feet, compressed into a tiny field of view. The air was still and heavy and silent.

At that moment, directly in front of me, not 20 feet from the island's edge, out of the fog at eye level burst two magnificent adult bald eagles: one a female, slightly larger

Flat Island, Pleasant Bay looking east

than her mate following close off her outboard wing. They flew by, wingtip to wingtip, out of the fog—as startled to see me as I them—and then careened sharply away and were gone in an instant. But I heard and in the damp air felt the cool rush of wind from their wings on my face.

In that single moment I felt a sensation telescoping itself outward, beyond Flint's outermost realm, into a foggy white light beyond boat times and the lists of names of species I had left a world away at the campsite. I felt I was being swept from the island and transported to some outer place in the universe.

Something else also happened that day, which did not make as great an initial impression, but kept working beneath the level of consciousness. That morning while waiting for the fog to lift and the lobster boat to appear, I had decided to make another transect through Flint Island's dense interior. In a part of the island that I had not seen previously, I came across a large pile of fieldstones that had been cleared from a pasture and the wooden remnants of an old house foundation. It was hard to believe that someone had once lived on Flint. When I got ashore and began to ask about Flint Island's history, no one knew of anyone who might have once lived on this remote rocky outcrop. Who were they? It was as if history had dematerialized.

Although it took many more years for those experiences to take shape in my mind, it began to occur to me that islands are a kind of an archetypal landscape we carry around in our minds—that they are spirited places whose inhabitants never fully leave—and it is important to consider carefully how to keep these worlds balanced between accessibility and inaccessibility because in one single moment of solitude, they provide our callous, name-collecting natures something as precious as insight itself.

The Pure Essence of Defiance

Another experience seared into the memory from that first island summer occurred toward the end of my survey work for The Nature Conservancy. I had been dropped off on Brimstone Island, one of a half-dozen islands in a group south of Vinalhaven. All were treeless with grassy meadows burnished a tawny gold in the late summer sun. I was to spend the day collecting detailed species lists of flora and fauna.

Brimstone is named for its beautiful, peculiar bedrock, which pokes like dark bones from beneath its thin skin of heath. Pieces of brimstone have been quarried into billions of bits by pounding seas and prying ice and piled onto a pair of steep cobble beaches on either side of the island. On a calm day you can land on these indescribably smooth blue-black stones which the sea's swash has polished to a high sheen. If you look hard enough, you can find one without so much as a hairline fracture to serve as a lucky piece as old as time itself.

As I walked around Brimstone's treeless expanse, I came to magnificent cliffs that face south with a view that stretches out toward the open Atlantic. I crept carefully along a ledge, one hand clutching my notebook, the other on the cliff, when I ran out of ledge at a crevice too wide to cross. I was about to turn back when I was startled to see a fledgling raven staring at me across the crevice at eye level about four feet away. For some time, neither the fledgling nor I moved. We stared at each other for long moments, neither of us flinching.

Gull remains,
Brimstone Island

Then the mass of black feathers launched itself off its ledge, but instead of flying, it fluttered downward with a broken wing like Icarus and landed a few hundred feet out from the base of the cliff, a mass of wild dark feathers scattered in the sea. Within seconds, a gull flying in toward Brimstone cut a tight circle and shrieked above the young raven, which was trying to paddle toward shore with its one good wing. The air, which had been quiet moments before, became animated with the alarm cries of gulls that were suddenly wheeling and diving at the hapless dark creature in the water. It was terrible to watch.

The shrieking of the gulls, which soon numbered a score, was met by the hoarse defiant croak from the raven, which knew the gulls meant to kill it. The raven turned on its back and met each swoop of a gull by arching itself upward out of the water to parry their attacks with its beak over and over again. Finally, two gulls worked in tandem; as one swooped in toward the raven, the other hit it from the back, breaking its neck. The horror was over. The raven, a limp, dark thing, looked like a spot of oil in the morning sunlight. The gulls did not even eat it.

So long as I live, I will not forget the raven's cry: utterly without remorse, without any quality except the pure essence of wild defiance, which drowned out even the shrieking of the gulls. It is a sound I will carry to the grave.

Over the past 30 years, I can think of another small handful of such experiences, which almost always occur alone and accidentally; which strike me dumb at the time, but then work like tide and fog through muffled sounds and obscured sight to bring me back to sensations that cannot be described.

Here in Maine, still within our arm's reach at the beginning of the 21st century, we find a multitude of these once lightly inhabited islands. They are places that offer deep

Lunt Harbor,
Frenchboro, 1984

lessons in natural and maritime history. Sometimes the smaller they are, the larger the window they open on the ineffable; the more enclosed, the farther they telescope our view out into the universe.

When I returned to forestry school the following fall, in addition to commercial forestry courses, I signed up for ornithology, evolutionary biology, geology, botany and marine biology to try to make sense of what I had seen during my first visits to Maine islands. Thirty years later, I still draw on my first island experiences in the watery expanses of the Gulf of Maine.

Frenchboro—Slip-Sliding Away

After graduating from forestry school my first job was working as a forester in the Allagash Waterway region of the north Maine woods. But I left the woods and returned to the coast when Hurricane Island Outward Bound offered me a job compiling natural history summaries of the 200 or so islands they had permission to use for their educational expeditions. I cruised the Maine coast for two summers, often in the company of an irascible older instructor, Alan Sterman, in his shoal-draft, 19-foot rowing-sailing vessel, DOVEKIE, which we could tether to the shore of nearly any island.

Early in this new field research work, Sterman—he was invariably referred to by his last name—and I landed on the back shore of Frenchboro, Long Island. Eastern Cove is a deep broad harbor, exposed to the northeast, between the main part of Frenchboro and the headland called Rich's Head, also labeled on the charts as Long Island Head. Fronting the cove is a steep-faced boulder beach topped with a massive pile of storm-tossed flotsam. The thousand-foot-long beach consists of perfectly rounded and smoothed boulders up to two feet in diameter that are testament to the brute force of wave energy that pounds the beach during a storm. Even on a calm day, the surge and swash of the tide creates a dull rumbling of the beach's granite spheres, an echo of the fury that must regularly visit this place in the winter.

Out on Rich's Head are stone walls, a corral and cellar holes. You cannot help but wonder what people inhabited this terrifyingly beautiful headland. A miniature community had seemingly melted back into the landscape, leaving behind a few signs like Dorset ruins on a half-wild hillside

Across the beach on the main part of the island, I found a trail that wound back toward Lunt Harbor and the town of Frenchboro, as the tiny lobstering community on Outer Long Island is called. Two miles across this unbroken forest, I came out of the deep spruce shadows to find several dozen fishermen's cottages clustered around a small steep-sided protected harbor where lobster boats lay at their moorings. I was startled to see several deer grazing in the backyard of one of the cottages unconcerned by my passing as I wandered down the road and found the Frenchboro post office, actually the attached ell of the post-mistress's small cottage, and watched deer wander through the settled part of the harbor.

The postmistress, while hesitant with information, did tell me that no one had lived out on the Head since the turn of the century when the Riches, who had settled there, moved into the harbor. Evidently, they chose to abandon their homes to be nearer the island store, church, and school, although I learned that Riches had maintained their own school out on the Head for several generations before they returned to the comforts of town.

At the head of Lunt Harbor was Frenchboro's one-room schoolhouse next to the church, graced atop its steeple with a wind vane in the shape of a large cod. However, almost half the harbor appeared to be abandoned. One abandoned building used to be a store, another a sail loft and boat shed. Although Lunt Harbor was the heart of the island community, like the Rich's Head community at the other end of Outer Long Island, Frenchboro itself seemed to be parting its mooring—slipping away before my eyes.

Deer strolling through the village on Frenchboro; Author with field notes on Shipstern Island

Hurricane Island Naturalist

In the 1970s and 1980s, the Hurricane Island Outward Bound School was a magnet for all kinds of intensely inter-esting, driven people, many of whom ultimately settled in Midcoast Maine and used their talents to help build and run a variety of significant institutions and enterprises. The cast of characters is too long to list, but at its head was Peter Willauer, a tall, rangy, handsome sailor who had summered at Prouts Neck as a boy and whose grand-uncle was Winslow Homer. After graduating from Princeton and teaching for a few years at the exclusive Groton School in Massachusetts, Willauer longed for something more meaningful to do with his life. He convinced the owner of 150-acre Hurricane Island, Jim Gaston, to lease him this rugged place, most notable for its abandoned granite quarry, to help bring Outward Bound to America in 1964.

Outward Bound had been developed by German-Jewish émigré Kurt Hahn, who fled Nazi Germany before the outbreak of World War II and started a private boarding school in England, using the outdoors and physical tests to impel young students into value-shaping experiences. Hahn's notoriety increased when the British merchant marine hired him to teach survival skills to its young able-bodied seamen who were dying at an alarming rate from German U-boat attacks.

To run all the complicated programs that operated out of the main base on Hurricane Island, and on two other island bases, Willauer had hired Bob Rheault as program director. After my first summer working for The Nature Conservancy, Rheault hired me to compile a natural history guide for the 200 islands Outward Bound

Northern Spring and Summer Gardens

MAY 2, 1978—On this spring evening, a light, faintly warm breeze has found a crack in the solid wall of a cold Canadian high-pressure cell and worked its way subtly into consciousness. The sun, now noticeably higher in the sky, has warmed enough of the sharp frontal air to dare you to look forward.

Island springs are painfully slow to unfold, so attenuated in their promise, so delicately pasteled that if you're not watching carefully you can miss them altogether. Colorless seas of leafless trees begin pulling ground sap up their limbs into slowly swelling buds until one day you notice the tops of red maple trees are beginning to give the faintest rosy hue on slopes where cold pockets of air don't get trapped. Poplars and birches follow after a few weeks with shades of pale green and yellow against the tarnished bronze of their smooth and slender trunks. Against Hurricane Island's stony hillsides, these are the signs that the damningly faint praise of spring has begun.

From the height of land, we can sometimes see spring fires burning back on the blueberry hills ashore, a ritual that seems positively Neolithic. On such nights there is a red glow in the distance as little Pentecostal tongues lick at the edges of the fields and disappear into the dark flanks of the woods. It seems like a re-creation, a celebration, a ritual enacted since dawn's dawn while waiting for a seasonal renewal.

JULY 11, 1978—On Big Garden's well-named back shore I found a full salad bar from a garden of earthy delights laid out. Here is an abundance of edible beach pea, orach, sea celery and goose tongue. Meanwhile, from the little inner bar you can collect sea blite and glasswort to go with steamers and mussels. But the best part comes from the cobble beach where a profusion of sea rocket grows.

I appreciate sea rocket's ecological strategy, for it is the ultimate colonizer. When an underwater volcano off the coast of Iceland erupted in 1972, the first plant to colonize the newly created island of Surtsey was sea rocket. Sea rocket grows along the temperate and polar coasts of the Atlantic and distributes itself by an ingenious adaptation of its seed capsules. Each flower of sea rocket matures into a two-parted capsule, the larger of which has an air pocket that allows it to float great distances to new habitats. The other part of the capsule, though smaller, is actually heavier, and it drops in place to germinate a new plant next season. A real bet hedger—like all islanders.

The lavender colored flowers have bright yellow centers. The spatulate-shaped leaves and stems of sea rocket are fleshy or succulent—which is one of their adaptations to conserve water in the dry strand environment. Like all members of the mustard family, the leaves of sea rocket have a hot sharp taste, which will remind you of the flavor of horseradish (also a member of the mustard family); a sharp, different, and exotic islander.

had permission to use. I started at $125 per month plus room (a tent) and board on Hurricane Island.

Rheault had been a Green Beret commander in Vietnam. During his career he had been famously court-martialed after taking responsibility for ordering the execution of a Vietcong double agent, and had been even more famously pardoned by Richard Nixon. Rheault was a scary guy to most people. Educated at West Point, he was, as we used to say, "wound very tight." But he was incredibly professional, very fair and loyal to a fault.

In addition to my duties compiling the natural history guide, I led nature walks to groups of students who were temporarily riveted on what they might find (and eat) before being set out on "solo" for three days on an uninhabited island. Beyond their interest in what was edible, inner-city kids wanted to know whether there were wild animals, bears and snakes on the islands. One asked if there were lions and tigers out there. Along Hurricane Island's shores grew a full salad bar of edible beach pea, orach, sea celery and goose tongue. Around the edges of tide pools, you could find sea blite and glasswort, which go nicely with the clams and mussels you might find in the in-tertidal zone. Or you could catch little wriggling rock eels from under rocks and boil them in a soup.

The Ecology of Salt and Fog

As background for these talks and walks, I read as many ecological descriptions of the islands as I could find. I learned about the significance of the long fingers of the sea and fog, which reached far into island forests to create special worlds not found on mainland sites. Fog provides an additional ambient source of water for lichens, mosses, and ferns that are capable of extracting moisture directly from the air rather than get-ting their water through roots. The mosses and lichens form deep emerald carpets

Fern bed, Long Cove, Vinalhaven

atop rocky isles and constitute a much more important part of island forests than of mainland forests. Storm seas, meanwhile, kick up airborne particles of salt that create forests of fantastic forms when implanted in the bark of young spruces. The resulting rounded globes suspended from the trunks and limbs of trees look like a forest in an *Alice in Wonderland* dream.

From the morning run and dips that were standard fare for all Hurricane Islanders, I began to appreciate that the composition of island vegetation is dominated by the influence of the cold Arctic-born water currents—the younger sister of the Labrador Current called the Nova Scotia Current—which explained why swimming off the Maine coast is such a character-building exercise.

Because Hurricane Islanders were such able "dead-reckoning" navigators, I also began to understand what warm southerly air piling in over the cold water means to sailors. The Maine islands are magnets for fog—not little cat's feet-like fog, but dense, impenetrable walls of fog. Sailors used to say there are two ways to navigate in the fog: facing forward with a Bible, or facing aft with a bottle of rum. Even veteran lobstermen, especially in the era before modern electronics, were leery of fog.

With light southerly or southeasterly flows of humid air, you can watch the fog rolling in, locking up first the outer islands and then the southern ends of inner islands before rolling over like a blanket. On the mainland, those who live "down peninsula" can drive to town and find that the rest of the world is having a warm, sunny day, as the heat of the land dissipates the fog, only to return home to the insular gloom of the fog. But on islands there is no escape. The fog approaches with the stealth of an Indian; and if you are out on the water, your worldview changes in a moment from one of passing interest at the interplay of green water, white shores, and blue sky to a view where all sight is obliterated and you are forced, in quiet, intense concentration, to calculate the number of ledges that lie between you and your home harbor. It can be terrifying.

There is, alas, still plenty of room for error, as one of the captains on the Vinalhaven ferry run learned, not once but twice during a recent summer fog mull, during which the GOVERNOR CURTIS grounded twice in Lairey's Narrows, the tight, rock-strewn passage between two islands in West Penobscot Bay where the ferry channel from Rockland twists and turns. After the second grounding an anonymous wit tacked a large piece of plywood up on the north end of Lairey's Island, complete with an arrow, which read "KEEP LEFT."

The Procession of the Equinox

As I became more interested in how the climate of the Maine islands affects their ecosystems, it was impossible to ignore the incredibly dynamic weather systems that rolled over the aptly named Hurricane Island every few days, especially during the

Burnt Island
off North Haven

spring and fall. So I became a student of the weather, and eventually, a teacher of how to read the weather as well.

The first thing you need to know is that Maine is in the zone of prevailing wester-lies, which simply means that the systems that cause Maine's weather originate to the west of us and move eastward. Either they come down the St. Lawrence River Valley, thus sucking into their vortex southeast blows of maritime air, or they charge up the coast and draw in gales of wind from the northeast.

For substantial parts of the year, the cold is colder and winds are windier on is-lands. So why do people still persist in hunkering down out there, waiting for the teeth to be removed from the bite of the dog? Part of it is habit, tradition, inheritance, and simple Yankee stubbornness, but the better part of it is participating in the drama, the Titan-like interplay of capricious elements that serve to give all who stand and watch a primitive belief in the "will of the gods," luck, fate, or call-it-what-you-will. The sea is possessed by its own mood and spirits, and we are almost nothing to it.

Then too, there is the matter of the summer, which many of the islands' enthusiastic temporary residents have discovered. Few landscapes can match the interplay of col-ors on "broken islands in the sea" on a high, blue sunny day. The thousands of events which change winter to late spring and short spring to a sweet summer are small and quiet. But in August all discretion seems to break loose, when the tenor of island life vibrates at its highest pitch. Flocks of the young of the year are out and about, schools of juvenile fish and tinker mackerel appear inshore, attracting bigger fish and seabirds that feed in frenzies, lobsters in new shells are crawling into traps, and every boat on the Maine coast and half those on the East Coast show up in previously deserted coves and guts. It is a time of manic activity, when all things are possible.

Metallic Moon

October 3, 1979— Those that have been around Hurricane Island for several years say that the fall equinoctial gales are late this year. Today a little low-pressure cell has been shoved off the coast by a cold front, and the night sky is flecked with stars and a metallic moon. There's a melancholy feel in the night air, with the unmistakable hint of fall falling down. In the understory of island forests, leaves molder into an earthen mulch signaling an end to the frantic double time of short summer nights and deliciously endless days. A few lightly turned poplar leaves, scattered on the island's bare ledges, dip and spin in little wind eddies.

I am still living in a tent in a spruce woods behind the main quarry face at Hurricane Island, aware of the change of the seasons in my bones. As the season changes, so too the activity around the periphery of the island. Lobstermen have moved their gear from within a boat's length of the curling waves on the island's shores where lobsters first appear after shedding their old shells before moving into deeper waters where they crawl when the shoal waters begin to cool in the fall. The resident wood warblers, which divide up the vertical niches in the spruce forest during the courting and nesting seasons, and whose calls I have just begun to learn, have evacuated from these parts. The warblers have been replaced by flights of migrants, which touch down temporarily on their way south. One sunny morning recently, I was startled to see a scarlet tanager—a bird I had never seen before but identified from the Peterson guide—foraging in a meadow on the island.

I have been going up to the top of the south-facing cliffs of the quarry that was worked by two generations of Swedish, Finnish and Italian quarriers, stonecutter and Carver's. On a little ledge partway down one of the cliffs is a shelf, partly obscured by a small spruce with just enough room for two people to sit and see the entire cliff. This is a secret spot to watch the accipiter hawks— sharp-shinned and Cooper's hawks—work the cliffs to pick off unwary young songbirds to fuel up for their migration. But on a day like today, after being pinned down by low pressure, the hawks will be on the move, and you want to be on top of the cliffs to count the incredible multitude of hawks and falcons slicing southwestward on the nigh northwest airs that will carry them far down the coast. From this rampart, I look out over the rim of the ocean to Vinalhaven where I have a winter rental and where I will spend the winter writing up my field notes.

Last night I went down to the shore at the main pier as the moon rose full and bright over Heron Neck Light across Hurricane Sound. The ghostly light chiseled the edges of the spiky spruce and pointed firs, and I drank in the the luminescent air until I could not hold a drop more. A path of scattered moonstones led me up the old wagon way the quarriers called Broadway and through the churchyard, where its foundations are now overgrown with wild grasses and young spruce, through the dappled light under tall spruce to my tent at the edge of the ice pond.

The wind still has a bit of heat in it, a little hint of upper prairie life and high wheat country it picked up sometime yesterday before it blew into Maine, but its bite also foretells the sting of a hard frost to come.

Sea glass

Fall's Failings

Islanders talk a lot about the weather because the weather determines so much of what you will and will not do; it reduces you to a little part of a much bigger world. For all but the most stupid or arrogant (and out there, the two are almost interchangeable), it commands respect.

Summer heat, regulated by the sea's thermostat, lingers well into October when island flowers are still in bloom, and gardens still produce long after those on the mainland have turned brown. There may be no other place where the meaning of Indian summer is so real. But then the grand procession of the equinox reminds us that the colors will turn to browns and grays and finally the incredible whiteness of being.

"Cold as a Dog"

Following Allhallows Eve, when gray November prunes the day length and the air grows more raw and unruly with each passing week, it is pure boneheadedness not to think through the differing conditions any day can bring. At the end of the year, as December's aperture closes down around the fleeting edges of daylight, darkness defines the field of view. But December's days also have an eerie depth of focus when island horizons loom larger; they rise up off the water to greet you, to invite you to the heart and hearth of island winter. Then one day in December it is all over, and the winter is brutally quick about its business: A cold front roars through and sits on towering haunches, picking its teeth. The sea is alight with tongues of sea smoke as she gives up the warmth she has harbored for half a year, and we watch and wait, imprisoned by the cold. It is called "sitting on a rock" in the North Atlantic.

Sprucehead Island

Northeasters, which ancient mariners called no' theasters (not nor' easters, because that is not how you repeat a compass heading), are most frequent during the fall and winter and result from a shift in the jet stream. Northeasterly gales can pack winds of hurricane strength and are a trial to be endured anywhere, but more so on islands. Northeasters bring in the worst of all weather, so-called maritime polar air, which combines winds both wet and cold from the waters surrounding Newfoundland, Labrador, and even Baffin Island. You cannot weather a northeast gale on an island without recalling the title of Ruth Moore's collection of poems (the author herself was born and brought up on Gott's Island), *Cold as a Dog and the Wind Northeast.*

No matter how tight your house may be, or how many layers of clothing you try to put between yourself and the cold-fingering rain or snow, you feel a northeast gale to your bones. Because of the way winds clock around the low-pressure cells that produce gales, the trailing edge of a northeasterly is a cold front that ushers in clearing air from the northwest—often cold enough to make you wonder if the gale itself were not the lesser of two evils. Snapping-clear high pressure from the dry polar continental interior cascades in behind a gale. In May or June, it can drive off the encircling fog within a matter of moments to reveal the long view, the large day. In the winter it whistles day after day, churning up seas known as "white horses" that gallop across a bay and freeze on the hulls and in the rigging of boats. When the winds howl, part of you is listening to the chafe of your mooring pendant or feeling the relentless beating of the sea on wharf pilings and fish-house footings.

Fish House Gossip

After my second field season of collecting information for Outward Bound, I rented the back wing of a farmhouse on Vinalhaven at the edge of Roberts Harbor. I spent the next two winters there with George Putz and his family. In addition to being my landlord, Putz was a gifted writer, anthropologist, maritime expert and storyteller. I could not have asked for a better situation.

George loved to host big gatherings at the farmhouse to thrust disparate clusters of islanders together, pour alcohol over the event and see what the spicy bouillabaisse produced. Everyone had a mythic identity in George's mind and he loved to brag his friends up. I was an island naturalist who knew everything that was edible on islands. At one of George's bashes where a lot of hard cider and whiskey had been passed around, I found a bunch of mushrooms in his field and brought them in to get a spore print, since I was fairly sure they were the common edible meadow mushroom. But before I knew what was happening, George had started serving them up to his guests. I suddenly panicked. I had never done this before. What if I were wrong—what if they weren't an edible species, after all? Long before Jonestown, I could see the headline in the newspaper about the naturalist who had witlessly killed a bunch of islanders by misidentifying a deadly species, so I ate as many of the mushrooms as remained to ensure I would be as dead as anyone else.

When the days grew shorter and the weather patterns were dominated by gales and northwesterly fronts screeching for days at a time, George took me around to some of the fish-houses on Clam Alley, Sands Cove and Indian Creek, which were clustered communally around the harbor. Some of the younger lobstermen were contemporaries of George's, who was respected for his maritime knowledge, humor and prodigious thirst, so I was glad to sit around the little stoves bespattered with buoy paint listening to gossip and passing the bottle.

Fish-house, Islesford

George Putz on Criehaven

The quality of fish-house conversation is inversely proportional to the weather. It is the only intense time that fishermen have to spend ashore socializing with each other. Impromptu sessions with fishermen who are better known for their nicknames, Tink, Gweeka, Hummer, and Fireball, were wonderfully entertaining. These were hardworking and inventive young fishermen who, with about a score of their contemporaries, had begun sharing the harbor privileges with older fishermen.

Some of the fish-house conversation was murderously slanderous. Somehow I knew it could not all be true; people simply could not have done all the things that were routinely ascribed to them. When I asked George about the discussions later, he explained a fundamental lesson about the island world. The word *gossip*, he said, derives from the ancient Anglo-Saxon, "God's sip," or God's family. If you are part of God's family, embraced in the arms of the community, you'll be gossiped about as a sign of belonging. Veracity isn't the issue; it's whether you count enough in the community to be gossiped about. The important thing is to know who was saying what about you and how to use the social intercourse of gossip as a currency to reply in kind to your friends and enemies. The worst thing in an island community is not to know what's being said about you. If you're outside the gossip, you are, quite literally, outside God's family.

Island Journalism Is an Oxymoron

George was a voracious reader with catholic interests—cultural anthropology, archaeology and maritime history were a few of the subjects that fired his imagination as a writer and editor. But island writing is a sensitive issue among native islanders, where the line of who is in the know—inside the family—and who is not—is impossible to straddle. After reading newspaper or magazine stories about Vinalhaven or other islands, George would routinely point out that island journalism is an oxymoron: If you know enough to know the real story, you cannot write it; and if you do not, you will get the story wrong.

George's professional life revolved around editing the *Mariner's Catalog,* with his friend Peter Spectre. They had already edited six or seven volumes of this wonderful compendium of maritime lore, tools and technology, which had been inspired by Stewart Brand's *Whole Earth Catalog.* So it was not surprising that the *Mariner's Catalog* attracted the interest of Stewart Brand, who was an avid sailor. A lively correspondence led to an invitation to Brand to make a winter visit to Vinalhaven, while he was on a trip east. The visit was a pretty big deal for Putz and Spectre, because Brand was already a countercultural avatar, and because they were going to discuss the possibility of George and Peter editing an ocean issue of Brand's new periodical, *CoEvolution Quarterly.*

The only thing I remember about the visit, however, was that when Brand asked George to use the facilities, Putz led him out onto the porch and showed him a patch of Jerusalem artichoke, which would benefit from additional nitrogen. Putz assured Brand that here in rural New England, real estate was purchased on the basis of whether you could use your porch in this fashion. After Brand left, he visited Jon Wilson, founder and editor of *Wooden Boat,* a magazine in which George and Peter had published many articles. When Putz called Wilson to see how the visit had gone, Wilson said they had a wonderful time, but that he was a little undone by Brand's western habit of relieving himself right off the front porch.

I learned that most islanders also lived on a kind of lunar clock, which is strange and inexplicable to those who have never experienced what it means to have the tide going with you, or worse, to have lost the tide, or to have wind and tide opposed and the boat unable to get you back to the mainland. Missing the tide only has to happen to you once or twice—when you lose a day's work, and then have to wait weeks till it all comes right again—to get the point.

In these fish-houses, it was evident that islanders also have a well-deserved reputation for being supremely inventive and making do with the materials at hand. Clarence Howard of Eagle Island in northern Penobscot Bay, for instance, was the first to use a brass rudderpost and packing box in his lobster boat in place of the iron pipe through the hull, which often leaked badly when boats were loaded. He was the first to use an automobile steering box rather than rely on slack tiller ropes, which could break on a hard turn. He was the first to use a jury-rigged Ford rear axle for a lobster-pot hauler, and when he turned his attention to the herring fishery, he was the first to set seine nets off a stern roll and the first in the area to use a depth recorder as a fish-finder.

View of Hurricane Sound above Wharf Quarry, Vinalhaven

Talents such as these are rare enough anywhere, but are uniquely handy on boats where new situations are always presenting themselves. It is helpful to remember that the entire crews of two successful America's Cup defenders were recruited from the fishing port of Deer Isle (when the town was still an island) in 1895 and 1899. These were skilled mariners, to say the least, even though the Deer Isle boys were reportedly let go in subsequent years due to their habit of second-guessing the skipper's orders.

I also learned another important island lesson that first fall. A young fellow with a long albino-white ponytail and his girlfriend had been bouncing around Vinalhaven since the summer trying to find a place to rent as winter approached. On a lark one November day, the pair set out in a canoe to cross to an island a half-mile offshore. But beyond the calm beach where they launched, the sea sprang up in a stiff chop and they capsized. Someone from shore saw them and several lobster boats were quickly scrambled from the harbor on the other side of the island. The pair were fished out and brought back ashore, warmed up with no real harm done.

Because the survival of the community depends on the survival of its individual members, I thought this gallant rescue would be a cause for celebration—certainly that would have been so on the mainland. But the lobstermen were angry. What I slowly recognized is that when individuals in an island community put others at risk, they also jeopardize the community and become liabilities that the entire community closes ranks to shun. The couple left the island a few weeks later.

Cellar-Hole Melancholy

It takes time to appreciate the intricate balances Vinalhaven's fishermen maintain between the fierce competition of the lobster chase and the need to cooperate when someone is in trouble. No matter how cold or tired at the end of a day of hauling, men would wait around on wharves, or at the co-op or in their fish-houses until the last boat came in. Without discussion, they watched the fleet in. And while waiting, there would be time for politics, philosophy, or fixing gear to get ready for the next day's hauling. The harbor was much more closely knit with invisible threads than one might think possible of a group of outwardly truculent and independent individualists.

George was my guide to local knowledge; he had carefully observed and described the inordinate influence a few primary personalities are able to exert on island life. A few years later he wrote about this in the first issue of *Island Journal*. "Many islands have been under the domination of certain individuals for as long as half a century. Their emergence and demise radically alter and direct the course of island history—the personal, economic and political lives of islanders—although the principals are seldom the obvious ones," he wrote. "Selectmen, town managers, ministers and the like are generally irrelevant to the real power domain of islands. But when minor fluctuations occur in an island economy, ostensible island leaders are generally powerless and marginal islanders are forced to leave the community, as people must "take care of their own. It's a tragedy for them and a sadness for island life."

Through islanders' eyes and from what I had learned from the reconstructed histories of generations of Vinalhaven fishermen, I began to understand some of the deep

Green's Island,
Vinalhaven

Carver's Pond and
Harbor, Vinalhaven

conflicts native-born Maine islanders felt watching the rising tide of newcomers purchase second homes from the ancestral holdings of old families who often have fallen, temporarily, on hard times. Or the dismay islanders feel when visitors appropriate or reduce access to the shores of previously productive island places where fish had once been shut off, clams dug and secret trysts arranged.

Winter Ice

During the winter of 1978–79, the sea froze around Vinalhaven while I was living there, for the first time in recent memory. Ice 18 inches thick covered not just Carver's Harbor, but Rockland out to the breakwater. In Carver's Harbor, lobstermen walked out to their boats for a period of a few weeks. A few lobstermen tried to chop their way out of the harbor, to find a mooring in water where it was still ice-free, but most were frozen like Shackleton's ship in the thickening harbor ice. The ferry made increasingly futile attempts to keep the harbor open, but it too finally gave up. Those who lived on nearby small islands like Green's, across the Reach, could, if they were crazy enough, walk over to Vinalhaven for supplies. North Haveners walked across the Fox Islands Thorofare just to say they had done it.

At the farmhouse on Roberts Harbor where I was living, the pipe from the well froze solid, even though the taps had been left running all night. For six weeks we had to haul water from a spring across the island. One of the island's elderly matriarchs died and was placed in a surface crypt until spring because pickax and crowbar could not penetrate the ground. Cut off in the back room of the farmhouse, the winter dark began to envelop the place; it wrapped around everything in a tense grip and did not let go. It was like nothing I had ever experienced; it was like what it must feel like to be in a spacecraft that passes behind the dark side of the moon before it can return to solar light and warmth again. It was profoundly unnerving. I thought of that island winter as my trial by ice—and I loved it.

CHAPTER 2

Downwind History and Ecology

*In the old days, a good part of the best men here knew a hundred ports
and something of the way people lived in them . . . Shipping's a terrible loss
to this part of New England from a social point of view, ma'am.*

—Sarah Orne Jewett, *The Country of the Pointed Firs*

*(Facing) Birch Cove, Fox
Island Thorofare, with
Goose Rocks "spark-
plug" light in distance*

While working as the staff naturalist at Hurricane Island, I was based in a small office on the second deck of Hurricane Island's main building with a view out toward Deadman's Ledge and the Heron Neck lighthouse at the tip of Green's Island. One day a letter arrived from the mainland with a questionnaire inquiring about the history of Hurricane Island. It was from Charles McLane, a professor of government at Dartmouth, who had begun spending his summers sailing to the islands with his wife, Carol, collecting historical information for what became the first volume of a four-volume history of the Maine islands.

I returned the McLanes' questionnaire and invited them to Hurricane Island. They arrived one day in their beautiful yawl, Suliko, and I liked them from the start. Charles was a Soviet government expert who had spent time with Carol in Moscow working for the U.S. government after World War II. Perhaps Charles knew too much for his hosts' comfort, as he left the Soviet Union and spent the remainder of his career in academia. Island history was a sideline for Charles, but with Carol's careful help, the two of them became deeply immersed in the enterprise. From the first moment we met, we shared information. I would tell him where I had found old foundations, or who owned various islands he wanted to visit. He would share the historical research he had gathered from town offices and his detailed interviews with islanders. We became great friends and island traveling companions summer after summer.

Three Hundred Island Communities

*Historian,
Charles McLane;
North end of
Metinic Island*

From McLane I learned that various European settlers—mostly French and English—were attracted to Maine's islands from the earliest explorations of the New World. The islands were of interest not only for their proximity to fishing grounds, but because their location conveyed defensive advantages in an insecure and potentially hostile new country. During the 17th and 18th centuries, islands such as Isles of Shoals, Richmond, Damariscove, Monhegan and Matinicus developed into important fishing stations and trading centers.

Other island communities consisted of a rich mix of multigenerational extended families, while still others were sophisticated multilingual places whose mariners navigated the oceans of the globe. During the days of merchant sail, islanders benefited economically from coastwise trading routes that went, quite literally, right by their front doors. All kinds of island products, from woolens to cordwood, from smoked fish to salt cod, from potatoes to cheese, could be put up and then traded in the fall to supply islanders with their winter needs. Islandness was deeply interwoven into the economic way of life on the Maine coast during the Age of Sail.

As I began to read—and later, under the aegis of the Island Institute helped publish—the four volumes of McLane's island histories, I gradually understood that there had once been 300 year-round islands, and that Maine's island heritage ran deeply in the state's history. I began to get a sense of the thousands of stories lived out in small but intricate island communities, the vast majority of which have been abandoned as year-round communities and then reinvented as summer colonies, conservation islands or private kingdoms.

Eagle Island Light, Penobscot Bay, with the foundation of the light keepers house abandoned in the 1960s, when the U.S Coast Guard also rolled the 2,000 pound bronze fog bell into the ocean below.

As George Putz had shown me on Vinalhaven, I learned all over again that island history is melancholy history because so many communities have disappeared. At the peak of island populations in the 1880s, deepwater channels connected Maine islands to the marine highways of the Atlantic coast and the rest of the world. But following the decline of merchant sail and a score of other compounding events, literally hundreds of island communities of extended families, industrial colonies, or simple fishing outposts disappeared.

To this legacy of loss, we should also add an additional 75 island lighthouse stations where families maintained a tenacious watch, including precarious perches on the outermost islands, where these sentinels exemplified the enduring character of a magnificent but frightening coastline. On Matinicus Rock, for example, 17-year-old Abbie Burgess, a lighthouse keeper's daughter, became a folk legend for keeping the light through four weeks of unrelenting winter gales that struck the Rock when her father had gone to town and could not return because of the fury of the seas. From scores of other island lighthouses come similar records of endurance, where duty and care were weathered deep into the family character: the Corbetts of Little River (Cutler), the Wasses of Libby Island, the Gilleys of Great Duck and Baker, the Nortons of Whitehead, the Pottles of Franklin, to mention just a few. These stories, too, have faded, as gradually the island lights were automated and lighthouse families "removed."

Why did they leave? The reasons are as varied as the stories of the people who occupied these stony places; but all the stories are rooted in the simple truth that island living, especially in the winter, is a hard, hard life. The ecology changes as you travel from west to east, but the stories of islanders are familiar from bay to bay.

Pleasant Point Gut and Gay's Island, at the mouth of the St. George River, with Muscle Ridge islands in the distance

The Bays of Maine—The Physical and Cultural Setting

Maine has an immensely long tidal coastline. In the first volume of *Islands in Time*, published in 1981, I wrote that Maine's coast was 2,500 miles long, collapsed accordionlike into a short 250 miles as the crow measures the distance from Kittery to Eastport. But Maine's saltwater interface has now been accurately measured from aerial photography that has been scanned into a computer. This digital wizardry has shown the coastline to be 7,005 miles long—an immensity no one had ever imagined.

Within and along this intricate shoreline are 4,617 islands, which collectively contribute almost a third of Maine's total coastline. The long, sinuous shoreline certainly is good for the fish and shellfish that depend on the nutrients washed off this acreage and for the fishermen who set off after the fish from hundreds of protected coves and bights—yet it almost defies generalized description.

As I began writing up the ecological and historical information from the 200 islands I had visited for Hurricane Island, it was also evident that the islands at different ends of the archipelago—a wonderful Greek word meaning a group of islands—had distinctly different ecologies. If you were blindfolded and landed on an island in Casco Bay, you would not mistake it for an island downeast off Jonesport or Beals. So I began organizing islands into groups within their distinctive embayments.

Isles of Shoals—The "Remarkablest Isles"

I first visited the Isles of Shoals on a sailing vessel owned by another forester, Ray Leonard, while bound from Portsmouth Harbor to Hurricane Island. We had planned an overnight voyage but got a late start and when the wind died unexpectedly at sunset, barely underway, we headed toward the little cluster of islands that straddle the border between Maine and New Hampshire. They do not look like much from a distance, but they quickly open themselves up to be one of the most enisled mini-archipelagos along the entire Maine archipelago.

We rounded up into the little harbor formed by Appledore, Star and Cedar Islands where we dropped anchor for a restless night. The Isles of Shoals were named for the schools or "shoals" of cod that appeared in legendary aggregations there, causing the waters to ripple with their passage. I later read that Captain John Smith was so taken by these islands during his expedition of 1614 that he referred to them as "the remarkablest isles," and named them after his remarkable self. The name Smith Isles has faded even as a footnote in history, although Smith Cove still commemorates his visit and affection for the place.

Before the American Revolution, Appledore Island had a population that fluctuated between 300 and 600 and cured 300,000 quintals (pronounced "kentals"; a quintal equaled 112 pounds) of cod a year, mostly for the Spanish and West Indian markets. William Wood, the self styled "Lord of the Isles," wrote, "He is a very bad fisher that cannot kill in one day with his hook and line one, two or three hundred cods. And is it not a pretty sport to pull up two pense, six pense, twelve pense as fast as you can hale and wear a line?"

A century later in the 1890s, Celia Thaxter, the daughter of the innkeeper who turned this tiny archipelago into Maine's first island resort, planted luxuriant gardens amid the rocky outcrops, and lured the literary lights of the day, including Nathaniel Hawthorne, John Greenleaf Whittier and James Russell Lowell to the fabulous family hotels that dominated the landscape for three-quarters of a century. Today Appledore supports a notable marine research station maintained by the University of New Hampshire and Cornell.

Isles of Shoals and harbor formed by Appledore, Star and Cedar Islands

Ragged Island meadow, outer Casco Bay

Saco Bay: "Nut Trees and Vineyards"

Early in my years as an island ecologist, I visited Richmond Island, the largest island in Saco Bay, to assess its ecological assets and potential as sheep pasturage for its owners on the adjoining mainland. Almost 200 acres in extent, Richmond's tall pasture vegetation seemed to spill off the edges of the island, with only a few small copses of intervening spruce. When I read Champlain's description of Richmond Island from 1605, I was surprised by his account of its "fine oaks and nut trees, the soil cleared up, and many vineyards bearing beautiful grapes in their season." Champlain was exploring the coast looking for a more suitable location for his country's Acadian headquarters after a disastrous winter on an island in the St. Croix River. He called the island "Isle de Bacchus" in honor of its grape vines. But he did not stay.

Richmond Island was settled two decades after Champlain's visit, in 1627 or 1628, and within a few years ownership officially passed into the hands of an influential Bristol merchant named Robert Trelawney. His agent, John Winter, established one of Maine's early fishing and trading posts there. Some of the most interesting pictures of island life in the 17th century are contained in the *Trelawney Papers*. Between 1630 and 1645, vessels built and launched from Richmond Island shipped cargoes of fish oil, pine clapboards, and oak staves, all of which were harvested from the islands and nearby waters. At the height of the island's prosperity, 60 men worked in the Richmond Island fisheries.

Full-grown and fat cod weighing between 40 and 60 pounds were sold in Europe; the smaller cod that were not good enough for the Spanish or Portuguese markets were sold to the Virginia colony. Dried fish of inferior quality—they may have been salt-burned and spotted or simply not as full-fleshed—were packed in casks and sent to the West Indies to be fed to plantation slaves.

From Richmond's shores, you can look out across the arcuate curves of Saco Bay to Stratton Island, which was settled in 1630 by an Englishman, John Stratton. Stratton cleared the land, established a small farm and traded a few goods with the Indians for furs. Today, Stratton is a multi-species heronry, including white herons and glossy ibis that have expanded their ranges northward.

Casco Bay: "All Broken Islands in the Sea"

I originally explored Casco Bay islands from a small sailboat that Hurricane Island instructor, Jonathan Nolan and I launched from the shore of his family's summer cottage on Cushing's Island. Nolan was the kind of charismatic Outward Bounder who could seemingly make a small sailing craft do anything he wanted. We sailed across to Peaks Island and to the larger islands of Great Diamond, Long, Chebeague, and Cliff. Portland, Maine's largest city and commercial center since early colonial days and one of the East Coast's most important deepwater ports loomed over our shoulders.

Nolan and I sailed past House Island, where Christopher Levett built a fortified house in 1624. Levett described the landscape as "all broken islands in the sea which makes many excellent good harbors where a thousand sail of ship may ride in safety." The word *Casco*, however, apparently derived from a Wabanaki term meaning "muddy bay," because their birch-bark canoes wound through passages at the inner edges of the bay where sediments collect. I also learned that *Chebeague* is an Indian word that translates as "island of many springs," and no doubt many of the bay's original white settlers were envious of this piece of Indian domain, since lack of adequate water was one of the factors limiting settlement of these otherwise highly desirable islands.

Richmond Island, Saco Bay;
Cliff Island, Casco Bay;
Damariscove Island, Boothbay

Until the end of the last French and Indian War in 1760, the whites settled only the islands that the Indians did not use. With few exceptions, white settlers used islands, particularly the outer islands, at the mercy or sufferance of the Indians, who commanded the islands by virtue of their superior numbers and mobility in canoes. In 1689, for example, 300 to 400 Indians gathered on Peaks Island in preparation for their successful attack on Portland. For most of the 17th century, the Indians simply had a more impressive navy than the settlers.

Casco Bay islands have been called the Calendar Isles, supposedly because there was one island for every day of a non-leap year. But then someone counted them and found there were 222—and that includes all the islands that are now connected to the main by bridges, such as Bailey, Orrs, Sebascodegan, Cousins, Littlejohn, and Mackworth.

Today, most of the state's oil is delivered here in coastal tankers. Several proposals to establish an oil refinery or LNG gas terminal on one of the islands in the bay, or on the nearby mainland, have been soundly rejected.

Boothbay, Sheepscot and John's Bays

My early voyages to the islands off Boothbay were in a 30-foot Hurricane Island pulling boat on an expedition to the western rivers region of the coast—the intricate tidal passages among the Sheepscot, Back, Sassanoa and Kennebec rivers. Bob Weiler, one of the most gifted natural leaders I had ever met, piloted the pulling boat. We anchored at the head of the south-facing cove of Damariscove Island, which looked as if it was open to the full fetch of the Atlantic Ocean, but was actually well protected at its entrance by submarine ledges that smooth the waters inside to millpond conditions.

Damariscove Island was named after Humphrey Damarill, an independent trader and fisherman who set up headquarters on the island's southern cove before 1614. Because the hapless Popham Colony had already failed by this time, Damariscove Island has the distinction of being the site of the first permanent settlement in Maine. Like Richmond Island off Cape Elizabeth, Damarill's Cove—or Damariscove—was ideally situated near an important winter cod spawning ground a few miles off the mouth of the Sheepscot River. When the District of Maine petitioned the Massachusetts Bay Colony to provide some sort of government for the area in 1687, Damariscove and Monhegan were the two places assessed with the largest tax, a reflection of their larger populations.

We sailed and rowed—mostly rowed—through the narrow saltwater river channels, catching a favorable tide when possible, anchoring when the ferocious tide was against us. I learned that Southport Island had sheltered a large fleet of schooners that fished the offshore cod grounds and was the homeport of several of the most successful mackerel seining vessels. When the menhaden or pogy fishery boomed, Southport fishermen sold these fish to supply the oil and fertilizer plants built in Boothbay. At one time, so the story goes, Southport Island fishermen had the highest per capita income of any port in Maine.

During the second half of the 20th century, the Boothbay region developed a vigorous tourist economy. Tour boats run between Boothbay Harbor and Monhegan and out to bird-nesting islands and seal rookeries. Several of the islands in the Boothbay region—Capital Island, Heron Island, Isles of Springs—have been purchased by associations and developed as private summer colonies in a manner similar to those of Casco Bay.

Muscongus Bay: "The Fishing Place"

As Hurricane Island's staff naturalist, I spent a good deal of time on Burnt Island in Muscongus Bay, where Bob Weiler directed a second Outward Bound base after the school outgrew the number of students that could be accommodated on Hurricane Island. The artist Jamie Wyeth, who painted at that time on Monhegan, owned Burnt Island and scheduled his lively visits to this mostly wild island with his even wilder New York artist friends when the Outward Bounders were off on expedition. With careful planning, the two groups got along famously.

Burnt Island was home to an abandoned Life-Saving Station, which Jamie's caretaker was slowly renovating. The Outward Bound instructors holed up in two little shacks known as the Rickety House and the Spook House when they were not with their students in tents above a beach on the north shore. Burnt Island had a wonderful supply of blue mussels, a field of milkweed from whose early flower pods you could make the most delicious steamed meal of broccoli-like flower heads, and a little cattail wetland where we collected stalks to make a cucumber-like salad. Weiler never failed

Burnt Island
Life Saving Station,
1939, Muscongus Bay

to take delight in my teaching these simple meals to his students, and his enthusiasm was infectious.

While surveying the islands throughout Muscongus Bay, we had to contend with the fact that the rivers that empty into this bay create a lobster heaven. These rivers are warmer than the Gulf of Maine, and since the bay is quite shallow, the water gets warmer the further up the bay you go. The rivers also carry a load of suspended nutrients, which, in combination with the moderate water temperatures, creates ideal lobstering grounds. *Muscongus* is an Wabanaki word for "fishing place"—probably referring to smelt rather than lobster, according to Fannie Hardy Eckstrom, whose indefatigable efforts to unravel Indian place names give us one of the best pictures of Indian uses of the coastal islands. But as anyone who has tried to navigate Muscongus Bay between June and November can confirm, there are probably more lobster pot buoys per square nautical mile here than any other place on this lobster coast.

Across a narrow body of water from Burnt Island is Allen Island, where a granite cross commemorates the first Anglican church service in the New World during George Waymouth's expedition, and where I would later spend several years working for its new owner, Betsy Wyeth.

Up in the inner edge where the Medomak River spills into a corner of the bay lies the hull of an enormous old schooner, the CORA CRESSY. Designed to carry huge loads of up to 4,000 tons, this 278-foot, five-masted schooner was launched in 1902. She competed against steam-powered ships that were faster, but the enormous "Downeasters" could haul larger cargoes. The CRESSY was used primarily to carry coal from Virginia to Maine and was said to be "cranky" and hard to handle when light. Several steam donkeys and a crew of 11 men was required to hoist the gaff-rigged sails. She had such a rake forward that a bow pilot was required to guide the ship inshore.

She rode out several ferocious gales, including the March gale of 1924, in which the famous six-masted WYOMING disappeared. The CORA CRESSY weighed anchor before the gale and rode the storm out offshore while the strain on the WYOMING's anchors probably pulled the bow out of her. Nevertheless, the CORA CRESSY was sold that year for $3,610. She was a floating nightclub in Gloucester, Boston, and Providence, before being towed to her present location where she was scuttled and used for a lobster pound. This scheme didn't work out either, and now, aside from supporting a small grove of birch trees on her bow, she serves as a breakwater for two lobster pounds just to the north of her.

Penobscot Bay: Granite and Lobsters

Penobscot Bay is my adopted home territory, so it is difficult to write about this most magnificent of all bays dispassionately. To begin with, Penobscot is Maine's largest bay, measuring 20 miles across from Whitehead to Isle au Haut, and trending 30 miles north to the mouth of the equally grand river of the same name. Encompassing almost 1,000 miles of shoreline, and encircling 624 islands and ledges, Penobscot Bay is also the second largest embayment on the Atlantic coast of the United States, after Chesapeake Bay. Five year-round islands ring the bay, including three of Maine's largest year-round island communities—Islesboro, Vinalhaven and North Haven. The latter two at one time were joined into a single town—North Fox Island and South Fox Island. At Penobscot's eastern flank is the year-round community on Isle au Haut, and at its outer edge, remote Matinicus.

I spent five years exploring every corner of Penobscot Bay and followed the Penobscot River north to the head of tide in Bangor. Through these explorations, it became clear that trees had been cut and islands were burned to create pasture on even the smallest "junk-o-pork" islands. By 1820, virtually every island greater than about 25

Cemetery, Calderwood Neck, Vinalhaven, where Mary Calderwood and ten of her children are buried

acres supported either people or livestock. The census for that year shows 207 hardy souls on the small islands surrounding North Haven and Vinalhaven.

Beginning around 1870, island farming and fishing efforts were eclipsed by the granite boom, which swelled island populations to the bursting point, including on Hurricane Island, where at one time 1,500 people reportedly lived and worked. Because granite could be transported conveniently on coastal schooners, island quarries developed much more rapidly than those on the mainland.

Forests have regrown on many of the islands once cleared for pasture, and some have cabins tucked in among the trees. I remember reading through the guest book at one of the bay's most remote islands, which featured a 12-year-long list of characters— some honeymooning, some stranded ("$1,000 in lost wages"), some washed ashore ("no food") and some merely bored ("arrived on an outboard with 200 hp engine of awesome power, stayed ten minutes, got cabin fever—good-bye forever.")

Merchant Row to Jericho Bay: The Heart of the Midcoast

I cannot count the number of times I have crossed the expanse of waters defined by Eggemoggin Reach to the northeast, and rocky Jericho Bay to the east and Merchant Row to the south, with the Deer Island Thorofare, as its name suggests, bisecting the archipelago's most island-y and ledgy geography. Though the islands in this stretch of water are not arranged in well-defined bays, when taken together they constitute the heart of the Midcoastworld of islands. Year-round communities persist on Swan's, Frenchboro (Long Island), Isle au Haut, Deer Isle, and Little Deer Isle (whose inhabitants still refer to themselves as islanders, even though they have either the best of both worlds or the worst of two worlds since the suspension bridge was completed to Sedgwick in 1937).

Hell's Half Acre
Island off Stonington

One of the interesting historical patterns of settlement in this section of the archipelago is that many north-facing shores appear to have been settled earlier and more densely than southern shores that face the sea. The determining feature for island farmers probably was the chilling effect of damp fogs, which roll in off the Gulf of Maine and set back crops on seaward-facing shores. The northern shores of Northwest Harbor and Smalls Cove on Deer Isle were settled before most of the rest of the island's southern shores, suggesting the initial island settlers placed a higher priority on growing crops than on catching fish. Even on neighboring Vinalhaven, a traditional fishing community from earliest times, the northern Thorofare side was settled before Carver's Harbor on the island's south side.

Swan's Island was named not for North America's largest waterfowl, but for James Swan, a Boston merchant and an early speculator in island real estate, who offered to give 10 acres of land to any fisherman who owned his own boat and settled there. He died in a debtors' prison in France before he could recoup his investment. But before leaving for France, Swan, who fought in the American Revolution and was a close friend of General Henry Knox, had planned to build a lavish summer home for himself on the island.

Today the 65 islands of the Merchant row group range in size from less than an acre to the 250-acre Merchant Island. Due to the many summer cottages that have been built on islands in Merchant Row and Deer Isle Thorofare, this area continues to be one of the more densely populated parts of the Maine archipelago—at least for a couple of months a year.

Lazy Gut Island with Eggemoggin Reach in the distance

Blue Hill and Frenchman Bays: The Arms of Mount Desert

No other stretch of Maine's coastal waters is defined so completely, so emphatically, by the land that rises up out of the sea as is Mount Desert and the desert-mountains above Southwest, Northeast, Seal, and Bar harbors. An ancient covering of the country rock into which the younger granite of Mount Desert intruded primarily underlies the islands surrounding Mount Desert to the west and south. To the east, a massive inclined sheet of an underground molten rock flow, which, like a slab of inerodable cement, gives them a ramp-like shape, defines the steep, austere topography of the Porcupines and Ironbound.

With the exception of Little Placentia Island, now called Great Gott, the islands surrounding Mount Desert were not settled until the conclusion of the French and Indian War in 1763. However, in 1688, when Sir Edmund Andros, governor of the Massachusetts Bay Colony, sent a whaleboat along the Maine coast east of Pemaquid to survey French occupation, the expedition found "Petit Plaisants" (the Little Beautiful Island) occupied. We don't know anything about the two families enumerated there, but they must have been inconspicuous or politic enough to have avoided the enmity of both France and England, who otherwise spared no efforts to destroy each other's unprotected settlements along the coast of Maine.

Sutton Island bar and schooner in Western Way off Mount Desert

Today, Acadia National Park occupies much of the land on Mount Desert, and brings millions of visitors to the region, while the seaside towns at the foot of Champlain's "desert mountains" have become some of the most expensive summer real estate along the Atlantic coast. The Cranberry Isles, consisting of the year-round communities of Islesford and Great Cranberry and the summer community on Sutton Island, struggle with sharing their confined island sensibilities with millions of visitors and visiting millionaires.

Running the Easting Down

When I came to Maine, I initially settled in Township Number 7, the southernmost unnamed township in Maine and one of only two with saltwater frontage.

Because the prevailing maritime winds blow from the west, it has been a linguistic convention for well over a century to say you're going "downeast" when headed in the general direction of Canada, or "up" to Boston, Portland or anywhere to the west'ard. One of the first things a newcomer learns along the Maine coast is that there is no north and south; there is only east and west. Some people think of Camden as "downeast," where a magazine of that name is published. But these places are not what the term means. Still everyone agrees that along the shores of Washington County, where you are at the end of the line, you are downeast, at the raw edge of America.

After passing the turnoff to Mount Desert Island if you're on Route 1, or if you're offshore cruising under Acadia's sheer granite faces, you enter a region of increasingly strong tidal sets. Once past either point, the psychology of the coast changes; you enter not just a different county, but a different province of the mind.

The climate here is more boreal. Larch and peat bogs are more common than the pine and oak forests of southern Maine—the fogs are more enduring and impenetrable; the society more sparse and egalitarian. There are precious few of the lovely old sea captains' mansions of Searsport, Camden or Wiscasset. Pulp cutters, clam diggers, blueberry rakers, and Passamaquoddy Indians live on and off the land, changing occupations with the seasons and with the fluctuating prices of commodities which are set in distant places by people who have never been here, and if they have, know they don't want to be here for long.

Along a partly wooded, partly barren landscape that has been worked hard for 200 years are a handful of remote villages, each of which can be captured in the loom of a single street lamp. Offshore narrow peninsulas finger out into the cold Fundy current to create cruel, treacherous pieces of water that force fishermen and mariners to maintain respectful sea room between them and the jagged shoreline. Jenny Cirone, an independent female lobsterwoman who maintained a flock of sheep for over half a century on Nash Island, once said to me, "One thing about 'downeasters'—well, of course I'm one, but then—well, they's awful grudgy."

The eastern Maine coast does not open itself quickly to strangers; but it welcomes you into the winter of its soul.

Glacial erratic, 1,532 feet above sea level on Cadillac Mountain with Porcupine Islands and Frenchman Bay in background; Abandoned quarry, Hardwood Island, near Jonesport

Narraguagus and Pleasant Bays

Before working at Hurricane Island, I had moved to the Pigeon Hill Road along the edge of its eponymous bay in 1972. Down the long peninsular road that terminates at Petit Manan Point, I cut pulpwood in spruce woods, dug clams in muddy coves, and

raked blueberries on small barrens. These were the graduate courses I took before I enrolled in graduate school, and they were my first tastes of Maine, both sweet and bitter.

From shore, I used to watch the waters from Pigeon Hill, Narraguagus and Pleasant bays spill back and forth into one another and create furious seas around Petit Manan Island offshore. These bays are bounded on the main by Cape Split to the east and Petit Manan Point, named by Champlain, to the west.

The first time I entered the small lobster harbor of Cape Split, a place name you can't find on any road map, I was aboard the motor vessel, HURRICANE, captained by the no-nonsense Ed Dietrich, of German extraction, with Chip Bauer, his first mate, who seemed to have left a broken heart in every port he visited. We were headed east to Hurricane's downeast base.

As we rounded into Cape Split, on the eastern shore was Oscar Look's wharf, where we tied up to refuel. Look was a lobster dealer, whose family has sold fuel, lobsters, and groceries from a wharf-side establishment for many generations, traded gossip with the few hundred people who make up the village of South Addison and dispensed wisdom to anyone who cared to listen. While we were fueling up, he told us a story from the day before when he had been interrupted by an officious yachtsman looking for ice and lobsters for his crew and in a hurry for service, during the lobster season when Look's lobster boats were also exceedingly busy. I gathered that the yachtsman had not been rude exactly, but he had raised his voice at his crew while landing at the float, had gotten in the way, and generally betrayed an impatient and lubberly attitude. After taking on his supplies, the yachtsman inquired about a mooring (there were none) and then asked if there was enough water for him to anchor up in the harbor in a little cove. "Oh, there's plenty of water up there," said Look.

Nash Island sheep run, Pleasant Bay, Addison

*Beals Island
fisherman's camp*

The following morning the yachtsman came back by Look's wharf, all steamed up, and complained about grounding out in the middle of the night. When Look nodded knowingly, the yachtsman said, "But I thought you said there was plenty of water." "I did, and there is," said Look with a wicked grin. "It's just spread kinda thin."

Eastern and Western Bays: Beals and Great Wass

The waters of Eastern and Western Bays surround four large islands—Beals, Great Wass, Steele, and Head Harbor—which together form the easternmost granite dome of the Maine coast. Beals Island was the last coastal island to be ceded to the mainland when a suspension bridge was arched over the swift tidal waters of Moosabec Reach in 1957.

Samuel Eliot Morison, a cruiser of the Maine coast as well as a preeminent maritime historian, suggested Champlain stopped in these waters on his second coastal voyage. Morison believed Champlain dropped anchor in the Cow's Yard between Head Harbor and Steele Harbor islands, which is still one of the few protected deepwater anchorages east of Schoodic Point. Champlain named the islands Cape Corneille, or Cape Crow, for the black birds that made their presence known to him in raucous fashion. Cape Corneille is now known by the less-attractive name of Black Head, but the birds he saw could have been either crows or ravens, which still associate with each other on the islands. You can still watch flocks of crows, exceeding a thousand in number, winging their way across the waters offshore when the evening lights begin to flicker, group after group heading for thick copses of island spruce where they roost in scores of little murders secure from two-and four-legged predators.

Mussel dragger and lobster boat in Moosabec Reach, with Jonesport in background

One Fourth of July, I was sailing through Moosabec Reach with Alan Sterman, the oldest Outward Bound instructor at Hurricane Island, who had left a successful career in commercial real estate to simplify his life. When he was not teaching courses, Sterman showed me the waters he had sailed; I showed him the islands I was coming to know. During our expeditions, Alan shared his philosophical meditations. He referred to himself as a "Jew-Bu," since he had been raised in an observant Jewish household, but had become a serious student of the Buddhist philosopher, Trungpa Rinpoche. I learned a lot from Alan, both on the fine points of sail and the Mahayana tradition in Nepalese spirituality.

We had sailed down to Cross Island at the east end of the archipelago and were beating our way back west when we entered the Reach with the tide against us. As we waited for the six-knot current to slack, we realized that a parade was getting organized on the main street and we went to watch. It was a wonderful small-town spectacle and included the winner of the beauty pageant, "Miss Outboard Motor," whose prize was a thoroughly practical engine for one of her lucky beaux.

Englishman Bay: Puffins or Rogues

Among yachtsmen, Roque Island is most well known today for its magnificent Great South Beach. Getting to Roque requires careful navigation through the rocky waters east of Schoodic, where anchorages are difficult to find and fog is prevalent. Navigating the way to the island is as much a rite of passage as a sailing passage. And your reward for completing the voyage is to anchor off the long, arcing, white sandy beach, which stretches for well over a mile between the shoulders of two immense headlands. Of course, in these days of electronic navigation gear, the challenge is not quite as real as it was 20 or 30 years ago.

Samuel Morison has suggested Roque Island may be an abbreviation of Isle des Perroques, a name that French explorers gave to places frequented by the "sea parrots," or puffins, they found on the islands of the North Atlantic. But Roque itself is not suitable habitat for puffins. A more plausible explanation is that the name is a corruption of Rogue Island, referring to its use by pirates, known then as privateers, who raided passing merchant ships. In fact, there is a record of one John Rhoades, who headquartered his pirate fleet at Machias in the early 1700s and conceivably used the high headlands of Roque to post lookouts—on a clear day, Mount Desert is visible from the summit of one of Roque's promontories.

Machias Bay: Volcanic Arches and Caves

Outward Bound's downeast base was on Cross Island in Machias Bay, where yachtsman and industrialist Tom Cabot had deeded 20 acres and an abandoned lifesaving station to the organization. Cross had apparently been named for a wooden cross that a French expedition—perhaps headed by Champlain himself—had erected on its southern cliffs. The names of the other islands at the entrance to Machias Bay derived from some of the area's earliest inhabitants—Stone, Libby, and Foster. It's hard to say how Scabby Island at the western edge of Machias Bay got its name, though it may have been named in the same spirit as Ragged Arse Island at the entrance to Penobscot Bay.

The Machias Bay islands, like those of Englishman Bay, have a more rugged and forbidding topography than islands farther to the west, reflecting the change in bedrock that underlies the coast east of Jonesport. The southern shores of most of these islands are formed of brittle, fractured, needle-shaped volcanic rocks that have been cut by intrusions of other igneous rocks known as dikes. Yellowhead Island gets its name from one of these sulfurous volcanic rocks. Many of the dikes have eroded away, leaving narrow, vertical-walled crevices and a world of arches and caves that invites exciting expeditions by foot around the shores of these lightly inhabited places.

On one circumnavigation of Cross Island with forester Ray Leonard and several

Great South Beach on Roque Island is over a mile long.

Old Man Island

AUGUST 24, 1995—The Cross Island mini archipelago lies at the extreme eastern end of the Maine coast—the last group of islands before the 20-mile long "Bold Coast," of Washington County, where there is scant protection from a long lee shore. The easternmost island in this little archipelago is Old Man Island, where on an exceptionally calm day, I land with ornithologist Richard Podolsky.

Behind Old Man's massive jaw of black granite we drop RAVEN's danforth in the rock and kelp holding ground and then row the skiff on the falling tide and scramble ashore.

Dawn at Old Man Island at the end of the summer is an exquisite piece of work—a tiny piece of an an unrecognized international biosphere reserve. The island is cleft by a huge fault where two massive blocks of black granite

have tumbled past each other. Here just past low slack the sea cascades into the Venturi of the V-notch cleft and funnels into an elegant tide pool on the inner shore, perched just above mean low tide where the still waters seem to be holding their breath in the hot still eye of the morning. I lay on the leeward edge of these cliffs, bo-

real and pungent with crowberry, while a lone eagle banks twice over the tide pool, disdaining company. A four-year-old bird, on the edge of its majority.

Then just like that, it happened. The tide changes; a little surge heaves up outside followed by a deep and throaty gurgle from within the granite jaws, and little white concentric force rings of spindrift begin to appear and radiate out into the middle of the pool, thirsty for new water, foaming with oxygen and carrying food and life. Each set of six or seven waves gets stronger and pushes the spindrift patterns further into the quarter-acre tide pool.

To watch the tide push in past these huge south-facing rocks where the rays of the morning sun off the sea sear the eyes is to watch the biological pulse of the sea conquer massive brutish rock.

The surge comes in sevens.

Outward Bound instructors, we explored the island's bold southern shore. Midway along this outer coast, we saw below us a little beach of fine stone and decided to climb down to it since it was near low tide and the sea was calm at the foot of the cliffs. When we arrived on the beach, it was like entering a chapter from Verne's *Mysterious Island*, as the narrow maw of a sea cave opened before us. We walked in cautiously, listening to the restless beating of the outside ocean, a large muffled roar, pulsing here and everywhere inside the rock walls. Sea anemones of pale and vivid colors were attached to the back wall of this 60-foot-deep cave. It was both eerie and wonderful.

Although we were at the most lightly inhabited eastern end of the archipelago on Cross Island, when the sun went down, enormous, thousand-foot-high towers lit with red lights loomed above us. This network of towers at the Cutler Naval Station felt like the watching eyes of Mordor, but they were actually communicating with American submarines under the oceans of the world.

Cobscook and Passamaquoddy Bays

I did not get to explore Cobscook Bay's inner sanctum or the swirling whirlpools of Passamaquoddy Bay by boat until I had graduated from small sailing vessels to piloting power vessels that could successfully navigate the largest—24-foot—tides in continental America. I will never forget the first time I took a 26-foot outboard through the 6-foot standing tidal waves at Falls Island, where half of Cobscook Bay drops into its other half. I was with Peggy Rockefeller of Maine Coast Heritage Trust who was aboard to survey its scenic character. Believe me, *trust* was the operative word.

Cross Island sea cave with Outward Bound pulling boats in background

Cobscook Bay is distinct from all other bays of Maine. Here the old river valleys run northwest-southeast, or perpendicular to the trend of bedrock along most of the rest of the coast. Cobscook is a system of concentrically curving bays, peninsulas, and islands formed from the partial submergence of these arc-shaped valleys and ridges carved in folded shales, slates, and sandstones. When sea level rose following glaciation, it flooded a cross valley that connected the inner and outer longitudinal valleys to create the topography we see today.

Cobscook Bay is an integral part of Passamaquoddy Bay, known to most Americans since Franklin Roosevelt's time for the power potential of its enormous tides, which he unsuccessfully proposed harnessing by building an elaborate set of tidal dams. More recently during the 1970s and 1980s, Cobscook Bay was at the center of the public debate of whether the Pittston Company would build an oil refinery in Eastport. Environmentalists rallied and the Pittston refinery proposal was defeated.

A decade and a half later, a new industry grew up around the bay, which also pitted environmental groups against industry—salmon aquaculture. Raising farmed Atlantic

East Quoddy Head light,
Campobello Island

salmon in ocean net pens became a huge business in the waters off Eastport and Lubec in the 1990s, employing hundreds from among Washington County's most isolated communities. Environmentalists questioned whether waste from the millions of farm raised Atlantic salmon which swim in pens would pollute the ocean waters or whether escapees from the farms would endanger the native-run stock of Atlantic salmon that still make their way up the Dennys River in the inner bay annually. The environmentalists prevailed again when the native salmon run on the Dennys and a handful of other rivers were listed as threatened. They were helped this time by growing economic competition from imported salmon abroad, and salmon aquaculture as an industry had shrunk to a shadow of its former self, although lately it has begun to recover

The Maine boundary at the southwest end of the archipelago runs through the Isles of Shoals, while the international boundary between Maine and Canada runs through the Lubec Narrows offshore of West Quoddy Head, separating Maine's easternmost town from Campobello Island, New Brunswick.

On Campobello Island is the site of the historic summer cottage and grounds of the family of President Franklin D. Roosevelt. As a child and young man, the future president spent every summer of his life on Campobello, which he called his "beloved island," and where he learned to love the sea and the outdoors. It is the island where he courted his future wife, Eleanor, who loved the island as much as he, where morning fogs enveloped them in its quiet embrace and gave them respite from the demands of their lives.

In 1964 the Roosevelt-Campobello International Park was established by treaty between the United States and Canada as a "symbol of the enduring friendship" between the two countries. This international park is the only one of its kind in the world. During the past half century, the park has grown through acquisitions and extensive renovations of the historic Roosevelt cottage and neighboring cottages and has become an economic engine for both eastern Washington County and Campobello Island, drawing over 100,000 visitors per year to this enisled corner of Maine and Canada..

The Hands of the Past

When I first began collecting ecological information on Maine's islands as a graduate student, I thought that their natural communities—the numbers and variety of plants, birds, fish and shellfish along these shores—would be fairly consistent. I thought that if you had been to one rocky, spruce-covered island, you would have seen what most islands had to offer for ecological diversity. I couldn't have been more wrong.

Slowly I began to appreciate that the nature of particular islands is peculiar, local, and idiosyncratic. No matter where you go along this immense archipelago, if you care to notice, you will be struck by the stark differences in the assemblages of plants and animals you encounter. I know I was.

On the mainland shores, the amplitude of an ecological event that disturbs a community—a fire, land clearing or a windstorm—is quickly dampened by the influence of adjacent communities, which rapidly invade disturbed areas, supplying new life to fill the gaps and to compete with the species that remain. But islands are different; in their isolation they record the effects of the past. Striking ecological differences are etched into the island landscape. In short, the effects of the past are indexed in the landscape.

Once you begin to see island communities as an ensemble of historical motifs, resulting from minor or catastrophic events, caused by human or natural agents, that reverberate down through the centuries of ecological time, the performances have the power to entrance you, and the differences between islanders and their environments starts to blur.

Southern Island,
Tenants Harbor

CHAPTER 3

Landforms:
Cliffs, Caves, Cobbles and Domes

And there in ragged grayness lay the quarry
"This pavin' motion," my companion said,
"Was goin' to make me rich and made me poor.
'Twas in the eighties I began to work here,
When the great cities paved their streets with blocks
A nickel a piece they were, and I could reel
Two hundred blocks or more each blessed day."

—Wilbert Snow, "The Paving Quarry"

Hurricane Island;
(Facing) Glacial
striations, Birch Cove,
Vinalhaven

While living on Hurricane Island, in exchange for the room (tent), board and access to Outward Bound's small private navy, I gave natural history lectures for groups of students passing through the island on their courses. It was a humbling experience. My audiences were generally bedraggled groups of all ages who had been awakened before daybreak, run grueling loops around the perimeter of the island, jumped into the frigid waters of Hurricane Sound before breakfast, then climbed vertical rock faces, hung from ropes between trees, and completed a boat capsize drill before I got them at the end of the day.

If you can imagine feeling as they did when they arrived after dinner in the dark and warmth of a dining hall, you would appreciate that they might not have been keenly attuned to the wonders of nature. Once, a student in the front row fell off a bench dead asleep and did not wake when he hit the floor. I learned to talk fast, racing through a natural history slide show to introduce students, mostly from cities and suburbs, how to use signals from the environment to anticipate the rhythms and sounds of the natural world.

Why There Are So Many Maine Islands

In spite of their exhaustion, Hurricane Island was a wonderful classroom for these students. I would sometimes take them to the top of the cliffs on the south end of Hurricane Island with a 270-degree view of a bay full of islands, and the very first thing everyone wanted to know was: Why are there so many islands out there? The simple answer: ice.

I asked the students to imagine a massive sheet of ice covering all of Maine and the Gulf of Maine out beyond the horizon, with a sheet of ice a mile high over the highest point of land. Before this shuddering hulk of ice ground over the landscape, Maine's topography had been much like that of the remainder of the Atlantic coast: gently sloping coastal plain with sandy beaches and salt marshes, with an occasional granitic dome and ridge or ancient crystalline pinnacle breaking the horizon.

Someone has taken the time to calculate that an acre of ice one mile high weighs on the order of seven million tons. Imagine the burden of this ice warping the land down along a weak zone in the earth's crust that trends approximately northeast-southwest, corresponding to the present trend of the coast. Then, within a very short period of time all that ice melted and flooded into the ocean. Not in the little floods we have every year, not the hundred-year floods that wipe out whole towns, but floods of incomparable magnitude surging into the sea. These floods coursed out of lakes twice the size of Moosehead—today the largest lake east of the Great Lakes—through river corridors many times the size and volume of the Kennebec and Penobscot and Saint John rivers—and

The Bubbles, glacially rounded mountains at the head of Jordan Pond, a glacially carved lake

filled the basins of the coastal lowlands.

Nine million cubic miles of ocean were pulled up onto the land and held in the ice sheets. When all that water was released in a geological instant, the sea level rose worldwide. But it was especially dramatic along the Maine coast, where the crust had warped downward. The glacial meltwaters sent incredible torrents of water into the sea, sending its long fingers into the land; the rising sea flowed up the old river valleys, all the way to Millinocket on the Penobscot and near Greenville on the Kennebec. It flowed over the outer banks, which had been dry land, and completely submerged the coastal lowlands to fill the Gulf of Maine. Isolated mountaintops, hilltops and ridgelines were stranded as islands in a vast gulf.

Long Island—Round Island

From my expeditions compiling the natural history guide for Hurricane Island, I could not help but notice that Maine's islands come in one of two shapes: They are either long and narrow like the islands of Casco and Muscongus bays, or they are rounded and domed. The domes of granite give shape to not only Hurricane, but also Mount Desert, Deer Isle, Swan's, Isle au Haut, Vinalhaven, Beals and scores of smaller granite islands between the Muscle Ridge and Jonesport. In contrast, the region from Casco to Camden is primarily underlain by the rootstocks of ancient fold mountains, the roots of which run in parallel lines of ridges with their intervening valleys now flooded. The craggy islands of eastern Maine beyond Beals Island are composed of the remnants of volcanic activity that have weathered like stone castles into fantastic shapes. The study of the rise and fall of landforms is called geomorphology, and there are few places in the East where geologists have such a field day in studying the restless movements of the Earth's surface as in the frozen rocks of Maine's shores.

To study geology is to dream about the Big Picture of the Earth's restless epochs, and the dramatic rock tableaux presented on the wave-scoured shores of Maine's rocky islands are a geologist's heaven. The Big Picture of rock history is sometimes revealed in small details. I have spent many pleasant days with geologists, plinking away at island shorelines. I recall one afternoon spent with Arthur M. Hussey II, a Bowdoin College geologist, who had been bent over a small outcrop on a Casco Bay island for a half-hour or more. When he stood up, he pointed to a series of lovely, sinuous crenellations in the outcrop and said, "This is a third-order fold of an ancient mountain chain and is good evidence of a continental collision." Such a gigantic conclusion from such a little outcrop!

Third-order fold, evidence of continental drift

Stone Ghosts

No one who has ever visited Hurricane Island can fail to be amazed by the scope of the quarrying operation that occupied workers and families there between 1870 and 1914, when the island was abandoned almost overnight. Huge steam boilers rusting on the south end of Hurricane, next to the largest flywheel ever cast, and stone monoliths, half carved and polished lying around the island, give silent, elegant testimony to a way of life that enlivened these shores and then receded into the encroaching spruce forest.

I caught a whisper of one of the thousands of Hurricane's untold stories one night with just enough moon in the night sky for walking around the island paths without a light. I was sitting in a little clearing among the spruce, which had invaded what once had been the quarriers' "town." Deep in conversation with a couple of instructor friends, I idly ran my hand over the moon-bleached bare granite, when my fingers felt a straight ridge in the time-smoothed surface. Leaning down to adjust my eyes in the moon glow, I could just barely make out four letters: RN and LN. Initials

Carved remnants, Dix Island;
Uncut granite, Starboard Rock, Vinalhaven

on the rock; surely a century-old sign of a tryst. But the most remarkable feature was that the letters had not been carved down into the rock; rather, the granite surrounding the letters had been lovingly chiseled away—perhaps worried away—leaving these four initials to rise in bold relief from the hard stone surface. In some ineffable way those unknown initials encapsulated all the poignancy of an island town that disappeared while all its stories and dreams and personal histories were scattered to the wind.

The modern-day owner of Hurricane Island, Jim Gaston, was equally fascinated by Hurricane's history. Gaston's father had bought the island in the late 1930s and conceived of turning it into a granite museum/club/resort for wealthy yachtsmen. The project foundered because he could not secure a liquor license from abstemious Vinalhaven. Not until Gaston leased the island to Hurricane Island Outward Bound, in 1964, did it slowly come back to life.

Jim Gaston was an interesting character. A pilot and a surgeon, he would fly to Rockland, get in a boat, often at night, and steam across the bay in all kinds of weather. People used to wonder how many lives he had used up in the process. I sometimes walked around Hurricane with Gaston, pointing out what I knew from stories I had heard on Vinalhaven, or had learned from Charles McLane, or had been uncovered by the vigorous tree cutting and pruning that the Outward Bound staff completed to keep the island's feral nature at bay. Gaston's great-uncle was Gifford Pinchot, the founder of the Yale School of Forestry and the first chief forester for the U.S. Forest Service. Since I was a forester, I got along well with Gaston.

One of the first projects I worked on at the Island Institute several years later was editing *Hurricane Island: The Town that Disappeared,* a fascinating history of the quarry era on Hurricane Island, by Eleanor Motley Richardson.

The Hard Facts of Quarry Life

My first winter on Vinalhaven, George Putz had taken me to one of the island's many cemeteries where granite workers were buried, lest I become too rosy-eyed about life on quarry islands. At the height of the granite era in the 1880s and 1890s, Vinalhaven had supported a dozen large quarries. Wandering around this main cemetery on the hillside overlooking Carver's Pond, we came upon a dozen or so of the strangest, most elaborate gravestones I had ever seen. George told me that the men who lay under them had also carved them. When granite workers began coughing blood from the dust they breathed every day, they started carving their own gravestones. If the monuments they left in the Vinalhaven graveyard are any indication, these hard men had a long time to consider their fate.

I began reading whatever histories I could find about the quarry era on islands, and learned that there had once been 33 major island quarries among Maine islands, stretching from Friendship to Jonesport. Large towns and workforces of 1,000 or more men, most of them immigrants, appeared almost overnight, and in many cases disappeared as quickly, on islands such as Clark, Dix, High, Hurricane, Crotch and Black. The Scottish, Italians, Finnish, Swedish, and Welsh artisans and laborers who came to the American shores of opportunity paid a high cost in labor, and often enough with their lives.

Maine's island granite belt ranges from the Muscle Ridge islands across to Vinalhaven, east through Stonington and the islands of Merchant Row, to Swan's, Black and Mount Desert Islands to Head Harbor Island off Jonesport. This hundred-mile section of the coast became the center of an enormous trade in stone: granite for bridges and breakwaters, for paving blocks and public places, for libraries and for the Library of Congress, for monuments and memorials, for foundations, sills, lintels, curbstones, and a hundred other uses. And everywhere went millions of cobblestones, the quarries' bread-and-butter work, to pave the muddy streets of burgeoning cities. In 1900 and the preceding few decades, more men were employed on the Maine islands in the granite business than in fishing and farming combined.

Although small island quarrying operations had begun as early as 1792, the first granite commercially quarried in Maine was cut in 1826 on Vinalhaven to build the walls of a prison in Massachusetts. Were these stonecutters aware of a historical irony in the making? With access to inexpensive water transportation, island quarries had a natural advantage. In the Vinalhaven area, which would become the center of

Hurricane Isle, Me.

Hurricane Island company town;
Carver's Pond cemetery

Sands Quarry Vinalhaven; Friendship Long Island, with schooner SEVENTY-SIX *dockside*

this trade, a second quarry opened in 1846 on Leadbetter Island, just across the Narrows on the west side; a third, the so-called East Boston Quarry, opened in 1849. There were three more by 1860 and seven others between 1860 and 1880. By 1890 Maine led the nation in the production of granite. Elegant structures such as the Metropolitan Museum of Art, the Cathedral of St. John the Divine in New York City, and the Lincoln and Jefferson memorials in Washington were once silent, solid hefts of rock on the shores of Maine's far-distant islands.

Subtle blends of whites and gray granite came from the exposed domes of Mount Desert Island, particularly from Hall quarry. Similar textures and colors came off Hurricane, High, Dix and Clark islands, and from Vinalhaven's dozen massive quarries, including one on Norton Point where quarrymen also cut black granite for monuments and facing stone. From Jonesport came a bloody red granite, while other quarries advertised blue and cinnamon hues. The flecks of quartz and mica within the feldspar mineral matrix of granite also produced a variety of textures, from fine-grained granodiorites to massively textured great gray granites with individual crystals as large as your thumbnail. And sometimes in a dome of granite with a different cooling history, individual crystals of dark micas remelted to produce patterns of frozen swirls like those in a chocolate pound cake. Pattern upon pattern could be bought depending on a buyer's whim or the job to be done.

The Rift, Lift, and Hardway

Walking along the flanks of the southern cliffs on Hurricane Island where the main face of granite cutting had occurred is like walking through a geology textbook. There you can see how granite lies in sheets of varying thickness over the surface of the land and how the stone naturally fractures along right-angle planes. What is it within us that likes a right angle?

An experienced stonecutter can tell how the grain runs in an unbroken piece of granite. Quarrymen used to speak of the plane of granite in terms of its "rift," which runs perpendicular to the horizon. Most Maine granite is oriented along an east-west axis. The "lift" of the granite (what geologists call the "sheeting" of granite) runs parallel to the horizon, and the "hardway" runs at right angles to the rift.

On Hurricane Island's sloping shoulders leading up to the top of the quarry, you can see where the sheets of granite widen toward the center of a main quarry face due to the natural jointing patterns in the rock. This trend of the lift, as quarrymen spoke of it, allowed them to cut single pieces of enormous dimensions. The four rough columns for the interior of the Cathedral of St. John the Divine, which were cut from Wharf Quarry across Hurricane Sound, were 64 feet long and 8 feet in diameter and weighed 300 tons. An earlier piece of granite cut for the monument to Major General John Ellis Wool weighed half again as much as the cathedral pillars and was at the time the largest single piece of granite ever cut from solid rock. Since granite quarrying everywhere has fallen on hard times, the best guess is that this record still stands.

You can still see one of the St. John the Divine cathedral's 64-foot rough columns in the puckerbrush near the end of the Sands Quarry Road on Vinalhaven. It is almost unimaginable how horses, oxen and wooden vessels could move blocks of this magnitude. Some date the decline of Maine's island quarry era to the failure to deliver the final columns for the Cathedral of St. John the Divine intact. They broke on the enormous lathe constructed to round the rectilinear blocks and were delivered in two sections.

One of the interesting historical sidelights of the island quarry era is the complementary role played by Chebeague Island in Casco Bay. There islanders built boats to carry granite, and during the early years of the era, they supplied all the boats that carried stone along the coast of Maine. Since Chebeague Island sloops had carried rock ballast from the shores of Casco Bay islands to the expanding Portland shipyards from the early days of settlement, perhaps it was only natural that they should have gotten into the business of hauling granite to build coastal forts and breakwaters.

By 1870, about 50 Chebeague Island craft coasted along the islands carrying granite. The vessels, originally rigged as sloops but later rerigged as schooners,

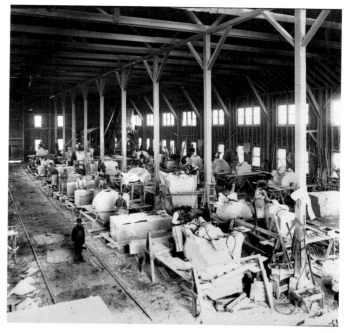

Cutting shed, Bodwell Granite Co., Vinalhaven;
Column sections for the Cathedral of St. John the Divine, New York, ready for shipping from Carver's Harbor

were beamy, full-bellied craft manned by crews who knew how to handle rock, and most important, how to stow cargoes. A load of 60,000 paving stones headed for Boston, New York, or New Orleans was not uncommon. Records show that in one 12-day period, 320,465 paving stones cut on Hurricane Island were shipped from its stone wharves.

The End of an Era

The first concrete house in the United States was built in Port Chester, New York, in 1874. Although there is no record as to whether it was a tasteful piece of architecture, the beginning of the end was at hand for granite quarries. Cement making was a skill that had been familiar to the Romans, though one lost in what we are fond of calling the Dark Ages. It was rediscovered in 1824 by an engineer in Portland, England—hence the term "Portland cement."

The introduction of the cheaper and easier-to-handle building material was probably the ultimate cause of the decline of granite quarrying on Maine islands, but it was not the only cause. The end of lucrative government contracts, the construction of railroads on the mainland, and labor unrest all laid blows on an increasingly desperate industry.

Nowhere did the end of the era play out more dramatically than on Hurricane Island. The island had been bought in 1870 for the preposterous sum of $50 by a retired Civil War general who had fought at Bull Run. Davis Tillson had a reputation of being a petty tyrant, probably all the worse for owning his own island, which he ran as he pleased. When Hurricane Island separated from the town of Vinalhaven in 1878, it had its own post office, bank, pool hall, bowling green, bandstand, ice pond, ball field, boardinghouses, and 40 cottages. Hurricane was justly famed along the coast for its cutting and polishing shed. It was said that no granite took polish as well as Hurricane's fine-grained gray-white granite.

For 45 years the only two superintendents

of works on Hurricane had both been Landers. First John Landers and then his son, Thomas, had run the day-to-day activities on the island, where the population at one point reportedly reached 1,000. As we cleared the forest around various stone artifacts on Hurricane, we located the Landers' family's large house foundation at the top of the slope along a steep cart trail called Broadway on an old island map. It was the only foundation in which a cistern had been carved in the bottom of the granite bedrock on which the foundation stood. As we cleared trees from more and more of the other foundations on Hurricane, we gradually uncovered the genius of their engineering. The Landers men had laid out a set of dendritic channels across the broad east-facing slope of Hurricane, turning much of the hillside into a catchment basin where rainwater was channeled to a reservoir for watering livestock and servicing the steam powered engines that drove the drills on the massive active face looking out to sea.

But when Thomas Landers died on Hurricane in 1914, it was excuse enough for the already financially troubled Hurricane Island Granite Co. to announce it was closing the company store and ceasing regular boat runs to the mainland. A kind of panic ensued as quarrymen, stonecutters, blacksmiths, paving cutters, tool sharpeners, tool boys, lumpers, stone boxers, teamsters, and their families had short notice to pack for the last boat. Many of them were forced to leave some of their worldly possessions behind and most never returned. The houses were taken down and sold wharf-side; the church was floated across the bay.

For years Vinalhaven people who visited Hurricane described an eerie pall hanging over the island. Tools were literally set down in place; huge, half-carved stones stood where they had been hauled into the carving sheds or set down on the way to the wharf. It was as if hundreds of people had disappeared overnight, which is precisely what happened.

Perhaps the most striking aspect of Hurricane's legacy, however, is that 47 years

St. Helena Island quarry;
Spruce growing out of
bare rock on top of main
quarry, Hurricane Island

after this massive industrial enterprise cut most of the island's trees, removed its soil, and brought in huge numbers of immigrant workers to cart off its bedrock, Hurricane became a premier setting for a world-famous wilderness program. Here is a true and lasting picture of the obdurate nature of Maine islands: Hurricane's cut and blasted granite faces are covered again by the equally obdurate spruce that grow out of fissures in bare rock; its motions are carpeted beneath thick mats of luxuriant mosses. If history has a way of repeating itself, the story of Hurricane Island during the first decade of the 21st century might be titled, "The Town that Disappeared Again." Outward Bound moved its mainland base from Rockland to a protected cove in Spruce Head, where courses could be launched more economically, and just a few years later, in 2007, the school let its long lease on Hurricane Island lapse. Although Peter Willauer, the founder of the Hurricane Island Outward Bound School, came out of retirement to start up a new group, the Hurricane Island Foundation, to offer scientific and educational courses on the island, the long decades of deferred maintenance suggest the path of re-creation there will be long and steep.

Crotch Island: Greatest Stone on Earth

In 1980, across East Penobscot Bay off Stonington, the Crotch Island quarry reopened and I went for a visit. Everyone who ever sailed through the Deer Isle Thorofare knows that the Crotch Island quarry was most famous for the shade of its granite—a lavender pink and milky white with occasional flecks of deep red, caused by the presence, in unusually high concentrations, of a particular variety of feldspar. The Museum of Fine Arts in Boston was built with Crotch Island pink, though the rough blocks were first taken to the famous cutting shed on Hurricane Island to be cut and polished. A few of these blocks are still lying around on the south end of Hurricane Island where the polishing sheds once stood. In 1966 Crotch Island was briefly reopened to cut rose-colored granite for the Kennedy memorial in Boston.

Antonio Ramos, the president of New England Stone Industries of Smithfield, Rhode Island, is the man who reopened the Crotch Island quarry on a more permanent basis. Ramos began his granite career as a sculptor, went into the stonecutting business in Rhode Island in 1969, and bought the first part of Crotch Island in 1979. He told me he saw a big future in Maine granites because of their variety of color and textures and because of the demand for red and pink and black granites rather than the gray and white that once dominated the business.

Earl Kelty was Ramos's first superintendent of works when Crotch reopened. "Nowhere is there stone like Crotch Island's," he told me. "I'd always heard about it. It's

stronger than Barre granite and it splits better. You almost have to bend this granite before it'll break, but when she lets go along the 'hardway,' you've got a clean face to work on." Running his fingers over the rough surface of one of the quarry stones, he said, "It's a pretty stone; it's kind of got a glow, a warm feeling to it. Tony got me to see that."

A natural salesman, Ramos will list the reasons granite is back as a monumental building material: It's cheaper than glass, more durable than cement, and is also a good insulator. New machines have been developed in the last six or seven years that can cut granite down to 3/8-inch thick—the thickness of a pane of glass—so it's lightweight, too. In the old days granite companies sold more cubic feet of stone, but the demand for granite measured in square feet has never been higher. "That Crotch Island stone is the greatest stone on earth," says Ramos.

The Geomorphology of Place Names

The study of the origins of place names can be entertaining, especially while cruising among the islands of Maine: How did most of these 4,617 discrete pieces of island real estate (not to mention innumerable pieces of the bottom of the Gulf of Maine) get their names?

If none of the currently inhabited islands had names, no doubt they would come to be called by some of the same names they were first given. An island with a bold granite southern shore that shimmers in summer sunlight should rightly be called White Island. There would be a number of Long and High Islands, a few Sand Islands, a scattering of Washerwoman Ledges where the surf foams up over a half-tide ledge, perhaps one or two Crotch Islands if this didn't cause too much blushing—although around the turn of the century this was reason enough to rename more than one Crotch Island.

Sugar Loaves, Fox Islands Thorofare; Popplestones on beach, Eastern Cove, Frenchboro

Still many other islands and ledges that were named for their geophysical features would have different names now. Who has even heard, in these days of imported textiles and polyesters, of a thrumcap, which was a round hat made of four leftover pieces of homespun called thrums? Would we still call the myriad of smooth-rounded ledges by these whimsical names: Sugar Loaves, Junk o' Pork, or the Ladle, inspired by kitchen products, or Colby Pup and Virgin's Breasts conjured up by inspirational forms? Probably not.

But one island that would be named the same in any era is Shipstern off Milbridge. The alternately layered ochre and white sedimentary units at the western end of Shipstern are among the most beautiful rock outcrops anywhere on the Maine coast. No one who has sailed under the lovely cliffs at this exposed end of the island fails to remark how the rock formation resembles the stern of some abandoned galleon at the entrance to Pleasant Bay, hinting of pirates and treasure and Spanish doubloons.

Popplestones, Cobblestones, Killick Stones

Long before quarrying began on Hurricane Island and its neighbors along Maine's Midcoast region, this rocky coast provided more humble products. One of the first was rocks that could be fashioned into small anchors known as killicks. Iron for anchors was almost unheard of, and in any case it was too expensive for the self-sufficient island economies. Rather, long and thin stones were used as homemade anchors; these were found chiefly in the western bays from Casco to Muscongus, where the trend of the bedrock nicely fit the desired shapes. One island on Muscongus whose shores are covered with just the right-shaped rocks is still called Killick Stone.

Stone ballast for vessels was another early local resource. Although Great Spoon Island off Isle au Haut was no doubt named for its high inverted spoon-shaped hill and long trailing handle that ends up as a cobble beach, on the early British Admiralty charts it was called Fill Boat Island. Another island off Jonesport is still known as Ballast Island. Both islands have exposed beaches where smooth round rocks were easily collected to ballast homemade sailing vessels.

Somewhere along the line, someone realized that large wave-smoothed stones, free for the taking off Maine's shores, could also be sold to city merchants intent upon cleaning up their streets. These "popplestones," as they came to be called, were the first (but not the last) Maine rocks used to pave the streets of East Coast cities. Popplestones were probably also the first ballast ever sold for profit, and they provided employment in the early 1780s to Maine islanders.

On the south end of Isle au Haut, where popplestones were once collected, you can have an entirely distinctive island experience. Boom Beach, in the small bight below the road that skirts the south end of Long Pond, consists of a collection of smooth, rounded boulders one to two feet in diameter, with a few enormous boulders up to five feet wide. Standing there when a big surge rolls in, as I did once, you can hear variations on a theme from Newton's music of the spheres; when surges recede, the rolling of the stones creates a deeply resonant tympanic crescendo that no human music quite captures.

Sandy Beaches and Rocky Headlands

Many of Maine's sea cliffs are awesome, even to the most jaded eye. Monhegan's White Head and Mount Desert's Otter Cliffs, each calling itself the highest sea cliff on the East Coast of the United States, come to mind. But the islands' innumerable pocket beaches are equally wonderful.

Hurricane Island supported one tiny strip of sandy beach at its north end, composed in part from ground up shells. This was typical of most of the islands I visited. Of 7,000 miles of saltwater shoreline, Maine has perhaps only 60 miles of sandy beach, mostly from Saco Bay southward. There are a handful of sandy beaches on Casco Bay islands, owing to the fact that the Androscoggin River used to empty into Casco Bay before its course was altered and the river hooked left into Merrymeeting Bay. Casco Bay beaches are mostly sited on the north sides of islands, so that sunbathing has never been as diverting there as other places.

In studying island beaches, I learned about wave energy. The outthrust jawbone of a rocky headland or peninsula, like a street fighter, dares something to hit it, and a stormy sea is only too willing to comply. A point of land focuses wave energy at its outer edge, while waves bend around promontories and headlands. As I watched them bend, they would lengthen, become less steep, and spill some of their energy, so that they were usually quite tame as they curled into a cove. It became apparent to me that the particle size on a beach is good index of the average annual wave climate; as it grades from cobble to gravel to sand or mud, the fury of the wave energy that visits each year is more and more dissipated. Thus a beach is really a kind of natural seismograph recording the climate of wave energy: Slight currents transport silt; a 2.5 knot current transports inch-round stones; a storm wave packs three tons of power to a linear foot of shore; and so forth, up the Beaufort Scale. A granite boulder on Matinicus Rock, calculated by a stonecutter to weigh 100 tons, was moved 12 feet during the lifetime of one of the island's lightkeepers.

Undoubtedly the most exquisite sandy beach on a Maine island is at privately owned Roque Island. It is the longest sandy beach on the archipelago. For many years,

Author on
Shipstern Island

George Head Island bar;
Lime Island beach, the
only limestone beach on
the Maine coast

I stopped in at Roque Island on voyages downeast, to visit with Roque's manager, Ken Rich. He had been Hurricane Island's Mr. Fixit, but had gotten a real job running the farm, livestock, icehouse, trail clearing and homesteading operation for the extended Boston-Maine family that has owned this primeval plantation for several centuries. One night a group of Outward Bound instructors had gathered at Ken's invitation at Roque's cookhouse while their students were out on solo. It was a beautiful August night with a full moon and we got it in our heads to ride horses down to the Great South Beach and gallop them in the moonlight.

One of the instructors, Clay, was courting another instructor, the beautiful Maggie, who was an experienced horsewoman. Ken led us to the barn, where under the pull of the moon, we decided we would ride bareback down to the beach. Clay assured Maggie and Ken that he could ride and Ken bridled Becky, a big workhorse, for him. As we rode off from the barn, I will never forget Clay's shaky voice as he tried to rein Becky for the first time. "B -e-e-e-cky," he said, his voice rising in register and cracking. That was all Becky needed to hear as she headed for the first low hanging branch on the side of the road and cleaned Clay quickly off her back. Ah, romance—what pain it causes!

Water from Stone—Bedrock Aquifers

Life was sustained on Hurricane Island by drawing water from the abandoned quarry that had refilled with water. But on nearby Islesboro, islanders during the late 1980s and early 90s were beginning to be concerned about how several decades of shoreline development had affected the ability of the island's bedrock to store the water needed to sustain human life. Where freshwater is concerned, the rocky underpinning of an island is a true lifeboat surrounded by a sea of salt.

It's actually a bit counterintuitive: The fine lines and fractures in bedrock, no matter how impenetrable the stone underfoot might seem, actually represent storage space for tiny packets of water that fall as the gentle rain upon our island plains. Add all this space up, and it amounts to something—more in places where large joints and fracture planes create more storage, and less where tight fracture patterns limit space in the bedrock to trap and hold water. There is not an endless endowment of freshwater, but enough on most islands larger than an acre or two to share all around.

However, this freshwater resource stored in the pores of rock is not uniformly distributed. Ask any water witch or dowser and they will tell you this is so. To find the mother lode of water in a rock body requires more than luck. A hydrogeologist will take into consideration the bedrock type and the dip and trend of the fracture patterns, while the water witch just feels the underground surge of life-giving water. Whatever.

Because freshwater is less dense than salt water, and because of other mysterious complications of physics, the water stored in island rock—its so-called aquifer—floats in the shape of a dome. The "lens" of drinking water is thus thinner at the edge of an island than at the center of an island. No problem, except for our inherent behavioral tendency to pay large sums of money to live as close to the shore as legally allowed. When you pump water out of the ground, you suck freshwater into a cone of depression around the pump zone. If you're not mindful of the physics of freshwater around your shorefront, you can easily draw salt water into your well, which is hard to cure because the more you pump, the worse the problem gets. Caveat emptor!

Lately, the finite nature of islands' freshwater resource has attracted the attention of the federal government, which considers inhabited island communities to be "sole-source aquifers." In mainland communities, the stakes are not so high. If communal

Sea Caves and Beaches

AUGUST 8, 1980—My first winter on Vinalhaven, a fisherman told me about a cave on an island from whose entrance you could see clear through to the other side at low tide. I was skeptical. I wondered if this were just another fish story. The place was supposedly on Seal Island about ten miles farther out to sea than Hurricane. I had seen Seal low on the horizon from the top of the cliffs of Hurricane, and I longed to go there.

Finally I have a chance to go, courtesy of Chip Bauer of the Hurricane Island waterfront crew, who has landed me on all sorts of difficult island shores. He puts me ashore on Seal Island's sloping granite in the slippery surge. I walk up the grassy slope and begin to explore the far-side ramparts, hiking out toward the edge of the little cleft called "Squeaker Guzzle" on old charts. Red-footed guillemots tumble out of the scree slope late in the season. I climb down a fault zone where two massive halves of the island had let go of each other, into the zone of sea foam where the breaking energy of waves makes the air alive and astringent.

As I look back over my shoulder I see the entrance to the cave; it looks like nothing at all at first, but when I climb up and in, onto a little tabletop, it is almost pitch black except for the slanting light at the entrance. Higher still is another ledge that two people can press into side by side by hugging

their knees. It is close and peculiar. As I sit on the ledge watching the tide come in, the air tumbles into the cave in a rush and slow uncurling boom. I feel like I am inside something very big, bigger

than anything I've ever felt, like a giant chambered nautilus. I can feel the sound before I hear it. This is the living, beating heart of the sea . . . *pfruump, whoosh.*

And then I want to get out, because I cannot help but reflect that when the winds and seas begin to build, this might be just the place to pass an eternity.

JUNE 4, 1981—Lime Island is the only island off the coast of Maine, with the exception of small parts of Islesboro, to be composed almost entirely of limestone. The bedrock is formed from ancient metamorphosed coral reefs with a beautiful wave-built cobble beach that extends along a good part of

the north and west side of the island. I went along on an Outward Bound expedition to Lime Island piloted by my instructor friend, Alan Sterman, to show him and his students the limestone beach and the limestone-loving wild columbine that grows in wild profusion above the highest wave-built terraces.

When we arrived for the natural history experience early one foggy morning, amid the wildness of the scene, we found a nearly unconscious fisherman and his outboard stranded on the beach. As he groggily came to consciousness, he introduced himself as "Two-Blade," apparently in reference to his general means of propulsion. He explained his personal survival ordeal to the incredulous students. He was navigating back in the fog at night from the mainland to a nearby island where he was the caretaker when his outboard struck a submerged ledge and sheared the propeller off. He was able to paddle to Lime with the one oar he had aboard. Lacking a bedroll, he consumed the case of beer he was carrying back with him to stave off the cold. Two-Blade actually had a spare propeller aboard but no shear pin. We had a nail aboard that served as the required pin and he happily launched his outboard back off into the fog. If the students did not remember the natural history lecture, they certainly would not forget the cultural experience.

Great Gott Island

water supplies on the mainland become limited or corrupted by some kind of contamination, there are usually alternative sources from a nearby river or lake or other underground aquifers. Not so for islands. There is only one aquifer, and worse yet, it is all connected underground. Thus, what your neighbor does to his land can translate to subtle or dramatic effects on your water supply. Just another example of why islanders rely on lifeboat ethics every day as if their lives depended on it, because this is, in fact, the case.

CHAPTER 4

Forests:
Firre, Oke, Yew and Spruce

We stayed the longer in this place, not only because of our good Harbour
(which is an excellent comfort) but because every day we did more and more discover
the pleasant fruitfulness; insomuch as many of our Companie wished themselves settled here,
not expecting any further hopes or better discovery to be made.

—James Rosier, *True Relation of the Voyage of George Waymouth to the Coast of Maine*

Author landing on
Allen Island;
(Facing) Ancient yellow
birch, Allen Island

While I was still working as the staff naturalist at Hurricane Island, I was hired by U.S. Forest Service researcher Ray Leonard to help establish a series of long-term research plots in undisturbed forests on Maine islands. Leonard, who worked in the forest service's lab in Durham, New Hampshire, was an avid single-handed sailor. Our research platform was his cutter-rigged double-ended Westsail 32, SATORI, which he kept in Little Harbor, Portsmouth. He would often single hand overnight to Hurricane Island, sometimes, he said, "under double reefed main and diapers." His envious forestry colleagues in Durham chided him that the real reason he was interested in establishing plots on the Maine islands was to be able to spend time aboard SATORI. That might not have been far from the truth—but what's wrong with having fun while you work?

From my earlier island surveys, I had a pretty good idea of where some of the most impressive old-growth stands of trees could be found along the archipelago. At the outset of the research, I knew that mature spruce forests covered perhaps 90 percent of the islands east of Cape Small, and thus, we intended to lay out long-term forest plots in primarily spruce forests. I also knew that white spruce, or "cat spruce" (so-called because the sap smells like cat pee), is the most salt-tolerant of the spruces, which is why these trees grow along the edges of the islands, while red spruces crowd the interiors.

The Boreal Island Forest

Balsam fir, an important component of mainland conifer forests, does not thrive on islands. Foresters say, "Three foggy nights will kill a fir tree." Although this is an exaggeration, the cool, damp, foggy climate, presents ideal growing conditions for various wood-eating fungi, which have a ravenous appetite for balsam fir and make short shrift of their lives.

I told Ray that we might find an old-growth red spruce stand on the remote southern end of Allen Island where I had landed a few years earlier, so we returned there to run a transect. After landing we crested the island's high southern spine, picked our way through wind-thrown tangles of fallen spruce, then crossed huge fern glades, acres in extent, and looked back at our footpaths, which made little wakes in the luminous green sea of waist-high hay-scented ferns. Then we headed down the western slope of the island where we stumbled into a protected ravine and first saw them—a dozen or so mammoth yellow birch trees spread up and down the slope amid scattered old-growth red spruce.

They were the most majestic trees I had ever seen in my life. Their gnarled trunks were between four and five feet in diameter, supporting enormous drooping boughs with leafy green crowns that grew into the light of spaces where 200-year old spruce had fallen. Their spreading branches gave them a drip line of some 150 feet in diameter. The whole grove was not more than 10 acres in size; it felt like finding a treasure chest filled with artifacts from a primeval island forest.

We knew that the granite cross at the island's north end, which commemorates the first Anglican service in the New World, marked Allen Island as the base for Waymouth and Rosier's exploration of Midcoast Maine in 1605. Soon I got ahold of a copy of Rosier's *True Relation,* published by the venerable Hakluyt Society with its richly annotated footnotes, and began reading Rosier's descriptions of their voyage. It was

Author and Ray Leonard on Allen Island

Fern bed, south end
Allen Island

immediately clear that this document provided the most vivid clues to pre-settlement forest ecology that we could have ever hoped to find. Rosier's narrative, in combination with the old-growth yellow birch grove we had discovered, provided rare views of how Maine's island ecology had changed over time. It was like finding a pair of time capsules—one a remnant of ancient forest that had miraculously survived down through the centuries, and another message in a bottle launched by Rosier 375 years earlier.

"Trees Very Great and Good"

At the end of his narrative, Rosier comprehensively listed the trees encountered during the expedition, including "Birch very tall and great," a reasonable description of the birch we had found on Allen Island. Rosier also described "Beech, Ash, Maple, Spruce, Cherry-tree, Yew, Oke very great and good," and the "Firre-tree out of which issueth turpentine in so marvelous plenty and so sweet as our Surgeon and others affirmed they never saw so good in England."

After discovering the old-growth birch grove on the remote end of Allen Island, I began to research as many accounts of original explorations as I could lay my hands on. Ultimately, I spent a month and a half in various university libraries, including Yale University's Beinecke Rare Book Library. I learned that common names for forest trees had changed from place to place and from era to era. The term *pine* was almost never used to describe the various species of this tree that were so important to British shipbuilders, coopers, and carpenters. According to nautical historian Roger Albion, when the British exhausted their supply of mast pines very early in their history and began to import Scotch pine from the Baltic, they generally referred to Scotch pine as *Baltic Firre*.

So the *firre* Rosier describes was most likely a pine, and almost certainly the stately white pine rather than balsam fir. Rosier records that "we pulled off much gum congealed on the outside of the bark which smelled like Frankincense. This would be a

Ray Leonard and the author at a U.S. Forest Service research plot on Hurricane Island

great benefit for making tar and pitch." Foresters know that white pine is extremely resinous, substantially more so than balsam fir, and often exudes its pitch from wounds or openings in its bark, which would have been significant to sea captains like Waymouth. As Albion pointed out, the Royal Navy was constantly on the lookout for supplies of natural products to reduce rot aboard their ships.

It also occurred to Ray and me that Allen Island's balsam fir was most likely to have been called a yew, since it resembles the English yew that grows to about the height of balsam fir in England and has similar flat evergreen needles arrayed in patterns. In contrast, the native American yew is not a tree at all, but a pretty shrub that is also commonly planted around northern homesteads. To make matters more complicated, it is possible that Rosier's yew, which is not a yew, might have been hemlock, which also resembles the English yew, but hemlock's needles are smaller and its foliage much more dense. So the weight of evidence suggests Rosier mistook our balsam fir as a yew.

A few days after their first exploration of Allen and Benner islands, Waymouth and Rosier landed "upon one of the Islands (because it had a pleasant sandy cove for small barks to ride in)." To Ray and me, this seemed to be an excellent description of the same anchorage we had chosen for Ray's 32-foot SATORI between Burnt and Little Burnt islands.

When Rosier and Waymouth went ashore, they found "hard by the shore a pond of freshwater, which flowed over the banks, somewhat overgrown with little shrub trees, and searching up in the Island, we saw it fed with a strong run, which with small labor and little time, might be made to drive a mill. In this Island . . . were spruce trees of excellent timber and height, able to mast ships of great burden." Here Rosier seems to provide a good description of the forests of Burnt Island where Ray and I also established long-term forest plots.

For an ecologist, Rosier's observations are the best firsthand information on forest, wildlife and marine ecology of the Maine coast before European colonization. His account may be the single most valuable measuring stick to gauge the changes in Maine's coastal ecology during the past 400 years, after European colonization transformed the landscape and the seascapes of this part of the New World.

The Original Island Forests

The Beinecke Rare Book Library was a treasure trove of other early descriptions of the Maine islands. I read at least a dozen surviving accounts of early English and French explorers to the northeastern region of North America, including most notably Bartholomew Gosnold's account of his 1602 voyage, Martin Pring's voyage of 1603,

Samuel de Champlain's voyages of 1604 and 1605, as well as Captain John Smith's account of his 1614 voyage. But none of these accounts are as comprehensive as Rosier's, nor as lyrically written in a vivid prose that still makes for lively reading 400 years later.

Many of these early accounts describe stands of white pines that were the region's most valuable timber. Clapboard Island, for instance, in inner Casco Bay, was one of the first islands named in the area. As early as 1630, John Winter was writing enthusiastic reports to England of the supplemental income derived from cutting clapboards out of Richmond Island's soft pumpkin pine for the export trade. A local history of islands downeast mentions that a white pine stand was cut on Bois Bubert, the large island east of the treacherous Petit Manan Bar. And a history of Swan's Island mentions that an early settler moved to the eastern side of the island and cut an immense growth of pines there.

Old-growth red spruce forest, Starboard Rock, Vinalhaven

The tall pines that lined the shores of coastal islands, as well as rivers and bays such as the Presumpscot, Sheepscot, Kennebec, Androscoggin, Merrymeeting, Abagadasset, Sasanoa, Montsweag, Back and Cross rivers, particularly attracted the notice of the British Admiralty, which had been perennially short of quality mast timbers for the Royal Navy. All of England's pines had been destroyed during the brutal sacking of the independent Scottish kingdom. The British were reduced to piecing together sections of masts from the much-shorter imported Baltic pine. When the Admiralty saw Maine's supply of white pine, they realized the advantage their navy would enjoy if they controlled this resource.

All white pines two feet or more in diameter were marked with a "Broad Arrow" by Royal Surveyors to reserve as masts for the King's Navy. In 1690 it became a crime to cut down these mast-sized trees. And Maine's inner islands were blessedly easy places to cut and load them. My historian friend and sometime island traveling companion, Charles McLane, uncovered the fact that Sawyer Island in the Sheepscot estuary above Townsend Gut was originally known as Ship Island because the Royal Navy cut and loaded mast pines there. And Georgetown Island, originally known as Parker Island, was a major supplier of white pine masts.

For nearly a century local resentment grew over the King's Pines until it spilled over into a Revolution.

Periodic Catastrophic Disturbances

As Ray Leonard and I continued to measure our research plots over a period of five years, I took every opportunity to plumb local libraries for additional descriptions of Maine's island history and ecology, and to consult with Charles McLane on what his island historical research had uncovered. Ray and I were particularly interested to know

Broad Arrow Pine

OCTOBER 12, 1979— While researching the locations of old-growth pine stands, I received a letter from forester Norman Frye of Fryeburg, who wrote that though he'd never seen it himself, he'd heard of a Broad Arrow pine growing on the upper reaches of the Saco River in Oxford County on the estate that once belonged to Henry Wadsworth Longfellow's grandfather, Peleg Wadsworth. This tree sounded like the same pine I'd heard about from another source, so I decided to try to find it.

By sleuthing through the Maine Historical Society records, I found out that Peleg Wadsworth had lived in Hiram near a broad meander above the Saco River. A call to a local contact established the location of the road and the driveway into the property in question.

I figured the chances of finding a tree that was actually a Broad Arrow pine were perhaps one in 100,000—I'd been chasing false leads for two years. To be a Broad Arrow Pine, the tree would already have had to be large prior to 1775, which meant that now the tree would be in the neighborhood of 300 years old. If the tree were originally marked because of its exceptional form and it was near water where it could be floated to the coast, how could it

have survived the intervening 200 years of pine cutting, not to mention weathering the one or two major hurricanes which hit each century?

I drove along the two-lane blacktop that crisscrosses the Saco River to Hiram and found the drive after asking for directions at the general store. The drive led to an old Federal house standing out in a cleared field surrounded on all sides by white pines. An older woman who answered the door pointed toward a ravine beyond the edge of the field where she said the largest pines grew.

Peering over the lip of the ravine, I saw a single monstrous white pine tree, exquisitely shaped, slightly tapered, and genuinely elegant—in short everything you might imagine a surviving Broad Arrow pine to be.

The giant tree, over 4 feet in diameter at chest level, and seven feet across at the butt, rose clear and straight for 80 feet, to a top over 120 feet up. At 110 feet, where the upper trunk was still 16 inches in diameter, the original top (which would have added another 30 or 40 feet in height) had broken off, probably due to a windstorm.

This tree was also well rooted at the edge of a small, sandy-soiled tributary of the meandering Upper Saco, which, according to knowledgeable foresters, produces the finest white pine in all of Maine. Its location at the bottom of a steep-sided ravine might explain why it was never cut or blown down in a storm.

When I determined from an increment corer that the tree was over 300 years old and would have been an exquisite centenarian when it was originally reserved for His Majesty's Ship over two centuries ago, I was firmly convinced I was looking at a tree that was marked with the King's arrow.

how often the forests replaced themselves from periodic natural disturbances such as windstorms.

Storms that coincide with a high tide can work changes that defy the imagination of our routine-bound minds. The storm of January 12, 1978, during which I had been hunkered down on Vinalhaven, had peaked with an especially extreme spring high tide. The tide, 10 feet higher than normal, caused such havoc that many coastal property owners couldn't recognize their land or find their homes afterward. As the storm raged for six hours, the rising tide equalized the barometric pressure over land and water. Just as the tide began to ebb, the cold front broke through the storm's trailing edge and the abnormally high tide began rushing out of bays, driven by a 60-knot northerly flow of high pressure. For those on shore, worrying over their boats, the effect of the front's passage was frightening. In north-south-trending bays, the water simply disappeared, as though someone had pulled the plug in a tub. Boats that had held on during the morning swung violently around, and a few disappeared with the cascading tide. A dinghy tied to a pier at high tide was hanging taut from its painter just 15 minutes later. The event was called a "100-year storm," though it was not a hurricane.

Ray and I had ridden out our share of seasonal gales, particularly when the autumn weather began to shift, but we also knew that disturbances ranged in intensity from the spate of yearly gales that batter the coast to an occasional bona fide hurricane. In the three centuries between 1635 and 1938, there were three storms so ferocious that they made it onto anyone's hurricane scale, Beaufort or otherwise. That's an average of a hurricane a century. Since then the New England coast has been hit by four more hurricanes, but none as severe as these.

The storm of August 15, 1635, was apparently the most destructive ever known on the Maine coast. It began early in the morning, when the winds picked up from the northeast and blew "with great fury" for five or six hours, driving up a huge tide 20 feet over normal that flooded islands and coastal croplands. Edward Trelawney of Richmond Island in Saco Bay wrote back to England that the storm "blew down many thousands of trees, turning the stronger up by the roots and breaking the high pine trees in their midst." The hurricanes of 1815 and 1938, and Hurricanes Carol and Edna in 1954 and 1955, caused great damage throughout New England, but did not affect the

Ray Leonard aboard his research vessel, SATORI

Maine coast quite so drastically, although the damage nonetheless included millions of wind-thrown trees. Hurricanes Hugo and Bob in 1989 and 1991 were comparative lightweights.

At the end of the 1980s, Ray lived through what mariner Dodge Morgan dubbed "Hurricane Son-of-a Bitch" and which Sebastian Junger immortalized in his book, *The Perfect Storm*. Leonard served as an unfortunate foil in this story. In October 1989, Ray had left Portsmouth Harbor on SATORI, bound for Florida where he planned to leave the boat for the winter. He had two young women aboard to help with the delivery, one with extensive marine background, one without a shred of experience. Once they were more than 100 miles offshore, two unnamed low-pressure systems combined and produced a terrifying storm with frightening sea conditions of 80-foot waves at times. SATORI was riding under bare poles with all her hatches battened down, and Ray had deployed a sea anchor to try to keep her bow into the wind and seas. But she mostly wallowed beam-to in the frothy sea and took a terrible beating. Her hull was sound and she was not taking on water. Nevertheless, the two women were convinced they were going to die, and begged Ray to allow them to put in a May Day call to the U.S. Coast Guard so they could be evacuated.

Many hours later a Coast Guard cutter appeared off SATORI's stern, and Ray assumed he would be able to offload his badly frightened passengers. But the Coast Guard would have none of that; they all had to abandon ship, under threat of SATORI's captain losing his Coast Guard license and ability to operate commercial boats ever again. With a heavy heart, Ray abandoned SATORI, but unlike everyone else, he knew the vessel would survive. As soon as Ray was ashore, he began chartering airplanes to locate SATORI; his friends chipped in on the search. Twice he saw her from the air, but by the time he had chartered a boat to get back out to the vicinity of the sightings, she could not be found.

Finally, a few days after the last sighting, Ray got a call from someone who reported that SATORI had beached herself near the Delaware-Maryland state line. Her rudder had been damaged in the grounding, but apart from that and the mess belowdecks, she was sound. Ray hired a D-9 and a barge to winch her off the beach, took her to a yard where she was repaired within two weeks, and then he single-handed her to Florida. A year later, his experience was derided in Junger's *Perfect Storm* story, which made the book's author millions of dollars, but nearly destroyed Ray Leonard.

Island Hardwoods—Heavy Seeds—Fragile Forests

If Leonard and I had learned something experientially about the weather systems of the Gulf of Maine that constantly wreaked havoc on our old-growth forest plots, it was that island spruce rarely live to be old trees. From Rosier's *"True Relation,"* however, we knew that the Waymouth expedition had also encountered hardwood forests. These might be longer-lived for being deeper-rooted.

Rosier had described "Oke," as both "very great and good" and "of an excellent grain, straight and great timber." We assumed the trees he described were most likely red oak, especially since Rosier also lists oak from Monhegan, where the maritime climate, shallow soils and exposed aspect do not favor white oaks, which are more demanding in their site requirements.

It was also clear to us that Rosier's mention of beech was accurate since he would have been familiar with its similar English relative. His ash was also undoubtedly the

Old-growth red oaks,
York Island, Isle au Haut

Red oak forest, Mount Desert Island; White birch growing from ledge at Clark Island quarry

white ash, which is the same genus of tree that the English had used for centuries to make their long bows. The Wabanakis used the wood from ash trees to make their arrows, "big and long with three feathers tied on, nocked very artificially and headed with the long shank bone of a deer," Rosier wrote. However, he noted that the Wabanaki bow "is made of Witch Hazel, and some Beech in fashion much like our bows." Hakluyt, the English maritime historian who compiled many of the original explorer's accounts, suggested that witch hazel refers to hop hornbeam, an extremely tough, resistant wood, similar to a species found in England that was often used for the handles of farm implements since the grain of its wood was so durable and strong.

The maple Rosier described from Allen and Benner, but not Monhegan, we believe would likely have been the red maple rather than sugar or rock maple, which requires deep, nutrient-rich soils that in all of our expeditions throughout the islands of Maine, we have rarely, if ever observed.

Although hardwood forests are rare on Maine islands today, I had stumbled upon an island hardwood forest several years earlier during my original island surveys for The Nature Conservancy. Mark Island lies at the end of a long chain of narrow islands at the terminal end of the Turtle Head Fault—a narrow sliver of upcountry rock which has somehow wedged its way 100 miles southward into Penobscot Bay over the past several hundred million years, the way seed gets squeezed out of a pod. Not particularly remote, Mark lies just three miles out in West Penobscot Bay, but it is very nearly inaccessible because of its steep craggy shores.

Mark Island's bedrock is completely different from the bedrocks in Muscongus Bay or the rest of Penobscot Bay. Its rocks are greenish-gray in color, and cut with long vertical fracture planes that have been riven away from the edge of the island, leaving large column-like slabs all a-kilter like pieces of an ancient temple. The first time I crawled up and under the spiny lower branches of the white spruce on the periphery of Mark's shoreline and stood in the interior of the island, I walked on soft soil bathed in emerald light with a complement of understory flowers like none I had ever seen. Solomon seal, red and white doll's eyes (white baneberry), trailing yew and dense beds of wild leek grew in profusion around the bases of a mature hardwood forest of beech, birch and maples. The deep leaf litter, dampened by the fog shroud, seemed soft and centuries old. Except for the muffled heave of the bay, everything was quiet. Walking slowly through the gray-green filtered light to the height of land, I proceeded toward the south end of this 35-acre Oz. It was the first island forest I had seen dominated almost completely by old hardwood trees.

Further historical work indicated that pre-settlement island forests were much more diverse than today with many more hardwoods. Rosier, Raleigh Gilbert, Smith, and Christopher Levett all mentioned the oaks found on both the islands and the mainland. When Champlain landed on the shores of Richmond Island in 1605, he was impressed by its luxuriant groves of oak and nut trees. Five years later when Gilbert and Sir John Popham were exploring the islands and nearby shore of Casco Bay for a plantation site, they described immense oaks and walnuts "growing a great space asunder, one from the other as our parks in England, and no thicket growing under them."

Both Levett and Smith mentioned the presence of chestnut in Maine's forests; Levett found chestnut trees on the islands of Casco Bay, and Smith described them inland, east to the Penobscot River.

On a British Admiralty chart of the Maine coast published in 1760, the island now known as Hardwood Island in Blue Hill Bay was charted as Beech Island, and many of the early island descriptions note the presence, and in some cases the preponderance, of beech groves. The 1805 *American Coast Pilot* gave instructions for coasting east toward Mount Desert as follows: "Steer east by south which will carry you between the Ship and Barge and 3 islands which you leave on your larboard which are covered with large rock maple trees." Swan's Island, according to a town history written in 1898 and the verbal recollections of its earliest inhabitants, was covered with a hardwood forest. Many of the town ancients could remember discovering enormous stumps where even in 1898 only spruce was found. The early records of both Baker Island off Mount Desert and Roque Island mention magnificent stands of the smooth gray-barked beech.

Today, many forest species that were earlier present and notable are gone. Walnut, oak, beech, hard maple, chestnut, hickory, ash, yellow birch, hemlock, and white pine are conspicuously absent from all but a few island forests. No doubt the most significant reason that walnut, hickory, oak, and beech have almost disappeared is that their heavy seeds float out and become established on islands rather irregularly. Once the last individual of a heavy-seeded species is harvested from an island, it may be an eon before time and tides interact favorably to reestablish the hardwoods there. Perhaps the chief lesson to be drawn from the disappearance of so many island tree species is that although trees themselves might be rugged, forests are more fragile.

A tremendous volume of wood went into each schooner; Wallace boatyard, Thomaston, building last wooden dragger, COLUMBIA

Phil Dyer: Vinalhaven Boatbuilder

The first winter I spent on Vinalhaven, I met Phil Dyer, a veteran island boatbuilder and got some of the sense of the heritage of wooden boatbuilding from someone who had built a dozen or more lobster boats for island fishermen.

Dyer, who is called "Philo" by everyone who knows him, lives on Indian Creek, where his boat shop is located. Indian Creek is a narrow, high tide bit of water that provided a "back door" channel between Penobscot Bay and Carver's Harbor before the Lane's Island bridge was built, but still provides a high water launching area for Philo's boats.

"You see," he explained to me one afternoon at his boat shop, "when you build a boat, it's like an artist painting a picture. His fingers are the tongue and it's speak-

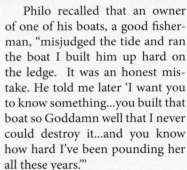

ing for him. His talent is coming out as a gift from God. It's the same way with building a boat. You gotta live it; it's part of you. Your hand is speaking for you. You're giving a part of yourself to that boat," he said.

Philo recalled that an owner of one of his boats, a good fisherman, "misjudged the tide and ran the boat I built him up hard on the ledge. It was an honest mistake. He told me later 'I want you to know something…you built that boat so Goddamn well that I never could destroy it…and you know how hard I've been pounding her all these years.'"

"I wouldn't build a boat if I had to slight it. I'm not interested. I want to give it man's best—my best. After all, you're dealing with a man's life. When a fisherman's down to the so'thard, and it comes off whistlin' 40, 50 knots, he wants to come home. And he don't wanna have to worry, did Phil Dyer put this boat together right?"

"The boats I build, when I see them go by, I call them my children."

Shipbuilding "Better Cheap"

Another reason that once abundant island hardwoods are now rare was the use of their wood to build a fabulous number of vessels of all sizes. As most histories of Maine are quick to point out, the first vessel built in the New World was the pinnace VIRGINIA, which was constructed during the winter of 1609 by the ill-fated Popham Colony and launched from the shores of the Kennebec River. Though several British explorers recognized the military significance of Maine's supply of mast timbers, Christopher Levett, the King's Woodward (forester) from Somersetshire, first saw the value of the diversity and abundance of tree species that could make Maine the shipbuilding capital of the world, as she indeed became:

"I dare be bold to say also, there may be ships as conveniently built there as in any place of the world where I have been and better cheap," he wrote. "As for plank, crooked timber and all other sorts whatsoever can be desired for such purpose, the world cannot afford better."

From the period after the Indian Wars until steel-hulled, steam powered ships ended the Age of Sail, hundreds of thousands of trees—pines, cedars, oaks and ash—were cut and fashioned into the intricate parts of the vessels upon which every island family ultimately relied. It was no exaggeration to say, as did one of Islesboro's shipbuilders, that a man could lay a keel and build his vessel on a timbered shore from which he cut both ship and cargo.

Although the islands' shipyards never came close to matching the commercial tonnage of ports such as Bath, Wiscasset, and Thomaston, the number of small vessels built and launched from islands is a good deal larger than the official records suggest. Fishermen built vessels for their own use out of any material they could get their hands on for the right price, which usually meant next to nothing. For enterprising islanders who were part farmer, part fisherman and part woodcutter, boatbuilding simply became another skill that had to be learned with the tools and materials at hand. Reuben Carver, the premier boatbuilder of Vinalhaven between 1820 and 1880, built a vessel almost entirely out of spruce—from a spruce keel and stem and stern pieces to spruce timbers and planks. As the joke went on the island, when she was launched, her crew hoisted a jib made of spruce and she sailed to Boston with a deck cargo of spruce cordwood. The story is probably not far from the truth.

Island shipyards on North Haven, Vinalhaven, Islesboro, Isle au Haut, Deer Isle, Swan's Island, and the Cranberry Isles produced an astonishing 185 schooners, averag-

Schooner race, Mackerel Cove, Swan's Island; Island forests produced "boat wood," with natural curves and bends

Kilnwood landing,
Rockland harbor, 1873;
Driftwood stump,
Dogfish Island

ing 90 to 110 tons, as well as a scattering of brigs, barks, and even full-rigged ships, such as the 200-ton LUCY AND NANCY. In 1790 a shipyard was built on Hooper Island in Muscongus Bay. By 1796, four schooners and a sloop had been launched from the shores of North and South Fox Islands. In 1800 David Thurlow settled on the island across the Thorofare from Deer Isle (which bore his name until it was changed to Crotch Island 60 years later), built a sawmill, and launched 17 vessels, including a 150-ton brig, before 1840. Similar efforts were under way at Vinalhaven's "Privilege," Deer Isle's "Privilege," Swan's Island, Isle au Haut, Islesboro, and the Cranberry Isles. In Casco Bay, the major yards were located on rivers, whose waters were more protected, but the islands were used as sources of raw materials.

As William Fairburn's monumental six-volume history, *Merchant Sail,* pointed out, very few of the Penobscot Bay shipyards could be considered permanent. Builders moved as soon as the timber of an area was depleted, only to relocate in some new area where the necessary stock of planking, knees and ribs, masts and keels was still found rooted upright along the rocky shore. Some idea of the great weight of these trees comes from the fact that shipbuilders often chose to move a shipyard to a new location in the midst of a good growth of uncut timber rather than leave the yard where it was and move the timber to it.

While the supply lasted, keels were cut from white oak, as were stem and sternposts. Keel stock was always in critically short supply, since suitably shaped large, clear white oak, free of defects, was rare, even in the so-called "virgin forest." For the rest of a vessel, the materials were not so critical. Floors were of red oak or beech, the topping planks of almost any available species: spruce, hemlock, white pine, or cedar. Ash was used for oars, rock maple for cabins and finish, hackmatack (larch) for knees, hornbeam or ironwood for handspikes, and locust or spruce limbs saturated with pitch for treenails. Masts and spars were of white pine when it was handy, but spruce spars became more common as pine supplies dwindled. Half the vessels built on Deer Isle, Vinalhaven, and North Haven had already been launched before 1830. Most island shipyards continued to operate until close to the turn of the century, but their heyday had passed. On the mainland, however, the boom lasted at least through the last decades of the 19th century.

Cordwood, Kilnwood, and Pulpwood

In addition to all the other uses for island timber, from the time of the earliest settlements the cordwood trade supplied Boston with winter fuel. Some 20 or 30 cords of wood might be cut routinely on islands with good anchorages for a deck load to carry upwind to Boston. It was good winter work when fishing and farming were slack. One of Pemaquid's settlers, shortly after the conclusion of the long Indian Wars, related that most settlers' "whole living depended on cutting firewood and carrying it to Boston and other towns more than 150 miles from them."

Island hardwood trees, especially red oak and beech, often were shaped—or "riven"—into staves. There are islands today in Casco, Penobscot, and Frenchman Bays whose name Stave dates from this use, although dark spruces have long since replaced their hardwood forests. Levett, the practical forester, wrote that Maine's supply of beech and oak was "excellent timber for joiners and coopers. No place in England can afford better timber for pipe staves." (In Europe, staves were used to make great casks called pipes for the storing of wine.) Later, when a brisk trade developed between the American colonies and the West Indies, cargoes of staves were sent south to be assembled and returned full of molasses. As early as 1784, a Captain Parker of Yarmouth (as we are informed by historian William Rowe) complained: "I have this day seen the choicest timber cut down and sawn into staves. Transient men come down in gangs and cut from the islands, of which there are now 19 on Chebeaggue, and several vessels cutting their load." One oak was so broad at its stump that a yoke of oxen could be turned around on it.

Three-masted VICTORY CHIMES *from shore of Great Gott Island; Allen Island, birch pile*

We don't know when the supply of timber along different parts of the coast was exhausted, but George Hosmer mentioned the abandonment of the Deer Isle sawmill in the early 1800s, "as the best of the lumber had been cut off in the vicinity." Samuel Eliot Morison reported that most of the first forest growth around Mount Desert Island had been cut off by 1870.

In Penobscot Bay most of the forested islands had been cut over at least once prior to 1870, to serve the voracious kilns of the lime industry, headquartered in the Rockland area. Ever since limestone was first slaked into lime mortar in 1793, the expanding lime industry depended on an enormous and uninterrupted supply of wood to fire the kilns. By 1835 some 150 kilns were producing three quarters of a million casks annually. Several hundred vessels ranged the coast for fuel for the kilns, which burned 30 to 40 cords at a crack. In the four Midcoast towns of Thomaston, Rockland, Rockport and Camden, 75 kilns were fired every two weeks for 9 or 10 months a year. This required at least 20,000 cords of wood per year landed wharf-side. Cordwood was stacked so high on the decks of the ragged-looking "kilnwooders," which delivered the fuel, that their helmsmen were forced to steer based on directions shouted from the bow.

The Cutter's End

The final serious wave of island forest cutting began around 1920 and lasted until the early 1960s. The Seaboard Paper Co. at Bucksport on the Penobscot River was set up to offload four-foot pulpwood from tug-driven barges. "Pulping" was a means of generating additional income on islands where populations and economic fortunes had begun to decline. Several hundred of the larger islands, including Frenchboro, Allen and Turtle Island—the latter which had been saved from the pulp wooders in 1964—were cut over between the 40s and 60s by crews who used horse teams or home-made tractors called skipjacks or jitterbugs. Probably no other island use did so much to generate the movement for island preservation than the wave of pulpwood cuttings of this period. A pulped piece of ground is unsightly. And sensibilities had changed by this time, since the coast and islands were beginning to become important areas for summer recreation.

Irving Smith, a pulpwood buyer for Champion International's Bucksport mill 30 years ago, recalled for me how island wood was sluiced into coves, boomed into rafts, and then loaded by conveyor. "Island spruce," he said, " is as good a pulpwood for high-quality paper as there is anywhere."

Rediscovering the Yellow Giants

In 1980, midway through my first contract with the U.S. Forest Service, Betsy Wyeth, wife of the artist, Andrew, purchased the 450-acre Allen Island off Port Clyde. She had heard that I had been collecting ecological data for Hurricane Island, which had

Old-growth yellow birch grove, Allen Island

used Allen Island for its "solos" and arranged to meet with me and Outward Bound's founder Peter Willauer to find out what we knew about the island's history and ecology. Peter and I decided to show Betsy the yellow birch grove at the southwest end of the island, which was virtually inaccessible from the harbor at the island's north end.

It had been several years since I had been to the yellow birch trees with Ray Leonard and I had never approached them from the exposed western side, so I did not know exactly where to find the grove on this rugged 100-acre end of Allen. We passed lots of regular-sized yellow birch—rare enough on islands—but hardly the majestic sort of trees that I had described. Betsy was accompanied by her caretaker, Raymond Kirk, who began to roll his eyes with every regular sized tree we passed. And then we found them. Thankfully, everyone—even Kirk—agreed they were every bit as magnificent as I had described.

The Wyeths, who received most of their education one-on-one and from books, all enjoyed imagining what these forests looked like when Waymouth and Rosier first explored here. In this glade, all of us could imagine that in a place like this, men in armor, glinting with sweat, had first met men covered in seal hides. Here deer have tugged at green growth and huddled down to fawn; hurt hawks have perched and waited out the long weeks for a broken wing to heal. It felt like a place where time passes in measurements not of human making. Here an epoch closes when one of these old monarchs falls limb by limb, or in one thundering gale of a crash that no one hears. And nothing changes, because these great birches make in their own moldering wood a perfect seedbed for the tiny winged seeds of their own kind from which a new monarch springs and slowly casts its own deep shade over these glades.

When, a year later, Betsy Wyeth asked me to undertake a detailed survey of Allen Island's forest and prepare a management plan, I jumped at the chance.

CHAPTER 5

Landscapes:
Farms, Fires and Flora

Other islands have one house and one barn on them,
this sole family being lords and rulers of all land and sea girds.
The owner of such must have a peculiar sense of proprietorship and lordship;
he must feel more like his own master than other people can.

—Henry Wadsworth Longfellow

Mysterious button found
on Allen Island;
(Facing) Delivering
Metinic Island sheep to
Allen Island

After seeing the grove of yellow birch on Allen Island, Betsy Wyeth did not know yet what she would do with her new fiefdom. Her goal was to create a working island, which she liked for its own sake—and undoubtedly also hoped might attract her husband Andrew Wyeth's eye and brush. Betsy's sounding board for the Allen Island project was Peter Ralston, an engaging freelance photographer about my age and a neighbor of the Wyeth family from Chadds Ford, Pennsylvania. Betsy's initial idea was to open up the historic pasture at the north end of island where a scrub birch forest had taken root in the once-cleared land. Prior to beginning the first island wood harvest in over 25 years, Peter worked as my tallyman on an inventory of the island's forest stands in order to estimate the standing volume of timber for a forest management plan.

Betsy hired Doug Boynton, a lobsterman from Monhegan Island where her son Jamie Wyeth painted, as the caretaker for Allen Island. Ralston and I spent two and a half years working with Doug as I supervised several logging crews he had hired from inland Maine to clear pastures, harvest timber and build a wharf to transport logs ashore.

During these years Doug moved about Allen Island like a crow between the shore cottage, where he and his wife, Alice, stayed, to the wharf or north point, tossing rocks out of the way, shoring up a fence post, or cleaning a drainage ditch. His pockets and windowsills were always full of little things he had found along the way—clay pipes, bits of hand-forged machinery or a fisherman's marlinspike.

One day Doug spotted a roundish object in the mud and pulled out a thin metal button embossed with gold filigree. It was a beautiful and haunting object. Could

Author and Peter Ralston on initial survey of Allen Island;
Betsy Wyeth planning Allen Island restoration;
Skidder and loader arrive on Allen

it possibly have come from the coat of one of George Waymouth's crew in 1605? Was it something the Indians had brought to the island as a trading item? Was it from Captain John Allen's Revolutionary War uniform? No one knew, even after it was sent to the Maine State Museum for examination.

Betsy's Folly

That first fall, Doug teamed up with Jimmy Barstow, owner of Monhegan's mailboat, the LAURA B, to build a scow to haul the harvested wood ashore. Doug also found a woodcutter and crew from Union who were willing to load his skidder and pulp loader on a landing craft and haul them out to Allen Island on a high-enough tide to lumber up the beach with the skidder towing the pulp loader across the rim of a mudflat. It proved easier to get on to an island than to get off it.

Skidder operator Earl Norwood and his woodcutter Leroy Weaver had soon harvested huge piles of birch and spruce from the north end of Allen and set large fires to burn the slash. Earl and Leroy worked exceptionally hard and were well paid for piling up great loads of tree-length birch, spruce logs and pulpwood, while Doug worked to build a wharf where the timber could be loaded and barged ashore.

Doug had to do almost everything at once to get the island up and running. He needed to re-build the house—really the fisherman's shack—where he and Alice lived; he had to move all supplies, barrels of fuel and workers back and forth from Port Clyde in all sorts of weather and sea conditions; and he had to supply the logging crew with food while Alice cooked for everyone.

Watching Doug work on the shore house amid all his tasks was like watching someone shingle in the dark. Even though Earl would say he was "happy as a toad in Jesus's pocket," he would also complain that Doug was "a great one for doing things four times to get half a job done." Little did we know.

The scow was finally launched from Port Clyde late in the fall, and Doug towed it out to Allen behind his lobster boat in a grand procession. Stories of Doug got around Port Clyde that fall. Young fellows who had missed the last of the week's mailboat runs to Monhegan asked Doug for a ride. "Well, I am going part way out," Doug answered truthfully. He offered to take them to Allen, put them up, feed them and pay them for their labor while they waited for the LAURA B. Only the mailboat would not come and not come. They had canceled the trip, Doug would explain, because of the weather, and it would be a few more days before the boat would come; but then the tide was wrong for getting into the wharf at Allen. Because Doug had the island's only VHF radio on his lobster boat, they had no way to radio for another ride off the island. I came to think of Allen as the island of Doctor No.

The unwilling recruits were quickly assigned mythic personae—"Grinny," "Frenchman" and "The Whopper" were three names I remember. Another one was called "Crowbar," the world's simplest tool. These were hardly the pick of Maine's skilled labor pool, but there was nothing else to do on Allen except move stones to build the wharf, which was the *sine qua non* of getting off the island. "Now I know how you keep your boots so clean," Doug said to one of his crew. "You're always sitting on your ass."

As the deteriorating late November weather wore everyone down, Doug and Earl became more and more like oil and water. Earl with his big skidder rightly considered himself king of the island's forest, while Doug, by virtue of owning the only means of transportation to and from Allen, was king of the waterfront—he held the trump card. Worse for me, Betsy had assigned me the role of paymaster so both Doug and Earl submitted their hourly bills to me for authorization. Earl had little use for a professional forester—he referred to me as "Mr. Man," but he was obliged to be civil.

Author and Earl Norwood discuss wood cutting operation;
Earl burning slash piles with his skidder;
Betsy Wyeth and Doug Boynton view raw landscape on Allen

Peter Ralston cuts first tree on Allen.

(Facing) Doug Boynton and Betsy Wyeth plan the new wharf; Burning abandoned shacks on Benner Island; Pasture clearing Allen Island's north point

Finally by early December, Earl had loaded the scow with 20 or 30 cords of tree-length birch that he had arranged to sell as firewood on the St. George peninsula. There was not a straight tree in the load. Earl looked at it and said disgustedly, "You could drop a cat right through the pile." Towing this load with its high center of gravity, Doug said, would be "like standing on a bar of soap in a bathtub." But everyone was eager to get the first load ashore before the weather turned worse to prove that island forest operations were still viable.

The first load headed toward port on a rising tide, towed at two or three knots, just over the speed of the tide itself. Doug tied the giant scow off at the Monhegan Boat Line wharf and rushed back to Allen before the enveloping darkness and rising winds could strand him on the mainland. That night, in a pounding sea, the scow worked at her seams and began to take on water. By daybreak she was completely awash at her decks. Only the upper racks of birch poked above the gray water. Eventually Doug and Jimmy Barstow got her pumped out and unloaded, but this devastating maiden voyage seemed to dim the prospects of resurrecting island forestry.

The rest of the winter dragged on as Earl and Doug struggled for primacy in the island dominion and I was ultimately forced to make a choice as to who would remain. I let Earl know he would be leaving. A few days later, I woke up in the house my wife and I were renting in Owl's Head to find my pickup had been rammed through a closed garage door into the owner's car, which was being stored there for the winter. Frontier justice.

But by the end of the first year at Allen Island, 40 acres of pasture had been cleared on the north point and a hundred cords of wood had been barged ashore. Before the new pasture seeded in, the point looked like a lunar landscape. This generated speculation and controversy ashore, where words such as *rape* and worse were tossed around. Walt Anderson, Andy Wyeth's best friend in Port Clyde, had a more sweeping description; he called it "Betsy's Folly" to anyone who cared to listen.

June Bug

Doug Boynton was a Monhegan lobsterman, and a group of lobstermen from Friendship lived in " camps" or shacks along the Allen and Benner island shores.

Lobstermen from Friendship and Monhegan have had a long and bitter history of territorial disputes around Monhegan's exclusive lobster zone, which Friendship fishermen were forever testing. As a young alpha lobsterman, Doug had undoubtedly done his share to maintain Monhegan's invisible territorial boundary, and had probably cost Friendship fishermen a lot of money on foggy days; at least they assumed he had. So relations between Allen's Friendship fishermen, who had occupied the harbor for a generation since the island had been abandoned, and the island's Monhegan-based caretaker, were always tense.

One of Betsy's first priorities, which she delegated to Peter Ralston, was to establish some kind of understanding with this rough-and-tumble gang of Friendship lobstermen. Betsy's mainland caretaker in Cushing was a hard man who nicknamed Peter "Rent-a-Friend." Peter, who could charm the scales off a snake, cemented a bond with the Friendship fishermen one night when he went gulp for gulp with them out of a gallon whiskey bottle they passed around. Then he impulsively chewed and swallowed a June bug whole. With that, he earned a new nickname, "June Bug." Andy Wyeth, who was always amused by Peter's antics and his gift of gab, often said of Peter that he thinks with his lungs, but that night on Allen, he could also think with his teeth and tongue.

Big Time, Little Time, Anytime

The Friendship fishermen loved giving nicknames to each other, some of which stuck; some did not. The wicked names, like mythic identities, spread like gossip through the wireless ether. One lobsterman with a lot of children who liked to brag about his exploits, and always made them seem larger than they were, was called "Big Time." When his oldest boy started fishing with him, his nickname was "Little Time;" the lobsterman's wife was known as "Anytime."

The Friendship fishermen may have been a trial for Doug Boynton as Betsy's island manager,

Benner Island's waterfront, which Betsy Wyeth eventually purchased

but they were also a group to be feared by the Outward Bound crew on Burnt Island next door. One Fourth of July, several of the fishermen celebrated their independence with an all-day bender and decided to have some fun with the Outward Bounders. Let us just say that Friendship fishermen and Outward Bounders came from culturally distinct backgrounds. Right before sunset, three or four lobster boats steamed into the Burnt Island anchorage, where several Hurricane Island pulling boats were moored. The lobster boats proceeded to whoop and holler and cut ever tighter circles around the moored boats, threatening to swamp them.

The Outward Bounders appeared on the wharf to investigate the commotion, but they were in no position to act since they had only a few peapods hauled out on the beach. Accounts differ, but a shotgun may have been waved from one of the lobster boats and the gun may or may not have discharged. If so, it may or may not have been aimed in the direction of Burnt Island. Whatever actually happened, relations between the Burnt Islanders and the Friendship fishermen did not improve after the Marine Patrol showed up to investigate the incident.

Outward Bound was an enigma to most lobstermen. There was a joke going around that I had heard on Vinalhaven about a fisherman who hailed an Outward Bound student sitting at the shore of an uninhabited island. "Is it true that they put you ashore on this little island with no food?" he shouts. The soloist nods yes. "Is it also true that you paid $1,000 to come to Outward Bound?" The soloist nods yes again. "Well, hell," the lobsterman says, "I'll put you out on an uninhabited island with no food for $500!"

Perhaps this story was fresh in the mind of one of the Friendship fishermen who had a camp on Benner Island across the harbor from Allen. He had brought his wife and two children down to Benner for a few weeks during the summer. One day his wife was surprised to find her husband making sandwiches back at the camp around midday. She couldn't really figure out why since he always ate when he got ashore at the end of hauling, but he said he was hungry and went back out to haul. Then she got it and quickly hiked around to the back shore of Benner where, sure enough, her husband was about to have a picnic with an attractive young Outward Bound student on solo.

Sheep Islands—Stove-Up Leg of Lamb

The plan for the reclaimed pasture on Allen Island's north end was to seed between the rocky outcrops the fall after it had been cleared, with the aim of having sheep grazing on it by the middle of the following summer. I began researching how island sheep had fared on islands historically, since they had almost completely disappeared from any island where I had been.

According to Maine agricultural historian, Clarence Day, the early sheep were "long-legged, narrow-breasted, light-quartered, coarse-wooled, roving and wild." After Thomas Jefferson's Embargo Act of 1807 isolated the young nation from the cloth trade abroad, sheep raising became more significant to Maine's economy. For two generations, Maine was one of the leading grazing states in the country. During that time, herds of the famed and prized Spanish merino sheep were introduced into Maine's local stock—in some cases selling for fabulous prices that only well-employed captains and merchants could afford.

The advantages of raising sheep on islands were almost too numerous to list. First, there was the matter of fencing, which was time-consuming to build and maintain, but none was needed for pasturing sheep on small or middle-sized islands. Then there was the matter of watering other farm stock—a chore unnecessary for sheep, since they are capable of providing for their own needs on what they ingest from dew on forage or from intermittent rains. Not only were sheep capable of getting their own water, but they reportedly supplemented their forage with kelp from the islands' intertidal zones. Also, island sheep were relatively free of parasitic worms, which on the mainland took a continuous toll. Finally there was the matter of their wool. Wool from island sheep was highly prized and brought a better price at the local woolen mills. The exposure of the island sheep to cycles of sun, rain, and cold produced wool that did not shrink as much as other wool, was cleaner, and produced good staple (clusters of locks) or crinkle (waviness) for easy spinning. The president of the Knox Woolen Mill declared that long-stapled island wool was superior in every respect. Perhaps the only downside of island sheep farming was that the animals were wilder when they were rounded up for shearing or culling, and a certain number were lost off the steep-sided islands' pastures. Stove-up leg of lamb and drowned wild sheep were trials of the trade.

Nash Island flock, originally established by Jenny Cirone, off Cape Split, Addison

By the 1860s, there were thousands of sheep on the Maine islands. In 1858 there were 2,000 sheep on North Haven, compared to approximately 250 cows and 25 horses. Kimball Island and Isle au Haut each had 400. In 1910 there were still 500 sheep on Great Duck Island south of Mount Desert, perhaps 1,200 on Monhegan and 300 on Ragged Island—known as Criehaven—at the edge of Penobscot Bay. Even as late as 1960, there were 1,500 sheep pastured on Maine islands, according to a state agricultural department estimate.

Sheep—"One Cut Below a Stone"

Doug Boynton and his crew had seeded the north point of Allen Island's pasture the previous fall, but neither he nor I were sheep farmers. As a professional forester with a reputation on the line, however, I prayed for green shoots to sprout the following spring on the scarred landscape. Slowly, slowly, the first twinges of green began to spread over the scorched brown earth and rocks like a watercolor wash. By summer, a verdant natural growth had begun to resurrect the pasture, even if the dark bones poked through its new skin. The pasture would quickly revert to shrubs and spindly spruce if there were not a pasture management plan in place, and clearly mowing was out

Bill Stuart prepares to help unload Metinic sheep on Allen Island; Author after unloading sheep

of the question.

It was time to learn what we did not know about island sheep.

Peter Ralston and I had taken Betsy to Metinic Island, six or eight miles east of Allen in Outer Penobscot Bay, to visit the best-known remaining island flock. The Post family, which owned the southern half of Metinic, said they would sell Betsy a group of old ewes and wethers following their annual Fourth of July shearing.

We arrived on Metinic on the appointed day and met Ralph Post, the lobsterman in charge of the sheep, who asked us if we knew what we were getting into. He shook his head doubtfully when we assured him we wanted to start an island flock. "Sheep," he remarked, " . . . one cut below a stone." He told us sheep could always figure out a new way to die or kill themselves on islands. Ignorance is bliss, of course. So we loaded the sheep in an old stake-body island truck with a fish net over them so they would not jump out and trundled them down to the beach where the Posts agreed to lend us a dory. Ralph told us we would need to tie the 20 sheep in the dory and then showed us the knot that would keep them from jumping overboard without also choking themselves to death as they strained against their tethers.

We hired Glen Hall's herring boat from Port Clyde to tow the dory and headed back across the bay. We borrowed an outboard because Peter wanted to get a photograph of the sheep, the dory and the fishing boat. Peter and I followed the fishing vessel and dory out into the bay as a willowy fog enshrouded the surrounding water and islands. The light was magical and Peter could see the shot he wanted—with a wide-angle lens close to the stern of the dory. "Closer," Peter kept yelling. "Get closer! Closer!" I got the bow of the outboard up on top of the stern wave trailing just aft of the dory, but it was still not enough. "Closer," he yelled again, and closer we got until we tumbled down into the trough of the stern wave and hit the gunnels of the dory a good blow, nearly capsizing it. But Peter got his shot.

When we arrived at the wharf on Allen, we cut the lines off the sheep, which clearly had not enjoyed their sea voyage. Their copious excretions had mixed with seawater to create a slippery green slurry in the bottom of the dory. To the extent that we had thought about unloading, we had assumed the sheep would have been so relieved to arrive at their new island home that after the first sheep jumped gratefully ashore, the rest would follow.

After we wrestled the first sheep out of the dory and onto the shore, we stood back, waiting for the rest to scramble up to join the leader. No dice. They were not going anywhere. As we considered Plan B, the one sheep that we had offloaded ran down the shore and jumped back into the dory. There seemed no alternative to tipping the dory up on its side to encourage the sheep to scramble out. But with every heave of the dory, the terrified sheep scrambled to its high side, which made it impossible to tip. Plan C involved two of us in the dory heaving them out one by one, which was easier said than done since they were not only shorn with no wool to grab onto, but the slick green slurry coating them made for a homely scene. Peter took pictures.

Doug Boynton seeds Allen Island pasture before sheep arrive; Peter Ralston on dragger that towed sheep to Allen Island

As soon as the sheep were finally all ashore, instead of grazing peacefully in the new pasture, they hightailed it into the woods and we only occasionally caught a glimpse of them for the remainder of the summer. They had found a bit of pasture on the extreme south end of Allen and had no intention of heading back toward civilization and the new pasture we had carefully prepared.

Venison in Small Pieces

Doug's wife, Alice, planted the first small island garden on Allen Island, one that

Exporting Island Sheep

JULY 2, 1989—On Allen Island, in shirtsleeves, down and dirty, we help round up 40-odd sheep for shearing in a pen down at the wharf. The idea of using sheep to keep island pastures open has begun to catch on with other island owners. So after all of Allen's flock have been liberated from their thick winter fleece, we cull the spring wethers and durable ewes to start a new island flock on Butter Island, 40 miles north-northeast.

With a baker's dozen of less-than-thrilled sheep penned in the stern of the vessel, FISH HAWK, we set off—at some pains to get up

on a plane—and head for the lee of the Muscle Ridge and then the northern islands.

As FISH HAWK rounds up and throttles back at the southeast beach of Butter, preparing to unload our cargo, picnickers from a nearby yacht stare in growing disbelief. The sheep, it must be said,

are not in peak form, just shorn and covered green inside and out from their sea voyage. The only possible debarkation plan is to get as close to the beach as possible and heave-ho the sheep one-by-one—over the gunwale and into the brine as a proper and cleanly baptism into their new island life. Twelve wobbly wethers and ewes thus make their way out of the water in search of higher and more certain ground and straight up through the cluster of pre–Fourth of July beach picnickers, who look at us as if we were barbarians at the gate.

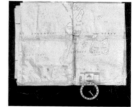

Doug Boynton and author after reseeding pasture;
Author's field notebook and maps

could be watered easily from one of the island's hand dug wells. Perhaps it was fitting that a Monheganer would replant this garden since the first island cultivator was Captain John Smith, who planted a garden in 1609 "on top of a rocky isle 4 leagues from the main [Monhegan] in May that grew so well that it served us for salads in June and July."

Despite the Monhegan–Friendship détente among the residents of Allen, tensions abounded among other fishermen whose traps circled the island. After Doug and Alice had gone inshore at the end of the previous winter, these tensions resulted in the remains of a deer carcass appearing in one of the island's two wells. The well water could not be used for drinking until it had been thoroughly disinfected, a job Doug put off until warmer weather. When Doug's father, a doctor, came for a visit, however, the message of which well had been compromised and which was good got confused. When he drank water from the wrong well, Doug and Alice were horrified. But Doug's father shrugged. "I've had venison before," he said. "Just not in such small pieces." Perhaps because he had spent so much time with the Public Health Service in far off places, his abdominal constitution was used to new flora and fauna. He suffered no ill effects.

Despite setbacks such as the sunken barge and the polluted well, the effort to mill lumber on Allen went well. It soon became obvious to everyone that the spruce timbers Earl and Leroy had stockpiled on Allen could be used for island building projects so as to avoid the unnecessary costs of shipping timber off the island and hauling loads of lumber back. Boynton located a portable sawmill whose operator was interested in setting it up on the island and soon we were in the lumber business.

The portable sawmill worked out surprisingly well: Approximately 50,000 board feet of logs were milled into rough-dimension timbers that went into the barn during the second summer, as well as a dozen other island and wharf maintenance projects. From the sawmill also came a set of fence posts for Alice's garden—to keep the deer out.

Colonial-era farmhouse and barn, Mosquito Island, Muscongus Bay

"The Phantoms of Pursuit and the Almoner of Life"

The Englishman Sir Ferdinando Gorges, who was cheated out of immortality as "The Father of Maine" when the Popham Colony he financed fell apart after one brief winter of 1607–08 was a planter at heart. He hoped to sow seeds of settlement in Maine, not with fishermen, but with farmers, out of an abiding belief that farming led to a Good Way of Life. In a letter to one of his associates, he bemoaned the Maine settlers' interest in other pursuits: "Trading, fishing, lumber, these have been the phantoms of pursuit, while there has been a criminal neglect of husbandry, the true source of wealth and the almoner of human life." Little did he know about Maine's harsh climate and thin soils.

Betsy Wyeth also imagined an island farm on Allen, but she was more practical and local than Sir Fernando, and she had a great interest in and appreciation of island history. I showed her various descriptions of island farming from local historical accounts. Of the several advantages of island farms, an important one was the abundance of natural fertilizers. Seaweeds were always free for the taking. Trelawney, ever the interested patron, was told that Richmond Island farmers fertilized corn with menhaden or pogies—"1,000 fish to the acre owing to their rich oil." Another farmer on Friendship Long Island in Muscongus Bay described his method of increasing corn yield: he harvested mussels in the spring and set them in heaps along the upper edge of a cornfield to leach slowly over the soil during the growing season.

The original survey records of Islesboro, at the time when the island was divided up into approximately 100-acre lots, describe over and over again the condition of the ground that would bring Maine's island farming era to a relatively quick end: ". . . 40

acres ledgy, broken. Not more than one acre in a piece fit for plowing." The efforts of clearing the stones from the discontinuous patches of fields on islands made Yankee industriousness not just a virtue but a life-supporting necessity. You can imagine the effect on islanders of descriptions of new land in Ohio. Elisha Philbrook from Vinalhaven wrote that in Ohio he saw: "One hundred acres of corn in one field so high that a man cannot hang his hat on them. Five acres of corn will cost not more labor than one acre will in Maine." And he added, "The land is free from stone." Hello, Ohio; good-bye Maine.

Pish

One of the best sources of information on early island farming is the writing of John Winter who faithfully corresponded with his patron Robert Trelawney about Richmond Island in the early decades of the 17th century. Among the "sorts of beasts" with which Richmond Island (and very soon others like it) was well stocked were hogs. Pork was one of the most important sources of meat for the early colonial farms. On the mainland pigs foraged in the woods during the warmer months, and often ended up as a fine pork dinner for wolves. However, if the hogs were set out on islands, particularly ones with oaks, they could feed themselves in relative freedom, fattening on the fall acorn crop just before they were slaughtered. From Winter's account, it seems that hogs were also fed clams from the intertidal zone, and they soon learned how to dig out these truffle-like delicacies for themselves. After three years Richmond Island was home to 200 pigs.

From my winters on Vinalhaven, I knew a little about the difficulties of raising pigs on islands, the most important being the cost of feeding them. Two of my wife's friends, Spencer and Dale Fuller, ran a herring carrier to supply bait to the lobstermen of Vinalhaven and surrounding islands. Because Spencer generally had extra herring, it seemed only natural to supplement the feeding of the family's pigs with the leftovers from the family's other business. All the Fullers' friends looked forward to a big fall pig roast.

Anyone who has ever eaten a gull's egg will know what happened next. Everything from the bacon to the tenderloin to the hams tasted like fish. The Fullers took to calling the pork by another name—pish—and with no other choice, they ate it all winter.

Raising bacon, Allen Island;
Clearing and burning a pasture on
Butter Island

Burning the Islands

Island histories are replete with descriptions of how islanders burned island pastures to enhance their growth, not just to pasture livestock but also to produce a cash crop of hay. In fact, during the 18th and early 19th centuries, hay was the first island cash crop that was shipped aboard just about any vessel at hand to feed livestock in and around Boston. Massachusetts farmers who were raising livestock either for dairy products or to sell

Before and after at the Allen Island pasture

at market were no doubt reluctant to sell the crop on which their own farm animals depended. Instead, at least in the early days, a good deal of it came from Maine islands. On a reaching wind, Boston's famous Haymarket Square was not much more than a 24-hour passage.

An incident that still resonates with Matinicus residents was the murder of Ebenezer Hall by a group of Indians in 1724. It seems that Hall, a fisherman, was also in the business of selling hay in Boston. To stimulate a flush of new growth, he was in the habit of burning over nearby Green Island, then as now an important seabird colony. Green Island was particularly important for the Penobscot Indians, who went there to collect eggs and young seabirds for meat. Unhappy with Hall's peremptory use of their traditional hunting grounds, they successfully petitioned the distant Court of Massachusetts to enjoin Hall from burning. When he ignored the court order and burned Green again, a party of braves, no doubt angered over the delay in enforcement, settled matters themselves by ambushing and scalping Hall.

It is worth stopping for a moment to consider the name Green Island, which is shared by no fewer than 19 Maine islands and could conceivably have described the look of an evergreen forest. Checking back again with the always-informative 1760 edition of British Admiralty Charts of the coast of Maine, several still named Green

Islands appear, but they are all outer islands currently inhabited by seabirds whose rich and copious excretions give them a well-fertilized, luxuriant look. Without a doubt, many of the treeless green islands of the Maine coast remained so by virtue of the nesting gulls, cormorants, and "shitpokes" (great blue herons) that inhabited them.

There are also about seven Burnt Islands so labeled on charts of Maine waters—a small percentage of the number of islands that were cleared either to raise a cash crop for Boston's Haymarket or later to pasture islanders' own stock. At least in the early days, all that was required to raise hay on a Maine island was an ax, hard labor, and a flint box. Over the course of a year or two, depending on the size of the island, the trees were felled. Large, valuable timber may have been rafted to a nearby tidal mill, but as often as not, timber was left to dry out, awaiting a hot spell to be torched off.

Where and when the process of clearing and burning islands began seems to have been a matter of historical happenstance. On the early charts of the Maine coast, Swan's Island was referred to as Burnt Coat, evidently a corruption of the French "Brûle Côte," or Burnt Coast. Some have attributed this original name to Champlain, although it does not appear on any of his charts. Yet it does appear on several other 17th-century maps. It is tempting to conclude that part of Swan's was burned for pasturage by an early independent fisherman trader who wished to leave a source of fresh meat on the island in anticipation of his return. Champlain, in fact, mentions that Portuguese fishermen left wild bullock and sheep on Sable Island in the 1540s.

The illuminating Atlantic Neptune series of charts calls Black Island in Casco Passage, "Grass Island." The *American Coast Pilot* presents this picture of eastern Muscongus Bay in 1809: "You may steer NE for Whitehead leaving George's Islands (Allen, Benner and Burnt Islands) on your larboard. The eastern island has no trees on it." Today, the eastern one has been reforested after a century and a half. Mosquito Island, which was described in the *Coast Pilot* as covered "with burnt trees," was described 60 years later by another eye as "a low rocky island covered with brush."

Seal Island Fire

Perhaps the history of burning islands for hay explained an event I had witnessed on Seal Island in outer Penobscot Bay when I was living on Hurricane Island in 1978. A Bermuda high had built over the normally cool waters of the Gulf of Maine and remained nearly stationary for weeks. The temperatures had climbed into the high 90s and the mercury had barely moved. Word arrived that a fire had broken out on Seal ,and since Hurricane had mobile fire pumps and Indian tanks, a crew of staff quickly mustered with gear and headed offshore.

From several miles off, even before the smell of the fire reached us, the island looked like a battleship afire. As we got closer we saw that the air over Seal was dark with circling, screaming, careening seabirds. Large rafts of eider ducks floated around the shore in confusion. I knew there were luckless petrels in their burrows in the turf that would likely not survive.

We lugged the firefighting gear ashore, but the fire had already gone deep into Seal's peaty turf and was traveling underground. We set up the pumps and hoses and tried to contain the fire. Despite our best efforts, it would erupt over and over again behind

Arctic Flowers

AUGUST 22, 1995—I had read in old botanical journals of rare arctic flowers that are found on some of Maine's outer islands, including Seal Island. Because they have adapted to short unpredictable summers and can set seed more quickly, they have leapfrogged down the chain of outer islands much farther south than on the mainland. In ecological terms, species such as pale oyster leaf, bird's-eye primrose, small gentian, Greenland sandwort, mats of astringent crowberry and the loveliest, most delicate of all the arctic flora, roseroot stonecrop have filled a vacant temporal niche on Maine's outermost islands.

Among these rare plants, I had found only crowberry on Allen. I reported this to the Maine State Critical Areas office in Augusta, which was documenting the location of rare plant stations on the islands. But I also knew that the most extensive roseroot stonecrop site I had seen anywhere on the Maine islands was located on Jordan's Delight, a small outer island east of Petit Manan Point. Whoever Jordan was I do not know, but the island is aptly named. I had been there several times with Hurricane Island expeditions, and had seen its sheer, 60-foot roseroot-covered cliffs

subtly change color as the flowers bloomed and set seed throughout the spring and summer seasons. The yellow-tipped male flowers of roseroot appear shortly before the red-tinged female flowers, which ripen into orange seed capsules. The walls of the island pulse in shades and combinations of yellows, reds, and oranges as the season progresses; it is unspeakably beautiful. From Jordan Delight's steep cliffs, North Atlantic's smallest alcid, the scarlet-footed guillemot, tumbles off ledgy nests most of the summer.

During a late summer cruise, as Peter Ralston and I trended by Jordan's Delight, approximately a decade after I had first filed the rare plant report, we were startled by the sight of a big new house amid the arctic flowers and seabirds. A two-storied be-gabled and be-windowed shingle cottage came into view above Jordan Delight's impressive sea arch, hunched down and gigantic all at once, with a "boathouse" hovering over one of the island's cliffs. It appeared that the seabirds would have to give way to newcomers, suggesting that to everything, there is a season, and that the season of seasonal island development was also heading east.

A few years later, thankfully, the Maine Coast Heritage Trust was able to buy Jordan's Delight and disassemble the "boathouse" and two story residence, returning the delight to the island's original name.

the fire line we carefully laid out. Fresh groups of volunteers appeared at intervals throughout the late afternoon and evening, including a crew from the Thomaston prison. But the fire just kept going deeper under. All through the night the air was alive with the sound and feel of petrels flickering through the shadows cast by the half moon and fire glow.

We worked in shifts throughout the night amid the screams of gulls and other seabirds wheeling madly overhead and throughout the next day until near sunset, when a large explosion rocked the island—an unexploded bomb left over from World War II, when Seal was used for target practice by navy ships and planes. Everyone was quickly evacuated. Before leaving, someone found the remains of a picnic lunch from those who had merely thought to burn off the hay.

For the next six weeks, when the air was southerly, you would occasionally inhale tiny charred pieces of peat dust, which appeared above Seal as a yellowish smudge on the horizon. Every once in a while a dull explosion from offshore would tell us the fire was still burning.

Artillery shells on Seal Island fired by the U.S. Navy during World War II target practice exercises ignited when the island was set on fire.

Whirling Helicopters and Flying Ants

As Allen Island's sheep and forestry operations unfolded, Betsy's husband, Andrew Wyeth, began to take notice, although he took delight in reminding Betsy that all the fishermen in Port Clyde continued to refer to the island as Betsy's Folly.

For Andy's birthday one July, Peter Ralston had an inspired idea. He asked the island woodcutting crew to cut a hole in the woods down at the south end of Allen

Landing Andrew Wyeth on the south end of Allen Island

Allen Island wharf with Benner Island in background; Betsy Wyeth and Allen Island lobstermen at Allen's new fishermen's wharf

Island, and then found a helicopter pilot willing to land there. On the day of Andy's birthday, Peter told Andy he had a present that would take just a few hours and all Andy had to do was to bring along his watercolor kit and paper. The helicopter landed at Andy's studio in Cushing, then flew the two of them to the south end of Allen where Peter showed Andy the yellow birch grove and left him alone. Several hours later, the helicopter reappeared and took them both back to Cushing.

Who could have predicted what happened next? All over Muscongus Bay for the rest of that day, and for weeks, if not months afterward, Friendship lobstermen's radios crackled with the news they had seen with their very own eyes: That no-good Monhegan Island fisherman running Allen Island had finally lost it and begun to smuggle drugs by helicopter in broad daylight! Even Andy got a chuckle out of that.

As I got to know Andy a bit through working with Betsy, I gained an appreciation of his sharp sensibility. One evening I related to Betsy and him a story about Ray Leonard that had amused me greatly, since it underscored my own sense of the potential for ambiguous endings to moral conundrums. Early in his career, Ray had been a forest ranger in his native Vermont and had been assigned the task of climbing one of the remote peaks in the Green Mountains at the end of the season to paint the fire tower. He dutifully took on the assignment, hiked up to the tower with his kit, including food, sleeping bag and gallons of paint, prepared to spend the three days he figured it would take to scrape, sand and paint the tower.

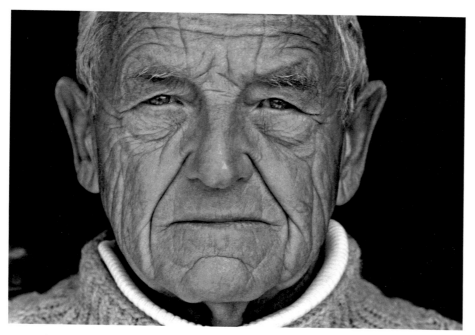

At the end of the rigorous three days, he was packing up his gear when he looked up and saw what at first looked like a dark cloud approaching. It turned out to be a cloud of flying ants which flew right to the tower and landed in the wet paint, sticking fast in such huge numbers as to turn it gray. Stunned, Ray asked himself what would have happened if the cloud of ants had arrived only a quarter of an hour later, after he had headed back down the mountain with no knowledge of their arrival? When he got back to headquarters, he said nothing about the ants. But Ray wrestled with his conscience all winter. Finally, the following spring, he went back to repeat the paint job, where-upon he found the tower had blown down during a winter storm.

I said I liked that story because it showed that the world allows a certain margin for errors of judgment.

"Yes," said Andy, not really amused by the story, "but it is very slight."

Birds:
Mews, Medricks, Hawks and Hernshaws

The civilized people have lost the aptitude of stillness, and must take lessons in
silence from the wild before they are accepted by it. The art of moving gently,
without suddenness, is the first to be studied by the hunter, and more so by the hunter
with the camera. Hunters cannot have their own way, they must fall in with the wind,
and the colours and smells of the landscape, and they must make the tempo
of the ensemble their own. Sometimes it repeats a movement over and over
again and they must follow up with it.

—Isak Dinesen, *Out of Africa*

Great blue heron,
Mark Island;
(Facing) Arctic tern
hovering

After a summer on the Maine islands, who could not help but be fascinated by birds? Their antics and presence are so central to the spectacle of island life. They are everywhere, doing everything. Birds aloft on wings or alight on water; birds beating their way north or south, soaring on silent feathers; wheeling in brilliant bursts of life, in tiny beating hearts, on huge shadowed wingspans; hatching off ledges, or down-lined nests, hunching over craggy barren aeries; flying, diving, dying, fishing, fighting, singing, mating, nesting, eating, and excreting, everyday, all around you.

I wanted to learn as much as possible about their behavior and history on Maine's islands. I began by reading Rosier's illuminating account of the bird life they originally encountered in 1605, and learned ornithology from some of the islands' great bird men, including Bill Drury at College of the Atlantic, and Steve Kress and Richard Podolsky at National Audubon Society's Hog Island research station.

Rosier's "Fowles"

Rosier's first specific mention of bird life refers to the moment he stepped ashore on Allen Island, presumably at North Beach, "where fire had been made." There, Rosier writes, were " very great egg shells bigger than goose eggs." Hakluyt's annotations surmised the eggs were from the great auk. But Ralph Palmer, the most careful student of the history of Maine birds, pointed out that two other Maine species, cranes and swans, also lay eggs larger than a goose, and Rosier lists both cranes and swans (along with the "Penguin," which Rosier mistook for a great auk) among the "fowles" in his notes of "profits we found."

Allen Island archaeological dig; Steve Kress, Richard Podolsky and Tom Goettel at Seal Island research station

Rosier wrote that "on the shore of the little island adjoining," that is, Benner Island, "we spied cranes stalking on the shore . . . where we after saw they used to breed." Rosier clearly distinguishes between cranes and herons (which he called by their English common name, "hernshaw") in the list of "fowles" in his endnotes. However, since cranes are ground nesters and prefer open spaces, while herons nest in trees and especially prefer forested islands for nesting, it seems more likely that the nests Rosier saw on Benner were actually those of great blue herons. Additionally, Arthur Spiess, an archaeologist who excavated an Indian site on Allen Island for Betsy Wyeth, noted that herons were a significant food source for Wabanakis who occupied the nearby Turner Farm site on North Haven at the time of European contact.

Shapes, Sharks and Shags

Rosier also listed Sharks" in his inventory of "fowles." There is a Shark Island lying between Allen Island and Eastern Egg Rock (where puffins are nesting again, thanks to the untiring efforts of Kress and Podolsky and their Audubon Society supporters). Shark's name undoubtedly comes from the English terms for cormorant—either a "sharke" or "shape." Bill Drury, who was then teaching at the newly established College of the Atlantic, suggested that Rosier most likely saw the double-crested cormorant—which was important to local Indians as a food source. But Drury also believed that the European cormorant, a slightly larger species, may have been present at the time of Waymouth's voyage and correctly predicted that these birds would someday nest again on Maine's islands. Drury's son, John, found the first colony of European cormorants on Great Spoon Island approximately two decades later.

Richard Podolsky at cormorant rookery, Machias Bay; Reptilian-like cormorant hatchlings

The first time I saw a cormorant chick up close, I was repelled by its appearance. Cormorant young are born without feathers; in fact, they are covered with reptilian-like scales and have a distinct tailbone protruding from their sterns. They look for all the world like little black lizards until they grow a juvenile plumage. Anyone who has doubted the truth of Darwin's theory of evolution should have a closer look at the homely young of the cormorant before insisting that birds are not descended from reptiles.

John Josselyn, who left a detailed description of Maine's flora and fauna after a visit to southern Maine in the 1680s, described how the Indians around Saco Bay harvested the cormorant (which he referred to as a shape or a shark). "Though I cannot commend them to our curious palates, the Indians will eat them when they are flayed. They roost in the night upon some rock that lies out in the sea; thither the Indian goes in his birch canoe when the moon shines clear." The Indian then quickly dispatched "the watchman," whereupon he was able, by "walking softly [to] take them as he pleaseth, still wringing off their heads; when he hath slain as many as his canoe can carry he gives a shout which awakens the surviving Cormorants, who are gone in an instant."

Fishermen called "sharks" shags for their habit of entering a herring weir, to chase (or shag) the fish. This "shagging" breaks up the school and allows the fish, in their confusion, to escape. Because of this behavior, fishermen eliminated cormorant colonies near weirs. The fisherman-sponsored pogrom against cormorants grew in intensity as coastal fisheries became commercially more important than the offshore bank fisheries. The fairly detailed ornithological surveys of the period between 1880 and 1925 indicate no records of any cormorants nesting in Maine. They were simply eliminated as a breeding species for 45 years.

Of a more primitive stock than other diving birds, cormorants have fewer oil glands to keep their feathers dried, which explains their habit of standing with wings outspread on buoys or ledges as if they are drying out their laundry. They build nests on the most exposed, least desirable pieces of colonial seabird real estate, nesting frequently on the same rocks with gulls, eiders, and guillemots. Occasionally they nest in trees, but their habit of fouling their nests spills over onto the trees and strips them of needles. Many a treeless Maine island has the double-crested cormorant to thank for its green, grassy look, but before the trees fall, arboreal rookeries look like ghost towns in the making.

"As If They Had Been Stones"

What I knew—or thought I knew—about fishermen and birds was not comforting. I had read that seabirds represented an important source of protein for the European fishermen and explorers, who often were hungry and suffering from scurvy by the time they made landfall on this side of the Atlantic. They foraged for fresh food wherever they landed, including birds.

Eider raft, Muscongus Bay

When Jacques Cartier arrived at Funk Island off the coast of Newfoundland in 1542, for example, he wrote of the great auk they found nesting there. "We came to the Island of the Birds which was environed about with a bank of ice, but broken and crackt, whereof there is such plenty that unless a man did see them, we would think it an incredible thing . . . they seemed to have been brought thither and sowed for the nonce. In less than two hours we filled two boats full of them as if they had been stones."

On the Maine coast the distribution and abundance of seabirds has more often been determined by the attitudes, habits and hunger of fishermen than by any other group. Most fishermen gear up to exploit temporary concentrations of marine life, and even when they catch most of a school of fish, the reproductive potential of the remainder is enough to replace their losses. But when fishermen treat birds like fish, the results are often disastrous. The temporary concentrations of seabirds on their nesting grounds, for instance, are nothing like the fish in the sea in terms of their reproductive potential, and to harvest them as if they were fish has resulted in irreparable damage, especially those on islands—which is what happened to the great auk.

One colonist in the mid-19th century wrote: "There is nothing that swims the water, flies the air, crawls or walks the earth that I have not served upon my table." He then went on to describe the meals he has made of boiled owls and roasted crows. The directions for roast puffin were to slit the carcass down the back, open it flat like a kipper, then prop it upright on the hearth and grill it in front of the fire.

Without a doubt, the most devastating means used by fishermen to procure eiders for the table, for the market, or for their feathers was through "drives." Unlike most seabirds, which shed their feathers one by one to replace the worn out flight suit, eiders molt, or shed, their feathers all at once. There is a period, usually toward the end of August, when they are flightless and raft up in extraordinary concentrations. When this occurred, a great number of boats would assemble from island and coastal settlements and station themselves so that the birds could be driven up on shore. Duck Harbor,

*Common tern
hovering over nest,
Matinicus Rock*

on the southwest coast of Isle au Haut, was one of the places selected for such drives, since it is narrow at the mouth and extends a half-mile into the land. Deer Isle historian George Hosmer wrote that the drives would begin in Upper Penobscot Bay near Eagle Island, from where the flightless ducks would be driven south, "narrowing the flock. When the fowls reached shore they were taken and killed and everyone engaged could have all he needed."

A single drive organized on Vinalhaven in 1795 reportedly took 2,100 birds, very close to the entire production of eiders for the West Bay that year. After the 1790s the drives became less and less successful as the eider population declined. Eiderdown, as well as the wing and tail coverts of geese, swans, and winter ducks, went to a ready market in the city for quilts and bedding. The bird world produces no better natural insulator than eiderdown, which fetched a premium price, but other species were hunted and sold as well. Charles Eliot's biography of the John Gilley family of Baker Island south of Mount Desert gave a good description of colonial island occupations, including the sale of a hundredweight of feathers from winter sea ducks. It took six to eight duck skins for a pound of feathers, which gives an idea of the intensity of the hunting pressure placed on the ducks.

The other serious colonial pressure on the bird populations came from "egging." Islanders would row out to one of various Egg Rocks in the early spring after the birds had begun to nest. They were careful to take a bucket of freshwater, which would determine how far along toward hatching the herring gull, eider, or cormorant eggs were. If they floated, they had been incubated too long and were returned to the nest; if they sank, they were fresh enough to be sold and were kept. Those eggs too far along were smashed so the birds would lay a new clutch of eggs that could be gathered at the next egging expedition.

Christmas Bird Count

With this background in mind, I did not know what to think when George Putz organized a Christmas Bird Count during my first winter on Vinalhaven and invited me to accompany him and a pair of lobstermen nicknamed "Sneak" and "Muckle." George figured that lobstermen, who are hunters by instinct and habit, would be unusually keen at observing nature's subtle signals to help us locate a respectable number of birds.

As the two fishermen, the naturalist and the anthropologist began the Christmas Bird Count, it became apparent that these fishermen had watched seabirds carefully. They told me that seabirds are considered good luck; lots of bird activity generally means there is lots of marine life, helping define good fishing areas. Sneak's ornithology had another practical application. He said he knew by watching the gulls around Seal, where he fished, whether someone had been disturbing his traps. "The bitch is we'd get hauled a lot down there; they stole a lot of our lobsters. You could be pretty sure when somebody had been out there," he said. "You could tell by the birds, by the gulls. Anybody that'd know anything could tell in a minute. If the birds was uneasy or setting off in the water, you'd know they'd been hauling you."

It had snowed a few days earlier, but the weather hadn't turned really cold yet. We started negotiating the long driveways leading down to Vinalhaven's grand summer places around Seal Bay and Winter Harbor, Vinal Cove and the Mill River, Perry's Creek and Crockett River. We prospected every headland and beach, where each of these places has a name—if not on the charts, then in local knowledge. Sneak, who'd given up hunting birds, still knew where they'd be rafted up out of the wind, or feeding in tide rips or on productive bottom. We even surprised an old great blue heron on the Thorofare, a rare record at the time for this big wading bird, which moves out of Maine completely when the last flats have frozen. Muckle told us that often old males do not migrate at the end of their lives.

Raft of eiders—females are brown, males are black and white; Black guillemot with sand eel; Razor-billed auks

Clearly these men were gifted field ornithologists, although they might have poked you in the eye for saying so.

Mother Cary's Chickens

The year after the 1978 fire at Seal Island, Bill Drury suggested that Ray Leonard and I might consider establishing one of our long-term vegetation plots there to follow the patterns of recovery. We secured permits from the U.S. Fish and Wildlife Service, which owned Seal, to construct a tent platform as a temporary base for mapping and

"Little Jesus Feet"

JUNE 5, 1979—From the cliffs of Hurricane Island, you can just barely see the white ribbon of Seal Island's granite bones far offshore. Ray Leonard and I have secured permits from the U.S. Fish and Wildlife Service, which owns Seal, to construct a tent platform to serve as a temporary base to follow the recovery of its vegetation communities following last year's devastating fire.

We located our tent platform in a slight depression near the center of the island, which provides some measure of protection from the beating of the winds that always seems to be blowing half a gale. The feel of Seal Island's soil and vegetation underfoot is distinct: peaty, musky, wind-worn and rank. Arctic species like the delicate-looking roseroot stonecrop cling to Seal's granite crevices and its tall grasses ripple in the ever-present wind in two crescent-shaped meadows. The wild growth in the meadows is difficult to cross because of the number of unexpectedly deep bomb craters, which reveal themselves only after you plunge, shoulder-deep, into them.

Last night was a partially moonlit night. Several hours after crawling into the tent, I was awakened by a strange melodic whirring noise over the tent. After listening intently for a time, while the sounds mixed with other more unworldly calls, I crawled out and sat next to the tent, surrounded, it seemed, by the voices of lost souls stirring at this late-early hour.

In and out of the stark shadows of the lunar light, I felt the flicker of flight wings amid overhead whirring sounds. Stranger still, from a boulder field beyond the ken of the tent comes another call—a slow purring noise, punctuated by a soft clucking sound that has me on hands and knees, ear down amid the solid granite. Sitting rock-still, a robin-sized bird drops out of the moonlit sky near my feet and scrambles into a crevice between the boulders; then another and another, seemingly oblivious of my presence, whirring down like rain and disappearing into the ground.

The air is suddenly filled with the sound of whirring flight as the petrels arrive from nowhere to relieve their mates in the burrows. Wings whirring in dark air. And then the songs. Like nothing you have ever heard. It is a low, faintly musical sound that moves by in waves, in winged waves, and is answered in a moment, at first softly and then with more insistence from the burrow. The air and the ground become alive with the song. A large flight of Leach's storm petrels raining in like shadows out of the night sky and scrambling into rocky burrows beneath your feet is eerie and extraordinary. When the winged whirring calls cease, all is silent for a few moments until a new call, a deep throaty chuckle, arises from amid a sea of rocks to reverberate underfoot. Then one or two more chuckles, then more, until an entire chorus of laughter, Mother of Mary, I swear, erupts underfoot. The hard jumble of rock fills with thrilling pulses of mirth, of reunion, of fluttering hearts racing in the moment of dark danger defeated. An ode to joy.

After the first night of a large petrel flight, I felt I had gone to sleep a careful field researcher, counting patches of arctic vegetation on the island's bare bones. But I awoke the next morning with the certainty that such careful measures, though respectable science, can never divine creation.

sampling the plants. Sailors all over the world have a special place in their hearts for petrels, which remind them of gentle Mother Mary and which, in a Cockney play on words, they call Mother Cary's chickens. But here on these windy spots in the Gulf of Maine, the fishermen call them "Little Jesus feet," because they seemingly walk on water and the superstitious say they carry the souls of the dead to new life.

Field Ornithology—Puffin Redux

After my first experience of a large petrel flight on Seal Island, I could understand how birds become almost a religion for some people.

In order to learn more about the history of island bird populations, I signed up for a field ornithology course with the National Audubon Society on Hog Island off Bremen in Muscongus Bay. The course was led by a shy, droll ornithologist, Steve Kress, who was beginning to get a reputation for his efforts to reintroduce Atlantic puffins to nesting islands where they had gone extinct. His right hand in the puffin project was Richard Podolsky, a manic, long-haired humorist with a Robin Williams-style delivery and a way with the mostly female schoolteachers who attended the two-week courses on Hog Island. The pair of them taught me a lot of practical field ornithology on the course trips around Muscongus Bay, including to Eastern Egg Rock, where Steve and Richard were testing techniques for hand-rearing, feeding and returning puffin chicks to the wild in hopes they would return years later to repopulate this historic colony.

The Atlantic puffin is one of the most common birds of the North Atlantic, with a total population of perhaps 15 million birds, but they have always been rare on the coast of Maine. Puffin colonies already had been eliminated from four or five islands where they had once nested by the time excessive hunting and egging had been halted at the end of the 19th century. The largest colony had been on Seal Island, which supported some 1,500 pairs. Herring fishermen destroyed the colony by draping nets over their burrows at night to catch the birds in the morning to use as bait.

Field research station, Eastern Egg Rock; Steve Kress with puffin decoys; Peter Ralston with puffin chick

At the time of my first visit to Eastern Egg, I thought that Kress's effort to reestablish puffins in Muscongus Bay was one of the most likable research projects ever conceived. Most people cannot look at a puffin, or even a picture of a puffin, with its ludicrous posture and its most magnificent bill, without liking it immediately and unreservedly. For five years, Kress and his odd collection of housewives, artists, serious ornithologists, accountants, and others had collected a total of 684 eight-day-old puffin chicks from Newfoundland, flown them to Owls Head, driven them from there to Bremen, loaded them in a boat bound for Eastern Egg Rock, and placed them in specially constructed

Atlantic puffins on Matinicus Rock; Puffin returning to nest with herring to feed young

burrows and hand-fed them, hoping that a few may one day return to breed.

Like other members of the alcid family, puffins' wings are a hopeless compromise between the conflicting morphological demands that flight through both air and water imposes. As I watched puffins fly toward Eastern Egg Rock, they looked to me like toy doodlebugs. But their lack of grace in the air was more than made up for, I understood, when they used their wings to swim through the ocean to catch darting schools of fish.

Four years after my first visit, I returned to Eastern Egg Rock, where Kress displayed his new strategy—a series of puffin decoys. "It's well known that birds will land near decoys. Duck hunters and shorebird hunters have known that for years. But I don't know if anybody's ever used decoys for stimulating breeding behavior," he said. "But when you think about it, of course it makes a lot of sense that birds, particularly colonial birds, would be keenly tuned in to very specific shapes." Kress pioneered the use of decoys and other techniques for seabird restoration projects on Maine islands that have since been replicated all over the world. The decoys were a success and puffins soon began landing on Eastern Egg, although none stayed to nest.

Then, after almost a decade of working and waiting, on the Fourth of July in 1981, the future arrived for Steve, Richard and company when Kress picked up the careening flight pattern of a puffin beating furiously in toward Eastern Egg Rock. But this time Silver Engraved Number 38 had its bill crammed full of herring. "Beautiful herring," Kress exclaimed over and over again, tangible proof that hidden away in a rock crevice at the south end of the island, for the first time in a hundred years, a new generation of puffin chicks had hatched from eggs laid by birds he had raised as chicks.

Gulls Versus Terns

Bill Drury at College of the Atlantic had also assembled an island ornithology corps from among his college students who worked on and off of Petit Manan Island, a U.S. Fish and Wildlife island with a tall lighthouse. Drury had carefully counted arctic and other terns and gulls over a long period of time on Maine islands, since the days when, as a naval enlistee in World War II, he had participated in target practice on Seal Island from a naval warship. Over the years Drury had chronicled the increase in herring gulls, whose numbers had been greatly reduced during the plume-hunting years, but had recovered more quickly along the islands of Maine—at the expense of terns. In a mixed gull and tern colony, he found terns forced to occupy smaller and smaller territories, and in some cases driven off nesting islands altogether.

Arctic terns were among Bill Drury's favorite species. They are slightly larger than their more southerly cousins, the common and roseate terns, and are distinguished by their 25,000-mile round-trip flight to and from their breeding grounds. The northernmost-nesting birds travel from near the Arctic Circle across the North Atlantic to Africa, back across the Atlantic to the coast of North America, and down to Patagonia and Tierra del Fuego before turning around and retracing their flight path. In the process, many of these small birds see more hours of sunlight annually than any other creature on earth.

I visited Bill and his students at Petit Manan Island one July day after an unusually dramatic set of events. A spell of pea soup fog had rolled in over the eastern islands and held on and on. The normally active gulls on Nash, Flat and Egg Rock had stayed close to the islands instead of searching the shores and waters for food or following fishing boats for easy pickings. Within a 16-hour period, the hungry, rapacious gulls on Flat Island had moved into the Petit Manan tern colony, taking a hundred chicks and annihilating the colony. Similar predation occurred on Egg Rock where gulls took adult laughing gulls in addition to tern chicks.

Drury was at the center of the debate among conservationists over whether gull populations should be controlled around a few historically important Maine island tern colonies. He advocated controlling the number of gulls. Fundamentally this became a deep philosophical dispute over the extent to which humans are responsible for the present natural or unnatural order of things and what if anything we should do about it. Advocating the use of chemical controls—or coating gull eggs with oil—by those people we normally consider "conservationists" seems to some to violate environmental ethics. In the philosophical and emotional debates that swirl around gull control, biology is a referee while philosophers are protagonists.

Gulls mob lobster boat to feed on discarded bait;
The common tern is generally unable to compete with predatory gulls on nesting islands.

Dread Flights

Kress and Podolsky were interested in terns because they nested in dense colonies, where their swarming flights—called dread flights—were able to drive off predatory gulls. A dread flight is an impressive display of collective defense. Once on the northern tip of Metinic, beyond the frail, weathered, abandoned houses, I watched a small flock of terns wheel above the beach as a lone gull cruising overhead triggered an instant reaction. The terns rose as a single keening, careening organism of many parts; they flew into the air as if shot from guns wheeling and screaming in a confusion of targets, a disturbing "dread flight" of delicate winged fish hunters protecting their nests and young from marauding gulls.

Terns, which were originally called medricks, have never fully recovered from the effects of the millinery trade during the few, brutal years that their feathers fetched a fine price in the garment district of New York. Hunting of winter ducks for feathers had been an important way of generating cash for islanders during the 19th century,

Mark Island: The Long Leggeds

August 20, 1975—Mark Island lies at the end of a long chain of narrow islands at the terminal end of the Turtle Head Fault—a narrow sliver of up-country rock which has somehow wedged its way 100 miles southward into Penobscot Bay over the past several hundred million years the way that a seed gets squeezed out of pod. Not particularly remote, Mark lies just three miles out in West Penobscot Bay, but it is very nearly inaccessible because of its steep craggy shores without any good landing spots. I row ashore in a peapod and have four hours before the motor vessel HURRICANE will retrieve me. I look for a narrow cut in the shore bedrock where the peapod can squeak in along the steep-sided shoreline. But then, up at the north end of the island, I find a small shingle beach almost covered by the tide and timing the approach between the surge and swash, get ashore with only one wet boot.

When I duck under the long hanging branches of white spruce that line the shore and straighten up, instead of the low-lit gloom of a dense spruce understory, the forest light is a golden-green and dappled as it plays off the broad leaves of large maple, birch and beech trees. I am in an ancient hardwood forest

As I scour the area around the only possible landing site and find no sign of a cellarhole and finding none, nor any sign of human life, I am standing in a spot that is still like the Indians knew it.

Into this reverie, an alarming and completely unrecognizable sound cuts the stillness and halts me in my tracks. From the top of an understory birch, a large, gangling great blue heron fledgling stares down its lancolate bill and emits another challenging alarm cry. Soon another great blue lets forth from off to the left and higher up, like nothing you have ever heard. The notes seem to start somewhere within the recesses of its sinuous neck, but are amplified by the sharp reedy bill and sound like nothing so much as a blast from an oboe that Shostakovich might have scored.

The ungainly young herons look down at me from above and stab at the branches where they are roosting to gain purchase. Quickly, I count the nests—15 in all—which are easily detected since the deposits of white guano in the understory around the nest trees are unmistakable signal flags.

After mapping the locations of the nest trees, I withdraw, not only to keep from further disturbing the herons, but because there is a palpable sense that in this secret avian nursery, the other beast that walks upright should be conspicuous in its absence.

Several years later, The Nature Conservancy, which owns Mark Island, asked me to return to count the nests again. I discovered that the number of nests had approximately doubled to 30 or so, but was also amazed to find that a pair of bald eagles was also nesting in the midst of the heronry. This seemed like a natural history puzzle, since heron bones turn up in eagle nests, but perhaps other predators like ravens and crows and nocturnal hunters like owls are worse. It is possible that the herons might benefit from the presence of a single pair of eagles that can discourage a large number of predators, even if they have to sacrifice a few of their young as part of the Faustian bargain.

Arctic terns'
dread flight

but collecting feathers for ladies' hats was an entirely new business. The few tern colonies that were not exterminated were located on lighthouse islands, such as Matinicus Rock, where keepers and their families protected the creatures that were often their only company from early May to September.

The excesses of the millinery trade generated the first widespread public outcry against the habits of those who thoughtlessly exploited wildlife resources for personal profit. At the end of the 19th century, Frank Chapman, the distinguished American ornithologist, conducted a survey during the course of two afternoon walks through the streets of New York. He reported that 542 heads out of a total of 700 had been decorated with feathered hats from 20-odd species, including terns, grackle, owl, grouse, and green heron. The slaughter of birds—not to eat but to decorate ladies' heads—was simply insupportable to many and resulted in a spate of national bird protection laws.

In 1898 William Dutcher of the American Ornithological Union hired several Maine fishermen and lighthouse keepers to protect terns and gulls from the milliners. The same year, Dutcher reported that he had extracted an agreement from New York City milliners that they would not buy the skins of any birds shot after 1899. Two years later, the Maine Legislature passed a model bird law, making it a crime to sell or ship bird skins. By 1902, Dutcher, who had personally seen to the protection of Maine bird colonies on Great and Little Duck, No Man's Land, and Stratton islands, became the chairman of the newly formed National Association of Audubon Societies.

Fait (gradually) *accompli.*

Audubon's Voyages along the Maine Coast

While at Audubon's Hog Island camp, I learned that no less a luminary than John

Matinicus Rock research station maintained by the National Audubon Society; Seal Island mixed seabird-nesting colony

James Audubon himself had inadvertently chronicled the decline of seabirds on the Maine coast.

The aspiring American ornithologist had been traveling around the country collecting specimens to paint. He left Boston on August 14, 1832, aboard a steamer for Portland, intending to continue up into the Bay of Fundy. A week later he wrote back from Eastport that, "Birds are very, very few and far between." The next May Audubon returned, sailing downwind for Eastport again, where he arrived after a three-day passage. He chartered a cutter and prepared an expedition, not to Maine waters but to the Canadian waters eastward. Among the islands off Grand Manan Island, Audubon searched hard for gulls. For gulls! Today, an early May expedition almost anywhere east of Cape Elizabeth would expect to sight not just two or three species of gulls, but terns, cormorants, eiders, guillemots, herons, ospreys in great concentrations, and, with a little local knowledge, even petrels, razorbills, and puffins, and perhaps an eagle. But back in 1833, the picture was quite different. For several of these species, Audubon had to go all the way to the desolate Labrador coast to find specimens to draw.

In researching the history of bird protection on the Maine islands, I was struck by the role played by the Audubon Society's caretakers on Matinicus Rock, where so much rare bird life had ultimately been protected. I went out to Matinicus to learn how these islanders, who did not have a reputation for being gentle tree-huggers, figured into this history. Matinicus native Clayton Young's family had come to the island in 1765, making it the second family there. Clayton ran the island store for many years and served as the island's postmaster, which he told me proudly had been in the Young family for 100 years when I spoke with him in 1992. His ancestor, Marky Young, had been the first warden appointed by the Audubon Society to protect the terns on nearby No Mans Land. His presence on the island had deterred the feather hunters and as a result of his dedication and vigilance, the colony survived—one of the few tern colonies that had not been exterminated.

Another important piece of the Matinicus bird story came from Dot Bunker, whose husband Albert Bunker had ferried Audubon Society people out to the Rock for years. "Albert always said he didn't know anything about birds," said Dot. "But one day he took a crew down to the Rock and he was pointing out this species and that. He knew them all," she said proudly, but then added, "He was too embarrassed to let on to the other fishermen that he cared about the birds."

"Gripes"—The Northern Bald Eagle

I happened to be at the Hog Island Audubon camp when, amid great excitement among all of us, someone delivered a fledgling eaglet that had been found on the shore of an island and captured by a fisherman who took it to a local bird-watcher. Kress called the U.S. Fish and Wildlife Service because the bald eagle was an endangered species, and it was illegal even to handle one. Soon Frank Gramlich, the U.S. Fish and Wildlife Service agent from Augusta, accompanied by a Central Maine Power Co. pole climber, arrived at Hog Island. They knew where the nest was—in a tall white pine with no lower branches. I quickly volunteered to go along and watch the repatriation effort.

Eagles stay in the same nest from year to year, constructing new floors with sticks cemented together with guano. Over the course of years, these nests can assume enormous dimensions, as one energetic ornithologist discovered by weighing a nest that had finally broken through its supporting branches. It weighed more than a ton. These nests can reach sizes of up to 10 feet across. We located our young eagle's nest with binoculars from the base of the tree where the young eagle had launched itself, but failed to take flight

The pole climber strapped on a pair of leather foot and leg braces with large spikes protruding from near his ankles. Then he wrapped a rope around his waist and cinched to a leather strap that served as a backrest. He stuck one spike and then another just above the base of the white pine, leaned back, kicked in a new foothold while his weight was off his legs, and step-by-step made a slow ascent of the 120-foot tree. At the top of the pine, the pole climber dropped a rope. Gramlich deftly removed the eagle from its cage, taking care to grasp its feet firmly in his practiced hands. An eagle's beak looks fierce, but the talons are the business end of an eagle's armory. He put the eagle in a bag, which the climber hoisted to the top of the tree to return the bird to its nest. We learned a few days later that the young eagle successfully fledged.

In 1979 there were 48 nesting pairs of eagles in Maine, a tragically small number. Even more tragic was that this was more nesting pairs than in any other state east of Mississippi (with the possible exception of Virginia and Maryland, whose eagles moved back and forth across state lines often enough to confuse the issue). Two-thirds of these eagles nested on the islands; the remainder nested around shores of large inland lakes.

Estimates of pre-colonial eagle numbers vary, but it is likely that there were perhaps 400 or 500 pairs in Maine before the Europeans arrived. Rosier is nearly silent about eagles, except listing them among the species the expedition saw. Josselyn reported that in 1668 a great shoal of eels (more likely alewives) was stranded in upper Casco Bay, and that an "infinite number of Gripes (eagles) thither resorted insomuch that, being shot by the inhabitants, they fed their hogs with them for some weeks." Naturalist Herbert Spinney noted the decline of eagles in the late 1800s in the Midcoast area because of lumbering. Large pines near the coast, favored as nest trees by eagles, were among the first to be cut for ships' masts. Some islands were cleared entirely. In 1806 the town

Young eagle delivered to Hog Island; Returning the young eagle to its nest after its first flight failed

Bald eagle on the shore of Vinal Cove, Vinalhaven; Osprey hovering over nest

meeting on Vinalhaven placed a bounty of 20 cents on eagles. This would imply more than just destruction of habitat.

By the 1830s eagles were all but gone from Casco Bay, where one naturalist had a few years earlier described being surrounded by a flight of 13 of them as he climbed a nest tree on Peaks Island. In the early 1800s there were 15 occupied nests on the Kennebec River below Bath, but they had all disappeared before 1908. By the 1940s the population for the entire state was estimated at 60 pairs, and the numbers steadily declined through the 1960s and early 1970s.

It was Rachel Carson of the U.S. Fish and Wildlife Service, and also a summer resident of Southport Island in Maine, who first publically connected bird decline to chemical pesticides—especially those species like eagles that eat at the top of a food chain, where pesticide toxicity is most concentrated. Although she was ridiculed by many scientists who had been hired by the chemical industry to refute her, other scientists eventually proved Carson right. They were able to demonstrate that DDT interfered with avian calcium metabolism such that in the worst cases, eggs are laid in jellylike masses. With the banning of DDT in the 1970s, slowly the number of eagles and other raptors began to increase, and today they are expanding their range back to places where they have been absent for a half-century or more. Finally, with more than 400 nests in Maine in 2008, a reasonable estimate of their pre-colonial numbers, eagles were removed from the endangered species list, although they are still protected under other bird laws.

American Osprey

It is interesting that Rosier does not mention at all the osprey or "fish hawk", the most notable and common large raptor on Maine islands today. Perhaps ospreys had been so aggressively hunted by the Wabanaki that they were rare at the time of Rosier's visit. But by the time I began working on Allen Island, both Allen and Benner Island across the harbor supported pairs of osprey, and bald eagles were routine visitors to the wild southern end of Allen Island.

Ospreys inhabit every continent of the world except Antarctica and nest up and down the East Coast. Their brilliant brown and white plumage and harsh *kree-kree-kree* cry is an irreplaceable addition to the dark contours of a spruce-lined cove. Captain John Smith evidently thought so when he visited these rocky shores three and a half centuries ago: "Yet you shall see the wild hawks [who] give pleasure in seeing them stoop 6 or 7 after one another, at the schools of fish in the fair harbors."

Ospreys have never been persecuted to the same extent as eagles. To most fishermen, it is bad luck to kill an osprey that has to make a living in the same unpredictable way. During the quarrying years, however, the superstition from which ospreys had benefited did not deter the coast's new immigrant quarrymen. The late Arthur Norton, founder and curator of the Portland Museum of Natural History, reports that after Hurricane Island Granite Co. fell on hard times in 1890, 9 of the 12 pairs of ospreys nesting across Hurricane Sound on Green Island's were shot by unemployed quarrymen "whose primitive conception of hunting was abetted by an abundance of cheap fowling pieces and ammunition."

One group of 8 or 10 ospreys in northern Penobscot Bay nests exclusively on inaccessible rocky shores. This population, which has increased over the past decade, occupies needle-shaped ledges characteristic of the volcanic rocks of the northern end of the bay. A good number of these ground-nesting pairs are no doubt related to untold generations of the ospreys that for almost a century occupied a nest on a ledge at the entrance to North Haven's Pulpit Harbor.

Peregrine Watch

The coastal islands of Maine form an important part of the flyway for northern-nesting hawks. The fall migration is more spectacular than the spring arrival, since hawk and falcon movements are closely tied to changes in the weather. When the wind veers into the northwest after a September gale, cold, clear air pours in over the ribbon of land and water, bringing high pressure, which means flying time. Suddenly every variety of winged creature seems to be slicing southwest, and the hawks are close behind to pick up the pieces. Soaring hawks, such as the red-tailed hawk and the broad-winged hawk, avoid islands and the water in between, but the accipiters, the midsized Cooper's hawk and the smaller sharp-shinned hawk, will fly by your head all day if you stand on a high hill—or the southern cliffs of Hurricane, where I watched them for many years. During the fall migration of the hawks and falcons, small piles of flight feathers mark the spots here and there along the islands where the hunted, on their way south, have become fuel for the hawk migration.

Along the outer rim of the islands, if you have sharp eyes and sit still, it is possible to see merlins, magical falcons that stoop to conquer the slow of wing. In an earlier era the merlins would have been accompanied by a larger number of peregrines, the fastest bird on wings, which is known to dive out of the sky at speeds approaching 200 mph. If you are quick enough, it is possible that you will see their shadow darken your retina for an instant, since their numbers are increasing along the islands where they used to nest, and the outer islands are an important part of the flyway for arctic peregrines.

I first observed a large number of peregrines from Wooden Ball Island in outer Penobscot Bay in the early years of the Island Institute after Bill Drury suggested that we try to document the peregrines' use of the outer islands as part of their flyway. Wooden Ball seems like a piece of rock dropped from outer space into the sea. Because fishermen from the nearby island of Criehaven once fished "the Ball" from camps they

Osprey nest on fishing boat, Chebeague Island

Lane's Island—Snowy Owl

FEBRUARY 13, 1985—No matter how much snow fell on the coast this winter during a northeaster, it is never enough to cover the bedrock bones, which protrude from the windswept northern meadows on the islands. And because the wind never relents, most of what does fall is blown into little pockets where the wind spins into little eddies. You walk along on the undulating surface of the snow with the ground underneath, until it suddenly gives way in an unseen dip and you are floundering up to your waist or armpits in a deep snowdrift.

After winter storms, especially, the outer islands are a stark landscape of browns and whites against the backdrop of a gray sea, but the white surface of snow records little dramas of life above and below. The industrious tracks of meadow voles reveal their paths under the snow from where they emerge to uncover the seed caches they stored the previous fall. A mink's trail, bounding up over the shoreline where it has been feeding alert the passerby to where crabs may be caught. And occasionally you see the delicate wings—like angel's wings—imprinted on the snow, leaving an ultimately unknowable message written in white crystal.

Out over the meadow on Lane's Island, the moon is a quarter full and on her back. A few of Orion's brightest stars are bright enough to be visible, along with a scattering of others in the dark firmament of space as low clouds scud by. As I climbed to the spine of the point and looked back to the few scattered lights on the distant mainland, a huge silent shadow glided a few feet overhead in the eerie lunar night. Somewhere the mind knew this presence to be an owl cruising the bare pasture for signs of meadow voles, but its size, caught as a long winged shadow on the ground, was a shock—the more so, because not a whisper of sound trailed off the long wings of this ghostly gray streak. Only the silent bare ground, and off in the distance, the faint rote of the sea.

The following week, I found the body of a beautiful snowy owl, dead of starvation, out on the point. It was the most beautifully feathered bird I had ever held.

Wooden Ball Island;
Falcon with rodent on
Wooden Ball

built here, the island has a little more of a settled feel to its stark rocky beauty than the more austere Seal Island, which lies awash off to the east. Looking at the white rollers combing all over the surface of the deep blue of the sea reminds one of the description fishermen use for such days: White horses, they say, are galloping down the bay.

The peregrines we observed came in fast and low over the dome of the east end of Wooden Ball; their speed and strength of wing, their mastery of the air immediately marked them as different. Peregrines are birds of open heaths, of tundras stretching out to the horizon; of wild fringing beaches of uninhabited coasts, and lately, of bridges and skyscrapers where a nearly inexhaustible supply of pigeons is seemingly too alluring to ignore. We watched peregrines worry migrating warblers and sparrows that flitted along Wooden Ball's central pasture. A pile of yellow-shafted flicker feathers at the western end of Wooden Ball looked like the remains of a midair explosion.

During the first year, we had tabulated 31 sightings of peregrines during a week of observations as they cruised over the open heaths of Wooden Ball. In the years afterward, as the peregrine network grew and our observation skills increased, sightings increased to 55 to 60 birds per season. Most of these peregrines were the darker color phase, indicating they were Arctic migrants, and the data collected by this small shifting group of field biologists provided five years of data elegantly supporting Bill Drury's original idea of the vast importance of these tiny little heath islands to one of the globe's grandest species.

Great Spoon Island

JULY 19, 1993—Peter Ralston and I arrived on Great Spoon at the request of its owner, with whom I had corresponded while compiling the natural history guide for Hurricane Island Outward Bound. He was interested in donating the island to a conservation organization and asked for advice, so we scheduled a visit.

While Peter documented the Great Spoon photographically, I walked to the southern end, skirting the hiding spots of the young black backs and herring gulls. I love the deep throaty chuckle of gulls that signals all is well, but everyone who has spent any time on the shore knows another call, more highly pitched and urgent when food is located, that signals other gulls to assemble. But then I heard another call, more wild and scary. When I heard it, I looked out to sea from one of Spoon Island's headlands and saw a half-dozen herring gulls wheeling and screaming over the water where a lone black back was floating on the glassy surface of the sea. Near this large glossy, black-backed gull a nearly full-grown herring gull chick was haplessly paddling its way back toward shore from where it had apparently wandered. The black back rose up out of the water and landed on the back of the chick, grabbing its neck and holding its head underwater for a while until the strug-

gling chick was able to wriggle free and try to paddle away.

Overhead the wheeling herring gulls did their best to distract the black back by swooping down, screaming out a call that I had heard only once before. The urgent meaning of the call was clear: "There's going to be a murder."

Again and again the black back rose up and landed on the chick and held its head down under the water and again and again the chick struggled free of its death grip and tried to right itself. But then the black back would rise up again and have another go while the chick's pink webbed feet waving in the air began to slow and finally ceased kicking altogether. For another five or ten minutes the black back tried to eat its quarry, but it couldn't tear through its skin and it soon abandoned the lifeless mass of feathers that floated slowly out to sea.

The experience of watching these endless cycles of birth and death unfold has a grim hold on the memory. I can think of no other ecosystem so close at hand as Maine's mixed seabird colonies where five or six species share such small breeding territories and are so intricately bound to one another. Why would the black back have expended so much energy killing this large herring gull chick, which it then would not eat? Was this simply a gratuitous murder? What triggers such intense aggression when herring gulls are already relegated to marginal breeding territories off the headlands in the low-rent areas on Great Spoon's shores? From such places it is impossible not to wonder about the evolutionary significance of such cycles.

Looking Backward and Forward

What are we to make of the history of our relationships with birds along the coast of Maine? One thing is apparent: In sheer numbers there are now more nesting birds on the islands than there have been at any time since shortly after 1800. Today upward of a million pairs of birds nest on some 500 islands between Kittery and Eastport. As in the rest of the country, the past has left a mixed legacy. It is true that we will never again see the likes of the Labrador duck or the great auk, which disappeared from the earth before we knew what hit them. Other species, such as the Eskimo curlew, may have been rescued from the brink of an irreversible genetic event: extinction. But their fate is still hanging from an excruciatingly thin thread.

Gull breast feather; River Cove, St. George River

Ironically, the most silent spring, to use Rachel Carson's worrisome phrase, as far as the birds on Maine islands have been concerned, occurred not as a result of chemical contamination of the environment, but as a consequence of thinking of island birds as an inexhaustible resource. The quietest springs on the Maine islands were the first few decades of the 20th century when island birds were hunted for their feathers or as food. But we enter the 21st century in much better shape. Many of the wonderful birds that totally disappeared from our shores have returned to nest in great numbers. Today hundreds of volunteers and professionals help monitor upward of 350 island nesting sites, ensuring the continuity of protection that first began in this archipelago when Matinicus Rock lightkeepers were first drafted into service. This multifaceted seabird protection effort is one of the most remarkable conservation stories on the entire Atlantic seaboard in this century, and it continues down to the present. It is a lasting contribution sustained by the traditions of local pride and cooperation—traditions that continue today.

CHAPTER 7

Mammals:
Sea Dogs, Coney, Stags and Grumpus

I remember a remark made by a girl about her father, a businessman of narrow sensibilities,
who casting about for a means of self-gratification, traveled to Africa and slew an elephant.
Standing there in his new hunting togs in a vast and hostile silence, staring at the huge,
dead bleeding thing that moments before had borne such life, he was struck for the first time
in his headlong passage through his days by his own irrelevance.
"Even he," his daughter said, "knew he'd done something stupid."

—Peter Matthiessen, *The Tree Where Man Was Born*

Harbor seal;
(Facing) Deer skull,
Monroe Island

In 1972 when I first came to Maine, seeing a seal was a rare event, even though Congress had recently passed the Marine Mammal Protection Act in an early flush of post–Earth Day enthusiasm.

The fishermen I knew in Pigeon Hill Bay who took me out on my early island expeditions told me that seals were capable of recognizing individual boats from which people have shot at them in the past; they often "knew" whether a fisherman had a gun before they could see it, and they could judge rifle range more accurately than most other quarry. Many people have forgotten that for most of the 20th century through the 1960s, the State of Maine paid a bounty of $5 to anyone who took the time to bring the nose of harbor seals to Augusta, and more than a few individuals made something of a living off this source of income.

The first time I saw a harbor seal close up was while working as staff naturalist at Hurricane Island. When one of the instructors reported he had seen a dead seal floating in Hurricane Sound, we retrieved the unspoiled carcass and brought it to the main pier. One of the other instructors was on summer break from veterinary school in Boston and we decided to perform an autopsy for the benefit of the students to determine how the seal had died. Later on we realized we could have been fined $10,000 for this exercise, so I don't recommend it be repeated, but it was nevertheless a riveting educational experience for all concerned.

I had assumed that the cause of death would become obvious from a bullet hole somewhere, but none was apparent on any part of the seal's body. Everyone was hushed and respectful as we tried to understand how death had come to this beautiful animal. The biggest revelation was how every part of the seal looked just exactly like the drawings of the inside of humans depicted in high school biology texts. Little wonder that Nordic and Celtic mythologies consider selkies to be humans in seal form. After starting the internal examination, we noted that the intestines, though fully intact, were empty. So was the stomach. The liver, lungs, heart all looked normal and healthy and there were no obvious tumors, diseases or injuries inside or out.

Finally, when we looked inside the seal's mouth, the cause of death was immediately apparent: A large blue-black abscess in one of its molars explained its empty stomach and intestines and the lack of thick fat over its ribs. Whether the seal had died of an infection or starvation, the rotten tooth caused its death. Alas poor Yorick!, where was your dentist?

When I came ashore from Hurricane Island to a house at the edge of Rockport Harbor, I used to take my young sons down to watch Harry Goodridge and his legendary trained seal, Andre. Harbor seals are one of the few species of marine mammals that can be raised successfully by humans and reintroduced to the wild. It is an arduous process, now all but illegal, but what people who watched Harry and Andre learned from their remarkable relationship has deeply enriched the scientific understanding of the habits and capacities of these clever creatures. Andre's migrations from his winter home at the New England Aquarium to Rockport Harbor became the stuff of legend, intently covered by local newspapers. When Andre finally succumbed at age 23, his passing was mourned throughout the region and even internationally.

Some may not remember Andre's predecessor, Basil, the first harbor seal pup that Harry Goodridge raised. Basil was swallowed whole by a shark while Harry was out lobster fishing. Harry was so infuriated that he rigged up a harpoon, and like the mythical Ahab hunted the beast down, struck it with full force, and towed it back ashore where it proved to be a great white shark, which, when it was cut open, contained pieces of the unfortunate Basil.

Great white sharks, incidentally, are occasionally sighted in the Gulf of Maine. But they used to be much more common in West Penobscot Bay when the Belfast chicken processing plant still discharged chicken offal directly into the bay, and the blood in the chicken parts attracted sharks, including great whites, which can taste blood in the water in parts per billion and follow the scent upstream to its source.

Abandoned seal pup rescued by Criehaven fisherman

Furbearers and Minkholers

In addition to seals, the other common mammal I encountered in my early years on Hurricane Island was not a sea-dweller, although it was marine-ish in its habits. The quarrymen had constructed a road around half the periphery of the island from granite tailings and talus, to move equipment and blocks of granite from cliffs to cutting and polishing sheds. The talus piles presented miles of underground tunnels for a significant number of mink to den and feed after trips to the intertidal zone to forage for crabs, urchins and small fish.

Years ago, during the rash of strikes that shut down operations on many of the granite islands, quarrymen used the derogatory term *minkholer* to apply to scab labor brought in to break strikes. No doubt the furtive and opportunistic activities of this breed of men resembled in the minds of union men the habits of mink, which today still emerge hungrily from tailing piles and scurry about the shore when a granite island falls silent.

In researching the habits of mink, I read about the extinction of the sea mink. Known only on the islands of the coast of Maine, sea mink were a third again as large as the common mink of the interior. The various Otter Islands along the coast must have been named for this creature, since Maine's real otter is restricted to a freshwater

Shipstern Island

JULY 31, 1982—I joined an expedition from Hurricane Island to Cross Island, 150 miles to the east, stopping along the way to record notes of the islands where pulling boats stop for the natural history guide I have been asked to write for Outward Bound.

After crossing the treacherous Petit Manan Bar, the bold cliffs of Shipstern Island come into view. Shipstern's nearly vertical sides and lack of any shelving beach makes landing nearly impossible, but in the nearly flat calm sea, I am able to get ashore.

No one has ever used this inaccessible island for pasturing livestock or cutting wood, so the forest has a soft spongy feel underfoot from centuries of trees that have moldered into a rich organic soil. Old yellow birch trees and white and red spruce are laden with long wispy growth of old man's beard, underscoring the ancient feel to the place.

Near the north end of Shipstern, I find a big pile of sticks that at first seems like it might be from a fallen eagle's nest. But on closer inspection, the telltale marks of a beaver's incisors on the sapling-sized trees is a pure surprise. Could an eagle have plundered these sticks from a beaver lodge, I wonder? But then I find a stump, rooted in the deep soil that has been gnawed to a sharp point indicating that this large pile of birch sticks is in fact a beaver lodge far out to sea. What the beaver was doing on Shipstern, which has no flowing water, is hard to imagine. Like other rodents, beavers produce a large

number of young, most of which disperse downstream after the adults drive them away from the lodge in which they were born.

Apparently this beaver reached the end of the line where a stream on which it was born entered the ocean and kept on swimming. Although there are many islands named Otter, there are no Maine islands named for beaver, which seem to regard salt water as a barrier not worth crossing. It seems likely that once on Shipstern, this particular beaver soon exhausted its food supply of the inner bark of birch trees and probably swam away, unless of course the pair of eagles that have also built a large nest in one of the old-growth yellow birch trees on Shipstern made a meal of it first.

habitat. Sea mink was a specialized trade item for various coastal Maine and Canadian Maritime Indian tribes that overlapped its relatively restricted range on offshore islands from Casco Bay to Nova Scotia.

Sea mink furs were not only larger, but the pelt was softer, warmer and more lustrous than the common mink, and therefore a highly desirable trade item for which the Wabanaki were well known. In fact, of all the bones excavated in the preliminary dig at Allen Island, sea mink bones were the single most common species, which led Arthur Spiess to conclude that the Wabanaki used the site primarily as a warm-weather hunting station. When over-trapping drove the sea mink into extinction in its highly restricted range by about 1860, its north-woods relative moved into the vacant coastal niche.

Allen Island Predators

When Peter Ralston and I helped deliver sheep to Allen Island, the first animal that we wanted to know more about was the coyote. A good deal of what we learned during those years came from shepherds, including Mollie Nelson, the proprietress of Offshore Sheep Services. For several years running, we hired Mollie to shear the Allen Island flock after the annual sheep drive brought the half-wild creatures through the rugged woods of the island to the corral at the harbor. At one time Mollie probably knew more about the practices and pitfalls of raising sheep on Maine islands than most anyone else alive—except perhaps for Jenny Cirone of Nash Island off Cape Split, who ran a flock there for over half a century.

At one shearing, Peter had just returned from York Island, where Jeff Dworsky, an iconoclastic, bearded lobsterman who fished from both Isle au Haut and Stonington, had told us the following story. On his way out to York Island that spring, he had been alerted to the possibility of problems in his northern sheep pasture by the presence of an eagle, which generally signaled that a lamb was down. When he and his partner arrived, they found that 28 lambs had been slaughtered overnight. Immediately suspecting coyotes, they called in a U.S. Fish and Wildlife animal control officer and drove the island with dogs to try to flush out the beast that had wreaked such havoc.

Shearing sheep on Allen Island; Lambs killed by a coyote on York Island

Mollie listened to the story. "Could be coyotes," she said. She had seen times when coyotes had gone "kill crazy" in a flock of sheep; but you could not rule out dogs. Either dogs or coyotes could have picked up the scent of newborn lambs and crossed the quarter-mile from Isle au Haut to York. The only way to tell, Mollie said, was from the tracks. The middle two toes of a dog are longer than the outer two; in a coyote, it's the other way around—the middle toes are shorter. It's not really easy to tell, she said,

Caretaker Ginny Mott
with her penned coyotes
at Allen Island;
Canine on exposed bar
at Isle au Haut

but you take a piece of grass and lay it so it just fits in the print of one of the outer two toes, then set it in one of the center toes. If it fits inside the toe print without touching the end, it's a dog; if it doesn't, it's a coyote. Although no one will ever know just what happened that terrible night on York, few people understand what apparently docile pet dogs are capable of doing when they get loose on an island.

A few years later, the tables had turned on Allen Island. A caretaking couple Betsy had hired to live on Allen, Gordon and Ginny Mott, had adopted a pair of abandoned coyote pups, which they kept in a large cage. As they grew into full-sized adults, visitors were amused to see sheep roaming free, grazing on the pastures, while a pair of coyotes eyed them hungrily from within an enclosure.

"Dogges—Some Like Wolves, Some Like Spaniels"

With the York Island story fresh in our minds, it seemed prudent to check back in with Rosier to see what he had written in his *True Relation* about the animals he had encountered, and in particular to see if he mentioned coyotes. Rosier listed Wabanaki dogs which he described as, "some like Wolves, some like Spaniels," but he also listed wolves apart from the dogs that looked like wolves. It seems clear that the eastern timber wolf, which had a close relative in Europe, would have been easily identified and may have been at least partly domesticated by the Wabanaki.

It is not surprising that almost from day one of settlement in Maine, colonists, most of whom seemed to have read the Grimms" "Little Red Riding Hood," were alarmed by wolves. "Their hideous howling made night terrible to the settlers," Edward Trelawney of Richmond Island off Cape Elizabeth wrote back to his brother in England.

Since colonial settlements were huddled along the coastline, the colonists had in effect placed themselves between the deep forest, where the eastern timber wolf sought cover, and the shores where it sought food. The outlying pastures where land was cleared for livestock became increasingly tempting targets for these predators. One of the chief reasons that Casco Bay islands were cleared for pasturage was that hogs and cattle there were less subject to depredations from wolves. Throughout eight or nine months of the year, a colonial farmer who pastured livestock on the islands offshore could rest easier at night in the knowledge that they would not be killed by wolves. But come the winter and the freezing of the bay out to the islands, the situation changed.

According to several accounts, wolves possessed a sixth sense about the ice. Year after discouraging year, Casco Bay farmers waited for an early spring breakup hoping to get even with wolves trapped on the islands when the ice gave out. But no matter what day, week, or month the ice bridge lifted, the farmers would find tracks of the wolves that left the islands at the last moment, depriving them of certain revenge.

"The wolves are of divers colors," wrote John Josselyn in his usual informative manner, "some sandy colored, some griseled, and some black." Since the diet of the wolf had a more immediate and direct effect on the fortunes of colonial farmers, they were hunted down intently. In 1739 a bounty of 5 pounds sterling was paid for a dead wolf; a few years later it was 8 pounds, and then 16, "if a man should kill three." These figures, almost unheard-of sums in colonial New England, illustrate how diligently the colonists tried to eliminate the wolf from its domain.

Cyrus Eaton, the historian for the St. George River Valley, described the last wolf hunt along the shores of West Penobscot Bay. In the spring of 1815 a she-wolf and five whelps were spotted. The alarm went up, and soon some 20 men and their dogs took up the chase, which lasted three days and ranged through Waldoboro, Thomaston, and St. George. At the end of it, the last wolf, one of the pups, took to the water and headed out toward the islands of the Muscle Ridge. Whether or not the pup made it, we are not told, but no wolves were ever seen again in the area.

Perhaps surprisingly after three centuries of relentless hunting and trapping, DNA

analysis of a specimen collected in 1993 confirmed that wolves are again residing in Maine. (Grandmother, what large teeth you have!) During the past two decades since, there have been no incidents to stoke negative public reaction of the sort that their reintroduction has caused in places like Wyoming and Montana, where ranching and sheep raising has resulted in unavoidable conflicts between ranchers and wolf lovers.

Deer and Their Ilk (Elk?)

Among the other beasts on Rosier's list, he mentions three species of deer, "Raine-deere, Staggs and Fallow-Deere." Raine-deere is undoubtedly the woodland caribou, a species that would have been familiar to Waymouth's men from the tundra of northern Europe where Lapland reindeer had long since been domesticated. We know that the bones of caribou, a species extirpated by sport hunting about 100 years ago, show up in coastal shell middens along the Washington and Hancock county coast beginning about 2,000 years ago, but their remains have not yet been unearthed farther westward.

Rosier's listing of two species of deer, is also not surprising since there are two different species in Europe, the red deer and fallow deer. But Rosier's list raises an interesting question since there is only one species of deer in Maine. The white-tailed deer resembles Europe's fallow deer. Could Rosier's stag have been an elk? Perhaps, but it is much more likely that Rosier's Wabanaki interlocutors referred to the moose, a species that was unknown in England or Europe, but whose bulls carry an impressive antler rack, even larger than an elk's.

Arthur Spiess, the archaeologist who worked on the Allen Island excavation, also conducted detailed research of the North Haven Turner Farm archaeological site. His research shows how important moose were as a food resource for the Wabanaki at the time of the Waymouth voyage—significantly and surprisingly more so than deer. Interestingly, Rosier's list of Wabanaki words compiled from the voyage included *Moosur*, which translates to "he trims the bark from trees while feeding." That's a good description of how moose browse.

A half-century after Rosier, Josselyn described the moose (which he called an elk) as "a monster of superfluity," and the tips of their antlers "are sometimes found to be two fathoms asunder." Rockland and Thomaston historian Cyrus Eaton wrote that in 1750 a group of six moose were sighted on an island in North Penobscot Bay. One feeble calf was captured and made into a pet.

One Sunday in the fall of 1982, we found moose tracks on the north point of Allen Island. Two of the logging crew saw what they at first took to be a horse in the field, but turned out to be a young bull moose with spiked antlers. It plodded up over the rise and disappeared into the woods. Two days later someone reported finding the floating carcass of a young male moose off Western Egg Rock, southwest of Allen. The moose, if it was not sick, could easily have drowned. But the incident stimulated plenty of conversation among the Friendship lobstermen on the island, most of whom would have been quite happy to have harvested 400 pounds of meat to stock the winter larder.

Later we heard the story of a fisherman from Southwest Harbor who was tuna-fishing off Mount Desert Rock, 30 nautical miles out when he saw a moose swimming out to sea. Knowing its chances of getting back to the mainland were less than zero, he dispatched the hapless creature and winched it aboard. Heading back to shore, he anguished over whether to call the Coast Guard, figuring things could get complicated, but finally relented when he thought about some of the unpleasant consequences of unloading the moose in daylight at the public landing. After he radioed the Coast Guard group in Southwest Harbor to explain the situation, there was a long pause on Channel 22. Finally the Coast Guard recruit came back on. "Let me get this straight," the recruit said. "You went out for bluefin tuna, for which you have a license, but you're coming back in with moose for which you have no license . . . ."

Since moose are such strong swimmers and are not hunted in the southern half of the state of Maine, it is not uncommon to find them visiting the islands. However, there is rarely enough habitat from them to remain there long before plunging back into the water.

The Great Caribou-boo

In the early 1990s, with more and more public attention paid to restoring wildlife populations nationwide, perhaps it is not surprising that people became interested in restoring caribou to Maine. Dick Anderson, who had been head of the Maine Audubon Society for many years, and then the commissioner of the Department of Conservation, was the chief promoter of the caribou restoration program. The idea was to gather the nucleus of a herd from Newfoundland, bring them to Maine where they could get acclimated and then release them into Baxter State Park, near where the last herd in Maine had been observed before disappearing in the 1880s.

The question of where the caribou might be taken before they were released into the wild had still not been decided when I got a call asking whether Betsy Wyeth would consider using Allen as a temporary refuge for the caribou herd. At that time, the Is-

Deer skeleton,
Great Gott Island

land Institute was managing Allen Island for her, and I agreed to ask her.

I did not think Betsy would seriously consider the possibility because it would put a very public spotlight on someone famously and intensely private. But as it happened, Andy's "Helga" collection of stunning nude paintings of one of his models—knowledge of which he had withheld from Betsy for over a decade—had become painfully public. I don't know if the Helga story had any bearing on Betsy's decision, but I was surprised when she said she would be interested in having Allen considered as the caribou acclimation site.

Over the summer of 1991, the project gained momentum. The Newfoundland government issued permits for the collection of about 30 caribou from its large herd on the Avalon Peninsula. Peter Ralston and I brought wildlife researchers from the University of Maine who would oversee the reintroduction out to Allen. They noted approvingly that the boreal spruce habitat on the island was very similar to the habitat on the Avalon Peninsula. The idea was to build a large enclosure in Allen's forested interior, which could be accomplished cheaply by running a high deer fence from tree to tree, with observation posts for the biologists to monitor the animals' health and behavior, including their forage preferences, before their eventual release.

I am still not sure what really happened to this plan—only that I was summoned to a meeting with Glenn H. Manuel, the commissioner of Maine's Department of Inland Fish and Wildlife and others running the caribou project. They said that Allen Island would no longer be considered a transitional site for the caribou, since Manual's wardens had picked up new "intelligence" that Friendship fishermen were bragging about poaching caribou from Allen for their freezers. I almost laughed out loud. Of course that was the joke among Friendship fishermen. Even I had heard the radio traffic. But no one I knew took this amusing radio bravado seriously. It was not that poaching was beneath any of those broadcasting their derisive humor, but if you really were planning to commit a serious wildlife offense, you would not advertise it on the radio to such a broad audience. Still, Manuel thought he had rooted out a nefarious plot nearly red-handed, and that was that.

After a traumatic roundup of the caribou herd in Newfoundland and an even more traumatic crossing of the Davis Strait in a truck with 26 tranquilized animals, the caribou arrived on the Orono campus where they spent the winter in a small enclosure and were fed by the University research staff until they were released the next spring. None of them survived their reintroduction beyond the autumn.

Bambi on the Islands

During my first summer collecting ecological information for The Nature Conservancy, I recall walking through the dense forests of Bradbury Island with notebook and binoculars in hand, and everywhere sensing a shadowy presence. The longer I was there, the more certain I was that something was watching me. After several hours of carefully cataloging the island flora, like a trick of the imagination, the trees dissolved away and revealed glimpses of tawny outlines of several does and fawns that had materialized from the background of brown and green forest.

The deer were alerted to my every movement, not only by their incredibly acute hearing, which their constantly twitching ears register; but by the alarm calls of three or four crows that followed me from above the deep canopy of the woods and made such raucous noise that a child would have known where I lurked. The crows and deer acted as if they were in league with each other, as indeed they may have been.

To some of us, it is hard to believe that deer can get around among the islands as well as they do, but it should not come as a great surprise. Healthy deer are quite good swimmers, perhaps not as strong as moose, but certainly capable of the across-the-bay marathons they

Feeding a small buck on Monhegan;
Deer at "White Hen" cottage on Sutton Island

occasionally undertake. Their center of buoyancy in the water is slightly forward of their center of gravity, which has the effect of allowing their front quarters to ride a little higher as they swim, and their long necks then make it easy for them to keep their heads in the air. The only part of their body that leaves a bit to be desired in terms of water travel is their tiny hooves, which provide their modest propulsion. The splayed feet of the moose allow these beasts to swim a little faster.

On the larger islands farther off the main, deer don t move on and off in summer, but choose to overwinter. Island winters may be more raw, but they are less severe on deer herds than on the mainland, where deep snow makes it impossible for deer to move from one feeding area to another, so their numbers increase year by year on islands, especially in the absence of hunting. Most of us tend to ignore the fact that in the case of island deer, we have eliminated their predators. Hunting prohibitions on islands often turn out to be ill-conceived efforts to freeze constantly changing systems. Sooner or later something has to give.

On Maine's year-round islands, an overpopulation of protected deer pits deer lovers against gardeners. During the last decade, island communities have increasingly wrestled with the emotionally charged issue of authorizing deer hunts to thin a herd. These discussions, whether they have occurred on Monhegan, Islesboro, the Diamond

Islands in Casco Bay, or Great Cranberry downeast seem to include the same cast of characters: those whose biology was primarily influenced by Disney's Bambi versus gardeners. The resolutions have not been easy, but have turned in several cases over the knowledge that the deer-borne ticks have helped spread Lyme disease. Monhegan ultimately voted to hire an exceptionally talented marksman equipped with night-vision goggles and a silencer on his high-powered rifle to eliminate the entire herd. On Sutton Island, seasonally inhabited by equally passionate deer lovers and gardeners, an informal agreement among caretakers enables an occasional thinning of the herd in November after everyone else has left.

Swan's Island has avoided contentious community votes, since deer hunting has always been privately tolerated there, especially for those who have families to feed. I was in line one day at the Swan's Island store when someone came in and started talking about the deer season, which would open on the mainland two days hence. The day before the official opening day had traditionally and informally been the day that many islanders went hunting. The fellow in front of me asked the owner at thecounter, "Deer season begins tomorrow?" The store owner eyed him for a moment, and since he did not recognize him, replied, "Not for you it don't."

Rabbits and Raccoons: Island Introductions

Introducing new species to island ecosystems is never a good idea, but that does not mean it has not been tried many times on islands, and the results are always deeply problematic.

Many years ago the rod and gun club on Vinalhaven decided that hunting raccoons with dogs in the winter would be good fun, so they released a few pair on the island. After a season or two of such winter diversion, the sport died away. The raccoon population took off, and now partridge or grouse are nearly unknown on Vinalhaven, and farm fowl disappear in ones and twos over the winter while residents have new visitors to their homes and gardens.

I married into a family that is well into its third generation as summer folk on Vinalhaven. During the Memorial Day open-up recently, we were startled to disturb a large female raccoon scaling an aging drainpipe halfway to the top of the second story soffit overhang. She performed a perfect five-nine layback move, scrambled onto the pitched roof, quickly scaled the peak and descended into our fieldstone chimney, where we could hear her hungry kits through the walls. You might think, as we do, that

Raccoons do not swim across open salt water;
Foraging signs on Buckle Island beach, Swan's Island

islands are feral enough without this addition to local fauna, but the raccoons were an improvement over the mink that moved into the basement one spring, until the size of the nestlings and fish they ate grew too large to be pulled through the gaps in the foundation.

The most destructive mammal introduction occurred a few decades ago on Criehaven, which is primarily inhabited by a dozen lobstering families who maintain the fishing privilege around the island shores. They interact easily with each other and with the few summer families that have been coming to Criehaven since Robert "King" Crie died and his heirs divided up his fishing empire. But ever since one of the islanders decided that rabbits would add a pastoral dimension, Criehaven has been plagued with a curse of rabbits. During one visit there, Peter Ralston and I almost stepped on several as they scurried across the island's paths through of the dense brushy rose and bayberry thickets. In the absence of predators, the rabbits had overrun and underrun every niche on the island. No amount of d-CON, nor trapping, nor other measures had made the slightest dent in the population.

During the previous winter, a pair of d-CONned rabbits had crawled into one of the island"s important dug wells. The vexed landowner offered to endow the Island Institute if we could procure the bacteria that had been introduced to Australia and successfully mitigated that much larger island's rabbit plague. Sadly, there was nothing we could do.

Bear Islands

The largest terrestrial mammal Rosier listed in his bestiary was "Beares." Writing of his experiences on the coast of Maine in the mid-1600s, Josselyn describes bears fish-

Cross Island, Machias Bay

ing for lobsters, which were plentiful enough to be stranded in tide pools: "The bear is a tyrant at a lobster and at low water will go down to the rocks and grope after them with great diligence."

Bears completely disappeared from island ecosystems in the early decades of the 1800s, when serious island settlement began. Isolated and rugged islands no doubt furnished more than a few secure denning sites. Both Marshall Island in Jericho Bay and Bradbury Island in North Penobscot Bay were originally called Bear Island. On today's charts, an island adjacent to Bradbury is still called Bear, as is a smaller island in the passage known as Western Way off Mount Desert, but neither of these islands has recorded the paw print of this mammal in more than 150 years. Various island histories record the dates when the last bears were shot, as if, like the Indians who fell before, their deaths meant the community was safe from evil. Two bears were shot on Swan's Island before the turn of the 19th century, and no others arrived to take their place. On Vinalhaven, a solitary bear persisted within the confines of the large swampland northeast of Carver's Pond until 1825, when it, too, was shot.

Maine supports the East's largest population of black bears, but most of these are found in the northern woods. However, Cross Island, a 1,500-acre forested island in Machias Bay, supports at least one shy bear—or else someone has gone to a lot of trouble to make bear prints around several of the island's waterholes. If they are here on Cross Island, they are likely to appear elsewhere on the islands sooner or later.

In 1918 a large number of great whales appeared in Penobscot Bay and were harvested; Author's son discovers whale vertebrae.

Blackfish, Grumpus and the "Right" Whale

It is difficult to overestimate the effect of seeing a whale for the first time. Baleen whales are absolutely graceful in their movement—which is difficult to believe, given their size—and they move effortlessly through the water. A slight wave of their flukes and they are 30 to 50 yards away. They appear from below or out of nowhere, changing buoyancy like a living submarine. To look at it another way, a submarine in the best of circumstances can only approximate the movements of a living whale.

I saw my first whale in 1975 off Mount Desert Rock. It was late afternoon and we were headed back to Pigeon Hill Bay. A huge humpback whale surfaced near the lobster boat I was on, and while we throttled back to watch what would happen, the humpback repeatedly raised its massive white flukes clear of the ocean and then smacked them down emphatically on the surface in a motion called "lobtailing" by whale biologists. The whale seemed to be having fun.

In another encounter after a day and a night of fighting a peat fire on Seal Island in outer Penobscot Bay, three of us stood on Seal's central bluff at daybreak, transfixed in the early light of dawn while the blood-red orb of the sun loomed up out of the water.

*Humpback mother and
calf off Seal Island,
outer Penobscot Bay*

The island ground was hot, scorched and smoldering. About a half a mile from Seal's shores, between sun and sea, a whale's spout caught and hung in the shimmering vapor in the orange glowing path—and then another and another spout hanging like willowy breaths from Neptune's deepest lungs. Humpbacks in a pod. We thought the sounds and smells of the burning night had drained off every ounce of feeling, but the appearance of the whales blunted the sharp despair. In the sight of those silent shrouds catching the glow of the ever-rising eastern sun, a lightness began the turning, turning toward morning.

Rosier mentioned whale sightings in his 1604 account and left us with one of the few eyewitness accounts of how Maine's Indians captured whales: "He bloweth up the water and . . . is 12 fathoms long," Rosier wrote. The Indians "go in company of their king with a multitude of their boats and strike him with a bone made in the fashion of a harping iron fastened to a rope, which they make great and strong of the bark of trees. . . . Then all their boats come about him, and as he riseth above water, with their arrows they shoot him to death."

The species most likely hunted by Indians around the islands of Maine may have been the pilot whale. Compared with the swift rorqual whales (finbacks, seis, and minkes), which tend to swim farther offshore, pilot whales move along the inner rim of the Gulf of Maine, appearing in late April or early May. Captain John Smith describes them as appearing in great numbers and "easy of approach," though he turned aside from his original intention of taking whales to catch cod, instead, which were even easier of approach. William Wood's comprehensive listing of marine life around the Isles of Shoals mentions the "shouldering whale" and the "snuffling Grampus," perhaps the 20-to 30-foot pilot whale (also called the blackfish), which is a common inshore species.

John Josselyn wrote that the Indians and colonists alike hunted dolphins and porpoises, species of small whales that inhabit Maine waters. Called sea hogs by the English, they were cut into thin pieces and fried. "It tastes like rusty bacon or hung beef, if not worse, but the liver boiled and soused with vinegar is more grateful to the palate," wrote Josselyn. Perhaps so, but it is harder to trust Josselyn's judgment on marine mammal matters after reading his description of ambergris, the waxy substance formed within sperm whales and occasionally found washed ashore on the Maine coast. Josselyn took it "to be a mushroom . . . that riseth out of certain clammy and bituminous earth under the seas, the billows casting up part of it on land and fish devour the rest." Few people at the time had any idea where this valuable substance, used as a perfume fixative, came from. Nor would anyone be able to say for sure until New England ships had harpooned and slit open enough sperm whales on their Indian and Antarctic feeding grounds to lay that particular mystery to rest.

One of the benefits of the international effort to preserve whales is that their numbers have slowly increased in the Gulf of Maine where many live for the better part of the year, and where the northern right whale resides year-round. Researchers at island whale-watching stations such as Mount Desert Rock, 28 miles off the coast, have documented the yearly increases, even cataloging the rare appearance of the blue whale, the largest creature in the evolutionary record of life. The blue whale uses the entire Atlantic Basin, north and south, as its cruising grounds, communicating with other individual blues in deepwater acoustic channels that can apparently connect individual whales that are a thousand miles apart.

Endangered Northern Right Whale

The story of the Northern Right Whale is complicated. Because it is a slow swimmer, produces the most oil and floats when dead, hunters have long considered it the "right" whale for killing. But the natural rate of reproduction of right whales is very low, and their population has been very slow to recover since becoming the first officially protected species in 1933. The entire North Atlantic population may be derived from only a few mature females that escaped persecution. Today the population of the northern right whale hovers between 300 and 400 individuals.

More than 20 years of networked observations by responsible reporters shows that right whales transit the Gulf of Maine in the spring as they migrate to their summer feeding grounds in the deepwaters off Grand Manan Island. Along the way they appear on Stellwagen Bank and other offshore locations, but they are rarely seen in coastal waters. A few of these individuals may stray into Maine state waters, but the available ecological data demonstrates they are most commonly found in the region immediately surrounding Mount Desert Rock. Recently an over-wintering population of right whales has been discovered in the Gulf of Maine that do not migrate southward.

*Lobster pot warp,
Criehaven*

Mount Desert Rock is also virtually the only place within Maine"s territorial waters that is adjacent to the 600-foot-deep regions of the Gulf of Maine. Biologists know that right whales feed heavily on a single prolific species of zooplankton known as *Calanus finmarchius*, which research has shown are notably absent in coastal waters, but are abundant offshore, especially in areas of vertical upwelling.

Further offshore right whales share the ocean with fishermen and offshore lobstermen, and are occasionally entangled in fishing gear. Whale researcher Scott Kraus, who has worked at the New England Aquarium, among other institutions, points out that virtually all right whales sighted in the Gulf of Maine show battle scars of entanglement on their skin. But frequently mortalities also are caused by oceangoing ships, which collide with whales while they are sleeping at the surface.

Because their numbers are so low, the loss of even a single right whale is serious, and violates the Marine Mammal Protection Act. Responding to a lawsuit brought by an ecological activist named Max Strahan, a federal judge ruled that the Endangered Species Act required the National Marine Fisheries Service to adopt new rules to protect right whales from fishing gear. Following a decade-long delay occasioned by years of fruitless negotiations between animal rights activists, ocean conservationists and fishermen, NMFS finally adopted a rule requiring all Maine lobstermen outside a narrow inshore exclusion zone to replace floating rope used to string lobster traps together with "sink rope" that will lie on the ocean bottom.

The regulations created a firestorm of protest from Maine lobstermen because millions and millions of dollars were involved in the rerigging—estimates ran from $7,000 to $14,000 per boat. Clearly highly endangered right whales have become mortally entangled in lobster gear, although most experts believe vertical lines pose more of a threat than bottom ones. Nevertheless, fishermen are rerigging pairs and triples with individual vertical lines, which may sadly increase the risk to right whales, simply because there will be more, not fewer, lines in the water. No one is happy, and more lawsuits are likely to follow.

Looking Back and Looking Ahead

The past 350 years of interaction between humans and island mammals has not been pretty. But the news is not all bad. While much of the big game was hunted to early extinction among the islands, bears are now back; moose, too. Wolves and perhaps mountain lions have miraculously reappeared in places like coastal Washington County, and the wily coyote, never before part of Maine fauna, has also taken up residence. We'll never know whether the original island foxes were red, gray, or silver, but as long as the islands host voles, mice, and birds for food, a few foxes will skulk out in cold winters when the ice bridges the worlds of the main and the islands.

Deer live on islands often in numbers too great for their own good. Only caribou among the original faunal complement are missing, despite an ambitious restocking effort. Rabbits and raccoons have been introduced on some islands with predictably

Harbor seal haul-out, Long Ledge, Jericho Bay

Terry Goodhue, on right, taught North Haven students how to clean and assemble a seal skeleton.

unfortunate results. And the slightly weasely mink has moved into the habitat once occupied by a separate species of sea mink.

The situation in the marine environment is murkier. Seals, now protected for almost three decades, have continued reproducing and recolonized areas with an astonishing fecundity. They haul out on an increasing number of ledges to watch our activities and to raise their bewhiskered pups. The whales are the greatest disappointment. After all these years of protection—since the 1930s for the right whale and almost as long for the humpback—there are still so few. We should be grateful, I suppose, that in these rich waters of the Gulf of Maine, the most ancient, and some say most highly developed, mammals of the world still sing, splash, and dance in the blue-green water column.

Our challenges now are not how to deal with scarcity as much as how to balance conflicting interests created by the resurgence of wildlife in a more complicated world.

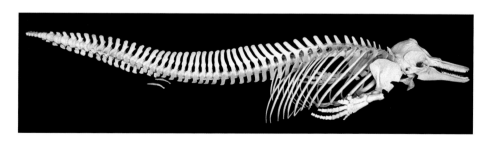

Rare beaked whale washed up on Vinalhaven, was rearticulated at the North Haven school.

CHAPTER 8

Fisheries:
Herring, Hake, Haddock and Cod

There is much temptation to stay away from home, the truth of which true men avoid
by going out no matter what. The worst of it is not in gale or storm but
when it is plainly severe and cold: early mornings when sea smoke works its way into
every man's and boy's blood and bone. At least a dozen compulsive work days a year
it creates a dwarf world where those on the water work in clouds,
and those ashore watch mastheads come and go like dorsal fins of extinct fish.

George Putz, *Island Journal*

Indian Island sea smoke;
(Facing) Herring dories,
Kent Cove, North Haven

It is hard to know what motivates men (and precious few women) to give up the relative comforts of terrestrial life, no matter how marginal, and venture out beyond the certainties of the known world; beyond the point where anyone is able to help you if you should need it; to float on the surface tension of the sea and cast nets down toward creatures of the deep; to be a tiny speck of effort within the immense and lonely expanse of the ocean. All we know is that our ancestors have been setting out upon the ocean to pursue fish great and small since before recorded civilizations, before adventurers left records of their exploits, and well before farmers tamed forests and valleys.

Most fishermen, it seems, couldn't live ashore even if they wanted to. Fishing is not so much a calling as a command. It appeals to those who are closer to their edges than their centers; to those souls in flight; to the restless, rootless waywardness in our being; to those outlawed; to those whose view of life is confirmed again and again by the acute sensitivities called forth from places of gray convexity far offshore where nothing is solid, nothing is certain; where everything is floating and the void is near at hand. The Arctic tundra in its elemental winter white is the closest terrestrial equivalent to the offshore fisherman's world.

*Vinalhaven fisherman
Tim Dyer with
332-pound halibut*

"Fish So Plentiful and So Great"

Rosier's description of the marine environments the Waymouth expedition encountered on its voyage through the Gulf of Maine proved to be as insightful and interesting as his detailed descriptions of trees, plants and animals. As the ARCHANGELL crossed into the Gulf, Rosier provides what may be the first European description of the Gulf Stream, which swirls offshore of Georges Bank. "We came to a riplin, which we discerned to head our ship, which is a breach of water caused either by a fall, or by some meeting of currents, which we judged this to be; for the weather being very fair, and a small gale of wind, we sounded and found no ground in a hundred fathoms."

As soon as the ARCHANGELL had anchored at Monhegan, you can feel Rosier's excitement as he remarks on the astounding marine bounty. "While we were ashore, our men aboard with a few hooks got above thirty great Cods and Hadocks, which gave us a taste of the great plenty of fish which we found afterward wherever we went upon this coast," he wrote. Two days later, the ARCHANGELL safely anchored off Allen Island, where Rosier describes the small fishing party that went out "about a mile from our ship, and in small time with two or three hooks was fished for our whole company three days, with great Cod, Hadock, and Thorneback." On their next fishing expedition, they "got about thirty very good and great lobsters towards night (when) we drew with a small net of twenty fathoms very nigh the shore." A few weeks later, Rosier relates that at Allen Island, "our men took Cod and Hadock by our ship side, and lobsters very great: which before we had not tried."

These observations about lobsters are highly significant because many fishermen, including most of the lobstermen who fish the waters around Allen and Benner, believe that the present abundance of lobsters in inshore waters is a result of the absence of cod, which can be significant predators of small lobsters. But Rosier's account clearly indicates that large cod and large lobsters occupied the same waters at the same place in abundant numbers. Cod and lobsters co-evolved with each other in the Gulf of Maine, and it seems unreasonable to conclude that an abundance of cod cannot also coexist with an abundance of lobsters.

Another interesting fisheries note occurs when Waymouth and Rosier invite a group of Wabanaki, who had been "fishing and fowling," aboard their ship at Allen Island to trade. Rosier writes that "they showed me likewise a great piece of fish, whereof I tasted, and it was fat like Porpoise, and another kind of great scaly fish, broiled on the coals, much like white Salmon, which the Frenchmen call Aloza." Rosier's observations suggest that the Wabanaki successfully hunted harbor porpoise from their bark canoes, no mean feat since porpoise are among the fastest swimmers and most highly wary among all marine species the Wabanaki hunted. Rosier's description of the "great scaly fish" may have referred to Atlantic sturgeon, which could reach sizes of several hundred pounds. The archaeologist Spiess notes that sturgeon were a tertiary food resource at the time of European contact for the Wabanaki of Penobscot Bay.

As Waymouth and Rosier departed from Allen Island after their monthlong expedition to begin their voyage home, they had one last opportunity to experience the Gulf's bounty. When they had sailed about 60 miles from the nearest land, they suddenly found themselves in 24 fathoms of water. "Wherefore our sails being down, Thomas King, boatswain, presently cast out a hook, and before he judged it at ground, was fished and hauled up an exceeding great and well fed Cod: then we were cast out 3 or 4 more, and fish so plentiful and so great. . . we were so delighted to see them," Rosier wrote. "All were generally very great, some measured to be five foot long, and three foot about." The fishermen at Allen Island believe that Waymouth found and fished on Jeffrey's Ledge, where several of them also fish in the spring. Jeffrey's Ledge is about 90 miles southeast of Allen Island.

Regardless of which fishing ground they had stumbled upon, the fishing was so

Drying fish on the shore of Matinicus harbor, 1898

Cleaning cod,
Fish Beach,
Monhegan, ca. 1890

extraordinary on this offshore bank that it "should be alone sufficient cause to draw men again." Rosier cannot help himself as his prose reached superlatives: "To amplify with words, were to add light to the sun: for everyone in the ship could easily account (that) in a short voyage with few good fishers (would) make more profitable return from hence than from Newfoundland: the fish being so much greater and better fed, and abundant with train (oil)." This was an exceptionally astute observation. When the English learned cod caught in the Gulf of Maine weighed two to three times as much as those caught on the Grand Banks, the drive to settle the Maine coast and islands began in earnest.

Maine Fish and Maine History

In the introduction to his monumental work on America's fisheries, George Brown Goode, whose research was sponsored by the first U.S. Fish Commission, wrote that the Narragansett Indian word for cod translates as "the fish that comes a little before spring," a name which "is suggestive in the extreme." Since before recorded history, cod were known to congregate in immense schools in late winter to spawn. This created a winter fishery in New England that supported settlements as far back as the early 1600s. Few people remember that the Pilgrims' first awful winter in Plymouth was saved only by a voyage to the fishing station at Damariscove Island off Boothbay Harbor, where they were resupplied with dried salt cod.

Unlike other groundfish species, cod migrate inshore to lay eggs toward the end of the winter months. Cod massed in enormous numbers in well-defined locations in accessible waters south of Isles of Shoals, off Richmond Island in Cape Elizabeth, off

Damariscove Island near the mouth of the Sheepscot River, and off Vinalhaven and
Matinicus in Penobscot Bay, in Mount Desert's Somes Sound, and in most of the other
bays of Maine eastward.

John Smith not only explored the coast of Maine in a small boat in 1614, but he also
caught enough fish during his stay to turn a handsome profit at the conclusion of his
voyage. He was one of the early popularizers of the idea of a Maine winter fishery. He
did not exaggerate when he wrote that cod that had fattened themselves all summer
long were more valuable when caught during the spawning season. "Each hundred is
as good as two or three hundred in the Newfoundland and you can have your fish to
market before they have any," he wrote. This essentially echoed Rosier's observations of
a decade earlier. Islands such as Isles of Shoals, Richmond, Damariscove, and Monhegan—all of which were handy to the winter cod grounds—became important outposts
for this new fishery.

The Rise of Island Groundfishing

In the three decades between 1770 and 1800, the population of Maine quintupled.
Suddenly there were many more mouths to feed. Before the Revolution there were
about 60 fishing vessels from the District of Maine. Only a few of these went to offshore banks such as Brown's, Sable or Roseway, and Georges was considered too rough
and dangerous for small craft. Instead, most vessels fished the smaller banks closer to
shore—Spot of Rocks, Saturday Night Ledge, Old Man's Pasture, Sou' sou' west, Kettle
Bottom, Schoodic Ridges, Clay Bank—from berths at Isles of Shoals, Damariscove,
Monhegan, North and South Fox Islands, Swans, Deer Isle and Mount Desert.

It is important to bear in mind the difference between the offshore fisheries and

Enormous cod were common in the Gulf of Maine until the 1920s and 30s; Lane and Libby curing salt cod, Vinalhaven

the so-called "shore fishery" or "boat fishery," which operated within 30 miles of the Maine coast and in which virtually every coastal and island village was involved. The inshore cod fishery represented a kind of local breadbasket where local boats, large and small, from small island towns could send vessels to fishing grounds in the Gulf of Maine. In 1817 Vinalhaven supported "15 sail of small schooners, the smaller fishing the shore," according to Edward Earll, one of the primary authors of the 1887 U.S. Fish Commission report. "Two or three of the larger were making voyages to the offshore banks." Deer Isle (Stonington) similarly reflected the division of effort between inshore and distant water fishing. In 1830, 12 large fishing vessels went to distant fishing grounds, while 40 smaller "boats" fished "along the shore," according to the U.S. Fisheries Commission report.

The early fishing enterprises of the islands, like those of small ports on the mainland, were characterized not just by their small size but also by the practice of fishing "on shares," whereby each crew member was paid on the basis of the value of a portion of the landings. This form of democratic "ownership" of the catch was an important reflection of the political culture of the region, and has survived as a continuing and nearly unique feature of many local fisheries, including lobstering, herring fishing and groundfishing. Of course a few capitalists emerged, such as David Thurlow of Deer Isle, who sent four fishing vessels to sea in 1829, including the 76-ton LYDIA. Captain Timothy Lane of Vinalhaven rose to prominence in the 1850s as a successful fleet owner and salt fish merchant. In 1851 Lane shipped $70,000 worth of dried cod to Boston, an enormous volume. But these enterprises were the exception rather than the rule.

By 1860, the democratic structure of the Maine fishing fleet, the skill of its crews, and the productivity of the local waters all contributed to the fact that Maine had more fishermen (4,607) than any other state in the nation. A great number of these fishermen were islanders. According to Wayne O'Leary, the leading cod-fishing region in Maine was almost invariably the Penobscot district. In 1860, Deer Isle (which included Stonington), where 45 percent of the population was completely dependent on fishing, supplied more fishermen than any other coastal village in Maine. In 1860 there were 11,375 mariners in the state of Maine—a fifth of the population.

20th–Century Groundfisheries

At the turn of the twentieth century the introduction of steam- and later diesel-powered vessels shifted labor demands on the fishing industry from the water to shoreside processing. On Vinalhaven in 1900, for instance, 200 fishermen in boats supplied fish for 100 jobs on shore, processing them into salt fish. A few decades later, many fewer fishermen at sea were needed to supply a much larger number of fish-processing jobs ashore.

The introduction of the otter trawl played a key role in the industrialization of the New England fisheries. A large net (approximately 67 feet across at its mouth, depending on the size of the boat), towed over the bottom and attached by cables to winches aboard a steam-powered fishing boat, the otter trawl was first developed in England for North Sea fishing in 1905. It appeared in southern New England the following year. Within a decade, virtually no new fishing boat in Maine was launched without one.

Vinalhaven historian Sydney Winslow reports that in 1903, the Vinalhaven Fish Co. was booming, having handled between seven and eight million pounds, which made it the largest fish-curing plant in the state and one of the largest in the country. That same year, the commissioner of Sea and Shore Fisheries reported that 12 million pounds of groundfish had been landed in Penobscot Bay ports by approximately 400 fishermen.

Fish delivered to Carver's Harbor;
Cleaning the catch, Vinalhaven

But by 1918 the commissioner of Sea and Shore Fisheries appeared to be concerned about the state of the resource. He issued a plea that the industry and Legislature "not disregard the urgent need of intelligent restrictions . . . [for] the protection of cod in the spawning season." The commissioner wrote that "it is a well established fact that during the spring months, large cod heavy with spawn seek the bays and rivers on the coast of Maine to spawn, at which time the gill net fishermen capture them in large numbers."

With the completion of the Maine Central Railroad in the 1920s, connecting Rock-

Blast From the Past:

NOVEMBER 6, 2009—Recently researchers at the University of New Hampshire, led by Karen Alexander, have analyzed logbooks from the fleet that fished out of Frenchman's Bay, just east of Mount Desert Island, in the 1860s. The authors used the Frenchman's Bay data to extrapolate landings from the entire Gulf of Maine in 1861. This fleet, comprised of 220 relatively small, wooden sailing vessels with hook-and-line technology, fished the inshore waters in a small corner of the Gulf of Maine and caught two to three times as much cod as we catch in the entire Gulf of Maine today! The results indicate that such landings were nearly equivalent to today's estimates of the entire spawning stock biomass required to generate today's maximum sustainable yield, suggesting that we are seriously shortsighted in our goals for restoring Gulf of Maine stocks. We have been arguing over the few fish that remain for so long we have lost sight of what we could have if stocks were really and truly rebuilt.

It is stunning to recognize just how much of the historical harvest was caught near shore—very near shore. In 1861, the average distance to a fishing ground was 20 miles. This means that in the 1860s

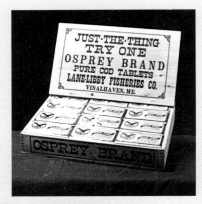

fishermen were fishing well inside the fishing grounds identified as productive just a few years later—and way closer to shore than Gulf of Maine cod can be caught in any numbers today. Alexander and her colleagues conclude that cod were once very abundant in nearshore waters but were dispersed in hundreds of "micro-grounds" that collectively supported enormous annual harvests. Such fish were caught sustainably for over a century by vessels fishing with baited hooks.

Our fisheries management system has failed to recognize that groundfish stocks in the Gulf of Maine are made up of bits and pieces, sub-stocks that operate somewhat independently. These sub-stocks spawn, feed, migrate and intermingle according to an ever-changing set of rules too complex for us to understand, much less predict. This diversity provides stability to the population as a whole. Sub-stocks can take advantage of locally productive conditions and, conversely, the effects of a poor year class in one sub-stock can be compensated for by better luck in others. Clearly, such diversity of sub-stocks cannot be managed effectively by applying the same rules to the entire Gulf of Maine. Local, area-based management is one opportunity for shifting some of the authority for fisheries management to a scale that can address sub-stock dynamics and abundance.

Although some stocks are recovering and some are fully rebuilt—according to our current standards—the work of these ecological historians, through painstakingly analysis of ancient logbooks, is incontrovertible evidence that we can do better. Much, much better.

land and Midcoast Maine to Boston and New York, the market for fresh fish greatly expanded. Groundfishermen looking to increase their catches began to target spawning runs of fish close to shore, far up the estuaries and around the shores of islands, with predictable results. Perhaps the only surprising thing is how long it took for the individual spawning runs to be located and fished to commercial extinction.

By 1930, there were clear signs that the fleet had grown too large in relation to the sustainability of the local stocks. While the state's fisheries commissioner continued to extol the building of new vessels with new technology, he also noted in 1934 that "[It] is an established fact that most species of groundfish are growing scarcer in our bays, harbors and inlets." The commissioner also noted that the "otter trawl, a blessing to the industry because of its efficiency, is a necessary form of harvesting, but under the present form of operation causes the waste of hundreds of thousands of pounds of small, unmarketable fish." He urged consideration of a regulation allowing no otter trawl to use a mesh of less than 4 3/4 inches in Maine waters. But the idea did not gain traction until 1978 when the first regulation on mesh size in Maine waters was adopted—four and a half inches. By then the end was in sight, though few could see it.

Vinalhaven fisherman Bert Dyer recalled for me days when the groundfishing was plentiful close to shore. "Beautiful hand-lining there, in the gully that's between Seal Island and the shoal," he recalled. "Christ, you'd go down there some days and load a boat with pollock. And big cod. Now you go down there, it's nothing. But, my God, in the spring of the year, you'd see sometimes 15 to 20 boats right there, hand-lining cod. March, April—load right up. It's too bad!" he said.

"We all trawled," he continued. "Tub trawls with 800 hooks to a tub, 34 inches apart on a gangion. Most of us in the summertime, when lobsters went to 30 cents, we had about 14 boats and we'd all go haking. We'd start middle of June and go through till October. We'd fish off the Ball and down to the Rock and what we called the Blue Ground and Skate Bank and the Bowdies. You could count on it every year, just as regular as could be. I don't know if it will ever be the same. Christ, if the farmers and fishermen

Bert Dyer and deckhand lumping fish, Carver's Harbor;
Fishing trawler,
DORA PETER,
Vinalhaven, ca. 1940

Eastport weir built with spruce spiles and birch brush;
Drying pocket of a stop seine, Rockport Harbor,
ca. 1940

can't make a go of it, who the hell is going to feed us. We can't eat plastic eggs. Plastic fish. Christ, you can't make a fisherman overnight. That's for goddamn sure."

Herring "In Such Infinite Numbers"

No other species of fish so readily demonstrates the immense productivity of the inshore waters of the Gulf of Maine as herring. The earliest observations of the region give a vivid picture of this abundance. In 1675 the naturalist John Josselyn, who lived on his brother's plantation on the shores of Saco Bay, described an inshore massing of the fish. "The herring, which are numerous, they take of them all summer long," he wrote. "In 1670 they were driven back into Black Point Harbor by other great fish that prey upon them so near the shore that they threw themselves (it being high water) upon dry land in such infinite numbers that we might have gone half-way the leg amongst them for near a quarter of a mile."

One of the earliest methods of catching herring was to build a herring trap or "weir." Originally this was a simple brush fence strung across the mouth of a cove—low enough that the fish could swim over it at high tide, but high enough to trap them when the water ebbed. In subsequent years, weirs were constructed of spruce spiles woven together with birch brush. Consider for a moment the productivity of these inshore waters where a fishery could develop that required little else but small trees cut from nearby shores and tended from boats that could be rowed a short distance to the weirs.

In 1825 the purse seine was introduced in Gloucester, Massachusetts, where it was first used to catch mackerel. By 1850, the technology was used to revolutionize the herring fishery. Like all fishing technology, herring purse seiners have gotten steadily larger. But the concept has one important biological feature, namely that herring spawn on or near the bottom and then rise at night to feed at the surface, which is where purse seiners catch them. One legendary spawning run of herring was measured at over 17 miles long. Many observers believe that purse seining takes a smaller percentage of spawning adults than mid-water trawling, the other major method now in use.

Some of the herring caught in weirs were sold to smokehouses in the island communities of Matinicus, Vinalhaven, and Deer Isle, to be preserved for shipment in the coastwise trade. But herring did not become big business in Maine until after the introduction of canning technology following the

Civil War. Herring weirs became increasingly sophisticated over the years, not only in their placement to capture the maximum number of fish, but also in their construction. Still, today they have almost disappeared from the Maine coast as larger and larger seiners and mid-water trawlers appear to break up the schools before they reach the shore.

Sardines

Herring spawn in the late summer in "three to thirty fathoms," according to Henry Bigelow, the great fisheries ecologist of the Gulf of Maine. They lay their eggs over many different types of bottom—rock, pebble, gravel—never over soft mud. A single gravid female lays between 10,000 and 30,000 eggs, which sink to the bottom and cling in clumps to everything from seaweed to pebbles to pot warp or anchor rode. Herring will grow to be 4 to 7 inches long during their first two years, when they are called sardines. By the end of their third year they are larger than 10 inches and frequent deeper waters.

Just before 1900, there were 68 sardine factories in Eastport, packing smoked herring that was shipped around the world. Then came sardine canneries, which revolutionized employment prospects along the coast. At one point there were some 75 sardine-canning factories along the coast, including several around the periphery of Penobscot Bay in Stonington, Belfast, Rockland and Port Clyde. The largest herring catch ever recorded from the Gulf of Maine occurred in 1946, when 219 million pounds were taken. The greatest number of these weighed about 1/2 ounce, which meant that something like six billion fish were caught. That's six thousand million—or, if you like, 6,000,000,000 individual creatures produced in two years of growth out in this rich green sea.

By 1997 only seven sardine plants remained in Maine. Most fell victim to changing consumer tastes and demand, as well as global competition Most of the remaining sardine plants packed for the export market. Then in 2010, the state's last sardine plant closed. Bumble Bee Foods, which owned the plant in Prospect Harbor, blamed the decision on federal regulations reducing the herring catch as regulators belatedly tried to save the fishery. It was the end of an industry that employed thousands of Maine workers for more than a century. Today, herring caught in Maine waters are used mostly for lobster bait.

Herring weir, Isle au Haut;
Herring weirs, Grand Manan Island, 1982

*Loading racks of herring
at a Grand Manan
Island smokehouse*

Once on Seal Island in the summer of 1980, I saw a glimmer of what herring fishermen must know in their bones: that the immeasurable richness of these waters is mysterious and godlike. The phosphorescence in the water fired the imagination as it lit the waves curling in on Seal's shores. While looking out to sea we watched a streak of eerie pale light begin to shimmer shapelessly beneath the sea's surface and move shoreward like a strange, silent, green force field. It was a slow, ponderous surge, a huge school of herring, which changed direction, flanked, disappeared and reappeared like a single cosmic mind trailing streaks of light through the black void of oceanic space—shimmering, sinuous pale light, flashing on and off in networks of neural activity, hundreds of fish, glowing like a single mind.

Fishing By Starlight

Alfred Osgood, a herring catcher from Carver's Harbor, Vinalhaven, is a legend throughout the far reaches of the Gulf of Maine and beyond. Perhaps no other fisherman has landed anywhere near the volume that Osgood has pumped out of the sea night after night, month after month, year after year. With handpicked crews from this island town, he roamed the herring grounds off Seal Island in outer Penobscot Bay, out to Halfway Rock and Jeffrey's Ledge off Portland, and up to Stellwagen Banks off Gloucester and beyond. Every fisherman in these ports and a hundred others in between is familiar with the name of his boat, STARLIGHT, and the legendary successes of its owner, captain and crew.

Some years ago, I went on a fishing trip aboard STARLIGHT, with Jason Day, STARLIGHT's alternate skipper at the time. We left Carver's Harbor when the sun was still a blinding bright orb in the western sky and headed toward an area southwest of Monhegan where the crew had seen fish the night before. Hours later STARLIGHT suddenly throttled back in the darkness. We were off Outer Pumpkin Ledge, southeast of Bantam Rock. Jason stared intently at the patterns of color on the forward scanning sonar and laconically observed, "This is the most fish I've seen in quite a little while."

The loom of instrument light cast an eerie glow in the pilothouse, as Jason began recording STARLIGHT's slow turns on the chart plotter, but the school was in water too shallow to deploy STARLIGHT's deep net, which was also the largest in the fleet at the time. STARLIGHT's net ran to an astonishing 40 fathoms, and Jason needed an additional few fathoms of margin to avoid tearing the bottom out of the $140,000 net.

Off to port and starboard the lights of four other boats bobbed and blinked in the inky night and all warily circled the fish, the ledges and each other. Suddenly the radio crackled intensely. Jason responded with a few words. Then STARLIGHT began to move ponderously off to the northeast toward one of the other boats, where we came up alongside the ANNA LISA, a 48-foot seiner out of New Harbor. Her skipper handed the ends of his seine net to STARLIGHT's crew. In the pocket of his net we watched approximately 160,000 pounds of silver-sided herring flipping near the surface. Since it was more than he could load aboard his modest-sized vessel, he was proposing to give the rest of the fish away. I was incredulous. Jason explained that recently most of the Gulf of Maine boats got together to form the Independent Seiners Association and that one of the things they agreed to do was to share catches that were too big for one boat to handle rather than tolerate the waste of herring dumped dead overboard. STARLIGHT took on some 400 bushels; at $8 per bushel, we had just received a $3,200 gift with little fanfare.

Although the 400 bushels were gratefully received, STARLIGHT still needed 3,000 bushels to satisfy its markets ashore. When we returned to a spot on the bottom deep enough to make a set, the question was whether the fish were still there, and if so, how many. The captain returned his gaze to the chart plotter. Meanwhile on the stern, STARLIGHT's crew waited quietly in the dark. Two men perched on the bug boat, the short, fast boat that will carry the twine in a large circle around the herring when and if the captain gives the word. Everyone else wordlessly waited with tense and watchful patience.

For the captain to give the signal, STARLIGHT would need to be "up-tide" of the fish to avoid fouling the net in the propeller as it shoots off the stern; the fish must be in 45 to 50 fathoms of water to protect the net; the sonar signal must indicate a large and dense-enough bunch of fish to make the set worthwhile; the location of other boats needs to be monitored; the compass heading must be remembered; and finally, the direction of movement of the feeding fish as they graze on the floating zooplankton pasture must be factored in. Soon a half-moon will rise, which can spook the fish, and Jason must factor this into his calculation too. You begin to understand why captains, in addition to their responsibility for the safety of the crew and vessel, receive a larger

Seine dories, Indian Creek, Vinalhaven; Herring shut off, Boothbay Harbor; STARLIGHT delivers bait to lobster float, Vinalhaven

Rockland harbor fishing vessels, ca. 1984; Rockland harbor fishing vessels, ca. 1994

share of a night's returns.

After circling for well over an hour in intense concentration, Jason swiveled in his chair, and quietly said only two words, "Let s go." The brake on the winch cable holding the bug boat on the stern let go with a rifle crack, and then it all came down to how quickly this small vessel could haul 2,400 feet of 40-fathom twine in a long arc around this body of fish before they swam away. A long three minutes passed before the leading ends of the net were handed up over the rail and Jason hastened back to the sonar. A slow smile spread over his face as he peered at the image of a bunch of fish neatly circumscribed on the screen. Then a whole village's worth of halogen lights went on, while the bottom of the net was pursed and we gazed out at two acres of white corks that floated lazily on the surface.

As the net came up, the herring flipping in the water sounded like a hard rain and the heave and surge of this massive school was enough to roll STARLIGHT over on her starboard side. As the herring flipped in the diminishing dimensions of the net, their shimmering scales, once collected for pearl essence, suffused the scene in a kind of opalescent glow. I understood why they say herring seining spoils you for any other fishing. It was an undeniably good night; this crew caught close to $24,000 of bait, the proceeds from which will be divided up into shares among the captain and the crew and STARLIGHT herself. This catch will supply enough bait to satisfy the August lobster market demand in Midcoast Maine for a day.

Fishing with Computer Chips

In 1981, I watched an old friend, Jim Salisbury, assemble an assortment of itinerant boatbuilders and fishermen to lay up the steel frames and hull plates of the JESSE, a 60-foot stern dragger on the shores of Pigeon Hill Bay—no naval architect, no detailed plans, not even a boat shed to escape the winter wind that bit like a driven nail to the bone. In early spring, when Jim's wife, Donna, broke the champagne bottle across JESSE's high bow and all the electronics were hooked up, Jim went groundfishing. After a decade of lobstering, Jim yearned to fish further out—to comb the dark shadows of underwater pastures for a more raw, less certain kind of living than tending gear inshore would provide.

Shortly after the launching of the JESSE, I stood in the pilothouse with Jim as he showed me the phalanx of technology he would use to get him around and over the fishing banks he was gearing up to exploit. In addition to CB and VHF radios, fathometer and the 24-mile radar set that were all beginning to be standard features on fishing boats, Jim had installed a Loran C receiver, which monitors radio frequencies from shore towers to give boats precise triangulated readouts of their location over any piece of bottom of the Gulf of Maine, or anywhere else at sea, for that matter. Accurate to within 50 feet, Loran technology meant that Jim could return to any fishing spot where he had previously had success with a precision that had been virtually impossible a few years earlier.

But the screen from which I could not take my eyes was a new color scanning sonar device. At the time few boats had them, because the early models were very expensive, driven by a pricey color computer chip that has since become inexpensive and commonplace. As Jim fired up the scanner and punched some buttons, the split screen showed a view of both the mid water column—whatever slice of depth he chose—and the profile of the bottom underneath. From the density of the return signal Jim could tell if the bottom were mud, sand, gravel plain, or hard, broken ledge. And from his knowledge of fish behavior, Jim knew what kind of fish he could expect to catch in each habitat. Even more amazing was the ability of the scanner to "see" schools of fish. By cross-referencing the sonar scanner with his chart plotter, Jim could find and relentlessly return to productive fishing grounds, even relatively small grounds. The fruits of Cold War submarine-hunting technology had been repackaged as fish-finding gear, which I realized much later spelled doom for Maine's legendary groundfish populations.

Hand-lining cod off Campobello Island; Dick Lunt baiting a groundfish trawl, Frenchboro, 1984

That day I had a vague premonition that fishing in the Gulf of Maine and out on the Banks would never be the same. With this kind of technological sophistication, there could be no place left for fish to hide. At the time we all were impressed with the way that Jim had harnessed a deep knowledge of fish ecology and technological innovation. Blind to the approaching calamity, we could sense the closing of the ocean frontier, but not see it. We should have listened to the voices whispering in our ears.

The Tragedy of the Commons

In 1984, I watched Dick Lunt bait one of his last trawls. For over 150 years, islanders from Lunt Harbor, on Frenchboro, had fished for cod, haddock, and an occasional giant halibut with baited trawls. But that fishery has since completely disappeared. It once sustained Frenchboro's small fleet for a six-to-eight-week period in the spring before the lobsters struck—which has always been later in the summer "downeast." Every time a small fishery disappears from a traditional community, residential development takes up the slack. That's not a bad thing, until the cumulative effect effaces the qualities that draw visitors in the first place, beginning with a self-reliant and vibrant individualism.

While watching the erosion of one fishery after another on the islands, I began to try to identify island fishermen who might serve as a voice for conservation from

Spring Spawning Grounds Migration—Willie Spear, Cousins Island

MARCH 22, 1996—We met Willie Spear at the boatyard on Cousins Island, where he was getting it ready for the upcoming fishing season, and listened to his story of getting started in the groundfishery.

"I had a chance to see the spring schools and the fall runs of fish. I will never get over seeing them so close to shore, the size and amount of them. That's what fishing was all about."

"It's just like a wall," said Willie, "ever since the beginning of time, fishermen just follow one ridge or one plateau to the next as the fish migrate up the coast. From time to time, the fish will be up against that wall when they first start to congregate to do their spring migration, I guess you could call it. There's cracks and fingers all along that fifty-fathom edge, you know, that go up into the shallow wa-ter—all the way from Jeffery's and we used to follow them as far as Mount Desert. We would start as far south as the Isles of Shoals and find the cracks and fingers and fish them with gillnets and trawls. Just followed one ridge or plateau to the next. Fish like different types of feed, like shrimp and so on. But the cod had their mind set on those 50 fathom ledges, that's where they would eat. Each fish has its own bottom. We filled this boat I don't know how many times with pollock in the fall. In November and December. One year we almost lost our boat with so many fish in it."

"Old-timers always said, 'Everything has to come to the shore to spawn.' Sometime around Easter Sunday, the cod used to show up. That was because Easter Sunday comes on the first Sunday after the first full moon after the spring equinox. So it's because of the moon that you start to see those fish. Where the water temperatures are right and the bottom is right, that's where you'd find them. Anytime from the first of March they begin to congregate, and you could follow them right up in. The eggs and milt would be less and less as the fish got closer to shore. The old-timers said that they'd work themselves up into Casco Bay . . . off here the fish would run west and northwest up into shallow water. By June off Cape Elizabeth the eggs and the milt would become less and less as they moved back out of the bays."

"To see the codfish and haddock . . . experiences you can never, ever replace. I thought fishing was supposed to be like that. After that we had to keep putting more nets on. And the handwriting was on the wall."

within the groundfish industry. Willie Spear of Cousins Island was one such person. He recalled, "Some of us tried to conserve, tow a five-and-a-quarter-inch cod end, but the philosophy was, if you left some fish behind, someone else was going to take them," he said. "By 1984 the groundfish were disappearing."

Ted Ames, who grew up fishing on Vinalhaven and became the Island Institute's first marine resource director, had a similar recollection. "We were working on pretty local runs in various bays as well as right down the coast. We worked out each one as we came along. We ended up being a lot more mobile than the fish," he said. "What happened was that the small boats that depended on the local stocks. . . those little guys had to get out of business and the big ones joined the parade to the next bay to do the same thing all over again. Eventually we ran out of new places to strip. We all did our share of it."

Without understanding the implications, fishermen caught all the fish, he said. "You could see that you were damaging the fishery but I don't think that we as fishermen, and those before us, as far as that goes, really understood what a toll we were taking on the whole system. By the end of it we were fishing spawning areas, nursery areas. . . it didn't matter where; if there was a fish there, we caught it."

Identifying Spawning Grounds

Ted Ames was concerned that nobody had ever recorded the location of inshore spawning grounds for cod. Published historical references from 1880 and 1929 described Maine's inshore fishing grounds, but neither referenced spawning grounds or identified their location. So Ames decided to pull together his own report. He began interviewing older fishermen to find out where they had found ripe or spawning cod inshore. "Those of us who fished knew, or knew people who knew, where the old spawning grounds were," he said. "A lot of people I talked to were 70, 80 or 90 years old. A great many of the spawning grounds have long since been wiped out. But I was able to document 1,100 square miles of spawning area in the coastal waters of Maine."

Ames's spawning-ground maps demonstrated that over half of the historic spawning grounds for cod and haddock had once been located in State of Maine waters. This project helped earn Ames a MacArthur Foundation "genius" award a number of years later. The Island Institute used Ames's information to convince the Maine legislature in 1998 to close all 2,900 square miles of Maine state waters to groundfishing in April, May and June, when cod and haddock come inshore to spawn. The vote came eight decades after the state had first considered protecting spawning grounds in 1917. The question was then as it is now: Was it too little, too late?

Ames and his wife, Robin Alden, went on to found the Penobscot East Resource

Dick Lunt with great grandson, Nate Lunt, Frenchboro; Ted Ames identified historic inshore cod and haddock spawning grounds in the Gulf of Maine.

Seine dories, Kent Cove,
North Haven

Center in Stonington, an organization which is working to restore groundfishing in the eastern Gulf of Maine where it has been commercially defunct for almost three decades.

Poster Child for Failed Fisheries Management

In contrast to Maine and the rest of New England, the fisheries of the West Coast, especially Alaska and other parts of the United States, did not develop significantly until well after World War II. Partly because the Pacific is a much larger ocean and the fishing grounds are generally further offshore and in exposed areas like the Bering Sea, fishing boats on the West Coast were usually larger than their East Coast counterparts, and they were often owned and financed by corporations, unlike the owner-operator model that has persisted here.

While few fisheries advocates in Maine have proposed emulating the corporate fishing model, it is accurate to say that the decades-long fight against regulations designed to reduce overfishing has left most New England fishermen with an image problem in

the minds of most of the public. Many of the proposed "indirect" controls on fishing practices—how many days fishermen can fish, where they can fish, and a bewildering number of other restrictions—have failed to stem the tide of decline in the resource. Clearly we must develop a better way to regulate our fisheries. Over the last 20 years, our fishermen have become poster children for a just-say-no approach to fisheries management, which has served neither the fish nor the fishermen.

The first ever cap on the total allowable catch for New England waters was instituted in 2010. Whether this new system of a direct control on fishing mortality will lead to rebuilding depleted stocks remains to be seen, but prices were up for those boats still in the fishery. An even larger question is whether any small fishing boats from small fishing villages on the coast and islands will survive the continuing consolidation of the fishing industry and be able to fish the legendarily productive inshore waters along the rim of the Gulf of Maine, to feed their families and and sell their catch to their neighbors and to other markets that have been supplied by Maine fishermen for generations.

CHAPTER 9

Island Edges:
Clams, Crabs, Lobsters and Urchins

Hell no, I don't know where all the rocks are; I just know where they ain't.

—Vinalhaven lobsterman, when asked how he remembered the location
of so many ledges when navigating in the fog

*Tar pot, Opechee Island
in Casco Passage;
(Facing) Tangle, Long
Island, Casco Bay*

On a profound level, fishermen and islanders share a worldview; these are people drawn to the edges of life. Islanders inhabit an "ecotone," which ecologists define as the zone where two different habitats intersect or merge, such as the edge of an island where terrestrial and marine zones meet. Such places are always richer in ecological terms, supporting a higher number of species than either habitat supports individually because species from both habitats overlap there. Shellfish such as the blue mussel and the soft shell-clam can exist subtidally, but competition and predation is less when they move toward the terrestrial zone in the intertidal zone, even if predation from gulls and diggers is more.

Islanders also occupy these narrow boundaries between the terrestrial and marine ecosystems and benefit from the increased biological diversity that circumscribes every island. But fishermen patrol the ultimate ecotone, where the solid earth is shrunk down to the hopelessly enclosed boundaries encompassed within the gunwales of a small vessel. And if this small known life fails to provide sustenance, or fails spiritually, fishermen are cast ashore, like Jonah expelled from the belly of the whale. It is a sadness of island life.

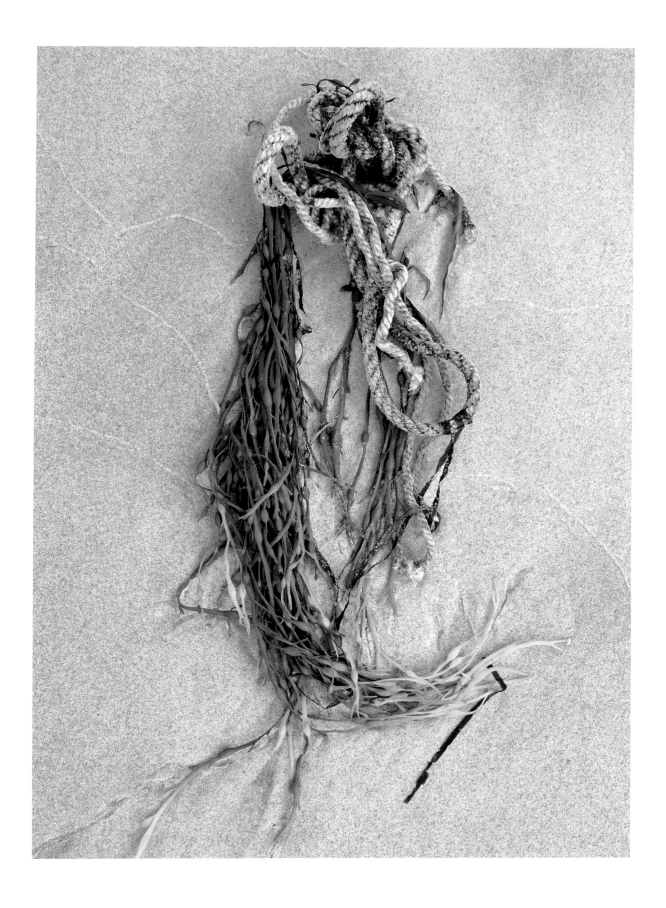

The Short Happy Life of a Clam Digger

One of my first jobs in Maine was digging clams during the spring and early summers of 1973 and 1974. Clam digging was a way to earn a living after mud season had shut down pulpwood operations, but before blueberry-raking jobs opened up on Washington County's barrens in late July. Along the Maine coast and islands, you start at the bottom and work your way up. In Washington County, the only marine trade lower than clam digging was digging worms, which was much harder work and paid less. I did not have the arms for it.

I dug in clam flats along either side of Pigeon Hill Road along the spine of the Petit Manan peninsula. With the purchase of a clam fork and a couple of hods, I was in business for less than the cost of my chain saw. I learned how to locate a good clam bed by estimating the size and density of siphon holes in the mud, how to sink a fork to avoid breaking the clam shells, and how many clams shy of the minimum two-inch size a clam dealer would buy. I dug the edges around boulders and ledges that other diggers passed by for more productive places in the middle of the flats.

I also got to know which shoreland owners would hassle clammers who tried to reach mudflats over land. Most Washington County property owners understood the importance of not appearing to stand between a clam digger and the place of his livelihood and did not mind a discreet passage along the edges of their property. But property rights were then and still are now a very touchy issue. I recall a *New Yorker* cartoon of a pair of clam diggers pointing up to a large house above them with the caption, "Somebody from New Jersey just bought it and now they act like they own the place."

I got so I could dig two bushels—four hods—on a tide in four to five hours, for which I was paid $28 per bushel in cash. Shorter, squatter fellows with much bigger biceps could dig three to four bushels on the same tide. After each day of digging I rested my back during a visit to the Rusty Anchor at the head of the Pigeon Hill Road, where I ordered a fried clam dinner to close the biological and economic loop.

Clamming on Little Deer Isle

Canned Clams and Steamers

The very first marine conservation law passed after Maine became a state turned the regulation of clam harvesting over to towns, ensuring that a community's inhabitants could take these shellfish at any time for personal and family use, and fishermen could harvest them for bait.

During the first several decades of the 20th century, an astounding number of clams were harvested from Maine's coastal flats. Figures from the Department of Sea and Shore Fisheries in 1903 show that there were 19 clam-canning factories along the coast, about half of which were in Knox and Hancock counties. All told between 1900 and 1906, the Penobscot Bay region produced several million pounds of clams. Upwards of 1,000 residents of both sexes were employed in the harvesting and the packing plants in the region.

By the 1930s, however, clam harvests had declined alarmingly. By 1934, the commissioner of the Sea and Shore Fisheries reported to the Legislature that most of Maine's hundreds of thousands of acres of clam flats were seriously depleted due to excessive digging. In 1935 the shortage of clams led the Legislature to pass the "2-inch clam law," which prohibited the sale of clams smaller than two inches.

In the 1980s, with new federal laws to protect public health from shellfish harvested in polluted places, almost half of Maine's clam flats were closed either due to pollution or to the absence of verifiable water-quality data showing the flats as free of bacterial contamination. During the following two decades, a host of volunteer groups of clammers and local activists mobilized to collect the water-quality data required to reopen closed flats. In 1996 alone, 10,000 acres of clam flats were reopened along the Maine coast. And perhaps more significantly, in 1987 a clam hatchery

Lobster and clam cannery, Isle au Haut; George Lewis managed the Isle au Haut lobster cannery from 1867 to 1883.

was established on Beals Island that supplies seed clams and expertise to towns interested in reestablishing clam populations and harvests.

Green Crabs and Ham

Marine biologists believe that one of the reasons that Maine's soft-shell clams have declined is a result of the expansion of the European green crab into Maine during the late 19th and early 20th centuries. A small crab found in virtually all intertidal habitats in Maine, the green crab has a voracious appetite for baby clams, and is among the world's worst alien invasive species.

Because the green crab is so ubiquitous under rocks in the intertidal zone, it provided a fail-safe opportunity for a stunt I used every time I brought a group of Outward Bound students to the shore for a lesson on foraging from the wild. I would turn over the first rock I came to find a half-dollar-sized green crab. (You will note that larger green crabs do not work as well for this trick, as you will soon see.) Carefully holding the green crab from the rear, pinching the top and bottom of its carapace to avoid its waving claws, I would explain that to prepare the crab for dinner, you did not even need to cook it, whereupon I would bite the crab in two and carefully chew the salty but tasty little crab, which is like biting a hard-boiled egg. This trick never failed to be an eye-popping success—except the one time a feisty young woman tried to repeat it, but bit the crab a little tentatively, whereupon the still-lively creature reached down with its one good claw and bit her smartly on her lower lip, leaving a ruby-red drop of blood as its final signature.

Clamshell midden, shore of the Basin, Vinalhaven; A bell buoy can save your life.

Saved by the Buoy

Clam diggers are legendary for their pigheaded tenacity. For the first issue of *Island Journal* I interviewed a 25-year-old clam digger from Waldoboro who became an honorary islander after being stranded on Bay Ledge Buoy south of Vinalhaven in January 1984 for more than 24 hours.

The fellow had left Waldoboro headed for Vinalhaven with a 10- to 15-knot wind, in a 15-foot outboard skiff, but he lost his bearings in a sudden snow squall. When he spotted a buoy, which turned out to be 12 miles south of Vinalhaven, he decided to tie up and wait out the weather. But his skiff was swept out from under him as he climbed onto the buoy and he was stranded there, coated with freezing spray, as night fell. Being a resourceful fellow, he used his belt to tie himself to the buoy so he could periodically walk around its slippery base. He tore off pieces of his sea boots with his teeth and lit them with a Bic lighter underneath his hooded sweatshirt every two hours to crank out

a few watts of heat that (barely) kept him alive. He was finally rescued after 27 hours on the Bay Ledge Buoy and went to New York, invited to turn his amazing story into TV gold as a guest on the *Today Show*.

The only problem was that his notoriety shone a light on his other activities back home, where it was alleged that our now-famous clam digger was also notorious for his alleged efforts to pry gold out of the teeth of centenarians buried in local cemeteries.

Lobster Territories

Lobsters have been an economically valuable fishery on islands for over a century, and lobstermen long ago staked out territories around island shores where lobsters come each summer to shed their old shells. An island's marine territory used to pass down from one generation to the next with title to land on the island proper. Even when islanders "removed," they didn't necessarily give up their proprietary lobster-fishing territories. Today, those few islands still in the hands of the original settlers' families maintain what to outsiders may seem like feudal control over public resources. But these marine "lands," circumscribed by hard-won boundaries, are essential historical, cultural and economic facts of island life.

The basic rules governing the lobster fishery are easy to understand. But the most important rules of all, upon which the astonishing success of the fishery depends, appear in no Maine statutes. These are the unofficial, unwritten, but universally applied rules of territoriality that give Maine lobstering its unique structure. As the anthropologist Jim Acheson has described in his classic *Lobster Gangs of Maine*, any Maine resident can get a lobster license, although not everyone can go lobster fishing. Understanding this paradox is the key to understanding the vast complexity of the informal means used by Maine lobstermen to limit entry and regulate effort.

Gull feeding area, Big White Island, West Penobscot Bay

Lobster boats leaving Carver's Harbor, Vinalhaven, for the outer bay and Seal Island grounds

The fundamental principle is to find a balance between number of lobstermen who can profitably fish a harbor's waters and the number of lobstermen needed to maintain a territory at its edges against pressure from lobstermen in adjacent harbors who keep "pushing the line." The tension between groups of fishermen can be palpable, particularly when the fortunes of one harbor are in decline relative to the next and boundary adjustments are attempted.

When someone sets gear in someone else's territory, a polite reminder might be issued: a couple of half hitches on the spindle of the offender's pot buoy. If the gear is not moved, sometimes a second warning is issued: The doors of the trap are open when it is next hauled. But then the pot buoy goes missing along with those of its similarly painted friends. A lobsterman's work thus takes not only a keen sense of lobster population ecology, but also careful timing, opportunistic use of fog, knowledge of where other boats are at all times, a knife, and, above all, teamwork from other members of the harbor "gang." Acheson and others have referred to the territorial system of Maine lobstering as "mutual coercion, mutually enforced."

Lobster Wars: "Some of Them Was Hard Dogs"

Boundaries on the water are traditional but fluid, maintained by informal agreements until one group can no longer adequately occupy and defend its territory. Then traps are cut in an escalating confrontation, which has from time to time involved gunplay. But mostly lobster lines are redrawn between harbors by a more discreet form of economic warfare, where one group of fishermen "nickel and dime" another group, if not to death, at least into retreat.

Lobster-buying station, Matinicus Harbor

I asked fisherman John Beckman why Vinalhaven boats would steam an hour out to Seal to haul gear when the lobster community of Matinicus was within sight of this valuable lobster ground. Although he didn't want to talk directly about how the line between Vinalhaven and Matinicus had been established, he described the long conflict over the territory between the two islands.

"Matinicus was bound that Seal Island was their territory, and we figured since it was taxed from Vinalhaven, we had the right to fish down there," he said. "But they was hard, some of them was hard dogs. Give us a hard time." But if I wanted to know more, he told me to go see Bert Dyer.

Bert Dyer is a slight figure of a man, and to see him anywhere along the Vinalhaven waterfront you wouldn't guess that he was widely regarded among other fishermen to have been one of the smartest and most successful fishermen of his day. Bert had fished out at Seal Island before John Beckman, but had since come ashore. He also recalled battles over territory.

"In the 1930s and 40s," Bert said, "there was three or four Vinalhaven fishermen and a few of the older Matinicus fishermen out there, and everybody got along finest kind. Christ, no trouble. Oh, there was little things," he said, "but no big harm done until they got over there and started a hell of a big cutting war."

After World War II, Matinicus fishermen decided to take over the territory, according to Dyer. "So they went over and cut the hell out of everything. Well, Christ, the fog would come in and we'd go down there and give them the same damn treatment. Cleaned them right out. Oh, we got into a helluva snarl there."

In response, Dyer's father and brother took their boats out to fish off Seal Island. "We had six boats, two boats a night laid right in the cove at Seal Island with rifles, and then the next night two more would come, like that, so's the other four boats could fish, while the two boats watched the gear," Dyer recalled. "That kept up for two sum-

Voices of the Lobster Industry

"You Didn't Live Very High"—Earnest Maloney

While working as a forester on Allen Island, I heard that a man who had fished off Benner Island in the early 1900s was still alive and living in Port Clyde, so I looked him up to try to piece

together some of the island's history. Earnest Maloney, who was 91 at the time, sat at his kitchen window with his daughter, Enid, Port Clyde's postmistress. Except for slightly stooped shoulders, his long gaunt frame looked like that of a man still used to being on the water. His eyes were alert like those of a fish hawk, and they peered down a long beaked nose.

"I don't know for sure," he started, "but I think it must have been 1910, I went down to Benner to lobster fish. It was tougher'n hell and you didn't live like a king. I'd like to have today the lobsters I sold for 12 cents; I'm going to tell you, you didn't have much of a job to count your money. In the summer there'd be 40 fishermen down there, but in the winter only six or eight of us. But we had a nice har-

bor down there. One of the best. Outside the mouth of the harbor, it'd be rougher than hell, but then the tide would run down through and it was just like putting a board through a planer. It would plane those seas right off smooth. You'd never even see them small boats dip their bowsprits.

"I fished outside most of the time—out to Monhegan in the winter. You'd come in from hauling and have to get a fire up in the stove to thaw out your oil skins so's the buttons would come apart. We used alewives for bait, but sometimes we'd have to cook them for supper if we had nothing else. They were bony. We used to say you'd have a hard time taking off your sweater after eating them. No, you didn't live very high."

"This Is My Ocean"—Sherwood Cook

Sherwood Cook, who fished out of Martinsville on the St. George peninsula, said his father and grandfather had lived on the lonely but beautiful north end of Metinic Island before they bought another smaller island, Little Green, several miles to the east. There, the family has maintained the fishing privilege ever since. Sherwood was a well-spoken but careful man who was

not at all sure he should be talking about the extralegal system of controlling a piece of the ocean.

"Metinic is owned by two families," he said, "and they have fishermen who fish on the share basis there. Big Green Island's done the same way, and there's three of us fishing like that on Little Green. On a share basis I furnish all the traps, as much as they want, and I have the bait

in tanks in my fish-house. And of course the island. It's good for them and good for me. And I don't mean just financially either. It's been fun working with these people.

"I don't come inshore and bother any of the fishermen and they don't come out and bother me. Oh, a few times when some-body wants to come in, I take two half hitches over the spindle and say, 'Come on, fellers, you're over the line. Move!' But if I didn't do this, this territory would be fished as open territory, and I don't think it would be good, because fishermen would move in with hundreds of traps. At least we've maintained a lobster farm there. We haven't exploited it; we haven't overfished it. But there's hardly any justification for somebody saying 'This is my ocean.' However, it's been done this way for a hundred and fifty years and it's a system that works."

"You Steer Your Own Ship Through Life"—John Beckman

John Beckman, now deceased, was one of Vinalhaven's highline lobsterman, who did not just survive but thrived, primarily by fishing at the furthest limits of Vinal-haven's lobster territory—the Seal Island grounds.

"One thing about Seal Island lobsters, because it's an outside place, you wouldn't get them soft goddamn shedders that ain't worth nothing like you get up in the mud, like you get on the back side of Vinalhaven and up the bay. Christ, lobsters don't need a very good shell where the water's warm, the water's calm, and ain't that many predators after them. But Seal Island is altogether dif-ferent kind of country. Christ, if a lobster's going to crawl out of his hole, he'd better be in good shape," he said.

Beckman was maybe 65 when I first met him, but looked a decade younger. Not tall, he had huge broad shoulders and hands that had a way of making even large lobsters look frail. The first thing

anyone noticed about him was his eyes: blue as the winter ocean, and deeply creased around their edges.

"To fish at Seal back then you had to be a young, strong man and you had to have a pretty good boat. PANDION, that was my boat then— it s the Latin name for fish hawk— she was a big boat then. Thirty-four feet," he said. "You wouldn't need to haul more than 100 pots and you'd have a boatload—800, 900, 1,100 pounds. Jeez, there was some monster hauls!

"And you'd catch lobsters there late into the winter, where the cold'll get them up here. Being down there, they get that deep ocean water circulation, even around shore. A man like me, and Bert Dyer, Christ, we was young and had young families. We had to keep going all winter. Which we did. But nights coming home from there. There'd be some hard pounds of it. You know, all the men in my time that I've known that was lost, was lost in nor' west-ers; fall nor' westers; freakish nor' westers, they was the ones that seemed to get men. You wouldn't think it would be. But the seas are just so steep and deep; they wash you all the time.

"You know, your environment makes you what you are. I believe in that. I don't hold with luck; I think you steer your own ship throughout life."

Scenes from the green urchin gold rush;
diver and his catch;
Urchin roe inside spiny shell

mers and then we built the camps down there. There was a bunch of Vinalhaven guys—Lyford Philbrook, Olaf Holmquist, Frank Thomas, John Chilles—they lived right out there on Seal and fished short warps around the island and we moved off and fished 35-fathom warps.

"After two years, it quieted down. They kinda backed off and finally we just took it over. You know once a gang gets entrenched like that, it's some hard to get rid of them. Two or three, why you can scare them off pretty much. But not a whole bunch of guys, especially when they're getting a living there. Now there's a lot of Vinalhaven boats out there."

Urchin Gold Rush

One of my roles as Hurricane Island naturalist was to teach disbelieving city kids that the rocky intertidal zone of every Maine island held a cornucopia of edible delights, not the least of which was the spiny green urchin, which were prolific. You just take the prickly pin-cushion-looking thing—actually an echinoderm with five-parted radial symmetry like a starfish—hold it upside down and with your pocketknife cut the shell radially along its equator. Then lift off the top and on the top of the shell, you have a yellow-orange delicacy of roe—or urchin egg cases the Japanese call "uni," which you scoop out and pop into your mouth. Simple, elegant and free. Little did we know.

In 1987, Japanese buyers came to Maine and paid a handful of divers to bring them bags of urchins from the waters of Maine during the winter urchin-fishing season. That first year Japanese buyers bought approximately a million and a half pounds of urchins worth a few hundred thousand dollars from fewer than 100 divers who raked the spiny urchins from the bottoms and edges around the Maine islands by hand. Then the rush for green gold was on. By 1994, 2,725 divers had arrived from all over the country including Alaska. They had heard about the gold rush, along with draggers who were licensed to harvest urchins and also wanted in on the action. Boats of every size and description, many barely afloat in winter seas, harvested 38 million pounds of urchins valued at $33 million—the second most valuable fishery in Maine that year after lobsters.

Then in a flash, the good times were all over. Three years later, the harvest had plummeted by half and has continued to decline every year since such that by 2009 fishermen scooped up fewer urchins worth less money than at any point in the previous two decades. The urchin resource has virtually collapsed along the coast and few islanders benefited from the bonanza, adding insult to in-

Hastily-rigged, unseaworthy urchin boat in Rockland Harbor during the gold rush

jury. It was a signal failure of the marine resource management system in Maine—one that has been repeated around the world, wherever Japanese buyers have discovered another virgin urchin resource regulated by inexperienced managers.

But in Maine, the story has a curious twist. Urchins are grazers—they feed on the tender shoots and fronds of kelp. After vast numbers of urchins had been stripped from the bottoms around Maine islands, kelp beds came back—prolifically. Dense beds of kelp that had been absent from coves and bottoms for decades now foul anchors and props if you are not careful at low tide. Kelp beds, it turns out, also provide shelter for lobsters during their vulnerable shedding season. The increase in shedder bottom following the removal of urchins from around Maine islands also coincided with a phenomenal increase in lobster landings along the entire coast. The scientific smoking gun is absent, but many marine scientists believe that the increase in lobsters is partly an unintended result of the end of the urchin gold rush.

A Million Acres in an Image

In 1996, Richard Podolsky and I got an appointment with Maine's Senator Olympia Snowe at her office in Washington to describe our work using a satellite imaging program we had designed called GAIA (Geographic Access, Information and Analysis). The program enabled anyone with the then-new color computers to view, pan, zoom and analyze satellite images at a million acres a scene. We were working in partnership with Bigelow Lab, and had helped introduce the software as a teaching tool in 137 classrooms throughout Maine.

We thought we could use the tool to detect surface oceanographic currents that influence the distribution of marine species, especially young—or larval—lobsters. Senator Snowe, as always, had done her homework and had on hand in her office a couple of

Composite satellite image of the Maine coast assembled by the staff of the Island Institute

University of Maine marine ecologist, Bob Steneck, with oversized "brood stock" lobster, one of the keys to the sustainability of the lobster fishery

officials from NOAA's National Environmental Satellite Data and Information Service (NESDIS). NESDIS ran a huge program of many of the government's satellites, but at the time was looking for local demonstration projects to demonstrate the technology's capacity for solving local environmental questions. The fact that Senator Snowe was the co-chair of the Senate's Oceans and Fisheries Subcommittee did not hurt, either.

We ended up, ultimately, with a five-year contract to use satellite imagery in combination with oceanographic buoys to try to unravel the ecology of lobsters in Penobscot Bay: Why were there so many there, and was the resource in danger of collapse? We contracted with a talented team of biologists, oceanographers, satellite imagery experts, state resource managers and fishermen to create the Penobscot Bay Marine Resource Collaborative. The collaborative successfully catalyzed a dialogue between scientists and fishermen over the future of Maine's most valuable marine species. We told the story in a book, *Lobsters Great and Small: How Maine Fishermen and Scientists are Changing Our Understanding of a Maine Icon.*

The Mystery of Larval Lobsters

Bob Steneck is one of Maine's leading lobster biologists. Affiliated with the University of Maine, Orono, he was part of a collaborative project that discovered the steady increase in lobster landings during the 1990s was not just a result of increased fishing pressure but represented "a real expansion of the population." Since the early 1980s Steneck, along with Lew Incze and Rick Wahle, then both at the Bigelow Lab in West Boothbay and also members of the Pen Bay collaborative, has been trying to solve a mystery that has confounded lobster biologists for over a century: How do tiny new lobsters "recruit" into the population? For a long time, marine scientists have known that Maine's lobsters were not large enough to be harvested until they were between

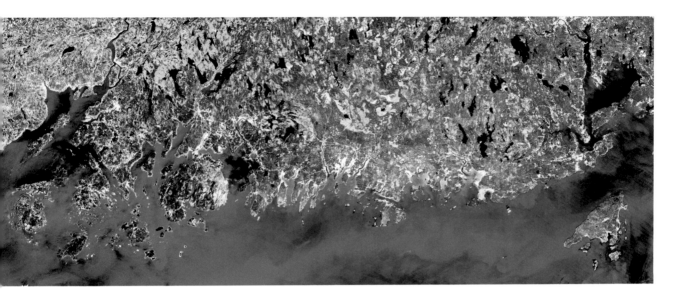

seven and eight years old. This was also the age at which most females spawn the first time. But no one really knew where baby lobsters came from and how they survived until they were old enough to spawn.

Lobster biologists had found young lobsters (four to five inches or so) in rock crevices in plentiful numbers. But where did they live between the time they settled on the bottom at a quarter of an inch and when diving biologists could find four-inch lobsters on the bottom? Where, in other words, were their nursery areas? Incze and Wahle had noticed an important phenomenon at Damariscove Island off Boothbay Harbor beginning in the early 1990s. They found that the bottom of the east-facing shores of Damariscove's long, narrow shoreline had many more lobster "settlers" than the west-facing shores. From that observation, they inferred that the new settlers had been brought there on the Maine coast's westward-flowing oceanographic current.

From satellite images of the Gulf of Maine, oceanographers with the Pen Bay collaborative have documented what intrepid swimmers have long understood: A plume of cold water comes down out of the Bay of Fundy along the Maine coast and curves offshore south of Mount Desert Island, running between Swan's Island and Frenchboro. The pattern "may act as a kind of a gate at the mouth of Penobscot Bay," says Steneck.

Putting these disparate observations together, Steneck, Incze and Wahle theorized that the dramatic increase in lobster landings that began in the late 1980s was a function of a ten-year warming trend in summer water temperatures in the Gulf of Maine beginning in the early 1980s. Because it takes a lobster seven to eight years to reach the size where it can be legally landed, it wasn't until late in the decade that the higher percentage of molted lobsters was reflected in the landing statistics. The scientists also proposed that cooler summer water temperatures in eastern Maine inhibit the first molt and reduces the number of new recruits, whereas the limiting factor to the south-

west may be the relative scarcity of cobble habitat for the critical nursery phase. But Midcoast Maine, say from Boothbay Harbor to Stonington, has both favorable water temperatures and ample cobble nursery areas to maximize recruitment of new lobsters into the population—and ultimately into the pot.

Perhaps the real test of the collaborative research was that it was accepted by the lobstermen who also participated in the project. In order to fully understand lobster distribution in Penobscot Bay, scientists wanted to know the pattern of distribution of juveniles—or "short" lobsters that fishermen threw back overboard. With Steneck's help, we recruited a team of college students to deploy on the sterns of lobster boats to count the number of short lobsters and egg-bearing or "berried" lobsters that they returned to the water. It seemed like dicey business to get lobstermen to participate. But Dave Cousens, the head of the Maine Lobstermen's Association, who fished out of Sprucehead Island, backed the program strongly and got on the radio to line up willing fishermen. The first summer, we hoped we could get 20 lobster boats to take interns aboard; we got 78—a figure that ballooned to approximately 150 along most of the Maine coast by 2001, when the project ended five years later.

Even more important, the Pen Bay project also clearly demonstrated that Maine lobsters were not being overfished in Penobscot Bay, a finding that was later repeated coast-wide.

Flat Island

I got my own introduction to the mystery of larval lobsters during a visit to Flat Island, off Cape Split, South Addison, around the time the collaborative lobster project began. We went to the island as part of an exercise to "ground-truth" a satellite image of eastern Maine—to catalog what different colors in the image actually represented on the ground. We had planned to land on the island during a new-moon tide in August close to dawn, when the maximum amount of the intertidal area would be exposed. The difference in acreage between high and low tides of the appropriately named Flat Island gives a hint of the enormous ecological effect of Fundy's tides: The island nearly doubles in size, revealing massive kelp beds waving fingered fronds just beneath the surface and exposing a whole new island along its outer shores. We wanted to get a "signature" on this habitat to estimate its total acreage.

As I stood on the island's outer shores just after dead low, the tide began to work its magic. Dimly at first, I became aware of tiny floating eggs washed along on the building current, first one and another, then more and more until thousands must have passed. I was transfixed in amazement: thousands of floating eggs were carried on the tide directly past our seaboots—the stirrings of life, reborn, passing silently by. Lobster eggs, carried on the undersides of female lobsters, released just before she sheds her old shell—seemed as prolific as a biblical miracle.

Lobster Landings: The Impossible Happened

The stability of the state's lobster harvest from the late 1940s to the 1980s was achieved by a steady and inexorable increase in fishing effort, and the use of computerized navigational equipment for precisely locating lobster habitat. Lobstermen were fishing longer, farther, harder (and probably smarter) than ever before in the history of the industry. The question was whether the remarkable increase in effort would lead to a population decline, as had occurred in virtually every other intensively harvested fishery.

Flat Island, off Cape Split, Addison, where lobster eggs swept by

Bass Harbor is the last large fishing village on Mount Desert Island

But then the impossible happened. Beginning in the late 1980s, lobster landings began to increase significantly year by year. Not small increases of a few hundred thousand pounds, but millions of pounds a year, so that the landings increased by 20 million pounds by the late 1980s, a doubling of the 20-year historical average; then, they increased by another 20 million pounds until lobster landings peaked in 2003. Carl Wilson, the state's chief lobster biologist, believes that because the reporting of lobster landings did not become mandatory until after 2003, the actual harvest that year was closer to 100 million pounds, a fivefold increase in a half-century, with corresponding increases in prosperity. On islands from Chebeague and Long to Vinalhaven and Swan's Islands in the Midcoast region, and all the way downeast to Beals, the leading economic indicator became the number of new Ford or GMC pickups lined up at the harbor landing; there were so many you could not find a place to park if you didn't own one.

John Beckman talked about the lobster boom of the 1990s when lobstermen caught lobsters "way up in Castine and Islesboro—way up there where lobster catchers mostly starve to death. North Haven, too. Christ, it used to be you could never be a lobster catcher in North Haven. They had to work for summer people. And now, Christ, you see a nice fleet of lobster boats up in North Haven. Because those lobsters took that change and that's where they are."

Beckman said he did not plan to chase the lobsters into North Haven's territory for political reasons. "I look back on times when they couldn't make a living lobstering, and we wouldn't let 'em down here. Christ, we wouldn't let 'em round the Point, round the corners. None of us. But guys on the west side, more than the east, are going up there. But I ain't going. I think I'm out of place."

Conservation from the Bottom Up

In 1994 the value of Maine's lobster catch exceeded $100 million for the first time in history, surpassing the 1993 total by a cool $28 million. That's a lot of pickup trucks. Around the world, 70 percent of the world's fishery resources are overfished, in decline, or under severe restriction to allow re-building. And yet one of the most intensively fished marine species in the Gulf of Maine has appeared in record abundance? How could this be?

If you can answer this riddle, you may either proceed directly to heaven or get elected to any town office anywhere along Maine's seemingly endless coastline. If you start collecting opinions about these observed facts, you could spend a lifetime trying to sort them out and never get there. But be-yond any immediate explanations, such as the absence of predatory cod or increased water temperatures, the way the lobster industry is structured and managed is fundamental to any understanding of why the lobster fishery has been thriving in recent years.

To begin with, commonsense principles of biology have been slowly and carefully structured into a few simple and universally accepted conservation regulations, which Maine lobstermen then rigorously enforce. First, Maine's lobster conservation rules protect small lobsters—"shorts"—before they spawn for the first time, as well as larger females—"broodstock"—which carry disproportionately larger numbers of eggs. Maine lobstermen also cut a "V-notch" in the tails of any female car-rying eggs on her belly, a mark that lasts up to three molts and makes her illegal to land. The most recent lobster conservation measure to be adopted in Maine required an escape vent in each lobster trap, to ensure that juvenile lobsters can easily leave the trap (after eating a lobsterman's lunch) without itself becoming a lunch for a larger lobster if it cannot escape. The vents also ensure that lost traps do not continue "ghost-fishing"

Pen Bay Marine Resource Collaborative community meeting on Monhegan

The lobster fleet and the village of Cutler

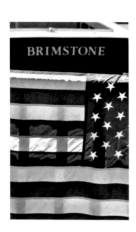

Patriotic display,
North Haven;
Moosabec Reach and
shoreline of Jonesport
from Beals Island

for lobsters, where each trapped lobster becomes bait for the next until the lost trap ultimately disintegrates.

The effect of these conservation measures, which stemmed from intense negotiations among losbtermen, is to increase the proportion of females to males in the population as well as their average fecundity, thus enhancing the reproductive potential of the entire population wherever lobster larvae are distributed.

Lobster Zone Councils: "A Village is like a Family"

One day at the end of the summer of 1996, Peter Ralston and I took RAVEN, the Island Institute's vessel, east toward Beals Island to meet with one of the most respected Downeast island fishermen, Herman "Junior" Bachman. The founding president of the Down East Lobstermen's Association, Bachman had been participating in Maine's effort to cap at 800 the number of traps fishermen could deploy and to design local lobster management zones along the state's 7,000-mile-long coastline. Robin Alden of Stonington, Maine's first female commissioner of Marine Resources, was urging the legislature to pass a new law creating a system for such local lobster management. The intent was to codify lobstermen's existing conservation principles along with a trap limit of 800 traps per fisherman. Alden had asked me to sit on a task force that also included Jim Acheson from the University of Maine and others to help design the rules and boundaries for the new zone councils.

The law that was eventually enacted created seven new lobster zones and provided the opportunity for fishermen to reduce the number of traps in each zone below 800 per person if they chose. The rules also allowed fishermen to limit entry for new fishermen in their zone and to establish other limits that are locally refined and self-enforced. The new zones, which went into effect in 1998, have attracted national—even international—attention as a model for fishery management. The zone system has demonstrated the capacity of local fishermen to make mutually binding agreements to conserve resources, a development that has been all too rare in this country's recent fisheries history.

During the meeting with Junior, we talked about his life lobstering from Beals Island over a cup of coffee in the pilothouse. "I got into fishing by being born in a small fishing village and being with my dad when I was a small boy. Of course I was like everybody; every kid in a small fishing village always has a few traps and a small punt when he's going to school. That's a way of life," Junior said. "Life in fishing villages wasn't all that bad. Nobody had money but eating was never a problem. You went fishing, hand-lining, lobster-fishing. Nobody went hungry."

A village is like a family, he told us. "We care for each other. It's the difference between Downeast heritage and other heritages. If we lose the lobster fishing, like we lost groundfishing, all these villages will become ghost towns."

Matinicus's 21st–Century Lobster War

After an unprecedented increase in both lobster landings and lobster prices during the two decades between 1988 and 2007, lobster prices collapsed with the onset of the nationwide financial crisis in early 2008. The nearly catastrophic price decline for lobsters hit fishermen hard. More and more lobstermen began to wonder whether they had a future in the business, and a desperate handful, perhaps motivated by fear about whether they could feed their families, resorted to violence, trap-cutting and dire threats to other lobstermen and competitors.

Nowhere were lobster territories more actively defended than on Maine islands—and for obvious reasons. The economic options for islanders have always been limited. Fishing has been one of the few reliable means of making an island living for 400 years. If you live on an island and someone "from away" begins to set traps around your island . . . well, you can understand the likely reaction, particularly if time, distance and fog give you better access to those waters than to perceived interlopers. Pushing the lines around lobster territories is as old as the lobster territories themselves, but ultimately lobster territories have been defended by the "law of the knife," where trap buoys are cut and territorial lines shift. Isle au Haut's nearly continuous loss of lobster territory to Stonington

Learning the ropes on Frenchboro;
Knitting lobster trap head, Criehaven;
Clayton Philbrook helps unload fuel, Matinicus

Lobster territories are
still defended by the
"law of the knife"

fishermen during the last several decades is one of the most recent examples.

Territories are not the only source of conflict in lobster communities. There is also the question of who gets to go fishing and how many fishermen a territory can support. The power to decide these questions used to be informally settled at the harbor level until the Maine Legislature gave that authority to the seven "lobster zone councils" of elected lobstermen. In addition, two island communities, Monhegan and Swan's, successfully lobbied the legislature for approval to create their own island lobster zones with much more demanding trap limits and other rules.

Lobster Zone Councils have the authority to conduct referenda among license holders to determine whether to limit the entry to the fishery. Today six of the seven lobster zones have voted for closed zones where either four or five lobstermen must retire before a new lobsterman can get a license. The only open zone in 2009 included Matinicus, where the question of who could fish escalated into a tragic and violent confrontation, when one fisherman shot and seriously injured another on the town wharf.

On Matinicus Island, the traditional informal rule has been that if you were born

on the island or married into an island family and lived on the island, you could go lobster-fishing. But you also could be "voted off" the island, Survivor-style, by the law of the knife. No one can be on the water at all times during the day and night, so if enough of your island neighbors do not want you to fish there, trap-cutting is a way to bleed someone economically until they can no longer afford to fish. It has been difficult for the state Marine Patrol to police these waters because undercover surveillance, as a practical matter, is impossible.

The shooting on Matinicus precipitated an intense discussion about whether the Maine Legislature needed to establish a more formal and legally enforceable means of deciding who can fish and who cannot—and whether formal rules would make any difference in blunting the law of the knife. But most fishermen believe the situation may only be alleviated when prices recover—if they do.

CHAPTER 10

Downeast Islands:
Common Interests—Separate Beginnings

When people are marginal, by race, by culture or by geography,
that marginality often creates a particular brilliance,
because they are restless by virtue of their special discomfort.

—Anthony P. Maingot, Trinidad-born scholar of the Caribbean

Author at first meeting
of the Island Institute,
1983;
Sutton Island beach with
Great Cranberry in
the distance

In 1983 four transplants to Maine—a writer, a photographer, a forester and an ecologist—pooled our energies to start the Island Institute. George Putz was the writer, editor and maritime ethnographer who had taken me in on Vinalhaven; Peter Ralston was a freelance photographer, who had documented our projects on Allen Island and elsewhere with his Nikon camera; Ray Leonard was the U.S. Forest Service research leader who used his small budget to establish research plots and sailed us to them in his 32-foot cutter, SATORI; and I was the ecologist who drafted a plan to create a new organization we called the Island Institute.

Two other crucially important people who helped launch the Island Institute were Betsy Wyeth on Allen Island and Tom Cabot, the industrialist, yachtsman and conservationist who was the largest private owner of Maine islands. These two provided the initial financial support for an organization that we imagined would serve as a clearinghouse of information about Maine islands and islanders. When Tom Cabot gave me a check for $10,000 to pay the first six months of my salary, he gave me an even more valuable piece of advice. "Many people are embarrassed to ask other people for money. But if you believe in what you are doing, never be ashamed to ask." I have thought of that advice on the brink of a thousand solicitations over the years. Betsy Wyeth provided us with ten signed, high-quality reproductions of Andrew Wyeth's print *The Reefer*, which were then valued at $2,500 apiece. Peter Ralston and I immediately began looking for buyers who might also be believers in such an organization.

When the Island Institute was launched, we believed we could differentiate ourselves from other island organizations by providing high-quality ecological information on how islands could be used responsibly without compromising their environment and communities. We imagined ourselves as an information clearinghouse and a forum for exploring the future. We had some ideas about how Maine islands might be used to support fishing, and how various other resources could be marshaled to support year-round life, including managing forests and pastures, and demonstrating new technology such as satellite imagery to identify the islands' natural resources. As newcomers, we fervently believed islands and their surrounding waters could be harnessed in ways that respected history and culture, while protecting scenic and wildlife resources. That is still our story today.

Sadly, Putz, a genius, if a flawed one, did not survive the first decade of the Institute's existence. Leonard never returned with Satori after his disastrous encounter with *The Perfect Storm*. But Peter Ralston and I have continued on for nearly three decades together at the Island Institute. If Peter has been the art, I have been the science. He has been the style; I have been the content. I have written the words; he has composed the images. It's been a great ride.

Keeping the Lights

We used two-thirds of our first-year's budget to publish the first *Island Journal*, which has become an annual publication celebrating Maine island life and culture. That first issue included a story about the U.S. Coast Guard's program to automate all of Maine's 64 lighthouses. Technology had rendered "manned" lighthouses obsolete, as the light and fog signals could be turned on and off automatically without the need for human keepers. But what no one had anticipated was that after automating the lights, the Coast Guard began demolishing the abandoned lighthouse keepers' quarters, one by one.

I learned about this demolition program the hard way—by stumbling into its results on the aptly named

Betsy Wyeth on Southern Island; Tom Cabot on Butter Island

Mistake Island off Jonesport and Beals Island. I had landed on Mistake and visited Moose Peak Light on several occasions during my time as staff naturalist at Hurricane Island. In 1983 I returned to check on the status of four rare plants that had been documented as growing around the base of the lighthouse tower and the keeper's quarters

on the outermost bluff of the island. But where the graceful, gambrel-roofed keeper's quarters had once stood
next to the tower, I found nothing but a massive hole in
the granite bedrock with blocks of granite strewn about.

Local lobstermen told me that the light station had
been blown up the previous fall. I could not believe my
eyes. To find out what had happened, I went to work
with a writer in Boston, Steve Perrin. Delving into Coast
Guard archives, he discovered that because Moose Peak
Light was not on the National Register of Historic Places,
the Coast Guard had approved a plan for a team of U.S.
Army Special Forces frogmen to "infiltrate" Mistake Island under the cover of darkness and destroy the lighthouse keeper's quarters as a training exercise. It was an
ill-conceived plan. The explosives cracked the lighthouse
tower base, breaking panes of glass in the lantern and
damaging the helicopter-landing pad.

After securing some funding, the Institute hired its
first intern to research how local groups might acquire
leases to these iconic lighthouse structures rather than
have any more of them so ignobly demolished. But the
task of working through the bureaucratic tangles of the
lease process was daunting, and nothing much happened
until 1989, when the abandoned lighthouse keeper's
quarters on Heron Neck Light on Green's Island off Vinalhaven were severely damaged by an electrical fire. The
Coast Guard assured us that the building would not be
demolished, but in 1994, after three years of trying to
find someone—anyone—to fix up the structure in exchange for a lease, the Coast Guard decided to tear down
the deteriorating structure. We felt betrayed.

Ralston had the brilliant idea of getting a NBC news
crew in Portland out to the Heron Neck lighthouse station to pose the question of whether anyone in America
wanted to fix up and lease the historic structure. On the
appointed sultry summer morning, with little wisps of
fog under the bright blue dome of the sky, the TV crew
got heart-stopping images of the beauty of the place and
ran the story the following day, followed by a showing
on the *Today Show*. The Coast Guard, inundated with re-
quests, called us the next day to offer a truce. They would

*Heron Neck lighthouse
keepers' building burns;
1989; Peter Ralston
directed the Maine
Lights Program*

not tear down the structure if we would help them find someone to assume responsibility for its maintenance.

Ralston then went to work with the Coast Guard realty office, which suggested
transferring the property to the Island Institute. We imagined we could then sign a

long-term lease with someone in return for maintenance. That is just about what happened, except that it took Ralston two full years and an act of Congress, sponsored by Senate Majority Leader George Mitchell, to win approval for the deal. Seeking to avoid a repeat of this grueling process, Ralston asked the Coast Guard to consider transferring Maine's remaining lighthouses to local towns and non-profits so that we could help find new owners and caretakers. The Coast Guard miraculously agreed, and the Maine Lights Program was born.

After another grueling two years of work, 28 of 36 lighthouse stations remaining on Maine's islands and coastline had new stewards. Many of these were in year-round communities including Monhegan, Vinalhaven, Isle au Haut, Swan's and the Cranberry Isles, to mention a few. Maybe the islands had more in common than had met the eye.

"I'll Call You When We Need Saving"

During the early years of the Island Institute, we published annual issues of *Island Journal*, started a program to support island teachers, and supplied ecological information to island towns and property owners based on the theory that high-quality information would support sound local decision-making. But just because we trusted island leaders did not mean they trusted us. Quite the reverse.

In a sense the issue was simple: The Island Institute, especially in its early years, depended almost entirely on financial support from summer people. Many islanders feared that when push came to shove, the Institute would represent summer interests to the detriment of year-round islanders. When we were out on the water in the Institute's vessels, FISH HAWK, and later in RAVEN, island fishermen would sometimes salute us with the universal finger of contempt. More than once bait was dumped in our cockpits as a "welcome" to the neighborhood. These incidents were distressing, but we knew they went with the territory.

Swan's Island selectman Sonny Sprague probably described the sentiment of most islanders about the Island Institute when I first called him to introduce myself. "I thought we were doing pretty good ourselves without having you around," he told me. "I'll give you a call when we need saving."

But slowly, perceptions began to change. One issue on Swan's Island helped initiate a nearly imperceptible shift in the late 1980s. A salmon aquaculture company approached the local lobstermen's co-op in 1988 with a plan to establish a salmon farm somewhere in Swan's Island's waters—anywhere the fishermen would agree to let them locate. Several other efforts to locate salmon farms in island waters had been soundly defeated by lobstermen afraid that fish feces and the detritus from fish feed would kill lobsters. But the Swan's Island fisherman's co-op voted to support the location of this new industry in a lightly fished area, with the expectation that jobs from the fish-raising operation—and even more important, salmon processing jobs—would generate what Sonny Sprague called "Christmas and kerosene money" for island families.

Two summer residents, whose properties overlooked the proposed site in Toothaker Cove, objected

Watching the first salmon arrive at Swan's Island from FISH HAWK; *Sonny Sprague, general manager of Island Aquaculture Company during net cleaning operation in Toothaker Cove*

to the salmon farm and intervened with the U.S. Army Corps of Engineers to delay the last required federal environmental permit for the fish pens. The delay occurred when the young salmon "smolt" at the hatchery were already morphing into their saltwater form. This was a critical time because the fish had to leave the hatchery and enter salt water if they were to survive and not lose an entire year. The permit delay meant the fish had no place to go.

Sprague organized islanders for a nonstop call-a-thon to the Army Corps' Maine headquarters and political leaders during business hours for over a week until the Corps called Sprague back and said they would issue the permit, but would he please, please stop with the phone calling? In the end, the permit was issued, not for Toothaker Cove, but farther out in federal waters while the environmental objections to Toothaker Cove could be sorted out. The Institute supported the decision of the Swan's Island selectmen and the lobstermen's co-op. Later, when Peter Ralston and I showed up one evening in June in FISH HAWK for the delivery of the young salmon, we began to notice a subtle change. We received some tentative waves from passing Swan's Island lobstermen. Later that summer, when the skipper of the PRINCE OF PEACE even doffed his cap, we sensed that word had begun to spread along the archipelago that maybe we were not all bad.

Abandoned schoolhouse,
Eagle Island;
Dorothy Simpson of
Criehaven

Small Wonders—Island Schools

During my two winters on Vinalhaven in the late 1970s, I saw that the island's school was the central institution for community life. It was where all the important events were held: town meetings, major public hearings, dances and graduations, to mention a few. No other island institutions hold more inherent hope and conflict than island schools where the future is glimpsed and lived every day.

But it was not until I learned about the history of Criehaven—the most remote of all Maine island communities, and the last year-round island community to go extinct—that I realized just how important schools are to their communities. And the smaller the community, the more important is the survival of its school. Of the 15 year-round island communities in Maine, 13 have schools; 8 of these are one or two-room schoolhouses.

Shortly after starting the Island Institute, I met the venerable octogenarians of Criehaven, Dorothy Simpson and Elisabeth Ogilvie. Simpson had grown up on Criehaven and Ogilvie had summered there in her youth during the 1930s and 40s. They told me Criehaven's instructive story.

After the start of World War II, the islanders could not find a schoolteacher—back then, almost always a single female—who was interested in living on such a remote island. Without a schoolteacher, the women and children were forced to go ashore for the school year. Without the women and children on the island, the store could not afford to stay open. Without the women and children and store, the mailboat couldn't afford to keep running during the winter. Without the women and children, store and the mailboat, the lobstermen eventually moved ashore.

In some senses, the Maine islands' most valuable exports, especially in the 20th century, have been their children. "A lot of our children go away," says Sonny Sprague. "I guess the ones that get the most education don't come back. I wish it were different than that. I wish everybody would go and get an education, and those that wanted to go, fine, but those that wanted to come back could. It wouldn't hurt for them to go and get an education—get it under their hat—and then come home and be part of the community."

Chellie Pingree, who lives on North Haven and became one of the Institute's first trustees, worked in the island school where her three children were educated before she became a state senator, and then First District U.S. Congresswoman. "There is nothing that comes close to an island school in terms of the value it can give our kids," she said.

So the first program we started at the Island Institute was the Island Schools program in 1985, which kicked off with a Maine Island Schools Conference. We collaborated with the Maine Seacoast Mission, which supported the event by transporting islanders and teachers from downeast islands to North Haven aboard its boat, the SUNBEAM. Right before the conference, I got a call from a pair of islanders from Chebeague in Casco Bay who were confused about the different logistical options for getting to North Haven. They understood the ferry schedule and the possibility of air service, but traveling via sunbeam—how did that work?

During the conference, the superintendent of the Islesboro School told the audience what it was like to put together the instructional team for a school where everyone wears many hats. "Well, it's very easy," he said. "All you have to do is hire a counselor who is also a gymnast, a janitor trained as a musician and a trilingual social studies teacher!"

Inter-island school event, Neighborhood House, Islesford; State senator from North Haven, Chellie Pingree

In subsequent years of the biennial Island Teachers conferences, we were impressed over and over by the variety of community-based school projects, which reinforce the unique sense of place that is ultimately a strength of island life—even if island teenagers occasionally grow weary of their limits. Community members become teachers and vice versa; learning becomes a lifelong occupation; school is less a place you go to be locked up than a place the community can permeate, allowing it to evaluate its prospects for the future. When you read about nationwide efforts to improve performance by encouraging schools to offer smaller classroom sizes, place-based education programs, and multiage classrooms where the older kids help teach the younger ones, you can understand why more and more educators understand that Maine's island schools are in the vanguard of educational reform.

In 1990, the Island Institute initiated an island scholarship program. Sometimes islanders asked us why the Island Institute would invest in a program that seemed destined to reduce year-round island populations, in apparent contradiction of our mission, since so few island students who went off to college could find jobs back home

Visiting the islands aboard FISH HAWK *and* RAVEN

using their skills, and thus rarely returned.

Pondering that question, I recalled a lesson Bill Drury had shared with me from his decades of studying island gull colonies off the coast of Maine. He observed that some gulls returned year after year to the same colony—and had the benefit of choosing the best nesting sites based on their "local knowledge." Other gulls would join the colony from time to time. These newcomers would start out in the least-desirable nesting sites at the periphery. Some of them stayed a season or two and left, but others moved up on to higher ground year by year, until they occupied the most favorable nesting sites.

All island life, like the life of the nation at large, is a balance of immigration and emigration. The surest path to community extinction is to erect high barriers for new community members to enter, as the Shakers in Maine discovered a century ago.

All Islands Are Different

Another reason it took a good ten years to convince island leaders that the Island Institute might have a constructive role to play in island life was an abiding belief that they had nothing to gain by collaborating with other island communities. Fostering inter-island cooperation, however, was one of the explicit assumptions behind the formation of the Institute. In the past islanders generally met with each other only over conflicts for scarce resources—lobster territory, ferry service or state support for their schools. And these encounters often pitted one island community against another. The message from islanders in the early years was almost always the same— "We're different from those islanders over there and we don't want to have anything to do with them."

So the Institute—essentially Peter Ralston and myself—began working with communities on an island-by-island basis, transporting ourselves on FISH HAWK or RAVEN, the Institute's boats, and initially downplayed any mention of cooperation and collaboration. All islands are different, we emphasized, which we knew to be true. But we also believed that islanders had common interests—supporting their often-fragile schools, negotiating ferry and mailboat schedules and explaining to the state and federal authorities the special circumstances of island life.

We began to develop relationships with teachers, se-

lectmen, fishermen, firefighters—anyone who would talk to us—from 15 different island communities, one by one, which we hoped might form the basis for more deliber-
ate collaboration in the future. After more than 25 years of working with Maine's island
communities, it is instructive to recall some of the occasions when islanders have come
together to respond to common threats and forge common interests out of disparate
histories. I will begin with the "downeast" island of Frenchboro, the first island community to ask the Institute for help, and then head west in subsequent chapters.

Downeast Islands

From any height of land on Mount Desert, you can take in all the "downeast islands." Frenchboro is directly south from the mainland—six miles off, but a world
away. Next furthest out is Swan's Island, a vigorous and successful lobster community.
In the very far distance to the west, you can see the highest of Isle au Haut's mountains.
The Cranberry Isles are two low-lying islands closest to Northeast Harbor and Seal
Harbor. In between the Cranberries and Swan's is Great Gott, ancestral home to the
island novelist Ruth Moore, but no longer home to a year-round community since the
1920s. Next to Great Gott is Placentia Island, where the Kellams, a locally respected
pair of hermits, lived for over half a century. These islands have been the easternmost
inhabited, unbridged islands along the Maine archipelago ever since Beals Island, off
Jonesport, was connected to the mainland by a new bridge in 1957.

Frenchboro—The Sound of Youth

Frenchboro became the first island community to open diplomatic relations with
the Institute. In 1983 Frenchboro's population hovered around 45; the population of
the one-room schoolhouse on the island had dwindled to a single student, and the
islanders knew the community was at a life-threatening crossroads. Without children,
there is no school; without a school, there are no young families, and without young

David Lunt, patriarch of Lunt Harbor;
One of Frenchboro's seven new homestead houses;
David Lunt's grandson Zach and family

families, an aging population peters out—just like a Shaker village. The story has repeated itself on Maine islands for more than a century.

In 1984 I got a call from David Lunt, first selectman on Frenchboro, who described his extremely improbable vision. He hoped the town could acquire a piece of land on the island, build a handful of new houses, and entice young "homesteaders" to settle there to repopulate the school. David lobbied the town and the school (where he was board chair) to approve the concept. He convinced the highly territorial lobstermen in Lunt Harbor, where he owned the only lobster buying and bait operation, to make room for a few more young fishermen with families. Then he convinced the Rockefeller family, which owned approximately 1,000 undeveloped acres on Frenchboro, to donate a 55-acre parcel of land on which the community would build affordable houses to attract new settlers. Because the new settlers would be selected in part based on the number of children they had or planned to have, the plan came to be known colloquially on the island as attracting "breeders." Lunt asked the newly formed Island Institute to appoint an ex-officio member to the board of the Frenchboro Future Development Corp, which would oversee the homesteading project.

After many years of work, Frenchboro succeeded in getting a loan to build seven new houses, including a house for the island's teacher; upgraded the town's ferry landing with a new 36-ton ramp; installed indoor plumbing at the schoolhouse; built a fire station, and created an area for helicopter landing pad for emergency medical evacuations. To help make this happen, existing year-round residents pledged to invest their own money toward refurbishing 15 existing homes. The Town of Frenchboro loaned the project funds, Lunt and Lunt Lobster Co. invested in new wharf facilities, and the town dredged the inner harbor, which opened up a more secure winter anchorage and successfully attracted some new residents and a new schoolteacher.

But by 1998, the school population had bottomed out again, with only a single student. Several of the new houses were rented by young, still childless families who were deciding whether to start families and make a long-term commitment to purchase and settle on Frenchboro. Nearly a decade after the first settlers arrived, the waters around Frenchboro had stopped receding, but the tide had not turned.

To make matters worse, in 1999 the owner of 950 acres of undeveloped land on Frenchboro—over half the island—who also happened to be the daughter of David and Peggy Rockefeller, put her half of the island up for sale for $3 million with a real estate

development company that planned to market 10 to 12 "kingdom lots" on the spectacular outermost shores of this outermost island. David Lunt buttonholed me when I had
arrived on the island, deeply concerned that such a development scheme would change
Frenchboro's economy from fishing to caretaking, irrevocably altering the island community he knew and loved. At the same time, David did not want the land conserved
in such a way that would eliminate the important tax revenue from the struggling community.

I had no idea what to do as I piloted RAVEN into Northeast Harbor to resupply. But
after tying up at the public landing, I ran into a great friend of the islands and seasonal
resident of Great Cranberry and described Frenchboro's predicament. On the spot, he
pledged up to one-third of the purchase price if I could put together other donors to
help protect the land—and help the community. My next call was to Jay Espy at Maine
Coast Heritage Trust, the islands' preeminent conservation organization. Jay and I
quickly sketched out a plan, which we brought back to David Lunt.

We believed we could approach the owner with an offer to purchase the land at a
bargain-sale price in order to conserve it, and then mount a campaign to raise the purchase price along with an endowment to pay the taxes on the undeveloped land, and
a fund to renovate the island school, church and library, which did not have running
water in the winter and lacked other critical facilities. All we needed was a total of $3.1
million. David and the islanders agreed that the taxes would not increase on the conserved land if we could purchase it, and we were all hopeful that by working together,
we could actually pull off this ambitious plan. The Maine Seacoast Mission helped with
a piece of funding for the church renovation and we all used our contacts to raise the
remainder of the funds by the end of 2000. It was a signal accomplishment.

Greeting the first state ferry run to Swan's Island, 1960

"We Were Not Just Swan's Islanders, We Were Americans"

Not too many years ago, the highly indented rugged shoreline of Swan's Island made it difficult for islanders to get from one part of the island to another. There were three separate villages on the island, including the village of Swan's Island at Burnt Coat Harbor, the village of Minturn across the long narrow harbor, and finally, Atlantic at the northeast end—each with its own school, store and post office. There were even two churches serving small congregations on the island.

The most momentous change to Swan's Island in the 20th century was the coming of ferry service more than a decade after the end of World War II. Wesley Staples, a returning veteran and member of Swan's Island's original ferry committee, explained his motivation for getting involved at the time. "Of course, we'd seen more of the world, had a wider perspective and didn't want to be left behind. But more important we didn't want to lose touch with America. We had fought for this new era and we wa,nted to be part of it." Wesley and his fellow veterans recognized, "We were not just Swan's Islanders, we were Americans."

It turned out that similar discussions had been occurring on Vinalhaven, North Haven and Islesboro. Leaders from the four island communities petitioned the legislature for a bond issue to build ferries and terminals to connect them with America. Toward the end of the 1956 legislative session, with support for the bond flagging among lawmakers, the islanders raised $1,100 from each island—a princely sum at the time—for a "downeast" lobster bash with plenty of booze at the old North Hotel in Augusta. The inspiration for this old-fashioned method of lobbying was Hancock County senator

William Silsby, for whom the Swan's Island's ferry would eventually be named. This bit of inspired public lobbying won the islanders the final votes they needed. The bond squeaked through in a special state referendum the following September.

Maine's First Trap Limit and Island Salmon Farm

In 1984, Swan's Island initiated another legislative campaign, this time on its own. First selectman Sonny Sprague convinced the legislature to create a special two-mile lobster-fishing zone around the island with the state's first officially sanctioned limit on the number of lobster traps an island fishermen could fish. Sprague's rationale was simple: "With a trap limit, we can catch almost as many lobsters at less cost. And if there are more lobsters left over, they'll reproduce better," he said. "Income tax day will tell whether the idea is any good or not." It took the rest of the state until 1998 to implement a state-wide trap limit.

Processing salmon, Swan's Island

Sprague was also a key player in the decision of the Swan's Island Lobster-men's Co-op to support the siting of the salmon aquaculture pens in Toothaker Cove. When after four years of operation the salmon company went into receivership, Sonny Sprague called the Island Institute; he told me that the farm's failure had been due to mismanagement and cited the reasons for the operations failure, mostly due to absentee ownership that misspent scarce funds. Sonny sketched out a plan where the islanders who worked on the farm could turn the operation around if they could acquire the farm at a foreclosure auction, since it was too important to the community to simply shut it down.

I put Sonny in touch with Frank Simon—and with his partner, Bill Marshall, who knew a lot about the fish-farming business. They helped Sonny put together a business plan, but no bank would touch the idea of rescuing the failed farm, so we helped Sonny raise $50,000, including $25,000 from Tom Cabot, who was a seasonal resident of Swan's Island and the first donor to the Island Institute. We also raised another $25,000 of non-recourse loans and off we went to the bankruptcy auction.

In one of the archipelago's truly great turnaround stories of recent decades, Sprague managed the salmon farm back to profitability before it was ultimately sold to a Canadian aquaculture company. Despite ups and downs for the salmon-farming industry in the state, the Canadian-based Cooke Aquaculture Co. still raises salmon on a site off Black Island near Swan's.

The Cranberry Isles: Great and Little Cranberry

The Cranberry Isles are home to Maine's only island town made up of two year-round communities—one on Little Cranberry, known as Islesford, and one on Great Cranberry. The Cranberries also encompass Baker and Sutton Islands, which lost their year-round populations at the end of the 19th and early 20th centuries respectively. Baker is now part of Acadia National Park, while Sutton supports a thriving summer community. Although both the remaining year-round communities on the Cranberry

Yacht Club Cruise

JUNE 2, 1993—A representative of the renowned New York Yacht Club, a young woman as it happened, was dispatched to Maine to visit each of the harbors where the Yacht Club planned to anchor for their semi-annual cruise to Maine's coast and islands. One of the most important tasks of the planning involved arranging for such necessities as ice, lobsters and shoreside facilities.

Burnt Coat Harbor on Swan's Island, the heart of a busy lobstering community off Mount Desert, was one of the harbors planned for the cruise, since it is one of the most protected, but spacious harbors anywhere on the Maine coast. The woman who was charged with arranging the logistics got in touch with the harbormaster and arranged to meet him at the Lobstermen's Co-op to discuss the logistics of the cruise

visit. Her first mistake was to get car reservations on the ferry both going and coming, thereby taking up valuable space on the boat needed by islanders, even though the harbormaster had offered to meet her at the ferry and drive her the 4 miles across the island to the harbor. Off-islanders, unaware of such subtleties, make such mistakes.

On the appointed day, the woman drove off the ferry, and 10 minutes later arrived at the Lobstermen's Co-op. She stepped out of the large car that had been

rented solely for the ferry trip. The woman who looked very much like she had come from the country's center of fashion, surveyed the almost archetypal scene of a New England fishing village arrayed along both sides of a protected harbor, while wonderfully elegant lobster boats steamed in and out of the harbor.

After all, the arrangements had been agreed upon, the yacht club representative began effusing about the beauty of the scene, how much she enjoyed being there, how much does real estate go for and the like. "I just love it here," she exclaimed. "It's so different. Why, even the way you talk is different." The harbormater shifted uneasily on his feet, not quite knowing what to say next. "Ma'am," he replied in a dignified manner, "the only one who sounds different here is you."

Isles have long and illustrious fishing histories, beginning in the 1970s, the two islands' trajectories began to head in opposite directions.

Islesford—"This Is the Good Life."

Ted Spurling was one of Isleford's grand old men. Descended from one of the community's founding families, Spurling had a varied career as a fisherman, merchant seaman, local historian, naturalist and writer. Because he was exquisitely tuned to the rhythms of the sea, in 1993 editor David Platt arranged with Spurling to write a column for the Institute's new community paper, *Inter-Island News*, and then later, *The Working Waterfront*, after the two papers merged in 1997.

When Ralston and I visited Islesford in 1994, Ted met us at the wharf with a piece of his marlinspike seamanship—a rope ladder ingeniously spliced together from a piece of lobster-pot warp. He showed us how to loop the rope ladder through one of RAVEN's stern cleats long enough so that it reached the water, but short enough to stay clear of the propeller. A number of years previously, one of Ted's best friends, a heavy older lobsterman, had fallen off his boat and nearly drowned because he could not get back aboard. He survived only because Ted finally heard him and towed him to the beach. Since then Ted had woven and distributed countless of these ladders along the coast.

Beal and Bunker barge landing at little Cranberry; Picking up passengers on little Cranberry; Ted Spurling, Islesford

Dan Fernald, a sixth-generation fisherman and artist from Islesford, contends that Little Cranberry's population grew in the 1970s and 1980s because some summer boys decided before or after college to stay on the island and earn their livings as sternmen. Dan Lief, who owns and manages the Islesford Dock Restaurant with his wife, Cynthia, echoed this observation. During the last several decades Islesford has always been a welcoming community, Lief said, not just to sternmen, but to other newcomers or transplants, as they are politely called in island communities. To Lief, the difference between an island with a growing population from one with a declining population begins with its attitude toward such newcomers. People in the Islesford community help young prospects find winter rentals, he said, and offer advice on cobbling together the myriad of part-time jobs that it takes to survive. Then islanders engage in matchmaking to help these transplants find spouses.

One of those transplants was David Thomas. Thomas became a lobster fisherman,

Islesford residents, Chud and Lil Alley, David Thomas with daughter, Rachel

married a young woman from a summer family, raised two children on the island, and has been involved in virtually every civic organization ever since. Most recently he has participated in the effort to transform the Islesford Neighborhood House into a year-round community center. "I came here in 1975 to teach school. I taught two years and just never left. To me, this is the good life."

For residents of both Islesford and Great Cranberry, like those who live on Chebeague in Casco Bay, or Monhegan off Port Clyde, or, to a lesser degree, on Isle au Haut off Stonington, parking on the mainland has become a recurring nightmare. So much so that the small town of Cranberry Isles voted in 2006 to raise $2.4 million in local tax dollars to buy an expensive piece of real estate on the Southwest Harbor waterfront for the purpose of developing additional parking.

The project resulted in an average increase of 30 percent in property taxes for both seasonal and year-round residents in the two communities, which showed how much islanders were willing to risk for 137 parking spaces and a foothold on Mount Desert's increasingly congested mainland connecting points.

Endangered Great Cranberry

Unlike Islesford, Great Cranberry never saw the surge of young people staying on the island in the 1970s, according to Dan Fernald, and now has only one fisherman left and little prospect of another taking his place. Great Cranberry, he said, "is now an island without an active year-round fishing population." Its two surviving boatyards (one is currently for sale) are now the only stable sources of year-round employment.

Great Cranberry's school is not officially closed, but is inactive due to a lack of students as the island struggles to survive as a year-round community, although a crop of toddlers will reopen the debate over reopening the school. One child of school age currently rides the mailboat to Islesford to attend school. Nevertheless, an active ladies' aid society, a determined historical society and an excellent local library have helped keep a community spark alive. Great Cranberry is in the midst of a shift from an island-based lobstering and boatbuilding economy to one where more of the jobs for islanders might be found on the mainland.

Great Cranberry's decline did not escape notice. In 1995 I worked with another Island Institute staff member, Lisa Shields of North Haven, as Great Cranberry confronted the impending sale of one of the island's two wharves. The wharf in question supported the island post office, the boat landing for the community's Southwest Harbor boat run and an artist's gallery that helped sustain several island families. Using models developed by the North Haven and Frenchboro communities, islanders formed

Beal and Bunker barge departing Northeast Harbor with work crew

the Great Cranberry Futures Group to focus on community and economic development, most especially a plan to acquire the wharf to support a more vibrant year-round economy.

Great Cranberry's wharf redevelopment failed to come to fruition and we wondered if we could have offered more support. Coulda, woulda, shoulda. The failure of the wharf project coincided with a rising tide of other difficulties—declining school enrollments, families departing, a cloud over the future of the island store, a divorce in the family of a potential native island leader, and then the death of another leader that deprived the community of a critical energy. When it rains, it pours. Great Cranberry's year-round population now hovers between 35 and 40. It is Maine's most endangered year-round island community.

Recently, island voters agreed to subsidize an experimental commuter ferry to help spur economic development. The hope was to make it possible for islanders to commute to the mainland, as well as for island students to attend Mount Desert Island High School.

Isle au Haut: Sharing Paradise Uneasily

While Isle au Haut is legally and politically a part of Knox County, along with the Midcoast islands of Penobscot Bay, it has always been tied to Stonington in Hancock County, and thus is more "downeast" culturally and geographically than "Midcoast."

The signal event in Isle au Haut's 20th-century history was the decision in 1943 by a group of summer families, many of whom dated to the "rusticator" boom at the end of the 19th century, to donate approximately half the land on this 6,000-acre island to Acadia National Park. By then the population on Isle au Haut had shrunk to 75 from 175 in 1910, when the introduction of modern marine engines enabled island families

Head Harbor,
Isle au Haut

to "remove" to the mainland while continuing to fish around Isle au Haut's shores. Ever since the park land transfer, the year-round community, clustered around the Isle au Haut Thorofare at the north end of the island, with a small outpost at Head Harbor, has shared the island, sometimes uneasily, with tourists from Acadia, who land at a separate wharf at Duck Harbor on the western shore.

The French explorer Champlain, who was struck by the impressive profile of this "high island," named it Isle au Haut. Most visitors, especially those with a smattering of French, pronounce the island's name as "Eel-ah-Hoe." But islanders refer to their community as "Aisle ah Hoe," perhaps because the island was settled by English and Scotch fishermen who wanted no association with the French, or because they did not want to put on airs. To this day, this linguistic convention immediately identifies whether a person's sensibilities are "from here" or "from away."

Isle au Haut was the last island community to install regular telephone service in the 1990s—not because it was more remote than other island communities, but because a majority of the islanders saw no pressing need to encourage more connections with the mainland, or vice versa. When Acadia National Park's new master plan was being negotiated in the early 1980s, the Isle au Haut community had a volunteer lobbyist in Washington who ensured that the park would limit the number of tourists allowed on the island per day and that they would land at a separate pier far from the town. Today Isle au Haut's year-round mailboat service from and to Stonington in the MISS LIZZIE and the MINK is partly subsidized by fares paid by Park tourists in the summer.

The isolation, which the old guard leadership on Isle au Haut sought to maintain during the second half of the 20th century, meant that islanders there had little use for the Island Institute. Beginning about 2005, however, new management at the boat company that owns and operates Isle au Haut's mailboats opened diplomatic relations with the Institute, hoping to qualify for state or federal subsidies for the boat service. For many years the boat company's annual deficits had been covered by contributions from summer families, but donor fatigue had begun to set in.

The six island communities served by the Maine State Ferry Service and the five island communities served by Casco Bay ferries receive public funds on the basis that ferries are quite literally "bridges" to the islands, and thus a part of the public transportation infrastructure. The Island Institute helped the mailboat company contact other private mailboat operations serving Islesford, Great Cranberry and Monhegan to make a successful joint appeal to state and federal transportation agencies. Then the Island Institute helped Isle au Haut acquire working waterfront bond funds to build a new public wharf and protect commercial fishing access on the older wharf in perpetuity.

Another factor that has reduced the isolation of Isle au Haut is its most famous resident, Linda Greenlaw, whose book about her years as the captain of a swordfish boat out of Gloucester, *The Hungry Ocean*, rocketed up the best-seller charts shortly after she was admiringly profiled in Sebastian Junger's *The Perfect Storm*. In Greenlaw's second book, *Lobster Chronicles*, also a great commercial success, she wrote the memorable lines about returning to her Isle au Haut home after 17 years at sea to settle down and start a family. The only problem: "There are three single men in residence; two of them are gay and the third is my cousin."

Greenlaw also makes a serious point in *Lobster Chronicles,* as Isle au Haut's territorial waters continue to shrink from encroachment by the very much more numerous and aggressive Stonington fishermen. Without an adequate fishing territory, the island cannot attract new residents to augment Isle au Haut's fragile year-round population, and without new families, the prospects for the survival of this fishing community— the key to the survival of the year-round community, will also continue to shrink.

But slowly, islanders on Isle au Haut have begun to grapple with balancing the isolation with cooperation with the outside world, which will likely be critical to islands' survival. Total isolation has its costs-and collective island action its benefits.

MISS LIZZIE, Isle au Haut Thorofare

CHAPTER 11

Midcoast Islands:
Lobstermen and Summer People

I truly believe that there is something about the culture of an island community
that needs to protect itself from people and ideas from away.
If there wasn't some resistance to change and to outsiders, you wouldn't be able to
maintain the integrity of a culture that's existed for so long.

—Chellie Pingree, North Haven

Benner Island,
Muscongus Bay;
Bremen Long Island,
Muscongus Bay

Penobscot is Maine's largest bay—almost 600 square miles from the head of the bay where the Penobscot River enters to its outer edges between Isle au Haut and Monhegan, where the bay mingles with the waters of the Gulf of Maine. The three largest islands-Vinalhaven, North Haven and Islesboro—and the three outer is-lands-Monhegan, Matinicus and Criehaven, with their small populations—all depend to varying degrees on two industries: lobster and summer people.

The waterways around Vinalhaven and North Haven are where I had my first experiences piloting a boat. Although I had grown up on the banks of the Hudson River where it widens out into the broad Tappan Zee, my enthusiasm for boating was extinguished early after my father bought the family's first 14-foot sailing dinghy and took me along on her maiden voyage. In the fever of rigging the mast and boom, running the sheets and shipping the rudder, we failed to notice a thunderhead rising up over the western horizon. We cast off the boat club float just as the first gust hit us broadside. Too green to notice the securely cleated mainsheet, we capsized within 50 feet of the dock. I'll never forget the smirking grins from the "dockbox" committee of teenagers on the boathouse porch as we swam around the anchorage, retrieving floating pieces of boat gear. I swore I would never go sailing again, and did not until wandering into Penobscot Bay more than a decade later.

Carver's Harbor
fishermen's landing

Some wit has remarked that a boat is a hole in the ocean into which you pour money; to which I might add that an island is an expensive piece of real estate surrounded by an illimitable need for a boat, ideally several. When I first lived on Vinalhaven, I worked on Hurricane Island only a few miles away by water. I desperately wanted to be able to come and go under my own power, which meant getting a boat; some kind of skiff with an outboard would do. My friend George Putz, co-editor of the *Mariner's Catalog*, eagerly volunteered to help, and showed me an 18-foot lapstreak and plywood skiff with a big 25-horsepower Johnson outboard that was advertised for sale at Hopkins boatyard. It was only $500—too cheap to be true—and was owned by a Waldoboro clammer, with all the karma that implied.

I should have known, but I bought it anyway, and will never forget the first voyage up Carver's Reach and across Hurricane Sound. Master of my own fate all the way to Hurricane! The only problem was that when I returned a day later, I noticed a couple of streamers trailing below the waterline amidships. These turned out to be pieces of fiberglass that had been hastily attached to the hard chine bilges and expertly painted to conceal their existence in order to keep her from leaking long enough to consummate the sale. When I returned to the harbor the next morning, my new transportation had sunk at the mooring.

Many boats and years later, I was returning to Vinalhaven again from Hurricane Island, this time with my young family, headed to the Lane's Island summer house. We were in FISH HAWK, the Institute's 26-foot Seaway, with a pair of 120-horse Yamahas aft and a pilothouse forward for protection from wind and waves. FISH HAWK was fast and able, but in our brash enthusiasm, we had painted ISLAND INSTITUTE in bold letters on her side. Kind of dumb, really. At the north end of Green's Island, just before entering Carver's Reach is a narrow cut called the Powderhole that runs between dangerous underwater ledges and the tip of Green's.

FISH HAWK was up on a plane about to enter the Powderhole just as a lobster boat approached from the Reach. FISH HAWK was faster, but the lobster boat was bigge—much bigger. I knew the lobster boat had no intention of throttling back, but I also knew exactly where the ledges were to starboard, knew I could get over them if I stayed up on a plane, and that backing down the throttle might have lots of unintended consequences. We passed port-to-port, gunwale-to-gunwale with less than a beam's width between us, both of us staring intently ahead. It was not until years later, after we had repainted FISH HAWK's sides with much smaller lettering, that we were acknowledged on the water around Vinalhaven.

But FISH HAWK and later RAVEN, the Institute's 37-foot Repco hulled lobsterboat cruiser with five berths below, enabled us to get to island communities and live aboard when necessary.

Vinalhaven—Becoming a Winter Jerk

Vinalhaven, together with its neighbor North Haven, make up the Fox Islands. The name derives from what might have been a long-gone species of fox described on these islands by Martin Pring in the early 17th century. The Fox Islands are the largest year-round inhabited islands off the Maine coast.

When I first became acquainted with Vinalhaven in 1975, the island community was just emerging from nearly a century-long economic decline. During its heyday in the 1870s and1880s, Vinalhaven was an entrepreneurial hub for two large industries—salt fish and granite—and all the support services that these kinds of labor-intensive enterprises required. By the mid-1970s about the only ways to make a living on Vinalhaven were lobsterfishing, building lobster boats for lobstermen or selling real estate as the first boom in island land prices in a century gathered momentum.

Putz introduced me to some of the younger fishermen, and for entertainment, we drove around the island—from Dogtown to Skin Hill and "Out Pequot" with cases of beer in the trunk and picked our way down rutted roads to visit summer estates.

Transplants in Maine's traditional island communities during the 1970s and 80s were often relegated to a kind of island purgatory, because they were neither summer people nor natives. Jamien Morehouse, an island school teacher and later my wife, was one of Vinalhaven's early transplants from a summer family. She told me islanders referred to people like her in the

Fifield's general store, Vinalhaven;
Fourth of July parade, Vinalhaven

early 1970s—partly fondly, partly not—as "summer jerks" because they only knew the island during its glorious easy weather, rather than enduring the hardships of winter isolation. But as more and more summer kids stayed over during the winter, their presence begged for a description, so they were called winter jerks. I became a winter jerk, even though I had no summer ancestry.

While riding the Vinalhaven ferry one summer day in the mid-1980s to visit my family on Lane's Island, Wooly Hildreth, whom I had met on Hurricane Island, introduced me to her husband, Hoddy (short for Horace). They were summer people on Vinalhaven of long standing. Hoddy's father had been a Republican governor of Maine and Hoddy had served two terms in the Maine State Senate before taking charge of the family business, Diversified Communications, which published *National Fisherman,* among other trade publications, and owned TV and cable operations. Hoddy asked about my ultimate aspirations for the Island Institute. I described the goal of getting islanders to cooperate with each other in order to leverage their small numbers in Augusta to effect major policy changes for Maine—a David-and-Goliath sort of thing. Hoddy was both amused at the naïveté of that idea and interested in its longshot political possibilities. Eventually he joined the board of the Island Institute and served as its chair for 17 years. Without him, the Institute might never have survived its adolescence.

Hoddy and Wooly Hildreth at Seal Bay, Vinalhaven

In recent years, the distinctions among natives, summer people and winter jerks on Vinalhaven, as on a majority of the other island communities, have become more muted. Part of the reason for this on Vinalhaven, in particular, is that all three groups have worked together during the past decade to successfully complete the most ambitious civic building program in island history. During that time, Vinalhaven raised local bond funds and private contributions to build a wonderful new school, while others pitched in to double the size of the island library, and then helped the town renovate a historic school building for new town offices. Vinalhaven has been on a roll.

North Haven—Bitter Battles Train Tested Leaders

North Haven is separated from Vinalhaven by only a quarter of a mile along the Fox Island Thorofare, but there is a world of difference between the two islands. North Haven's geology supports some of the best soils found on these typically scoured islands, which is why in early years farming competed with fishing as an economic driver.

At the end of the 19th century, the pastoral beauty of North Haven's seaside farms attracted the first generation of "rusticators" who sailed "down" to Penobscot Bay and began buying up the shorefront for prices that seemed astronomical by local standards, but were bargains for Bostonians. Today the 350 year-round islanders support themselves with a mix of lobstering from a dozen or so boats and a large service economy based on building and caretaking for the still-expanding summer community.

(Facing) J.O. Brown boatbuilding crew, ca. 1922; J.O. Brown 100th anniversary party, 1988; J.O. Brown–built lobster boats

In recent years, farming also has begun to make a comeback.

After the Civil War, the fishermen of Pulpit Harbor, unlike their neighbors at Carver's Harbor, built a specialized fleet of fishing boats. These elegant mackerel schooners excelled in the speed on the water required for supplying fresh fish to Boston's Irish and New York's Italian immigrant communities, particularly on Fridays and on saints' days. For a short period of time in the 1870s, North Haven had a larger tonnage of vessels and a more valuable fishing fleet than Vinalhaven's, a fact that has escaped serious notice.

But in a blink of an eye, everything changed. The Pulpit Harbor year-round community, which supported a population estimated at 200, is virtually gone today. The history books shed little light on exactly what happened. But we know that the mackerel fishery on which North Haven fishermen depended mysteriously collapsed almost overnight between 1888 and 1889. North Haven islanders began selling their land to some of the region's first rusticators, who transformed Pulpit Harbor into a pastoral landscape by removing the buildings on its working waterfront during the last decade of the 19th century and the first two decades of the 20th.

A local history merely records the following: "The Beverage store, storehouse, ice house and wharf no longer exist. . . . The William Piper fish-house and store, which stood on 'Frye Point'. . . were demolished and burned between 1900 and 1906. . . . The store on the bank above the Harbor that had been run by Roscoe C. Babbidge since 1891 was taken down in 1906 and transported to Vinalhaven. The fish shacks and storage sheds, which stood along the north side of the Harbor also disappeared around 1918. The Edward Witherspoon house was demolished in 1918. . . . The Josiah Parsons house on the road up the hill was torn down in 1918. . . . The old schoolhouse, built in 1867 on the curve in the 'old' Pulpit Harbor Road was also torn down in 1918."

With the passing of the Pulpit Harbor community as the center of North Haven's economy,

Lobster Boat Races

JULY 12, 1994—Fox Islands Thorofare: When I got back from Allen Island, Peter Ralston called me from the lobster boat races in the Fox Islands Thorofare. A terrible accident had occurred, he said. At the end of the last race, the "Fastest Boat Afloat" race, where boats of any design can compete, the winning boat driven by a lobsterman from Cushing had idled back toward the finish line amid the happy profusion of hundreds of boats bobbing on both sides of the racecourse. Just as the captain of the winning boat powered up to leave the course, his bow was raised, and with obscured vision, his boat went up and over a small outboard with four people and literally cut it in two.

Peter saw the whole terrible sequence of events unfold as if in slow motion from a friend's boat and immediately went over to the scene of the accident, where three heads popped up out of the water. But one of the passengers was missing. In the pandemonium, everyone seemed frozen, so Peter jumped in the water where the stern half of the small outboard was almost completely submerged. He dove down repeatedly but could not find the missing person. When he surfaced and climbed aboard on the committee boat piloted by Foy Brown from North Haven's Brown's Boatyard someone yelled, "Get the stern up!" They attached a line to the submerged skiff while Peter jumped back aboard and

scrambled aft and began cutting through the mass of lines in the boat with a knife that Foy tossed him. When he cut the gas line, it cracked like a rifle shot and Peter saw a pair of legs slide back from under the boat. Peter grabbed for the body, but could not reach her. John Emerson aboard a nearby boat helped lift the lifeless body of a young woman aboard who had been tangled underwater in the gas line. When Emerson and the others got the young woman back ashore, others administered CPR, and miracle of miracles, Stacie Robbins of Stonington came back to life. She had a nasty gash in the side of her face, lost part of her ear (later reconstructed), but she was alive after being underwater, others determined, for over five minutes. The Buddhists say if you save a life, you get to come back as a person again in your next life, which is a good thing for Peter, but even better for Stacie.

the year-round community re-created itself on the southern side of the island along the deepwaters of the Fox Islands Thorofare. The J.O. Brown and Sons boatbuilding business celebrated its 100th anniversary of ownership by the same family in 1988. The yard's first boat in 1888 was an elegant yacht for the Weld family, which had settled at Iron Point on the Thorofare. Before being turned into a boatyard, Brown's big waterfront shop was the site of a lobster cannery.

Throughout the early decades of the 20th century, rusticators have become an important force in all of Maine's remaining island communities. But I am aware of nowhere else where so much cultural history was removed from the face of an island to recapture a fleeting pastoral vision of a preindustrial coast.

For whatever reasons, during the past two decades North Haven has experienced some of the bitterest political infighting of any of the Maine islands. The most protracted battle erupted during the spring of 1997 when the North Haven school board voted 3–2 not to renew the contract of the school principal, Barney Hallowell. At the time a 23-year veteran at the school, Hallowell, whose family had been longtime summer residents, was also perhaps the most visible and respected island educator in Maine.

The battle was ostensibly about the school curriculum—an experiential learning model espoused by Hallowell versus a back-to-basics approach backed by the new majority of the school board members who decided they could do without Hallowell's innovations. Many native islanders were understandably upset by the prospect of the North Haven School sponsoring trips "off-island" where their children would be exposed to other ways of life and perhaps one day choose to live somewhere else. Such exposure was not a major concern for families of transplants who had come "from away." But it was an acute concern for many natives because many island kids who left for college—and there were an increasing number under Hallowell's guidance—decided not to return to North Haven after they graduated. Although the confrontation

Chellie Pingree, owner of North Island Designs, a mail-order sweater knitting company, with her daughters; North Haven school principal, Barney Hallowell

had a native–transplant dimension, some transplants sided with natives and vice versa for many complicated and personal reasons.

The battle escalated. People chose sides. Many island families, especially those with a mixture of natives and transplants, were bitterly divided. Island friendships fractured; drivers stopped waving to each other. A lawsuit that challenged the legality of Hallowell's dismissal was settled in Hallowell's favor. But the issue roiled into the next town meeting when islanders by the slimmest of margins elected new selectmen and school board members who favored Hallowell's approach. Of course the vote really did not end the schism—it just smoldered underground like a peat fire.

Some of the lingering discontent flared up again over a drama program that brought a colorful, retired Broadway director, John Wulp, to North Haven to teach kids and community members the fine points of staging dramatic plays. Wulp became a lightning rod for the political battle in part because he sponsored trips for students to perform in one-act competitions around the state and took them to New York for theater shows. One such show, *Islands,* written and produced on North Haven as a collaboration between Wulp and singer-songwriter Cindy Bullens, attracted huge attention.

John Wulp: "A Person's Life Is What They Do"

Wulp had been a highly acclaimed, award-winning theater director and producer on and off Broadway with Tony, Obie and Theater Critics awards to his credit. His blockbuster production, *Dracula,* for a time captured and defined the New York theater world. But between triumphs he traversed the territory of failure and, as a result, exiled himself to a seemingly desolate place where austerity either drives you under or you reach the deeper routes of self-renewal.

"I came here to Maine out of a sort of desperation, really. I owned this house, but I was broke," he said. "I had nowhere else to go."

When Hallowell offered Wulp a teaching job, he jumped at the offer, even though he had never worked with children, because he needed the money.

"I began to have success with the younger kids, grades one through six," Wulp said. "Now nearly every kid in the school, except those whose parents won't allow them to, has participated. I would say 90 percent of the school has been in plays of one sort or another. And one year, we won the regional One-Act Play competition, and another, the State One-Act competition. We've done very, very difficult material: Shakespeare, Oscar Wilde. Most of

John Wulp prepares for a performance

the plays depend on language, and the kids have learned to do this in a forthright sort of way. When you see kids up there on the stage, you cannot believe the kids are not getting a good education."

Wulp said that his work on the islands has helped him find himself.

"A person's life is what they do," he said. "It's a very lonely business. So making real contact with people is the only thing you can do. How do we become good? We don't find examples around us. It's very seldom that you find something that helps you. Camus said we are all trying to become saints without religion. What finally saves you, I think, is seeing things as they are."

When the leaders of the North Haven Arts and Enrichment group announced plans to renovate a vacant building next to the ferry landing, the former island grocery store, into a community center with a theater and stage for performances, the old battle lines quickly re-formed. Ditto when the school board announced plans to build a new island school.

Both the Waterman's Community Center (completed in 2004), with its Wulp Islands Theater, and the new school (completed in 2008) under Hallowell's continued leadership, have been great successes in reinforcing a sense of community, despite the community strife that had focused on both institutions.

Against this backdrop of turmoil, perhaps it is not surprising that two of Maine's most able political leaders of recent years tested themselves first in the cauldron of North Haven's local politics. Chellie Johnson was a bright-eyed, blond-braided 17-year-old in 1971 when she moved to North Haven with her boyfriend, Charlie Pingree, who was descended from one of the island's first summer families. She recounted the story in *Island Journal* of how shortly after getting settled on a back-to-the-land farm, she went to the North Haven School and offered to volunteer in the kindergarten. When

(Facing) North Haven town meeting vote on the future of the school; Nancy Hopkins-Davisson, one of the leaders of the Waterman's Community Center project;Renovating the old Waterman's store; John Wulp and cast

Saddle Island

AUGUST 22, 1999—Peter and I left Rockport Harbor on RAVEN in the early afternoon with three of our boys aboard, headed to North Haven for an evening performance of one of John Wulp's plays, *The Wind in the Willows*. Midway across West Penobscot Bay, we rounded up in Saddle Island's small anchorage, where I wanted to show the boys some of the island's magical natural features. I rowed them ashore while Peter tidied up aboard RAVEN. We clambered through the interior lush forest to the backside of the island, where we inspected an osprey's enormous ground nest and the rare hexagonal jointing of a rock formation that looked like bees had built it and then headed back across Saddle toward where Peter waited.

From within the island forest, we heard the drone of a low flying aircraft and I could just make out the flash of a fuselage through the trees. The plane banked and then I could hear it returning almost overhead until there was a sudden eerie silence. Then I heard Peter screaming to me, "Philip! Come quick! Philip! Come quick!" I had a terrible feeling in my stomach as the boys and I ran like wild men back to the beach. We quickly launched the skiff. I told the boys to sit on the beach and not move an inch while I retrieved Peter from RAVEN and we frantically rowed toward the southern end of the island where Peter had seen the plane, piloted by his friend, Peter Orne, go down.

We climbed up the nearly vertical sides of Saddle Island's southern cliffs to where the small plane was buried nose down in the spruce trees overhead, still streaming aviation fuel. We climbed up over the broken wing to the cockpit, but we were too late for the pilot who did not have enough lift under his wings and fell out of the sky.

the principal got back to her, he told her the school board had unanimously rejected her offer. He quoted one school board member as saying, "That girl who drives the red pickup truck is never stepping foot in the school." Twenty years later, married and the mother of three children, Chellie became chair of the school board.

A few years later, Pingree ran for and won election to the Maine Senate from North Haven, although most of the district was on the mainland. Her opponent badly underestimated her, calling her a "Pollyanna," which enraged many supporters—especially women. As she rose through the Maine Senate hierarchy, Pingree's colleagues elected her as Senate Majority Leader. Although she lost a U.S. Senate race to Susan Collins, Pingree was elected to the U.S. House of Representatives from Maine's First District in 2008, and was among the few Democrats in Maine reelected in 2010 when Republicans took over the House of Representatives. Chellie's daughter Hannah followed in her footsteps, serving eight years in Maine's House, including four years as House Majority Leader. She has recently become the Institute's first second-generation trustee.

Islesboro—Never Far from the Sea

Residents of Islesboro, at the head of Penobscot Bay, live on a narrow slice of ridge with over 50 miles of shoreline for its 14 square miles of land. Wherever you are on Islesboro, you are never geographically far from the sea. Perhaps the geography explains why this small community bred so many skillful and successful merchant captains who commanded three-, four-, five- and six-masted schooners and other ships that carried East Coast trade to and from the far corners of the seven seas during the 19th century. The elegant houses built by generations of successful captains and boatbuilders grace the shores of Islesboro, which still supports three excellent year-round boatyards, even though the island's residents are mostly captains of commerce rather than captains of commercial sail.

Gilkey Harbor, Islesboro, with Seven Hundred Acre Island in distance

QUICKSILVER water taxi dropping passengers at Lincolnville beach on the first run of the morning

Shortly after starting the Island Institute, I contacted a friend, Jeri Hamlen, who had taken an Outward Bound course from me some years earlier and who came from an Islesboro summer family. She listened to my goals for the organization and offered to host a dinner on Islesboro during the winter of 1985 with year-round residents. I gave a pitch about the waves of historical development on Maine's islands and how I thought seasonal residential development pressures were going to be the next wave. The take-home message was the importance of getting ahead of the wave and controlling it rather than ignoring it and being controlled by it.

After my presentation, an islander from a prominent year-round family who also was Islesboro's most successful realtor assured the group that Islesboro would not experience the kinds of problems I mentioned, since Islesboro's history of large family ownerships went back generations, he said, and would insulate the community from development. In terms of specific knowledge of Islesboro's land-use history and ownership, I was out of my depth by a great margin. The local realtor's opinion held sway among the 20 other listeners, who basically agreed that Islesboro was not going to experience ill effects from the development boom. I did not get one among them to become members of the Island Institute, except for Jeri Hamlen, who became an early Institute trustee. We can take care of ourselves, was the message, but we'll call you if we ever need help—like never!

A few years later, a 130-acre summer family property on Hermit's Point was sold to a real estate "developer," who proposed to subdivide the land into ten or so lots. The fact that the developer was also from a well-known summer family in Camden, as well as connected to the levers of power in Washington, D.C., only made the situation more alarming. Almost overnight, the interest on Islesboro in finding strategies to guide development gained traction. Islanders hired the Island Institute to collect baseline natural resource information. This work included a first-of-its-kind groundwater research project that eventually led to an innovative ordinance protecting Islesboro's aquifer recharge areas. The concern also led to the eventual creation of the Islesboro Islands Trust to acquire important parcels of land on Islesboro and the surrounding islands.

Almost 20 years later, in 2006, another 100-acre parcel on Islesboro went up for sale on a peninsula on the eastern side of the island. Most people—including the local land trust—considered the $9 million price tag lunacy. But a developer paid the asking price and produced a plan for 20 lots, later scaled back to 12, and history repeated itself.

Like both Vinalhaven and North Haven, Islesboro has also invested heavily in its K–12 island school, completely renovating the historic stone "cottage" donated by the Kinnicutt family. Vicky Conover has taught computer science and other technology courses at the Islesboro School for the past 15 years while raising two sons on the island. She has also been a key advisor for an Island Institute–sponsored technology education program called CREST (Community for Rural Education, Stewardship and Technology). CREST, funded by a five-year, $2 million

Islesboro School; CREST information technology program summer institute

grant to the Island Institute from the National Science Foundation, was designed to stimulate innovative approaches to information technology experiences for students and teachers. Between 2005–2010, the program created a series of partnerships involving 16 island and coastal high schools and middle schools to create place-based learning experiences that use technology to answer community resource stewardship questions.

The program has been very well received, including on Islesboro. Ruth Kermish-Allen is the Institute's education director. "Students can learn technology until the end of the day, but if they don't see a way to apply it in their everyday life, what use is it to them?" she asked. "We make sure there is an interdisciplinary project so students get exposed to science, technology, engineering and math in many different ways and integrate it into an existing curriculum in all the different classes. This [CREST] has given them something they are really proud of, and now they can go out and show that not only to their community, but to the rest of the world, which is exactly what they are doing."

Monhegan: "No One Goes Till Everyone Goes"

Monhegan, 12 miles offshore, is geographically the archipelago's smallest year-round island, barely over 500 acres in extent with a community of 70 or so year-round islanders. The island's high dark cliffs and austere seascapes have inspired thousands of

artists in the century since Rockwell Kent, George Bellows and other New York artists created a beachhead here in the late 1800s. Fishermen, artists, poets and other cultural misfits have shaped the essence of Monhegan's community. Over half of the island is preserved in its natural state, thanks largely to land donations by the family of inventor Thomas Edison and managed by the Monhegan Associates. Huge cliffs and fairy houses in the cathedral interior forest continue to inspire and delight both visitors and residents.

Monhegan famously has two seasons. The artists' season extends from May to October, when upwards of several hundred visitors per day come to explore the numerous galleries within walking distance of the mailboat landing. The other season is the lobster season, which used to operate between January and May, but which now opens in October, when the island's dozen fishermen set their traps in the island's exclusive lobster territory within two miles of its rocky headlands.

Unlike Matinicus, most of Monhegan's fishermen are transplants. The family of Shermie Stanley has the longest tenure on the island, extending back for only three generations. Who gets to fish these waters and who does not as the seasons come and go is a solemn matter that is still decided in a traditional manner at one of the island's most venerable institutions—the Fish House at Fish Beach—when the date for Trap Day is also decided.

No one goes until everyone goes. That's the way Trap Day always has worked on Monhegan. Sometimes the weather holds up the start for days after the official opening day. Very occasionally there's a delay because someone, perhaps an older fisherman, has been sick and doesn't have his gear ready. But the first good day after October 1, when everyone's ready, Monhegan's fall and winter lobster season begins, just as the season on the mainland begins to wind down. It's an energized time of year on the island; gear has been piled down all along the rocky roadsides, lining the hill, and down the sides of the wharf. The sea is streaky where the spume has blown, and hopefully lobster prices have climbed steadily throughout the fall.

After Doug Boynton returned to Monhegan to fish the winter season following two years on Allen Island, I asked him to describe the hardest thing about winter fishing. He said it was the days of freezing spray when you can't see anything. "It's not the cold," he said. "The invention of the hot water tub to dunk your mitten was the greatest invention on the modern lobster boat." But hauling through a string in limited visibility in the bone-numbing cold gets to you. "One day," he said, after a long stretch of freezing spray and vapor, "I got so mad, I went up on the bow and smashed the ice off the windshield with a hammer—which fixed the windshield permanently. The next morning it was 34 degrees, so I guess I broke the cold spell." But, he added, "Now I keep the hammer stowed below out of reach."

For most of the 20th century, Monhegan had the only legislatively defined exclusive lobster territory—a two-mile boundary circumscribing northern, eastern and western areas off Monhegan, but undefined on the southern end that spills out into the deepwaters of the Gulf of Maine. During the winter of 1995, Friendship fishermen—in a reenactment of the ancient law of the sea that only fishermen really understand—laid claim to this undefined territory south of the island. A dramatic confrontation ensued with knives drawn in the drear light of dawn, as lean and hungry boats from both communities warily circled one another in acute watchfulness.

In a tense set of meetings and hearings, commissioner of Marine Resources Robin Alden negotiated a truce, while Monhegan quickly petitioned the legislature to establish a formal three-mile zone around its southern territorial periphery. During the winter of 1996–97, virtually the entire year-round community of Monhegan moved to Augusta to keep a full court press on the legislators. They kept a daily tally of the commitments they received in support of their legislation. Twelve-year-old Kyle Murdock, the youngest son of one of Monhegan's lobsterman, established himself as the elevator operator in the State House and lobbied everyone who rode up and down. The Island Institute's community programs director at the time was Marge Kilkelly, who was also a state senator. She helped script the islanders' lobbying campaign. Monhegan finally won. The legislation was passed in both branches by overwhelming margins. Even the legislator who represented the town of Friendship voted for Monhegan's lobster conservation zone.

Trap day at the wharf on Monhegan; Lobsterman Robert Bracy and son loading traps

Matinicus and Its Air Service Lifeline

Matinicus, served by only one Maine State Ferry Service trip per month, is the outermost inhabited island on the coast of Maine—22 miles off the mainland—and is arguably one of the most independent island communities in the world. Some might say Matinicus has more in common with isolated island communities like Pitcairn in the Pacific than with other Maine island communities.

For most of its history, several island families—the Youngs, Ameses and Philbrooks—many of whom can trace their routes back to the community's founding families—have dominated Matinicus. Another key island family, the Bunkers, have been on Matinicus for only a century and thus are newcomers, relatively speaking. Almost all of the 40 to 50 year-round islanders are involved with lobster fishing. But what a fishery it is! Lobsters crawl into shallower warmer waters to shed their shells at the beginning of the summer and then crawl off into deeper, warmer waters in the fall when the north-

Monhegan Trap Day

JANUARY 6, 1983—I saw him a few weeks later, when he came ashore and was grounded out at the lobstermen's Co-op in Port Clyde painting GRYPHON's bottom. He was stagey and cat-like, maneuvering for room around the wharf, eyes darting about, half wild. He said he was being denied fishhouse privileges on Monhegan by the other 11 fishermen, a serious situation because without being able to store gear and bait at the fish-house, he would have to stage his solo fishing from the mainland, which involved incalculably greater risks and expense.

No one had ever survived on Monhegan when access to the fish-house had been withdrawn. He said there had been trouble. He didn't say what kind. But he said he would fight hard to get his berth back, and I didn't doubt him. Whatever his crime, the punishment had been terrible, swift and merciless. "There's one thing that islanders are really good at," he said ruefully, "That's when we get together to exclude someone.'"

This December, though, under the long afternoon shadows at the Monhegan wharf, he piles his gear alongside the other 11 lobstermen's traps, warps and buoys. No one says a word to him, there's just the baleful silences of another austere winter's day. Everyone is waiting; it's always like this before Trap Day—waiting; waiting for the wind to stop shrieking so the gear can be set out in Monhegan's exclusive fishing territory, so the men can go fishing again, so island families ease their cash-flow hemorrage. Some years it has taken ten days for the wind to let go or the sea surge in the harbor to steady.

But now four days into the waiting, the season finally begins early this morning. Everyone is down at the harbor early; steaming coffee in thermoses, the day promises to be a bright blue with a steadily freshening northeasterly at 20 knots, but time enough to get many loads of gear in the water fishing.

School, of course, in the one-room schoolhouse up the hill, has been called off so everyone can help load gear when the boats jockey alongside the wharf for their turn to load. Even the schoolteacher who has a lobster license is going to set a dozen traps in the harbor. More gear is piled at Fish Beach, including the gear of the lobsterman who has been voted off the island. You can feel the edgy energy all around, when an amazing thing happens—the schoolteacher in her skiff rows out from the wharf where her own gear is piled and along the shore to Fish Beach. She beaches the skiff and grabs three big wire lobster traps from the excluded man's trap pile and one by one loads them on her skiff. As everyone ashore takes a deep inner breath, she rows quietly out to his boat and lifts them up over the stern to him. The tension on the wharf eases as everyone takes a deep breath and gets on with the business of lobsteing that sustains this small community

Redemption does not come easily on islands, but maybe its tough vigilance makes such turning points even sweeter.

west gales start to blow. Matinicus sits astride two big channels of lobster migration where the waters of East and West Penobscot Bay meet at the edge of the ocean, and the fishery handsomely rewards those sturdy enough to follow it closely. Although lobster-harvest statistics are not compiled on a harbor-by-harbor basis, one might hazard the guess that Matinicus lobstermen enjoy the highest landings per capita of any fishing village on the coast of Maine.

Matinicus survives as a year-round community by virtue of an air service link from the county airport at Owls Head, where a bush pilot operation delivers islanders their daily mail, freight and groceries whenever the flying is decent—certainly not every day, and infrequently in the winter. The air service also delivers mail to Vinalhaven and North Haven, but is Matinicus's most vital link to the rest of the world. In 2003, the island air business was sold to a new owner, who after two years of red ink fired his general manager, Kevin Waters, and two weeks before Christmas abruptly informed islanders of his decision to suspend daily air service for the remainder of the winter. The decision seemed especially ill-timed—Christmas presents could be neither sent nor received, medication for a diabetic on the island was interrupted and island life went into a tailspin. That is when Vance Bunker, one of Matinicus's old-line community leaders, called Peter Ralston to see if the Island Institute could help.

With a little research, it soon became apparent that the island airline operator had not realized that suspending daily U.S. Post Office mail delivery two weeks short of the stipulated year-end date was a big federal no-no. Waters in the meantime was trying to lease an airplane and buy insurance to resume air service to the islands, including Matinicus. However, he needed the critical mail contract to the three Penobscot Bay islands in order to make the business financially viable. The existing air service owner, recognizing that he might not have acted in his own best interest, quickly expressed

a desire to resume operations. The U.S. Post Office representative charged with the decision of whom to award the contract asked islanders from the three affected communities to help vet the proposals for the following year's delivery contract during a meeting in the conference room of the Island Institute.

In an emotional appeal the air service operator who had suspended operations announced he would resume service to Matinicus the following day. But Vance Bunker, a bear of a lobsterman who was one of Matinicus's representatives, pointed out that the landing strip was privately owned. "You might be able to land on Matinicus," he said. "But your plane will never take off." A few days later the U.S. Postal Service canceled its contract with its previous operator, and awarded a new contract to Kevin Waters's new company, Penobscot Island Air. Then Matinicus residents passed the hat and quickly raised $17,000, enough for Waters to buy an air insurance policy—and operations resumed.

In 2009, Vance Bunker was involved with a tragic and violent confrontation over Matinicus's lobster fishing rights, discussed in chapter 9. Although Bunker and his daughter were acquitted of all charges, the violence has undoubtedly left a deep wound on the island that will take a generation at least to begin to heal.

The Kingdom of Criehaven

Criehaven, inhabited for nine months of the year, is the name given to the small town on Ragged Island, two miles farther out than Matinicus. The two islands were one town until Criehaven became a separate town in 1896. The split was caused by the difficulty of making "satisfactory arrangements for the instruction of [its] children," according to Matinicus's first histo-

rian, Charles Long. The new town was named by and for its most successful inhabitant, Robert Crie, grandson of John who had lived on Matinicus. Robert Crie began as a farmer with his new wife, Harrriet, in 1848 on Ragged, most of which he eventually cleared for sheep pasturage. He soon became the dominant landowner on this 300-acre island. By 1879, according to Charles McLane's meticulous deed research, Crie owned the entire island, which he ran as a fiefdom, leasing out parcels of land around the harbor to fishermen, who had no choice but to sell their catch to him for salting or packing lobsters in crates, sometimes for as little as two cents a pound. "King" Crie, as he was called, prospered, even when others did not.

In 1925, Robert Crie's son, Horatio, who was Maine's commissioner of Sea and Shore Fisheries, convinced the islanders to "de-organize," and to become an unorganized township to save on taxes. Dorothy Simpson, who grew up on Criehaven, dates the decline of Criehaven to this fateful decision. After de-organizing, she said, Criehaven "got state schools—state this, state that. Everything was lovely but nobody had time to have a town meeting anymore and everything began drifting apart."

As indicated earlier, Criehaven was the last Maine island to go extinct as a year-round community, after its school shut down for lack of a teacher during World War II. Various fishermen lived year-round on the island through the early 1960s, with their families joining them, but it would be a stretch to call Criehaven a year-round island community after its school shut down.

Today, Criehaven is inhabited for three-quarters of the year by 12 lobster fishermen and their families, who occupy small plots of land ringing the harbor, which only has room for their dozen boats. Much of the Crie land on Ragged was bought up by a new landowner toward the end of the 1960s. That family has occupied the island seasonally ever since, living in a big farmhouse on the hill and maintaining a cordial relationship with the fishermen and their families on the shore.

(Facing); Criehaven and Matinicus;Penobscot Island Air owner, Kevin Waters delivering the mail; Criehaven's mailboat, the BUTTMAN

Swept Away

On AUGUST 12, 2010, a tropical storm off the coast of Africa first attracted weather-watchers' notice, before it deepened into a tropical depression on August 15th and attained full-fledged hurricane force five days later on August 17th. Hurricane Bill, as the storm was named, spun its way toward the Gulf of Maine and Nova Scotia, pushing an enormous body of waves ahead of its track.

On Sunday morning August 23rd, Braden Aldrich, who was working on Monhegan, watched the 16-to 18-foot waves from Hurricane Bill pound in on Burnt Head on Monhegan's back shore with two friends. Braden was out on one of Burnt Head's rocky shelves high over the water, and as his friends watched helplessly, an enormous wave approached and swept him away. Cole Lord, Monhegan's fire chief, saw a young woman running toward him calling wildly for help for Braden who had been swept overboard. Cole ran to the nearest house, burst in and called lobsterman Matt Weber.

Lord said, "Braden is overboard underneath Burnt Head and we need to get a boat out there." Weber jumped in his truck and "was flying down the road, dodging people everywhere," he recalled. "By the time we got to the beach Angela and Cole were there. We launched into a skiff and Cole dropped Angela and me in my boat. I told Cole to bring a skiff in

case we needed to get it in close to the cliffs. I started my boat and did something I have never done before—I just opened her up cold full throttle; the oil pressure gauge was just pinned. *I hope she holds together* is all I thought."

When Weber came out of the harbor and looked at the seas off Burnt Head, he said, "I was shaking. To see those seas breaking, I said there's no way he's alive. No way he hasn't been sucked under or smashed on the rocks. I thought, I don't want to pick up a dead body."

By this time there was a crowd of people on Burnt Head so Weber switched his radio to the Monhegan channel and shouted "Where is he?" Chris Smith, one of Monhegan's other lobstermen, was up

on Burnt Head with a radio. "He's in the 15 bottom between Burnt Head and Gull Pond," describing where lobstermen set their traps along the 15-fathom contour on that part of the back shore. But Weber could not see anything or anyone in the water because the seas were so big and the troughs so deep. "You're going to have to walk me in." Finally, when Weber was within 100 yards, he could see him just outside the line of foam; he was waving his arms, the first time anyone could tell he was still alive.

"I swung around and backed down until he was alongside. We each grabbed one of his arms and heaved him up onto the gunwale. That's when I noticed he was buck-naked. I was so surprised, I dropped him, but Angela held on. He'd probably swallowed a bucket of seawater."

When the wave took him, Braden Aldrich had the presence of mind to dive down and away from the rocks and swam underwater as long as he could hold his breath. When he finally came up, his shoes had been sucked off, and his shorts and then he took everything else off so he would not be dragged under. "The backwash probably saved him," said Weber. "That, and the fact he was 22 and in great shape. But to see those seas breaking, you'd never believe anyone could swim through them."

Monhegan's harbor is exposed to storms, which takes a toll on its small fishing fleet.

A Single Link in the Chain

Undoubtedly the three big islands of Penobscot Bay will survive as year-round communities into the foreseeable future—and beyond. Although they are all plagued by declining school enrollments, their schools still offer excellent educations. On the smaller islands, as elsewhere along the archipelago, small changes have big effects. The violence on Matinicus has torn the fabric of island life. The Bunkers have made plans to "remove." But my bet is that Matinicus as a community will survive. There is simply too much good lobster bottom and the original families are too rooted (or too ornery) to leave.

Monhegan is currently more vulnerable. Several years ago Monhegan's most successful young fisherman lost his boat during a winter storm. It turned out that a single defective weld in his mooring chain broke. Life for that fisherman, and his energetic wife and their two children, was already economically stressed, but became untenable, and they "removed" for a more-reliable living on an island in the Caribbean. One of the island's older fishermen said ruefully, "We could have built a whole community around that family." Monhegan's year-round community is also changing as a result of the shift to the earlier lobster season opening, which means that some lobstermen can fish the fall and the spring, and skip the painfulness of fishing in the deep of winter. If there are no children in the island school, Monhegan could well become a three-quarters year-round community like Criehaven.

CHAPTER 12

Casco Bay Islands: At the Urban Edge

Island communities are all endangered species.
In the future we are going to be under incredible pressure.
If people find there is something to value—this way of life—
that has been sustained in my family since 1756,
then we are going to need all the help we can get.

—Donna Damon, Chebeague Island

(Facing) Ragged Island,
once the summer home
of poet Edna St. Vincent
Millay, outer Casco Bay

I first approached Casco Bay from the north and east—the opposite compass points from which most navigators arrive at this part of the coast. Small Point defines the bay's eastern end, marking a geographical divide in the way that the longer, narrower and more treacherous Petit Manan Point marks the divide between Acadia and Downeast. On one side of Cape Small are the rare and elegant white sandy beaches of Popham and Sewall—beaches that trap the perfectly rounded alluvial grains from the Kennebec, Morse and Sprague rivers. On the other side of Small Point are narrow channels that twist between the long ledges of Hermit Island and Basin Point and finger underwater, far beyond the tips of the points to which they are attached.

Ragged Island lies at the bay's eastward edge. Maine's most famous poet, Edna St. Vincent Millay, bought the island where she spent summers to let the lyricism of Maine island seascapes inspire her, as they had in Penobscot Bay when she wrote "Renascence" as a 19-year-old in Camden. Across the way from Ragged is Eagle Island, now a state historical museum, but once the summer home of Arctic explorer Robert Peary, who may or may not have been the first man to reach the North Pole, depending on whose story you believe.

A Calendar of Islands

Most Mainers view Casco Bay from a mainland perspective at its western edge. From Munjoy Hill in Portland or from windows in Portland's downtown buildings, the panorama of islands in the bay presents one of the most compelling vistas in Maine. Ridge upon rolling ridge of dark island shapes are separated from each other by silver slices of Casco Bay, the deepwater channels and wide watery boulevards that outline Portland's inhabited island communities. Casco Bay Islands have been called the Calendar Islands because there were supposedly 365 islands in the bay—one for each day of the year—which proved to be an exaggeration after some stickler counted them up and found there to be 220-some islands—depending on how big a ledge you might want to include, or how small a grassy islands counts.

Peaks Island is a 20-minute ferry ride from Maine's biggest city. The Diamonds and Cushing's, created to be summer gems of Casco Bay, lie just beyond. And from the top of the Observatory on Munjoy Hill, Portlanders can see all the way to the outermost populated island, Cliff, where a year-round community of 50 struggles to stay afloat. In between Chebeague and Long Islands, the bay's two largest fishing communities occupy the rich lobster grounds of the mid-bay. The vagaries of history have separated these latter two islands politically: For most of the past century and a half, Chebeague was the only island jurisdiction in the mainland town of Cumberland, while Long, and its year-round neighbors, Cliff, the Diamonds, and Peaks, had all been part of Portland for as long as almost anyone can remember. But in recent years, Long and Chebeague have more to share thanks to newly won municipal independence.

Fields of Fire—The Military History of Casco Bay

In 1775, following the outbreak of revolution, Britain's Royal Navy bombarded and burned the defenseless settlement of Portland—then called Falmouth—leaving more than 130 structures in ashes. Ever since, city residents have incorporated the outlying islands as front lines from which to defend themselves from another devastating naval attack. In 1807 forts were constructed on both Spring Point and House Island to protect the entrance to the harbor's main shipping channel.

Fifty years later, in the run-up to the Civil War, military engineers built Fort Gorges on top of the Hog Island ledges as an added protection at the entrance to Portland Harbor, although no gun was ever fired from its nearly impregnable ramparts. By the 1880s more fortifications bristling with new long-range breech-loaded rifled guns were deployed on the back side of Cushing's Island, where Fort Levitt was established, and from the shores of Cape Elizabeth at Fort Williams to protect the outer approaches to Portland Harbor.

The largest fortifications in Casco Bay, however, were built on the north end of Great Diamond Island prior to the Spanish-American War, and named Fort McKinley after the recently assassinated president. Built to accommodate seven companies, or 700 enlisted men and their families, the complex had its own water, sewage, power and recreational facilities, along with its large guns trained on the Hussey Sound entrances to the bay.

As the drums of the First World War beat more loudly, additional gun batteries were constructed on Peaks, Long, Chebeague and Cow Islands to protect the "back-door" entrances to Portland Harbor. The military then built observation posts on Jewell Island to help to direct the fields of fire from all these island gun batteries, but most especially from Great Diamond Island's combination of 3-, 6-, 8-, and 12-inch gun batteries.

Robert Laughlin spent summers observing the target practice from the Fort McKinley guns. "One outstanding thrill was the ability to pick up the sight of a mortar pro-

Fort McKinley and Diamond Cove, Great Diamond Island

jectile about one-quarter [of the way] up in its trajectory and follow it to the top of its course and down again to the point of disappearance just before it splashed into the sea near the target that was being towed by one of the Army vessels," he wrote. "Rowing out to pick up fish that were killed or stunned by mine explosions was also very exciting, particularly when one of the big codfish revived when about to be captured."

In the late 1930s with war again looming in Europe, War Department planners recognized the key strategic value of the deepwaters of inner Casco Bay and their proximity to the major northern shipping channels across the North Atlantic. The need for defenses in this part of the bay became particularly important after passage of the Lend-Lease Act, providing supplies and war materiel to Britain. The U.S. Navy built a seaplane base and huge fuel storage tank farm on Long Island that was capable of fueling the entire North Atlantic fleet within 24 hours if necessary.

During the half-century after the Second World War, most of Casco Bay's military facilities were turned back to civilian uses. Fort Williams in Cape Elizabeth became a town park, while Jewell Island became a state park. Fort Levitt on Cushing's Island was acquired by the Cushing's Island Association, which sold the military buildings and officers' quarters as residential real estate and placed a conservation easement on its outer shores. Battery Steele on Peaks Island was sold to an environmental group, while the southern shore was developed. Fort Lyon on Cow Island became the base of a summer program for city youth run by Ripple Effect.

Oil and Water—The Birth of Maine's Environmental Politics

Deciding the fate of the two largest military properties in Casco Bay—the Long Island tank farm and the Fort McKinley complex on Great Diamond—sparked intense political battles with long-term implications for Maine's environmental policies.

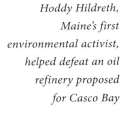

Hoddy Hildreth, Maine's first environmental activist, helped defeat an oil refinery proposed for Casco Bay

In 1969, King Resources, a Denver oil company, purchased the 173-acre Long Island tank farm from the U.S. Navy for $203,000, and announced plans to build a supertanker offloading facility a mile from downtown Portland. Within days, a group of concerned citizens formed an opposition group called Citizens Who Care, which was headed up by Hal Hackett, a Bates College biology professor and seasonal resident of Little Diamond Island. Citizens Who Care initially tried to get the Portland City Council to rescind zoning approval for the oil depot. Although that effort failed, the group quickly attracted more than 2,000 members. This focused political pressure on Maine's governor, Kenneth Curtis, and U. S. Senator Edmund Muskie, both of whom were initially attracted to the potential positive impact of cheaper foreign oil.

Delivering oil to the Portland Pipeline terminal in Casco Bay

Among the many questions raised by the public and the press was who would pay the cleanup costs for any spilled oil. Although there were other oil refinery proposals on the drawing board along the Maine coast, the King Resources plan appeared to present the greatest risks for a spill because oil would be transferred three times. First, oil would be pumped out of supertankers into storage tanks. Then it would be pumped into barges for transportation to the mainland, where it would be pumped yet again—perhaps to the Portland Pipeline that delivered oil to Montreal, or to a refinery. Beyond the immediate pollution threat, people all along the coast were also concerned about the effects of industrial development on Maine's environment. Would this mean that any local municipality with 200 acres of undeveloped land and deepwater frontage could volunteer itself for a major oil refinery without regard for the effects on neighboring communities?

Hoddy Hildreth, whose political routes ran deep, helped put together Maine's first environmental lobbying organization, the Coastal Resources Action Committee (CRAC). He quickly recruited a board of luminaries (partly by promising them they would never have to attend a meeting), including the writer E. B. White, visionary Buckminster Fuller, and photographer Eliot Porter among others. CRAC raised $40,000 and then hired Hildreth and another lawyer, Democrat Harold Pachios, to lobby the legislature to pass two bills of vital importance to the future of the Maine coast. The first was an oil conveyance law to establish an oil pollution fund based on a half-cent-per-barrel tax on the transfer of oil between ship and shore, and the other was a law to establish environmental criteria for siting any major industrial or other development project larger than 20 acres. After an intense legislative session in 1970, both the Oil Conveyance and Site Laws were passed and signed by Governor Curtis. They remain two of the most important environmental laws of Maine. Ten oil companies promptly sued the state, contending the oil conveyance law was an unconstitutional violation of the federal interstate commerce clause, but the Maine Supreme Court upheld the law in 1974 and the U.S. Supreme Court refused to review the decision.

King Resources applied for a permit under the new site law for its Long Island facility, which was reviewed by a citizen's board, the Environmental Improvement Commission, the forerunner of the Board of Environmental Protection. King Resources had told different stories to different people about whether it ultimately planned to construct an oil refinery in a subsequent phase somewhere on the mainland. Hildreth noted this during the hearing on the license. "Who knows what King Resources is really up to?" he asked, prompting considerable applause from the audience. Ultimately the commission voted 6–3 to deny the permit, on the grounds that it posed unacceptable risks to Casco Bay and its islands. While Maine's U.S. Senator Muskie would become known as a strong proponent of environmental laws at the national level, Hildreth had become Maine's first environmental advocate at the state level.

Almost 20 years later, the new town of Long Island would acquire the tank farm on the island along with the other military buildings, using the buildings and acreage for public purposes. That left Fort McKinley, the largest military facility, after years of abandonment and vandalism, to become the site of another battle between public and private uses of the historic, scenic and environmental resources of this strategically located island in the heart of Casco Bay.

Great Diamond—Newest Year-round Island Community

I first met Margery Foster of Great Diamond Island at a coffee shop in Portland in 1984. At age 70, she was a blue-eyed, white-haired ball of focused energy, and she was seriously upset. The Portland Planning Board was close to approving a plan to renovate the abandoned buildings at Fort McKinley on the north end of Great Diamond into a gated community of luxury condominiums and residences. Foster thought the Fort McKinley plan and its attendant zoning proposals would doom not just Great

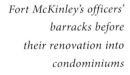

Fort McKinley's officers' barracks before their renovation into condominiums

Diamond Island, where she lived for six months a year, but the rest of the islands in Casco Bay to a legacy of intensive, unsustainable development that she had encountered elsewhere as a well-known and highly respected academic economist.

Before retiring to Great Diamond, Foster had received her PhD in economics and public policy from Harvard University, had taught at Wellesley College, become dean of the women's college, Douglass, at Rutgers, and served on various large corporate boards. By the time I met her, she had nearly completed the restoration of a six-room John Calvin Stevens cottage on Great Diamond. She argued that the condominium developers' plans for the 198-acre Fort McKinley property were ill-conceived and inadequately financed. Between 1985 and 1991, I served as a kind of sorcerer's apprentice to Margery as she cunningly surveyed the environmental battlegrounds around the old fort and fought with a ferocity that her opponents ignored at their peril. She was a grand old lady in combat boots who quickly became a founding trustee of the Island Institute during its formative years. Margery Foster was a fearless and daunting foe of other ill-planned development schemes in the region after that initial Great Diamond proposal ended, as she accurately predicted, in bankruptcy.

Before the bankruptcy, however, the Island Institute, the Maine Audubon Society and the Conservation Law Foundation teamed up to negotiate a series of agreements with the developers, limiting the environmental impacts of the project. The first agreement in 1989 successfully challenged Maine's Department of Environmental Protection's policy on overboard discharge.

Margery Foster, a leader in the effort to limit development of the islands of Casco Bay; Fort McKinley parade grounds ringed by officers' quarters, with gun emplacement around periphery of the island

This led to an improvement in the bay's water-quality and to the formation of an activist local group, the Friends of Casco Bay, to monitor conditions throughout the bay. The organization continues this work effectively today. The second agreement in 1991 cut in half the number of houses that could be built on Great Diamond's scenic shores, required deeded open space to protect old-growth pines and other scenic features, and prohibited building on the Fort's historic gun emplacements, among other provisions.

Ultimately, the protracted battle led to the creation of a pair of communities with seemingly incompatible lifestyles on the two ends of Great Diamond. On the north end, some of the condominiums around Fort McKinley's beautiful parade ground and some of the new shoreline homes became year-round residences, which no one expected. On the south end, a number of summer "cottages" were also renovated into year-round residences. With a growing permanent population of perhaps 45 people, Great Diamond Island became Maine's newest year-round island community.

These two communities on Great Diamond have spawned three island organizations that represent different slices of the fractured island. The Diamond Island Association represents primarily the cottagers from the summer community on the south end. The Diamond Cove Homeowners Association represents homeowners on the Fort McKinley side of the island, while the Great Diamond Island Association was organized by a handful of the original year-round islanders and is primarily focused on monitoring the effectiveness of Portland's road, trash removal, fire and safety services on Great Diamond.

One intractable issue that has dogged efforts to create civic bonds between islanders on Great Diamond is the use of motorized vehicles. Residents on the Diamond Cove end of the island, where the roads are privately owned, use golf carts to get around

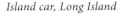
Island car, Long Island

the large amenity-oriented development. The Diamond Island Association members on the south side of the island, where the dirt roads are public and cherished mostly by pedestrians, have no use for motorized vehicles and have tried to ban them. The contentiousness surrounding the inherently different "lifestyles" on the two ends of the island has led to what one island wit referred to as the "Persian Golf Cart Wars" and a plethora of lawsuits that have sadly ground away at the potential for civic discourse on the island.

Long Island—The Little Island that Got Away

One of the effects of the Great Diamond Island condo battle was that Portland for the first time came up with special island-wide zoning proposals. On Long Island, the zoning plan ignited intense debate over lot sizes and the island's finite groundwater resources. In the midst of this intensely political debate, accumulated frustration over the chronic lack of basic city services on Long Island spilled over into secession talk, which spread like a fever among other Casco Bay Islanders. Then when the City of Portland revalued the islands in its jurisdiction in 1991, in effect doubling the tax bills of hundreds of islanders, the talk became a loud and persistent drumbeat.

Portland's initial reaction was to shrug off the complaints. Portland city leaders argued that Long Island, with a year-round population then of 150 or so, did not have enough residents to manage its own affairs successfully and needed the city's help for such things as educating students, firefighting, garbage removal and emergency medical services. But this kind of big-city paternalism backfired in the Legislature, which is heavily weighted to the interests of small rural towns and granted Long Islanders the right of self-determination. In a community referendum, the island's registered voters favored initiating the secession process by a 6–1 margin.

But then the political questions began to cascade: What would secession cost? Who would run the school? What would the town budget be? Who could register to vote?

Nancy Jordan at the Long Island Library and Community Center; Mark Greene, Long Island town office

Would taxes go up or down? Would the new town owe Portland for a part of the city's debts? A determined group of new island leaders, including Mark Greene, Christine McDuffie and Nancy and Bob Jordan, among others, schooled perhaps by their own experiences of self-sufficiency over the years, prepared answers to the questions as they arose. A second and final referendum was held November 1993, and the results were overwhelming: by a 4–1 majority, Long Island voters elected to form their own town, Maine's 455th, and chose July 4, 1994, as the day of their official independence.

"Before [independence], the best you could do was complain about the way Portland was doing things. Now it's in our hands—within our power," said Nancy Jordan. "We can make things happen."

The scene at the Long Island Town Offices on Independence Day 1994 was unforgettable. More than 500 islanders and their friends assembled outside the little white building that serves as the new town office in an old military building on the shore across from the ferry landing. The day was as gaudy a display of the island's naturally green, blue, and white colors as could ever be hoped for, and there was more red, white and blue bunting than surfaces to display it.

The ceremony was scheduled to begin promptly at the stroke of noon with the raising of the American flag at the entrance to the State of Maine's newest town hall, accompanied by the band playing "The Star-Spangled Banner." Just as the flag topped the pole with every eye in the audience staring upwards, the air was cracked apart by the deafening roar of four jets, which appeared and disappeared out of absolute nowhere 500 feet overhead. The display of split second timing left few without lumps in their throats, thinking about all the sacrifices that have paid for such privileges of independence.

In the years following Long Island's independence, the islanders indeed made things happen. Taxes went down by 20 percent, while services actually increased. Long Island built its own transfer station for managing and recycling waste. And to Long Islanders' great pride, they purchased and have operated an emergency evacuation vessel—long a sore point in relations between the islands and the city, whose fireboat had sometimes been slow to respond to emergencies.

But Long Islanders acquired something even more valuable than better services at lower cost: They trained themselves to be civically engaged, to be involved in setting their own course and managing their own affairs. This does not mean that politics are any more benign; if anything, on islands, political differences are more bitter because they are more personal. But I am not aware of any support for trading greater amity for less independence.

Perhaps the most powerful symbol of Long Island's emerging civic pride is its new library and community hall, strategically located next to the K–5 schoolhouse, where students can walk through a hallway and into the spacious reading spaces, where sunlight floods in through big windows. Nancy Jordan, who led the fund-raising campaign for the new building, recalled, "We talked about it for years. Everybody always said we need more room at the school, we need a bigger library. We also needed a winter gathering place. There was no place on the island big enough to have a winter thing—like a potluck supper." So the islanders held bake sales and auctions, sequestered tax dollars, wrote foundation proposals, and ultimately raised the $800,000 necessary for the project.

I learned a valuable lesson while piloting RAVEN back from one of Long Island's fund-raising events. We had spent the night at Long Island's new town float and headed off the next morning for a series of meetings on Great Diamond and Peaks. We were cruising with Peter Ralston at the helm and me at the navigation station when something thumped hard and the boat began shuddering violently. Peter throttled back immediately and we checked our wake but could see nothing we might have hit.

As first mate I was delegated to go overboard to check the rudder and propeller. I checked everything as carefully as I could in the heart-stoppingly cold waters of Casco Bay and came back aboard to report that nothing was jammed in the rudder or shaft and that all three propeller blades were intact. It was not until we limped slowly into Handy Boat in Falmouth and had RAVEN up in Handy's expensive slings that we learned what was wrong. Three propeller blades were indeed intact; it was the fourth blade that was completely missing, a victim of metal fatigue. I was reminded then and at least once a year for the next decade that outboards have three propeller blades while large marine engines always have four. The captain donated the propeller to me, which continues to inspire smirks from others and humility in the navigator.

At the Stone Wharf,
Chebeague Island

Raft Up in Casco Bay

JULY 14, 1992—As Peter Ralston and I make our way toward Chebeague Island on our 26-foot vessel, FISH HAWK, we are hailed by one of Chebeague's fisherman-philosophers, Ernie Burgess. Not much happens in the waters around Chebeague Island or on the islands around Chebeague's fishing territory that escapes Burgess's notice. Like most successful lobstermen, it is second nature to Burgess to keep track of small details even when they appear to be totally absorbed in the business of tending their traps.

When Burgess hails us, he wants to tell us what's happening on Stockman Island, just across Luckse Sound from Chebeague. He tells us that this low, brushy 30-acre island has been an important seabird-nesting island in Casco Bay for decades, mostly to eiders, but also gulls and other species. But recently the seabirds have all disappeared and he made it his business to find out why. It turned out that raccoons had taken up residence on the islands and lived off seabird eggs and other things they could forage out of the intertidal zone. Burgess believes that the raccoons did not get to Stockman Island accidentally; he suspects they were introduced, in order to make the island more valuable for development.

To add insult to injury, Burgess tells us that Stockman's designation as a Resource Protection Area was inadvertently left off Cumberland's recent zoning map, so there is no legal way to prevent the construction of a residence that has been proposed for the island.

You might not think that lobstermen would be concerned about seabird protection or land conservation, but Burgess is not atypical of many island lobstermen who care deeply for maintaining the local ecology they monitor on a daily basis. Gunwale to gunwale in the mid-morning swells, we come up with the outlines of a financial strategy for how conservationists might pool their efforts and resources to purchase Stockman to preserve it as a seabird-nesting habitat.

After returning to Rockland a few days later, we contacted Jay Espy, the head of the Maine Coast Heritage Trust, the most active land conservation organization on the islands of Maine. He was immediately interested in the story we related from Burgess, particularly because the Trust recognized that entire undeveloped islands in Casco Bay were increasingly rare. He promised to help.

Coda: A few years later, through a lot of hard work by the leaders of the Chebeague land trust, one of whom was Ernie Burgess, and with financial support from the Maine Coast Heritage Trust, a deal to buy and protect the island was finally struck and Stockman will be conserved as an island for the birds in perpetuity.

SUSAN ADAMS
CHEBEAGUE ISLAND

*Chebeague waterfront
and Chebeague Inn*

Chebeague—Part of the Main, or Not?

Sh–big. That's how you pronounce "Chebeague" when you're on the island. Like the pronunciation of Aisle ah Hoe when you're on Isle au Haut, these are important linguistic conventions for calculating the social distance between natives and those from away. Because summer people began coming to Chebeague in the 1870s, almost as early as they came to any Maine island, and because many summer family histories on Chebeague extend back four or five generations, there is a special term for such community members; on Sh–big, they are called "summer natives."

One newcomer to Chebeague, who grew up in Jordan before he married into an island family and moved there permanently, described how he adapted to island life. It was no problem, he explained, since there are only four tribes on Chebeague, and he made it a point to sit down with the leaders of each tribe to get to know them socially, which smoothed his transition into the community. It was just like dealing with tribes in Jordan, he said.

Long before Chebeague Islanders went to the Legislature in 2006 seeking approval to separate themselves from the town of Cumberland, Chebeaguers had spent a good part of the 1950s and 60s trying to build a bridge to connect the island with the mainland. But Chebeague's lobbying campaigns to convince the Legislature to approve bonds to finance the bridge all ended in failure—once by a single vote in the Maine Senate in 1957—and would undoubtedly never be supported today, according to Donna Damon, a 12th-generation islander and local historian.

I originally met Donna, who is part of the Hamilton clan which settled on Chebeague in 1756, at the first Island Schools Conference in 1985. She recalled the shock of meeting other islanders who felt like she did. "We used to feel like we were alone. My friend and I sat and listened to this speaker talking about island kids transitioning to the mainland," she said. "We both sat there with tears in our eyes because we had never

*Blanchard Bates and
Donna Damon, who
helped establish the land
trust on Chebeague*

heard anyone say that this was even an issue." Casco Bay Island kids who go ashore for their middle and high school years in Portland or Cumberland often feel stigmatized by their peers for their lack of supposed sophistication. And participating in extracurricular activities can be a nightmare of logistics for both parents and students.

During the late 1980s and throughout the 1990s, Donna was at the forefront of efforts to protect the Casco Bay islands from development pressures facing so many other southern Maine towns. She introduced me to Blanchard Bates, a kind and lovely man who was a retired Princeton University professor, but whose family roots extended back generations on Chebeague Island. I worked with Donna and Blanchard, two founders of the Chebeague land trust, to conduct an ecological inventory on a 26-acre property on Rose's Point beach. The land, which was privately owned but had been used by islanders for years, became the land trust's first protected property.

Chebeague largely sat out the secession movement that swept through Casco Bay in the 1990s because some islanders seemed to prefer the devil they knew (the town of Cumberland) to the devil they did not know—how they might govern themselves.

"There was always talk," says Mabel Doughty, a feisty octogenarian married to a respected retired fisherman, Sanford Doughty. "But it never got off the ground, until the thought that we might lose the school [became a reality]. . . that is what propelled it." In 2005 the mainland-based school board voted to restructure the Chebeague Island School and send fourth and fifth graders to the mainland to complete elementary school. Chebeague reacted as if a death sentence had just been handed down.

To Damon and other islanders there was an even deeper issue. The rapid escalation of property values in Cumberland, an upscale suburb of Portland, threatened Chebeague's destiny in an even more fundamental way. It was not simply a case of Cumberland seeming to use Chebeague's property taxes as a piggy bank, but rapidly increasing property values throughout Cumberland and Chebeague were taking a toll, as well. Those native islanders lucky enough to still own shorefront were slowly being taxed out of existence. Cumberland had once been a farming community and Chebeague a fishing community, but now their economies and ways of life had diverged even further. Median income on Chebeague in 2005 was $32,000, compared to $73,000 on Cumberland's upscale mainland. Cumberland had abandoned the town meeting form of government, while Chebeague islanders felt underrepresented on the town council. The two communities had simply drifted apart and Chebeague Islanders voted by an 86 percent margin to appeal to the legislature to start the process of secession.

In the meantime, the islanders began negotiating with their mainland counterparts in earnest. Unlike Long Island's pitched secession battle with Portland, the negotiations between the Cumberland town council and a committee of Chebeague Islanders were mostly civil. Separating themselves from the mainland school district was difficult, but ultimately an agreement was reached. The Maine legislature approved the bill enabling Chebeague to become its own town in 2006.

The Crown Pilot Cracker Escapade

Chebeague Islanders may have gotten a sense of their political and economic power a decade earlier after a group of islanders at the Chebeague store noticed the absence of Crown Pilot Crackers, their favorite chowder cracker, and learned they were no longer available from distributors. When Donna Damon followed up with Nabisco, the maker of the crackers, they told her the company had discontinued the Crown Pilot, having concluded it was not profitable enough. Understand, that did not mean the cracker was not profitable, just that its market was not growing beyond its New England base, so Nabisco discontinued it along with 400 other products. The point to Damon and Chebeague Islanders was that the Crown Pilot Cracker is the only cracker they had ever had or would ever put into their fish or clam chowder.

Nabisco's (former) oldest brand of cracker

Damon wrote an article about the Crown Pilots for *The Working Waterfront,* the Institute's newspaper, and started a letter-writing campaign. Damon got in touch with food historian, Sandy Oliver on Islesboro, who discovered that the Crown Pilot Cracker was actually Nabisco's oldest recipe, dating from the time the company bought out a small bakery in Newburyport, Massachusetts, where the cracker was made as early as 1792 for New England seafarers.

As Damon recalled, she soon got calls from *Yankee* magazine, *The Boston Globe* and *The Christian Science Monitor.* Then Maine humorist Tim Sample heard about the story and approached a CBS producer who summers in the Boothbay area.

During the Christmas season of 1996, *CBS Sunday Morning* aired its first story, which was the same week *Yankee* published their story. According to Damon, "This 1-2 punch set Nabisco spinning and in January they cried uncle!"

Nabisco announced that it had restarted its cracker factory in Pennsylvania. But Nabisco was also desperate to turn the bad publicity around, so they brought Damon, Oliver and other cracker activists to Boston for a news conference and chowder fest at the Chart House restaurant on the waterfront. But wait—there's more! Nabisco then chartered a ferry that churned its way to Gloucester, Newburyport and Portland where deckhands unloaded wooden crates of crackers to locals rounded up for the CBS cameras. Damon, who wrote up the story, also recalled in *The Working Waterfront,* "In

Peaks Island car ferry

Portland they had their execs unload the cases of crackers and bring them to the waiting Chebeaguers."

Eleven years later, in 2008, the Crown Pilot Cracker had disappeared again from New England's store shelves, but Nabisco, now part of the multinational Kraft Foods, did not return phone calls from Damon or Oliver.

Peaks Island—The Politics of Diversity

For most of the past half-century, Peaks Island has been Casco Bay's most diverse community, although it lacks the lobster-fishing fleet that anchors Casco Bay's other traditional island communities.

At the end of the 19th century Peaks boasted the only amusement park in Maine, and businessmen had built 10 hotels—including four large ones along the waterfront—and bragged of Peaks as the "Coney Island of Casco Bay." During the early part of the 20th century, when steamboats had their choice of four landings along Peaks Island waterfront, realtors sold vacationers small houses on quarter-acre lots along the island's southern and western shores. But the end of steamboat connections in the early 20th century led to a long decline in the island's housing stock. During the Depression and after World War II, Portland city officials took advantage of cheap housing prices on Peaks to relocate the City's welfare clients there where they mixed uneasily with island natives.

Relatively inexpensive housing prices on Peaks persisted through the 1970s and led to another wave of settlement—this time by artists and craftsmen who helped propel Portland's Old Port revival. Into this eclectic mix of natives, public housing residents, artists, hippies and retired summer folks came young urban professionals in the 1980s and 90s, attracted to the relative ease of commuting to high-paying jobs in booming Portland. This economic and cultural diversity has made it difficult for Peaks to be of one mind about any issue—much less one of such an emotional nature as secession.

The secession movement of 1991 swept across not just Long Island, but also Great Diamond, Cliff and Cushing's, all of which appealed to the Legislature along with Long Island in 1992 for permission to hold similar secession referenda. Portland was in a huge pickle. The city couldn't publicly suggest that the islands were a cash cow for city coffers; but city officials also knew they had alienated many islanders by suggesting the reverse—that the islanders were a drag on city services. So behind the scenes, they developed a new, highly effective line, suggesting to legislative leaders that if the remaining islands seceded, the city would need additional appropriations to maintain basic human services needs. A lot of money, know what I mean? Partially because none of the other islands were as united as Long, legislative permission to hold additional referenda on independence was buried quietly and deeply in Augusta in 1995.

But then secession reared its head again on Peaks between 2005 and 2007. Again taxes were the spark that lit the conflagration. Other hot topics included disagreements with the city over islanders' desire to keep roads dirt, rather than paved, the location of the wastewater treatment plant on a prime waterfront parcel, and the difficulty of attending night meetings on the mainland.

Unlike on Long and Chebeague, a vigorous group of residents on Peaks Island opposed secession. In June 2006, bitterly divided Peaks Island residents narrowly voted in favor of secession by 393 votes to 290—a 58 percent majority. Nevertheless, the Legislature again denied Peaks its independence, after the Portland City Council agreed to create a Peaks Island Council to provide a measure of self-governance. Secession leaders have vowed to press the issue again.

Cliff Island—Geography at the Edge

Located at the outermost edge of Casco Bay, Cliff Island is shaped like a tilted "H." Two parallel northeast-trending ridges—the outermost leg is shorter than the inner-

Cliff Island is shaped like an "H"

most leg—are connected by a wide sand and gravel bar across the middle. The most secure anchorage for lobster boats is south of the bar, although it is exposed to stiff southwesterly winds, and provides only a limited amount of space for the ten or so lobstermen who keep their boats there.

After abandoning the notion of secession in 1992, Cliff Islanders turned to what has always been their most pressing priority—how to keep Casco Bay's smallest community alive. An hour-and-a-half ferry ride from Portland, Cliff Island's community survives because it has been able to maintain the bay's last one-room school and its small post office.

In the mid-1990s, in an effort to cut costs, the U.S. Postal Service proposed closing post offices in remote rural areas if a larger, more-efficient post office were available within 10 miles. Like many other rules that might make sense on the mainland, this proposed rule would be devastating to island communities like Cliff, where traveling an hour and a half to Portland to get your mail is out of the question. On the smallest islands, the post office is a kind of community center where islanders congregate not just to get their mail, but to greet each other, do a quick bit of business and check in on who might need help. The threat to close small post offices, not just on Cliff, but on Swan's, Frenchboro, Great Cranberry and Islesford led to an inter-island campaign that Senator Snowe helped champion to exempt islands from the new rule. The postmistress of Islesford, Joy Sprague, came up with the idea of selling stamps by mail—to summer residents and other friends of the islands—that increases the revenue for isolated island post offices should the time come again when they are targets for new budget cutters.

Cliff Island also supports the bay's smallest lobster fleet. On other outer islands, lobster fishing persists through the late fall and into the winter. In one sense, Cliff Island should be no different, since island lobstermen theoretically should have first crack at lobsters crawling into Casco Bay in the spring and last crack as they crawl

Josh and Heidi Holloway with their students and family

offshore in the fall. But it doesn't work out that way.

Casco Bay's lobster regulations were developed with an eye toward the geography of long narrow sounds in which fishermen can set long lobster trawls—traps attached to bottom lines that run in strings along the bay's mostly northeast-southwest trending water courses. Unlike the islands to the east, Casco Bay island communities have small island territories surrounded by large areas of mixed fishing where boats from mainland communities also traditionally fish. The history here is more free-for-all than in other regions of the coast. In fact, before statewide lobster-trap limits were finally established in 1998, some Portland-based lobster boats fished as many as 3,000 traps and Casco Bay was known as the "Bay of Pigs."

In 1994 Peter Ralston and I headed to a meeting on Cliff Island to discuss conservation strategies for the uninhabited outermost leg of the island. At the meeting, the head of the Cliff Island Lobstermen's Association described a terrible snarl that had developed between island fishermen and their Portland counterparts. With groundfish catches so reduced, more and more fishermen from Portland had reconfigured their boats to go lobster fishing. Large offshore boats with long trawls had set their gear over Cliff, Long and Chebeague island grounds and a showdown seemed imminent. In fact, a few weeks later, Marine Resources commissioner William Brennan placed a 3 p.m. curfew on lobster boats in Portland Harbor to avoid an escalation of the confrontation. "If the Island Institute cares about sustaining year-round island communities," the Cliff Island lobsterman told me, "you'll help us do something to protect island fishing grounds."

That was a nearly impossible task, but several years later, under the leadership of a new commissioner of Marine Resources, Robin Alden, a task force was appointed (I was a member of the group) to propose a statewide trap limit and boundaries for seven local lobster zones.

The zones elected their own councils to help establish rules. While no one could possibly legislate the informal boundaries between lobstermen from different harbors, the zone council in Casco Bay was able to defuse the most egregious tensions between different "harbor gangs." And Cliff Island's lobstermen are still hanging on at the edge of the bay.

Cliff Island's school has been a small wonder for over three decades. When Earl and Judy MacVane, the island's two gifted schoolteachers for most of that time, retired in 2004, the question in islanders' minds was how to replace them. But in 2007, Cliff Island hired another teaching couple—Josh and Heidi Holloway. Some years earlier the Holloways had set out on a sailing adventure from Hawaii and ended up teaching in various island communities in the South Pacific, including on remote Kiribati Island. When the couple was expecting their first child, Heidi's mother convinced them to stay with her on Great Diamond Island. From Great Diamond, it was only a short jump to Cliff, where Josh currently teaches a handful of first-to-fifth grade students, while Heidi serves as art teacher and what is known in school terms as education technician. In an interview in *The Working Waterfront*, Holloway said, "It's like a teacher's dream. To me, it's like what homeschooling would be. The kids are your kids."

Hard Edges

The issues of secession and independence have dominated Casco Bay island histories during the past 25 years. Because Long and Chebeague have won independence they control their tax rates, development plans and hence their fates to a greater degree than ever. But independence does not necessarily mean that everyone is "happier." Although islanders are now making their own choices, those choices are inherently political and thus affect the lives of their neighbors, which can exact a high price in a

Lobstering in Portland's inner harbor

community where bad blood can last a generation.

Portland's attempt to thread the needle of independence with a compromise by creating the Peaks Island Council that would advise the city of islanders' concerns has not succeeded. Initially the Council included a mix of secessionist and "unionist" voices, but after the first year, secessionists, all of whom ran unopposed, dominated the seven-person council. Perhaps because Council members viewed their charge as that of a mini city council with rights and responsibilities, and Portland officials saw their role strictly as advisory, misunderstandings were inevitable.

Secession talk has again erupted and is unlikely to go away at any time in the foreseeable future. You might say it goes with the territory.

CHAPTER 13

Maine's Islands at the End of the 20th Century

It turns out that, when it comes to islands, what we all seek are people just like us,
whomever we may be, and not very many of them! That is the instinctive lusty power of islands.
Our dreams of islands are nearly always dreams of exclusions.
We must beware of our island dreams—they could just happen.

—George Putz, Vinalhaven

One of over 25 annual issues of Island Journal; *(Facing) Dogfish Island shoreline*

The first time I went to Augusta almost 30 years ago to address a legislative committee about an island issue, an elected representative asked me incredulously, "You mean people live on those islands in the winter?" But that was long ago and in a different land, politically speaking.

There used to exist a rarely voiced but prevalent undercurrent in the state capital that went like this: Maine islands are home to two kinds of people: out-of-state summer people who maintain private estates that exclude other Mainers, and quaint but hopelessly unrealistic types who choose to ignore greater economic opportunities on the mainland and then expect help to maintain their hopelessly uneconomic way of life. Legislators did not appear to have much sympathy for either group.

I like to think that publishing three decades of *Island Journals* has helped shine a light on the tenacity of islanders who have protected Maine's island culture and inspired a broad cross section of the state's residents about the importance of this heritage. Not just because the islands attract out-of-state tourists with extra dollars to spend, but because islanders have passionately and successfully defended their small communities and island way of life in spite of the long odds they face.

For a time in the 1980s, Maine's remote islands and coast were used by drug importers, a group of whom were apprehended in Bremen while unloading large bales of marijuana

Islands and Development

Maine's island culture remains intact in spite of the blandishments of seasonal residential development, and not because of it, as in so many other island places around the country and the world. All you have to do is to look slightly to windward—to places like Martha's Vineyard and Nantucket—to see where Maine's island communities might be headed. Or to the islands of the Outer Banks of North and South Carolina, the Georgia Sea Islands, Florida's Keys and Ten Thousand Islands; or the San Juans in Puget Sound, or Santa Catalina off Southern California, where one independent island culture after another has been punctured or broken.

Many island communities elsewhere in America were simply swallowed whole, like exceptionally sweet oysters. Route 1 bridge innovations broke the spine of conch culture in the Keys. On innumerable other barrier islands, bridges have enabled cheek-to-jowl beachfront cottage culture to extinguish local fishing towns. Dafuskie Island, where black islanders still spoke their own African dialect of Gullah into the 1980s, became a golfing community. Closer to home, the summer culture of Martha's Vineyard and Nantucket more closely resembles Greenwich and the Upper East Side of Manhattan than Falmouth or New Bedford.

I had a particularly memorable scrape with an island development proposal in the late 1980s, when one type of island development was mistaken for another. A friend of mine who had just earned his student pilot license suggested we take a sunset flight out over the islands of the Midcoast. We took off from Owls Head and flew east over Vinalhaven, and the islands between Stonington and Isle au Haut and saw uninhabited Marshall Island in the distance. Marshall, which had a small dirt airstrip, had recently been purchased by a developer who proposed to sell a handful of "kingdom lots" on the 1,000-acre island.

As my pilot friend circled overhead, it was obvious that the runway had just been upgraded. He went in for a closer look and decided to practice a remote landing. We landed effortlessly and got out to stretch our legs. When we heard the drone of another airplane engine coming closer and closer, we decided that discretion was the better part of valor and took off to head back toward the flying club hangar. No sooner were we airborne than a plane appeared off our tail. My pilot friend tried raising the harassing aircraft on the radio without success and decided to execute a giant aerial inside circle maneuver that put us on the pursuing plane's tail until it peeled off and disappeared over the horizon.

Just as we were on our final approach at Owls Head, I noticed the plane had reappeared on our tail. It landed closely behind us and followed us over to the hangar. When the student pilot cut the engine, a pair of very angry border agents from the Drug Enforcement Agency appeared at each of our doors with drawn weapons. The student pilot had been on the wrong radio frequency and they were not at all amused by his aerial stunt. They were also convinced that we had visited Marshall Island to retrieve a load of contraband, which for a short time during the late 1980s and early 1990s had been a secondary island development scheme for uninhabited, remote islands.

Is There Any Real Estate for Sale?

Seasonal development is initially a boon to isolated communities, bringing in extra dollars and fellowship. But in time, darker realities intrude. Those in the booming service economy, particularly younger couples, soon cannot afford island property. The cost of service jobs spirals upward. Property taxes escalate. Waterfront access becomes increasingly scarce for commercial fishermen and boatbuilders as one wharf after another changes hands to be used for a few months a year.

Traditionally accessible beaches are posted with NO TRESPASSING signs. Resentments build between islanders and summer people. Even island conservation becomes a double-edged sword; as more land is conserved, the price per acre of unrestricted land skyrockets further. The most recent summer residents often become the most ardent supporters of new restrictions on development and acquisition of new conserva-

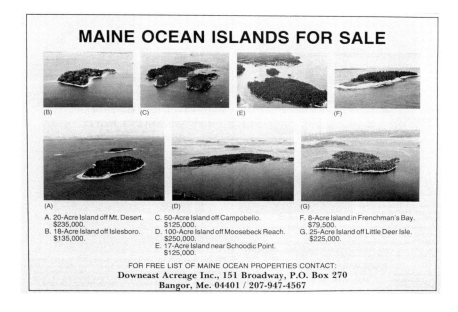

Ad from Down East magazine, ca. 1982

tion lands. To cynical islanders, this looks like pulling up the ladder, as it were, as soon as you are safely aboard.

In a manner analogous to the vast number of biological extinctions that have occurred on islands, a large number of indigenous island communities around the country, and indeed, around the globe, have also gone extinct—and most of them during the last 50 years.

Summah People—Some Ahrn't

The paradox is that as much as the islands have been transformed by the summer "trade," Maine islanders also need their summer people and other mainland friends to help sustain them as the next century unfolds. So it is important that everyone understands one another. Most of this book is intended to describe island history and culture to people who are not native to these communities. But it is also important for native islanders to understand the potential of new recruits to their communities.

My wife's family bought an old white elephant of a place four decades ago on Vinalhaven. She was still a teenager the first summer when they began the long and laborious renovation process. Although the house had been abandoned for twenty years, the windows had remained intact until just before my wife's family arrived for the summer, and then every window in the house was broken. Decades later she learned that a group of island boys had hurled rocks through the windows because they believed my wife and her girlfriends had slighted them at the swimming quarry the previous summer.

There are probably more jokes about summer people circulating through Maine island and working waterfront communities than blonde jokes or lightbulb jokes in most other communities. We all love to tell stories on summer people ("Why do all the fishermen in the harbor park their boats facing in the same direction?" . . . etc.). The sly humor in these jokes and stories reinforces the sense of place among those whose fami-

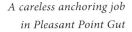

A careless anchoring job in Pleasant Point Gut

Summer event on
Great Cranberry Island

lies have the distinction of long histories (and memories) and who have consciously chosen the privations of year-round living in cold and economically stressed conditions over greater opportunities elsewhere.

These amusements have almost evolved into various forms of folk wisdom as we parse the status accorded to various sub-populations. When my wife told a neighbor that our four boys would be natives even though their parents were not, the neighbor repeated a line often heard by people from away: "Just because a cat has kittens in the oven don't make 'em muffins." On Vinalhaven, "fish hawks" is the islanders' term for natives returning to the island for the summer. "Year-round summer people" is the term used on many islands for transplants, who have decided to live and raise their children in the communities where their parents and/or grandparents summered. "Summer natives" are those multigenerational people who have been assimilated into an island community to help run the gamut of historical societies, churches, and other community nonprofits that help sustain year-round life.

In Maine, "Never" Takes Seven Years

When I was in forestry school, a professor of mine who had a lifelong history of introducing innovative approaches to tradition-bound forest management companies in Maine provided a lesson about how change occurs in Maine. The first time he was told that a certain new technique would "never" be adopted in Maine, it took about 10 years later to be assimilated. The second time, his proposed new approach took about six years to be implemented, and finally, a third innovation occurred in about three years. From this, he wryly remarked, "In Maine, on average, 'never' takes seven years."

So the question remains—are summer people a blessing or a curse? Or neither? Or both?

Summer people moving to coastal and island communities unquestionably skew local economies by increasing the prices of waterfront property and pushing up shorefront taxes for those few Mainers still fortunate enough to own waterfront land. But there are positive sides to summer people that Maine's small communities along the coast sometimes ignore. Of course, they bring wallets and checkbooks drawn on incomes from away. But far more important and overlooked is that summer people get attached to the communities where they live seasonally. As they get older (and wealthier), they stay longer. They winterize their homes; they come for Thanksgiving and Christmas. They frequent local libraries (and support their annual funds), they attend community theater events, and in the process they become more committed to their adopted communities. When many of them retire (often early) to those same communities, we tend to ignore them. After all, they are from away.

We ignore the potential of this group of deeply committed, year-round summer people at our peril. Our worst fear is that if we give these people half a chance to get involved in the dynamics of community life, they will try to change things to look like the places they just left in order to avoid. On Swan's Island, this truism is referred to as "Marky's Law," after Mark Stanley, who first gave it a local voice.

Although Marky's Law is not an irrational fear, few people come to Maine for the long dark winter to take over from local folks. They come, instead, because they are attracted to places where people are still "real." Where you can have a respectful, often amusing, always interesting conversation with your car mechanic, plumber, carpenter or lobsterman; where life revolves around school plays, community musicals, hymns by the choir, potluck suppers. They come, in short, to be part of the pulse and pace of small-town life. And they bring energy, professional talent, resources and connections.

High school and middle school students commuting on the morning boat from Chebeague

Islesboro students headed to an inter-island prom on North Haven

Maine currently has the oldest population of any state. This is not only because young people continue to leave for better job opportunities elsewhere (fewer than used to, but still a sadness), but also because the boomers who are beginning to retire in record numbers are attracted to the kinds of small American towns that used to be so prevalent half a century ago, but have been mostly swallowed up in suburban sprawl where you don't know your neighbors and where the corner store long ago became a discount chain outlet.

It should be possible to harness this potential human energy and apply it to the problems facing coastal and island communities, including the problems of affordable community housing and working waterfront access these non-natives helped to create. In the process, I bet we will also find library volunteers, technology consultants, business development specialists, fund raisers, great substitute teachers, and even, now and again, a new community leader or two.

Schools That Hold Island Communities Together

Islanders who might not agree on much else instinctively know that schools are the glue that holds their communities together. As we saw on Chebeague, islanders ultimately voted to secede from the mainland district when the mainland school board threatened to close down Chebeague's elementary school. Twenty-five years ago, the state of island education was precarious. After heartbreaking setbacks but with dogged perseverance, the strategy worked. In the late 1990s, Matinicus kept its school open even though there were no children enrolled until a new generation of young people could fill the gap.

Frenchboro's story is clearly the most dramatic along the entire archipelago. French-

Small schools conference, Isle au Haut; Frenchboro school students

boro's one-room school was down to a single student when islanders seized on a plan to build new houses to attract settlers to repopulate the school. The seven new houses were slow to fill, but eventually they all sold—several of them to the grandchildren and grand-nieces of David and Sandy Lunt. Some islanders also credit Frenchboro's schoolteacher with helping to turn the social tide, first in the school and eventually on the rest of the island. "She taught children always to look people in the eye and to introduce themselves and shake their hands," islander Rob Stuart told me about one teacher. Although islanders had always waved to each other when driving by, some islanders had avoided simple eye contact in other contexts, especially with people they did not know well. From that simple step, other changes began to happen. One of the schoolteachers, Becky Lenfesty, remembers her first baby shower. "People I did not even know came. They just wanted to hold the baby to see a new life on the island," she said.

As the echo of the echo of the baby boom continued on Frenchboro, Becky, who has three children herself, decided to start a preschool program in 2003 to help youngsters develop the kind of social skills that are important, especially in the small, multiaged teaching environment of Frenchboro's one-room schoolhouse. Two of David Lunt's grandsons, Nate and Zach and a granddaughter, Kristy, all had children in school or pre-school and were then among the 10th generation of Lunts who have lived on the island. When I visited the school in 2008, I was charmed by students in the younger grades who lined up to introduce themselves and looked me right in the eye as I met Austin, Myron, Amber, Elijah, Hannah, Saylor, Teressa and Brody.

Also key to Frenchboro's revitalization has been the community's willingness to address difficult cultural problems. As Alan Davis described it, "I remember a lot of the older fishermen. It was a pretty rough place. They came in from fishing, bought their bottles and drank until they ran out of money and then went fishing again," he said. "Sternmen can earn $30–40,000 in a season of fishing. That's a lot of money for a young kid, and some of them wanted to raise a lot of hell. There was alcoholism and drug abuse. It's been flushed out of Frenchboro. The Church had a lot to do with it."

Frenchboro certainly faces challenges as it moves into the future. One islander described the community as being "like a helicopter with 40 different pieces moving in different directions, but somehow it flies." Clearly Frenchboro has a future, and it is captured in a collective sound, says Becky Lenfesty. "All the older people say they know when it's 11 o'clock when the kids get out for lunch because they can hear the kids laughing and shrieking outside. It's the sound of youth!"

Information Technology to Reduce Isolation

Recently, island schools received a boost from an unexpected source. Beginning in

2004, the National Science Foundation recognized the quality of island education by awarding participating island and remote coastal schools with one of their most highly competitive grants—totaling $2.5 million over five years—to encourage middle and high school students to pursue information technology careers.

Ruth Kermish-Allen of the Island Institute helped design the program, based on the islands' strong tradition of place-based education strategies as a launching pad for teaching computer mapping (GIS), digital storytelling (iMovies) and website development skills. Someday these talented students may well bring these skills back to their communities as IT professionals when the digital world flips the paradigm of geographic isolation as a disadvantage to a digital place-based advantage. Heather Knight, Islesboro's school principal, considers the technology education program a good example of how to engage kids in authentic learning. "This is the biggest example we have of what education is supposed to look like," she says.

For the past 15 years islanders have invested heavily in their schools. During the most recent decade, Vinalhaven completed a new K–12 school, with a performing arts center and a fabulous library significantly financed with private funds, which now anchors the heart of the island community. North Haven more recently built another new K–12 school in a community that has long been a national model for innovation in placed-based education. Islesboro completely renovated its school and has attracted mainland students who commute across West Penobscot Bay, seeking to benefit from the island school's small class sizes, excellent teachers and demanding curriculum.

Ruth Kermish-Allen, education director, Island Institute; Island students and teachers at CREST summer institute

The remaining island schools—most of them one-room schoolhouses—have also continued to invest in better paid teachers, teacher housing, curriculum development and videoconferencing equipment. Collectively the 13 island communities with schools have invested well over $40 million in capital expenditures for new facilities and technology.

Twenty years ago, relatively few island students went off to college, and among those who did, fewer graduated with a four-year degree. The culture shock of leaving the security of a nurturing island town and living in a college community was often too intense. I remember one group of four islanders who graduated from an island high school a number of years ago and went off to college; three were back on-island by Christmas. So the Institute recently launched a mentoring program at the University of Maine and a website and Facebook account to help island students connect with their island peers from around the archipelago and to contend with the pressure cooker of college life. Today island communities have a higher percentage of college graduates than the state or nationwide average.

Another important ingredient in island student's success is the large increase in scholarship support for islanders from many sources, including the Island Institute and the Maine Seacoast Mission. The Institute recently launched the first "Island Partner Scholarship:" $5,000 to the most outstanding island student on his or her way to college, with a $2,500 award to the runner-up. These awards recognize students who have combined "civic leadership and community involvement with academic achievement." The first award went to a student headed to Brown University. This student, Zachary "Buoy" Whitener, was a self-employed lobsterman on Long Island and an elected town representative to his political party's state caucus. He was also president of the Junior Classical League, captain of the rugby team, and an honors student at Portland High School. He reflected on his island education, saying, "Islands create an atmosphere of both independence and dependence; learning to rely on oneself while reaping the benefits of a close community is an important part of growing up." Danielle Rich of Chebeague Island was most appreciative of the close student ties. "We were 'island kids' to the core. We were all friends. We spent summers on the beach together, went to each other's birthday parties and played tag at recess," she said. "There were only seventeen kids that made up grades one through three and we're as close as brothers and sisters."

As of 2010, 650 island students have received Institute scholarships totaling over three-quarters of a million dollars to attend 128 institutions of higher education in 27 states across the country. Clearly island schools are preparing students to succeed anywhere.

Offshore Connections

A friend of mine used to observe that islands are great places to live during all phases of one's life except one—when you are a teenager—the age when Paradise Island turns almost overnight into Alcatraz. That is why teenagers will continue to leave their islands to see the world.

The fundamental question is whether those who leave will have the desire, skills and determination to return to their island communities after they complete their education and taste some of the freedoms the world offers. If island schools remain vibrant places to learn, many young islanders will certainly return to raise families, provided that they also can find an affordable place to live and a way to put food on the table. Amid the challenges and privations of island life, if island schools continue to provide small classes and individual attention focused on helping every child succeed in her chosen path, not only will young islanders return, but other young families may also decide to migrate there as well. In every sense of the issue, today's island kids hold the islands' future in their hands—and the quality of island schools is the most important determinant of whether the islands will survive.

A major technology investment coordinated recently by the Island Institute resulted in the installation of videoconferencing units in every single island school. The six smallest island schools, on Cliff, Monhegan, Matinicus, Isle au Haut, Frenchboro and Islesford, can now take classes they choose with each other. A teacher on Matinicus can specialize in math and science while another on Monhegan can offer English or history. Instead of a classroom with two students, island kids might be in a class with a dozen island students from across the archipelago. Who knows; someday they may be in the same classroom with kids from an Alaskan or North Carolina island, or an island in Micronesia.

We are learning how to reduce the social "costs" of education on remote island communities, while celebrating the undeniable benefits of helping to shape creative, engaged and unique island voices and leaders. If there is one lesson we learned in the second half of the 20th century, it is that the value of a network—especially an island network—increases exponentially with the numbers of those who are connected.

Only connect!

CREST summer institute for students and teachers focused on information technology training

North Haven Island Fellow, Emily Graham, part
of the original Island Fellows cohort in 2000
with one of her students;
Island Fellows, Keely and Mike Felton, North
Haven and Vinalhaven Fellows, 2001-2003;
Island Fellows 2010-11

An Extra Set of Hands—Island Fellows

The goal of the Penobscot Bay Marine Resource Collaborative, which the Island Institute coordinated between 1996 and 2001, was to understand the ecology of lobster distribution. An unexpected result was the participation of over 150 lobstermen. Lobstermen from up and down the coast took young research interns aboard their boats and shared detailed observations about their fishery—something we never thought possible. This collaboration between young scientists and fishermen helped reveal important clues about the structure of the lobster population, which many scientists feared was on the verge of collapse from overfishing, but which lobstermen viewed as robust and healthy.

The program succeeded because these recent college graduates were on the lobstermen's turf, and they were not experts; they simply recorded information that lobstermen chose to share. So we wondered, what if we placed recent college graduates, trained to listen to islanders, to live year-round in island communities and to work on local priorities? Thus was born the wonderfully successful Island Fellows program.

Since its inception in 1999, the Island Institute has placed over 80 Island Fellows in 22 different island and working waterfront communities, to work in island schools, town offices, libraries, arts and music programs, historical societies and lobster co-ops. In addition to their "day jobs," Island Fellows have become part of the community fabric. They have coached soccer teams, baked pies for community suppers, acted in community plays, joined bands and volunteered for town events. Approximately 10 Island Fellows have become permanent members of island communities and now a half-dozen babies (junior Fellows!) have helped sustain the next generation of island life. Of the second cohort of Island Fellows, the North Haven Island fellow, Keely Grumbach, married the Vinalhaven Island Fellow, Mike Felton, who taught an aspirations course for middle school students for two years, before eventually being hired as the principal for the new Vinalhaven K–12 School. The fellows have been well received. "They excite the kids and make them want to learn more," said Vinalhaven lobster fisherman Walter Day. "When I was in school, all kidding aside, the average age of teachers was 60 or 70."

Emily Graham, who had recently graduated with a master's degree in library science, was one of the first Island Fellows. During her two-year fellowship she was hired to be the school librarian at the North Haven School to help the school win accreditation. She stayed an additional year to work as the computer teacher. "Those kids . . . I worked for three years for those kids," she said, "to give

them a view of the larger world, perspective to prepare for college and a stronger sense of self, of who they are and what they can offer the world."

Cherie Galyean, who grew up spending summers on Great Cranberry, spent her island fellowship working successfully to digitize the Vinalhaven school library collection. "I learned the value of showing up," she said. "A potluck supper can't build community if people don't turn out; it's just an empty table. A Fourth of July parade is not a celebration if no one is watching or parading. Showing up is the simple key to a community's success. And in my experience, no one shows up like they do on islands."

Island Fellow Morgan Witham, who stayed on Isle au Haut after her two-year fellowship, asked herself why, as a 20-something Maine native, she was not living in Portland. "The best answer I've found so far is that living on Isle au Haut demands I be unapologetically human," she said. "Every day I experience the highs, lows, and muddy in-between. It affords me plenty of time alone, but there is no hiding from the complexities, trespasses, kindnesses and contradictions of my friends and neighbors. Or from my own."

Maine Islands Coalition

Like all traditional communities, Maine islands have well-developed centers of authority. Only sometimes they are not the ones you would expect. Selectmen and -women are the ostensible leaders, but frequently the more deeply rooted sources of authority operate through proxies and are otherwise invisible to outsiders.

The first effort by islanders to organize across island territorial lines was called the "Inter-Island League." It was formed in the early 1990s by a group of Casco Bay Island-

Rob Snyder, executive vice president of the Island Institute; Hannah Pingree of North Haven followed her mother into politics

ers who were worried by the island real estate boom of the late 1980s, as exemplified by the condominium development on Great Diamond Island. They reached out with the help of the Island Institute staff to other islanders in Penobscot Bay and Downeast. But because these island "leaders" were self-selected, their ability to speak for others in their communities was limited. Furthermore, since all the Casco Bay islands at that time were governed from the mainland, their political pressure points were different than for the rest of the independently governed island communities. Thus the Inter-Island League slowly withered away.

The Maine Islands Coalition, however, arose organically at the end of a conference organized by the Institute in 2003 for islanders who wanted to find ways to create affordable island housing. They were worried that rising real estate prices were driving young people away and making it difficult to attract new families.

Rob Snyder, who became the Institute's vice president for programs in 2004 and executive vice president in 2010, worked with islanders to shape the new coalition. Rob came to Maine via China where he was an aspiring PhD student. One day he realized that he could spend his entire adult life studying rural Chinese life and still miss the important nuances that signal how Chinese communities actually operate. So Rob and his wife-to-be, Cathy Caveny, decamped from China and moved back to New England where Cathy had grown up. Then they implemented a "three-hour rule." They drew a circle from Cathy's hometown in New Hampshire with a three-hour driving radius and began looking for work beyond that circle. Thankfully, the Maine coast east of Brunswick was on the map where they started looking.

Rob worked with the first chair of the Maine Islands Coalition, Roger Berle of Cliff Island, who had helped develop the coalition's bylaws. Berle and other Institute staff worked with selectmen from island towns to encourage them to appoint formal representatives to the group. The coalition set up two subcommittees to draft recommendations both for the Maine legislature—where Hannah Pingree of North Haven had followed her mother into politics and become an impassioned island advocate—and for the Island Institute. The two subcommittees focused on island affordable housing and protecting working waterfronts.

Working Waterfront Coalition

In a 2005 report, *The Last 20 Miles*, the Island Institute conducted an inventory of working waterfront parcels in every town and island on the coast of Maine. We carefully documented the 869 parcels of land that collectively comprise the last 20 miles of working waterfront access along the Maine coast and islands. Only 81 of these parcels had all-tide, deepwater frontage, access to fuel and parking space—the characteristics that define the most valuable parcels. Sixty-nine of these properties are privately owned, rendering them most vulnerable to conversion for seasonal and/or recreational yachting purposes.

A 2005 statewide vote, informed by *The Last 20 Miles* report, amended the Maine constitution to enable local towns to tax commercial fishing properties at a lower rate. This constitutional act is the most significant change in state policy during my lifetime affecting Maine's 15 island and 127 working waterfront communities. It was followed by a series of additional votes to approve a series of bond issues to fund the protection and acquisition of significant working waterfront parcels.

The publication of *The Last 20 Miles* also became the rallying point for the emergence of the Working Waterfront Coalition, a cross section of marine and commercial trade associations, along with the Maine Islands Coalition, which banded together

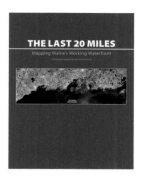

The Island Institute's working waterfront report that helped change Maine's constitution and begin the protection of the coast's working waterfronts; Intensive waterfront development in Portland Harbor led to a successful campaign to protect the state's largest working waterfront

"I Want to Thank My Grandfather and Father for Not Selling Out"

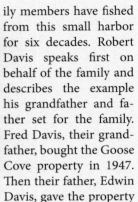

AUGUST 9, 2009—On a sunny day at noontime, over 150 lobstermen along with their families, neighbors, state officials and working waterfront activists, gathered at the Davis Wharf in Goose Cove, Tremont, for a lunch of family-prepared lobster rolls and chowder to celebrate the first working waterfront easement placed on a commercial fishing wharf by a Maine fishing family.

This event is one of the few conservation celebrations in my memory among the many notable celebrations I have attended along the coast where the parking lot and roadside are dominated by bumper-to-bumper pickup trucks rather than Volvos and Lexuses .

Robert Davis, along with his brother Wayne are third-generation lobstermen whose family members have fished from this small harbor for six decades. Robert Davis speaks first on behalf of the family and describes the example his grandfather and father set for the family. Fred Davis, their grandfather, bought the Goose Cove property in 1947. Then their father, Edwin Davis, gave the property over to his two sons. "He could have sold this property and lived a comfortable life, but he didn't," Davis said. "Without his unselfish generosity we would not have this wonderful shorefront. Now Wayne and I have done the same thing for all time."

Now setting an example for their sons, whose young sons also say they want to lobster from Goose Cove, Wayne Davis sums up his feelings about this day. 'When I go to my grave, I'm going to look back and say I got something accomplished today," he said. "Today's the day I'll remember. Today's the day." Finally, Robert's son, Matt, the next generation who is fishing off this wharf, summed up his sentiment in a few succinct words: "I want to thank my grandfather and father for not selling out."

to pass the constitutional referendum and bond money. These measures passed with overwhelming public support—exceeding 70 percent approval. One of the indirect benefits of this political victory was that islanders received very dramatic confirmation that making friends on the mainland is an asset, especially in the Legislature, where counting noses in the heat of the battle is the only thing that counts.

Decline of Salmon Aquaculture

One part of Maine's working waterfront that did not thrive at the end of the 20th century was the salmon aquaculture industry.

In 1993 Swan's Island, which hosted the westernmost salmon farm on the Maine coast went bankrupt; Sonny Sprague led the effort to buy the farm at auction. With a line of credit finally negotiated from the bank that was auctioning the farm, and an agreement by the Island Institute board to guarantee the liabilities of the enterprise, the Island Aquaculture Company was in business. Sonny Sprague became the general manager, and as the Island Institute's representative to the company, I temporarily became its president. Two years later, Sonny Sprague had turned the operation around, had paid off all the loans, and ran the operation for six years until it was sold to the largest salmon aquaculture company operating at that time in Maine. By the late 1990s, salmon aquaculture had grown to a $100 million industry primarily in Washington County, second only to lobsters in the value of Maine's marine resources.

But this was also the time when large national environmental organizations began to take aim at aquaculture, which was expanding rapidly, not just in Maine, but also in many Third World countries where mangrove estuaries were being replaced on a massive scale by huge corporate shrimp farms. In Maine, the U.S. Fish and Wildlife Service proposed listing Atlantic salmon under the Endangered Species Act, which would impose steep new costs on the industry to prevent escapement. In addition, environmental groups were also concerned that the excess feed and feces that accumulated under some salmon farms where currents were sluggish or feeding practices were mechanized posed a pollution threat to otherwise pristine Maine waters. They threatened to sue in federal court if the fish farms failed to apply for special licenses required of all "point sources" of pollution. The big salmon companies—mostly multinational companies—decided to fight rather than switch tactics, and they lost. Facing large fines, increased competition from cheaper salmon imports from Norway, Scotland and Chile, and implacable opposition from lobstermen and summer people, most of the salmon companies in Maine threw in the towel and relocated operations to other countries.

Today the salmon aquaculture industry is less than half the size of its former self and only a single Canadian company maintains operations in Maine, although one of the Swan's Island farm sites at Black Island between Swan's Island and Bass Harbor continues to operate. You can argue the merits of this environmental battle from either side and not find consensus, but what is undeniable is that the largest influx of investment to perennially impoverished Washington County came to a premature end at the end of the 20th century. Nevertheless, existing salmon operations are slowly expanding their production and are a permanent part of Washington County's economy.

Island Artists along the Archipelago

Fishermen, boatbuilders and other maritime tradesmen and -women are not the only vital economic segment of Maine's island and working waterfront communities. Every island has also been defined by its artists, who are inspired by the quality of

Jamie Wyeth and his father, Andrew, at N.C. Wyeth's home, Port Clyde

(Facing) North Haven artist, Eric Hopkins; Bo Bartlett and his wife at his studio on Wheaton Island, Matinicus Ashley Bryan, at his studio, Islesford

island light and by the powerful imagery of an island's maritime traditions. A century and a half ago, Fitz Hugh Lane sailed along the Maine coast in the 1840s and pioneered the school of art called Luminism. Lane was followed by the impressionist, Childe Hassam, who painted at the Isles of Shoals. A few years later Rockwell Kent lived and painted on Monhegan, and with his fellow romantic realist George Bellows helped establish Monhegan as a major artists' colony. Later John Marin, inspired by cubism, painted on and among the islands along with other abstractionists, including Marsden Hartley on Vinalhaven and William Kienbusch on the Cranberry Isles. For the past quarter of a century, pop art icon, Robert Indiana has lived on worked on Vinalhaven.

Jamie Wyeth, son of Andrew and grandson of N. C. Wyeth, is Maine's most successful and respected island artist. He recently described the importance of Maine's islands to three generations of the Wyeth family. "In order to work, I have to isolate myself, and an island does that. It gives me focus. When I paint islands what really interests me are the communities—the inhabitants. And they are different . . . . Being alone; being able to entertain oneself produces very interesting individuals."

In order to help Maine's island artists and craftspeople to connect to a wider marketplace, Peter Ralston suggested we open a store on Main Street in Rockland in the new building we moved into in 1999, with the help of the credit card bank, MBNA, and its legendary founder, Charles Cawley. Since that time, in addition to the 100 or more Maine island artists and crafts people whose work is displayed throughout the year, the Archipelago gallery has launched shows of some of Maine's leading island artists including Bo Bartlett of Matinicus, Eric Hopkins of North Haven, and Ashley Bryan of Islesford, to mention a few.

Archipelago has also provided a mainland venue to one of the archipelago's most creative pair of entrepreneurs—Steve and Kate Schaffer of Isle au Haut. Having fetched up on Isle au Haut from California, via Bucksport, with an interest in

culinary arts and searching around for a way to make a living, they decided to become chocolatiers. And what chocolate they have produced from their tiny kitchen (about to expand) out in the woods of Isle au Haut, at the foot of a mountain called Black Dinah, which became the inspiration for Black Dinah Chocolatiers. When Martha Stewart profiled their product in a recent Valentine's Day edition of her magazine, Black Dinah had arrived at the edge of success as they struggled to meet the surging demand for their chocolate and also stay rooted on Isle au Haut.

Island Indicators

In addressing the question of how the islands are doing from an objective point of view, we began to scour public databases for quantitative information. The result is a series of publications, *Island Indicators,* which monitor key indices of Maine island life. Island indicators, of course, are just that—they are suggestive, not definitive statements about conditions of island life. Here are a few highlights:

After the 2000 U.S. Census figures were first released, overall island populations increased between 1990 and 2000 by 7 percent. Of the 13 islands where individual island data is available, populations were stable or grew on eight of them. The increases were on Isle au Haut (50%), North Haven (17%), Peaks (16%), Vinalhaven (11%), Islesboro (6%), and Chebeague (5%). Long Island and Cliff were stable over this period. Populations declined slightly on Swan's, Frenchboro and Matinicus and quite decidedly on Monhegan and the Cranberry Isles. Most of this decline was on Great Cranberry not Islesford.

The median age of all but one island community—North Haven—is higher than the average for the State of Maine, whose average age already is the nation's highest. It is important to realize that in some cases the skewed age structure can represent the addition of recent retirees who contribute significantly to island activities as well as an absence of younger people. The oldest populations in 2000 were found on Great Cranberry, Chebeague, Monhegan and Matinicus.

Islanders are decisively better educated than the rest of Maine—89 percent of islanders had a high school education as of 2000, compared to 85% in Maine overall. We should note that Maine ranks near the top of the nation in the percentage of high school graduates. In terms of higher education, 32 percent of islanders have college degrees, while only 23 percent of all Mainers are as well educated. Islanders are also great patrons of their libraries. The average library circulation in Maine's small communities is approximately five books per capita. All eight island communities for which statistics were available reflect circulation rates at least twice that high. Monhegan's figure of

Kate Schaffer, with her husband Steve, started Black Dinah Chocolatiers on Isle au Haut

40 books per capita is the highest among the islands, followed by Islesford, Great Cranberry and Islesboro.

Based on median household income in 2000, most island communities are less wealthy than Maine overall, which trails the U.S. average by over 10 percent. Nine island communities trail Maine's median household income; the lowest average household incomes are reported on Isle au Haut, Monhegan, Swan's and Cliff. The highest median incomes—all above the state average—are on Peaks, North Haven, Islesford and Islesboro.

If we look at where islanders earn their incomes, it should come as no surprise that lobster fishing and tourism are the islands' two most important economic drivers. But the concentration on so few industries is troubling. Some islands, notably Monhegan, Isle au Haut and the Cranberry Isles, had exceptionally high percentages of retail sales from summer tourism, in excess of 70 percent of their retail sales during the short season.

Another troubling indicator is that the percentage of lobster-fishing licenses as a total of overall commercial fishing licenses increased on most all islands between 2001 and 2005. Lobster licenses comprise more than 85 percent of total commercial fish licenses in 10 of the 14 year-round island communities. This reflects fishermen's growing dependency on the one remaining productive commercial fishery in inshore waters.

Monhegan forecast; Building affordable houses for the homesteading project on Frenchboro

Finally, we collected figures on the rate of increase of property valuations on Maine islands between 2001 and 2005, compared to Maine as a whole. The huge increases exceed the state average on every Maine island, with the exception of Frenchboro and Matinicus. The largest-percentage increase in property valuations occurred on Isle au Haut, Islesboro, Long, Cranberry Isles and Monhegan. The Maine State Housing Authority publishes an affordability index that compares median income with median home price. The least affordable islands are Great Cranberry, Great Diamond, Matinicus, Peaks and Swan's. Housing is more affordable, on average, only on Vinalhaven.

Interdependencies

The Maine islanders I know don't dream of a mythical 19th-century self-sufficiency, nor are they naive enough to believe they are all captains of their own ship. Successful islanders, rather, become masterful at recognizing and managing their interdependen-

Great Duck Island

cies. Health-care delivery systems will never be better on islands than on the mainland; transportation costs per family will always be higher on the water than on the mainland; some food and energy will always need to be imported. So how will islands manage?

The persistence of Maine's island communities in the face of a rising tide of cultural homogeneity is testament to a simple truth: The real and renewable wealth of the islands has been and is still found in the water. Without a healthy and productive Gulf of Maine, island communities would no doubt still exist, but it is difficult to perceive their distinction.

At the dawn of the information age, islands could easily become convenient places where writers, telecommuters and Internet entrepreneurs could out-compete native islanders for scarce resources like housing, shore privileges and education. Waterfronts might look more picked up, less chaotic than some of them do now, and there might

be plenty of seasonal jobs, paying well enough to carry islanders through the long hard winters. But such islands would be Potemkin villages. It is almost too easy to predict how well-intentioned noise and lighting ordinances under the banner of maintaining the public weal of peace and quiet might pass muster in some already-gentrified towns; and you would bet your left nostril that bait barrels would be strictly regulated. The important point is to recognize that in small communities, it doesn't take much to tip a community balance.

No one believes that the island communities of Maine will rewrite regional economic history. Markets will have their way. But when the scales start to tip toward outcomes that no one wants, an active citizenry—and their far-flung friends—need to be ready to intervene with creative and innovative strategies to create a future in which we want to live.

CHAPTER 14

Will the Islands Endure?
The Next Generation

I don't believe an island is really an island, unless it's a year-round community.
If it isn't a year-round community, it's just a piece of real estate
with some trees on it and some people that come in the summer.

—Sonny Sprague, Swan's Island

Robinson Point Light,
Isle au Haut;
Great Gott Island view

P eople still ask if Maine's island communities can really be expected to survive in the long run. Another way of framing this question is to ask whether Maine's island communities have enough significance to others beyond the relative small number of people who inhabit them year-round to avoid becoming merely seasonal enclaves of the privileged served by a highly competent class of caretakers, as has happened to so many other island communities in America.

The question has taken on additional urgency at the end of the first decade of the 21st century, when food, fuel, ferries and other energy prices have been climbing inexorably and the price of lobsters has sagged in a historically weak economy.

Because food and energy are the two largest imports to island communities—as for the state of Maine as a whole—how islands deal with these large drains on their finances will be central to the question of whether they, and the rest of Maine remain viable places to live, work and raise children.

As we have seen throughout this history, island life is economically stressed even in the best of times. Not only do almost all the basics of life cost more on islands, but the means of earning a living are also more starkly limited. And yet, most Maine island community populations have either been stable or slowly increasing during the first

decade of the 21st century. This growth comes both from a higher number of young islanders who are choosing to stay on-island after they finish their schooling, as well as from newcomers who are moving to island communities to embrace isolation. How can that be?

The answers lie in the essential quality of island life. Islands select for individuals and families that are highly adaptive to changing conditions. In the most stable of times, island environments are more tempestuous than those on the mainland. Islanders' lives are more tuned to natural rhythms than elsewhere in America. Ferries and mailboats, not to mention individual boats and vehicles, break down at the most inopportune moments. In Mother Nature's outback, you learn to develop backup plans. And when your primary and your backup plans fail, you rely on your extended family or neighbors. You hunker down; you get by; you adapt; you keep trying.

New Island Indicators

Given the inconveniences and difficulties of island life, it was reassuring to learn that preliminary census data available at the end of the first decade of the 21st century indicated that island populations have continued to increase incrementally. Since 1990, the population on Maine's islands has increased by approximately 7 percent (from 4,188 to 4,492), compared to an 8 percent increase for the state as a whole. However, the increases were not uniform—the Downeast and Casco Bay islands' population increased by 5 percent, while the Penobscot islands year-round populations decreased slightly. Much of the overall increase resulted from the return of older islanders and other retirees to these small communities, where many of them originated as natives or summer people. Although these older islanders bring resources, skills and experience

Beals Island wharf

to their island communities, the aging demographic also results from a decline in the number of school-age children on islands, which places additional pressure to justify high per-pupil costs in school budgets at town meeting.

Since 2001 housing costs and property valuations have continued to skyrocket on Maine's islands—increasing by 166 percent on the islands compared to 116 percent for Maine as a whole. This stark statistic helped lay the groundwork for a successful bond campaign mounted by the Maine Islands Coalition and organized by the Island Institute. Under the leadership of Rob Snyder, the Institute's executive vice president, and with the support of outgoing Speaker of the House, Hannah Pingree from North Haven, the Maine Legislature recommended and the voters approved a large new revenue bond for affordable housing throughout the state. This bond resulted in a special carve-out of over $2 million for Maine's island communities—a first in Maine history.

After the 2008 financial crisis, however, housing prices fell everywhere, including on the islands. If there is any silver lining to the economic pain endured by nearly everyone at the end of the first decade of the 21st century, it is that houses are slightly less unaffordable to year-round islanders. Now an islander with an average income can afford 70 percent of the purchase price of an average island house, compared with 50 percent a few years ago. This is not a huge comfort, since no one purchases part of a house, but the number of year-round houses on islands being converted to seasonal residences has at least slowed for the time being.

Also surprising in the new census data is the finding that the median income of islanders is more closely aligned with the median income of the state as a whole than at any other time in the last two decades. Undoubtedly the increase in incomes was in part a result of the large lobster landings' favorable prices for most of the decade—at least until the last few years. There is always, however, a catch-22 in reporting income figures for islanders: Because virtually all living expenses from food to energy are higher on islands, if you do not have an above-average income, the chances are that you cannot afford to live on a Maine island in the first place.

Dirigo—New Island Leaders

Dirigo—"I lead"—which is Maine's State motto, is not a phrase you are likely to hear much on islands, where those who are eager to lead are often passed over and those most reluctant to serve are called upon for thankless duty. Personalities loom larger on islands than in mainland communities. What is important is who you are, not what you propose to do. Almost every islander nurses private hurts and public grudges, which require generations to heal when the terms of polite discourse that reinforce community bonds has been stretched beyond the breaking point.

The lessons of island community life observed during the last three decades suggest that the single most important difference between those communities that are thriving and those which are not is the quality of their leadership. Why some people become good and effective leaders and others do not has been central to the curricula of every business school in America—and still there is no good textbook explanation. Humility seems to matter—except when boldly moving forward matters more. Communication skills matter, except where quirky introverts turn into brilliant leaders. In other words, we really have no idea.

John Griffin, Natalie Ames, and family, Matinicus

Successful island leaders rely on a more complex calculus for deciding who will be awarded a trash contract, for instance, or will become a code enforcement officer or chair of the school board. The qualities that matter are a mix of whether you have deep island roots—or at least a sense of important pieces of an island's history, passed on through oral traditions. Can you shoot the breeze with your least-endowed neighbors while waiting for the ferry? Can you identify those on whom the community can count from those likely to stir up trouble? Newcomers who have not absorbed the stories and myths of the community are rarely encouraged to participate.

At the end of the day, the need for islanders to fill leadership positions—even in the smallest island communities—always outstrips the supply. On Swan's Island recently, one of the community's leaders counted up the number of positions on the 25 boards and committees that the island needs to fill each year—127! For a community with a year-round population of 350, half of whom are children or elderly, there are not enough leaders to go around. On Vinalhaven, the largest island community, there are 68 boards and committees. And imagine on Matinicus or Frenchboro, where year-round populations can decline to 35 in the dead of winter; the demands on leaders are enormous.

No wonder islanders are loath to volunteer; once you have agreed to take on one civic task, the demands are almost endless. And once a community has found a successful leader to fill an important position, there is no quitting, until he or she is either entirely burned out or drops dead. For these reasons, generational transfers of leadership are much more difficult on islands than other communities. But given that the islands are facing a very large generational change, sharing strategies for training a new generation of leaders is going to be critically important.

The sections that follow include a handful of stories of those who are likely to be among the new leaders of Maine's island and working waterfront communities.

Reinventing the Maine Lobster Brand

At the beginning of the 21st century, the existing business models for catching everything from cod and haddock to lobsters has begun to change yet again. For most of the 20th century, the way that fishermen made more money was to buy bigger boats that could go farther out during a longer season to increase landings. For fishermen this strategy meant installing larger engines with more horsepower to drag bigger nets over rougher bottoms. For lobstermen it meant setting as many traps as possible with huge bait bags stuffed full of expensive herring to carpet-bomb fishing territories. But these practices have begun to change. It appears that island fishermen, from those communities supposedly notorious for resisting change, will be among the first to adapt. In the end, change and adaptation are more constant on islands than anywhere else.

Chebeague Island lobsterman, John Jordan, one of Maine's islands' new lobster leaders

Not so long ago, lobstermen and their shoreside dealers had to sort their catches into different crates depending on quality. Hard as it might be to believe, not all lobsters are created equal. First, hard-shell lobsters travel much farther through wholesale distribution channels to their final destinations, so they are worth quite a bit more than soft-shell lobsters, also known as shedders. Shedders have a tendency to die when they are shipped to destinations beyond a single day's journey. Bigger lobsters—"selects"—are worth more than the standard pound-and-a–quarter lobsters called "chicks." One-clawed lobsters—"pistols"—and damaged lobsters—"culls"—are worth still less. I could go on, but you get the idea.

As Maine's lobster harvests began to increase steadily throughout the 1990s, lobstermen and their dealers began to ship an increasing number of their lobsters east to Canadian processing plants, especially after shedders traditionally struck in July. The Canadian processing plants, which are subsidized by the Canadian government, were only too happy to buy Maine lobsters, regardless of quality. The Canadian plants had huge processing capacity and had begun aggressively expanding their markets for lobster tails, claws and other processed lobster meat by selling to the booming cruiseship industry and large restaurant chains like Red Lobster and abroad to Europe.

Inevitably, "crate-run" sales to Canada became a normal business practice for the Maine lobster industry. And why not? Even though the price in Canada was lower than other markets, lobstermen and dealers saved money because they no longer needed to sort their lobsters into different grades, nor did they have to spend time finding different markets for all the different sorts of lobster. "Marketing" lobsters became a matter of loading 18-wheeled trucks with 40-foot trailers and sending them across the border—more and more each year until at the peak, upwards of 70 percent of Maine's lobsters were sold to Canadian dealers and processors. Everyone was making money, almost quite literally hand over fist.

But a not-so-funny thing happened on the way to the market—or the way back to the market, as the case may be. Because most of the Maine lobsters sent to Canada were re-exported back to the U.S., Maine's lobsters came back as Canadian lobsters or Atlantic lobster, or simply as some generic lobster. Slowly but surely, one of the most valuable brand identities in the western world—the Maine lobster—began to lose its image in consumers' minds.

Then a really unfunny thing happened. Because Canadian processors buy Maine lobsters when they are cheapest, during the summer and early fall when supplies flood the market, and sell during the fall and winter, they depended on short-term loans to finance the inventory. The cheapest financing available during the first decade of the 21st century came from Icelandic banks. When Lehman Brothers went bankrupt and the financial industry was driven to its knees, the Icelandic banks failed and the Canadian processors could not get short-term financing. The result was that the market for a vast swath of Maine lobsters evaporated almost overnight.

Truth be told, there were other complications to this story, including the fact that high winter prices for lobster when supplies are lowest had already encouraged the biggest customers of Maine (now Canadian) lobster to substitute cheaper shrimp imports from around the world. But the result was that by 2007–2008, Maine lobstermen could only get $2 a pound for lobster—the lowest price in 20 years. Younger lobstermen, often heavily mortgaged for large new boats and gear, had never even dreamed of prices that low.

John Jordan (on left) with Chebeague fishermen and Stonewall Kitchen chefs -owners, Jim Stott and Jonathan King, who helped the lobster company develop new products

Calendar Islands Maine Lobster—A New Business Model

One of the few positive results of the dawning recognition that Maine lobsters had lost their brand identity was a willingness among some lobstermen to talk for the first time about investing in new marketing and branding strategies.

One of these groups of lobstermen is from Chebeague Island in Casco Bay. Their leader was John Jordan, a college-educated lobsterman with an entrepreneurial streak and son of a summer family gone native. He convinced fellow lobstermen in Chebeague's lobster co-op that the only way they were going to control their economic fate would be to invest more in their business and market more of their own product.

The group's first investment was to buy their own bait company. This might strike those unfamiliar with the business as an odd place to begin. But as fishermen will tell you, lobstermen do not catch lobsters, bait does. And nothing binds a lobsterman to his dealer more tightly than bait. No bait, no lobsters; but also, no lobsters, no bait—a not-so-subtle way dealers have of controlling fishermen who might want to sell even a portion of their catch to someone else and then discover bait is no longer available.

Next Jordan and his colleagues secured a lease for a place on the Portland waterfront where they could sort their lobsters into different grades and begin finding their own markets. Jordan talked with some of Chebeague Island's "summer natives," businesspeople who appeared sympathetic to the new company's plans to market and brand their own lobsters. With the advice and then financial support from some of Chebeague's successful businessmen and -women, and from the Island Institute, Jordan explored lobster markets more deeply. This included establishing a relationship with Stonewall Kitchen, a successful food-marketing business, founded in York, Maine, two decades ago. Stonewall Kitchen gave the group access to their test kitchens and their experienced team of chefs, where ultimately seven new lobster products, branded as Calendar Islands Maine Lobster, have been developed, including lobster pizza and lobster pot pie. These products have begun to appear in places like Hannaford supermarkets and other retail chains.

Part of this "story" is that the lobstermen are deriving an additional share of their income from these retail sales. Their business model, if it's successful, aims to handle upwards of 15 or 20 percent of Maine's lobsters a year.

Linda Bean's Perfect Maine Lobster

The other person who seemed to take the lessons of the lobster industry downturn seriously was Linda Louise Bean, granddaughter of Leon Leonwood Bean (known as L.L. to the rest of the world), founder of Maine's other great retail brand. In 2008, the Bean heiress launched her own vertically integrated lobster company, "Linda Bean's Perfect Maine Lobster." Never one to avoid controversy, Linda Bean has recently bought up five lobster-buying stations in the Penobscot Bay lobstering communities of Vinalhaven, Owls Head, Tenants Harbor and Port Clyde, built a freezer plant and bait cooler on Vinalhaven, and promised never to buy Canadian lobsters. Then she contracted with a Rockland processing plant to package retail products, including her own lobster stew, flash-frozen lobster claws, and other lobster products that she intends to wholesale to upwards of 2,000 grocery stores throughout the country. And if that

were not ambitious enough, she has opened the first five of what she projects to be 100 franchised mini restaurants offering Linda Bean's Perfect Maine Lobster Roll.

Whether Bean will be as successful as her grandfather remains to be seen. But the big difference between Linda Bean's Perfect Maine Lobster company and Calendar Islands Maine Lobster—both of which are based on a vertical-integration business model to achieve greater financial success in the industry—is that island lobstermen, who have taken part of the risk, will own part of the Calendar Islands company, while Linda Bean, who took all the risk, will also reap all the rewards.

Investing in Sustainable and Diverse Fisheries

Ultimately the future survival of the Maine islands depends on diversifying beyond the dangerous overreliance on the lobster fishery to revitalize other fisheries. It is important to remember that as many codfish were caught sustainably year after year within sight of Mount Desert Island in the 1860s as currently exist in the entire Gulf of Maine. The capacity of the Gulf of Maine to produce cod and haddock and flounder has not failed; it is just that our technology to catch fish has outgrown our ability to manage ourselves.

(Facing) Adam Campbell
and daughters harvest
oysters from Mill Pond,
North Haven;
Glen Libby helped
convince Port Clyde
fishermen to invest
in a new brand

In conservation history, the late 20th century will be remembered as the era when, to resort to a terrestrial metaphor, we ate our seed corn. In fishery after fishery, we have succeeded in catching the veritable next-to-last fish, mostly because we did not know any better.

Overfishing, however, has a long history in the Gulf of Maine. The halibut fishery was the first in the region to collapse in the 19th century with technology no more advanced than baited hooks on trawl lines. The mackerel fishery was also depleted from overfishing, also in the late 19th century. The population of halibut, a slow-growing, modestly reproducing species, has never fully recovered; mackerel did, largely because there is no longer enough consumer interest in it to support a significant commercial fishery in the Gulf.

Herring once were caught in weirs and stop seines in island coves all along the coast, keeping large gangs of local fishermen employed. But this is another fishery that has disappeared from inshore waters during my lifetime. Then there was the gold rush in harvesting urchins and a boom in the fishery for glass eels returning from the Sargasso Sea.

Unlike Newfoundland, we have not yet reached the end of the road, where quite literally whole communities have simply been "removed" from the landscape, leaving empty houses behind as if a neutron bomb had gone off. But nevertheless we have suffered terrible losses.

The point is to remind ourselves that healthy island fisheries are a renewable resource. No coast should live without productive local fisheries; indeed, we cannot live for long without them. They represent a true and replenishable source of wealth—not just in economic terms, but also in cultural terms. The fisheries are ancient and enduring symbols of independence and of a heritage and lineage from which we turn away as exiles flee their homeland. And in more practical terms, there is no immutable biological reason that we cannot expect to recapture the immense bounty of fish that the inshore waters of the Gulf of Maine once sustained. We have gotten so used to lowered expectations from this legendary source of wealth that we have forgotten that it ever existed. We need to remember and to imagine what a restored inshore fishery could look like, because the immense productivity of the rocky bottoms and basins of the Gulf of Maine has not diminished. And the sea still laps at our feet, beckoning some of us to set out for the prospect of promise and heartache.

In the meantime, the question is how to revive the fisheries without killing the remaining fishermen and communities that depend on them. To fish or not to fish, that is the question.

Port Clyde Fresh Catch—"We Were Sick of No Fish"

In 1991 an environmental group called the Conservation Law Foundation (on whose board I serve) filed a lawsuit seeking an end to overfishing in New England. It was a swallow-hard moment for a small group of advocates who dared sue the federal government. To everyone's surprise, the National Marine Fisheries Service quickly agreed that the agency had failed to conserve the region's fisheries and signed a consent decree, which included a plan to rebuild stocks of cod, haddock and other groundfish in New England waters. We dusted off our hands and congratulated ourselves on a job well done.

But sadly, after nearly two decades of ceaseless wrangling, the most noticeable accomplishment of the new regulations has been to push smaller fishing vessels out of the fishery. By 2005 there was not a single active ground fishermen based in any port between Port Clyde and the Canadian border. You cannot buy a fresh groundfish off a boat anywhere between Rockland and Eastport. The curious system now in place rewards the biggest, least-conservation-oriented vessels—called "roving bandits" by some academics—that can fish anywhere throughout the Gulf of Maine and the outer banks, at the expense of community-based vessels that have lacked political representation at the decision making level.

Into the midst of this unfolding tragedy, Glen Libby, a fisherman from Port Clyde and his brother, Gary, had an idea. So they sat down the talk with "the boys," as the local fishermen call themselves. "We were sick of no fish," said Glen. "We needed to form an organization so that we can have a face politically." Their vision was to catch fish sustainably, create new markets, and keep Port Clyde in the fishing business.

The organization they created, the Midcoast Fishermen's Association is the east-

"The Boys," members of the Midcoast Fishermen's Association who invested in Port Clyde Fresh Catch

A deckload of
Port Clyde Fresh Catch
shrimp, with very little
bycatch after gear
modifications

ernmost fleet of groundfish vessels on the Maine coast. Initially the group consisted of a co-op of 10 local family-owned boats in Port Clyde, and with substantial support from the Island Institute, a group of fishermen have done the unthinkable: They have voluntarily increased the mesh size at their cod ends to eliminate bycatch, they have agreed to rerig their boats to be less destructive of the marine habitats where they fish; they have eliminated rock hopper and chafing gear that plug nets and kill juvenile fish; and they are experimenting with making shorter tows at slower speeds to save on fuel and to harvest higher-quality fish. In addition, several MFA boats are participating in a research program, designed in part by scientists at the Island Institute, The Nature Conservancy, and the Gulf of Maine Research Institute, to quantify how these changes make an ecological difference.

Although the management system neither recognizes nor rewards these voluntary efforts, MFA also decided to present their case directly to consumers. Again with help from the Island Institute, the fishermen set up the nation's first community-supported fishing program in 2008, whereby customers buy shares in the harvest similar to the community-supported agriculture model. Calling the CSF "Port Clyde Fresh Catch," they sold out the shares they thought they could reasonably handle and have raised substantial funds prior to going fishing. Port Clyde Fresh Catch customers pay a set price per pound for whatever comes in—cod, haddock, pollock, gray sole, or monkfish tails—for a superior product, instead of at least twice as much per pound at the supermarket. Fishermen also sell their fish at the Portland Fish Exchange where the remainder of MFA's fish is sold, but for a far lower price than at the CSF.

The ultimate test of this model will be whether it enables fishermen to catch fewer fish of higher quality with less environmental impact and to get more for it before the last community-based fleet is regulated out of existence. Many of us believe that the Port Clyde Fresh Catch model may be the basis for developing a sustainable fishing industry among the islands and coast of Maine for the 21st century.

Island Food Systems

Not only were many islands relatively self-sufficient in terms of providing their own food during the 19th century, but the larger islands actually exported food crops to urban markets in Boston, New York and Philadelphia. As Charles McLane's history of the Maine islands notes, it was a rare island that did not support a milk cow for butter and cheese, a calf for veal, a few pigs for hams, bacon and sausage, and small flocks of sheep and chickens for lamb, mutton, wool roasters and eggs. Today food and energy are the islands' largest import from mainland communities. But history shows that it does not have to be that way, especially when the costs of fossil fuel-based transportation are factored into food prices.

Toward the end of the 19th century, one of the largest and most productive Maine island farms was the Turner Farm on North Haven. North Haven's geology—and hence its soil—were highly conducive to farming. North Haven's rocks are a mixture of green-stone and green-schist units, turned up vertically by crustal movements over the eons and weathered into nutrient-rich soils. This is quite different from the scoured granite topography of Vinalhaven across the Fox Islands Thorofare—or Isle au Haut, Swan's or Frenchboro for that matter.

The first tax list of the Fox Islands published in 1784 revealed that North Haven had 68 taxpayers while Vinalhaven had only 42. Interestingly, all of Vinalhaven's ma-

Heirloom tomatoes ripening in movable greenhouse, Turner Farm, North Haven

jor farms were on the north side of the island fronting on the Fox Islands Thorofares, where soils and bedrock were similar to North Haven's. The date of the first agricultural census on the Fox Islands was also the year that Samuel and Mary Thomas arrived on North Haven from Marshfield, Massachusetts bringing their house with them in pieces. They re-erected the house on a wooded parcel with sloping south-facing fields on the east side of the Fox Islands Thorofare called Fish Point, where a large Wabanaki village would eventually be discovered by archaeologists in the mid-1970s.

The first two generations of the Thomas family on North Haven each produced ten children, and one of Samuel and Mary's great-granddaughters, Clara, married a Turner from next door. They and their descendants managed the "Turner" farm until Clara died in 1915, although the property stayed in the family until 1984.

In 2008, financier Donald Sussman, the fiancé of U.S. Rep. Chellie Pingree, who had started a farm on North Haven years earlier with her first husband, bought the Turner Farm. Since then, they have managed the property as a working farm, with pigs, chickens, turkeys, cattle, goats, three movable greenhouses, and extensive vegetable gardens. Much of the produce is sold locally at Nebo Lodge, a local restaurant and inn, and in the summer at the North Haven farmer's market. What goes round finally comes around. Also, on North Haven in 2010 were a local sheep farm, oyster farm and other farmers raising organic produce.

The Turner Farm is the largest island farm currently, but there are many others on the larger islands that sell through local farmers markets. The real challenge will be to link farms with larger wholesale distribution outlets on the mainland, because even a small farm can produce more lettuce, radishes, or other garden crops than island appetites can consume. But the pendulum is definitely swinging back toward local food (and fish) from local producers. The banner under which they all unite is "A face, a place and a taste"—buying fresh food from someone in your community.

The late Matt Simmons, who founded the Ocean Energy Institute, and his wife Ellen

Katrina Heads North—The Cost of Energy

Part of the impetus for fishermen to invest in their own distinctive local brands or for farmers to produce more island food has been the rise in fuel costs, which more than doubled in real dollars during the first decade of the 21st century. Maine fishermen and farmers see the effects of fuel costs on a daily or weekly basis: Higher costs mean lower incomes.

The late Matt Simmons, a longtime trustee of the Island Institute and founder of the Ocean Energy Institute, was a prominent oil industry analyst who came to the coast of Maine as a summer resident. He predicted that within the next dozen years the cost of diesel and heating fuels will likely exceed $10 a gallon, and that without new sources of alternative energy, Mainers would spend between a quarter and half of their income on energy.

In Maine, approximately 40 percent of our electric power is generated from natural gas turbines, an energy source that policy advocates in the 1990s successfully argued should replace the region's dirtier coal- and diesel-fired generating plants. When Katrina hit New Orleans in 2005, the shock waves from the storm surge ultimately traveled all the way "downeast" to Maine. These shock waves followed the route of a patchwork of interstate natural gas lines that link the Gulf Coast to Maine. Because the damage from Katrina interrupted the supplies of natural gas from offshore in the Gulf of Mexico, those at the farthest ends of the supply chain saw prices spike—a price shock that lasted for nearly a year.

The impact on ratepayers at the Fox Islands Electric Co-op, which serves Vinalhaven and North Haven, was severe. People already accustomed to paying more than twice the statewide average and three times the national average for their electricity saw their monthly electric bills nearly double during the winter of 2005–06. Many islanders saw their bills increase from $250 to $300, $400 and even $500 per month, according to Sonny Warren, a Vinalhaven lobsterman who serves on the electric co-op board.

Islands everywhere are small pieces of land surrounded by water; they are also everywhere surrounded by oceans of wind, and especially off the Maine coast where islanders feel not just little cat's breath wind, but everything from snapping southwesterlies to full-on gales. By harnessing the winds again, it is worth asking ourselves whether we can build island communities of the 21st century.

At the request of Maine's then Speaker of the House, Hannah Pingree of North Haven, the Island Institute convened island electric cooperatives to discuss the potential for generating electricity from the islands' abundant wind resource. Wind had powered a good deal of Maine's original wealth during the 19th century and the days of commercial sail, so the idea of harnessing island wind resources was perhaps not as radical as it was elsewhere. As a result of Maine's utilities deregulation law, however, electric generating companies and electric transmission and distribution companies had been split into separate enterprises under the theory that competition would lower prices.

A group of Vinalhaven islanders, led by Del Webster, who is descended from one

Del Webster in his electric car and Bill Alcorn who purchased the hilltop property to encourage their community to harness the island's wind resource

of the original island families, and his business partner Bill Alcorn, studied their island's wind resource, collecting hourly wind speed data from a ridge-top anemometer for three years at an abandoned quarry they purchased with the goal of establishing a wind farm. When experts at the University of Massachusetts Rural Energy Research Lab suggested Vinalhaven's wind resource was commercially viable, the local planning commission wrote an ordinance to control how that resource might be developed. Surrounded by wind, the Fox Islands and then Swan's and Frenchboro petitioned the Legislature for special permission to both generate and distribute their own power.

One of attendees of those early island electric coop meetings was George Baker, a seasonal Frenchboro resident and the volunteer treasurer of the Swan's Island Electric Co-op, who also had a day job as a professor at the Harvard Business School.

Fox Islands Wind

One of the primary reasons that there were some 300 year-round island communities off the Maine coast before the turn of the 20th century instead of today's 15 is that everything Maine produced or needed came over the water on ships rigged to catch the wind. Wind built island communities during the 19th century, providing the energy that connected Maine islands to the rest of the world.

George Baker, who left a tenured position at the Harvard Business School after 22 years to lead the Fox Island Electric Co-op's project that aimed to create energy independence and price stability for the year round residents of Vinalhaven and North Haven, quoted a maxim every business school student learns their first day: "There are no $20 bills on the ground, because if there were, someone would have already picked it up." But Baker thought the vigorous wind resource might just be a $20 bill waiting to be picked up on some Maine islands. The question was how hard it might be to pick up.

Fox Islands wind turbines, Vinalhaven; Fox Islands Wind ribbon cutting, 2009

In July 2009 island ratepayers on Vinalhaven and North Haven voted by a margin of 382-5 (over 98 percent) to go ahead with the project. As one local wit remarked, "You couldn't get that margin of vote in favor of the American flag." During the summer of 2009 three 1.5 MW turbines were erected by Cianbro Corp. on a hilltop quarry location that Webster and Alcorn had purchased for that purpose. "We have never worked in a community as supportive as this," said Chad Allen, project supervisor for Cianbro, as the turbines were going up during the summer and fall of 2009. Allen's favorite story of the incredible logistics involved with moving the enormous turbine parts from different parts of the country and the world to the wind farm site involved one turbine base section's detour on its last mile. The base section, 25 feet in diameter, was loaded on a 130-foot long specialized trailer with an articulated radio-controlled set of rear wheels to enable the rig to navigate twisting roads of Vinalhaven at between two and three miles an hour while all traffic stopped in both directions.

At the last curve in the road, the rear wheels of the trailer hit a soft spot on the shoulder and slid precariously into a ditch. Nothing was damaged, but Allen knew that it would take many hours to get a piece of equipment in place to gingerly lift the trailer out of its hole. And he was deeply upset about the inconvenience the mishap would cause to all the islanders backed up on either side of the only north-south road between the two ends of the island. You can imagine his astonishment as he noticed that islanders on either end of the immoveable traffic jam began walking toward each other and trading cars to keep headed toward their destinations. Islanders from the north end who were headed to the ferry on the south end simply traded vehicles with islanders going the other way with their groceries—melting ice cream and all. Cianbro's construction crew jumped in and helped haul everything from groceries to building supplies between vehicles on either side of the legendary traffic jam. Allen, a master logistician, had never seen anything like it.

Lifeboat Ethics

Once the turbines were up and running, there were still issues to be worked out. A handful of year-round neighbors complained bitterly about the disruption from the noise of the turbines. Their complaints resulted in front page stories in the *Maine Sunday Telegram*, the *Boston Globe* and ultimately the *New York Times*, including this quote from Cheryl Lindgren, one of the affected neighbors, ""The quality of life that we came here for was quiet. You don't live in a place where you have to take an hour-and-15-minute ferry ride to live next to an industrial park. And that's where we are right now." With their peace and quiet impaired, their retirements interrupted, their property values, they believe, compromised by "the miserable hum," it seems to these neighbors that the overall community is deriving benefits at their expense.

What went unreported in these stories was that a handful of other year-round neighbors as close or closer to the turbines reported not being bothered by the noise. A survey of island opinion after the first winter of operation determined that over 90 percent of the ratepayers on the two islands were as supportive or more supportive than when they had originally approved the project, largely because the windfarm had cut electricity bills to islanders by between 25 and 30 percent, as originally envisioned.

In the midst of the controversy over the noise from the turbines, the drama took an unexpected turn. At a March 2011 Fox Island Electric Co-op board meeting, the most aggrieved opponent of the wind project had just delivered a 50-minute presentation

View of turbines from ferry channel, Carver's Reach, Vinalhaven

During the Age of Sail, wind power helped Maine islands deliver their products to the world

on the noise issue to the directors of the co-op when he slumped over in his seat and quickly turned blue from a heart attack. One of the co-op board members leapt up and began administering CPR chest compressions and m-outh-to-mouth resuscitation to this neighbor and within a few minutes got the opponent's heart beating and undoubtedly saved his life. You could not make this kind of drama up.

It was quite literally a heart-warming moment. But different people have drawn quite different lessons from this real life drama. To many of the network of wind power opponents, both on and off island, the lesson is that the controversy around wind power risks the health—indeed the very lives—of those who live near the turbines. The blogosphere fired up quickly with a post from the heart attack victim's wife, "I feel that (he) gave his life the other night. He died for these issues, for trying to bring light to the truth. It was luck and grace that the efforts to bring him back were successful."

But others in the community drew the exact opposite conclusion from the story. To many islanders, the very nearly tragic heart attack at the Co-op meeting reinforced the lesson islanders know in their bones: that an island community is like a lifeboat and no matter who your worst enemies might currently be, community members are all in the lifeboat together and have to make accommodations in tight circumstances. Your bitterest opponent aboard might have to save your life, so it is important to keep things in perspective. "That wasn't the purpose of putting them up there to bother anybody," said lobsterman Bobby Warren who is also on the board of the electric co-op. "The purpose was to help us all."-

People who move to island communities from elsewhere often imagine their new lives will be simpler and more peaceful than in those places —usually an urban or sub-

urban community—they have left behind. But nothing could be further from the truth. The last place you should go to get away from your neighbors is an island community. City folk can choose to be anonymous and invisible; island folk never can. To be a hermit, you need your own island.

We always hope that stories of this sort have a warm ending; that people on the lifeboat will all pull together to save each other. But we are complicated creatures. How do the individual needs of a few people in a lifeboat weigh against the collective needs of all the others on board? The small minority on a lifeboat that requires the rest of their ship mates to make a sacrifice for their well being might logically fear that the majority will decide to throw them overboard with or without a life ring and their fear may make them even more unreasonable. Those pulling the oars to bring the lifeboat into a safe harbor would undoubtedly never countenance such an extreme response in ordinary circumstances, but everyone's patience is tested during the long days at sea—especially in March. In the meantime, the remaining passengers onboard scan the horizon for any hopeful sign before onboard civility is compromised further.

Whether the Fox Islands Wind project will prove to be a turning point in Maine island history—and perhaps in Maine history itself—remains to be seen. The question of whether we can build not just more island wind projects but ocean wind projects as well, and in the process, change the way we heat our homes and run our vehicles loom over us.

Many people—certainly in the wind-power industry—have firmly believed that no one could build a commercial wind farm anywhere on the New England coast, especially where there are significant numbers of well-connected summer people. At the very least, the Fox Islands Wind project has put that belief to rest.

Offshore Wind

One of the first questions that anyone asks after seeing a photograph of a barren Maine island in the 19th or early 20th century is what happened to all the trees. The simple answer is that people cut them down and used them not only to power many industries, but also as a readily available source of energy. Hard as it is to believe, the first deck loads of cordwood were being shipped from Maine to Boston by the early 1700s because the Massachusetts Bay Colony had run out of easily available fuel locally. The scarcity of fuel wood for winter heating was New England's first energy crisis three centuries ago.

Coal came to the Maine coast as an industrial fuel beginning in the 1880s, after most coastal timber had been stripped from the landscape, and a new railroad linked the coalfields of West Virginia and Appalachia with the seaport at Newport News on the Virginia coast. This new source of energy also brought wrenching economic changes. Steamships that burned coal transformed ocean transportation, driving even the fastest clipper ships into an early grave and idling wooden shipyards throughout New England. Ironically, the cheapest way to transport the huge volumes of coal needed to supply textile mills and hundreds of other manufacturing enterprises throughout the country was on specially designed "Downeasters." The four-, five-, six- and ultimately seven-masted coal schooners were launched from Maine boatyards for almost 30 years before even these sailing ships became obsolete.

The coal era ended after World War II in most of New England when we began heating our homes with oil. Most coal dealers became oil dealers. The switch to this new source of energy was expensive to those who had to replace central heating systems with new oil-fired boilers, but oil was plentiful and cheap and cleaner than coal. It was probably the least difficult energy transition the country has ever made, which has led most of us to expect that developing newer sources of energy ought to be a relatively painless process.

Although the Gulf of Maine has more areas with significantly stronger and more reliable winds, the states to our south have much larger energy markets close at hand and wind resources blowing over shallower waters that may be less expensive to develop on a per-kilowatt-hour basis. Nevertheless, the transition from a fossil-fuel-dependent economy to one with higher percentages of renewable energy will be expensive and wrenching. There will be terrible political battles—witness Cape Wind, the poster child for renewable energy gridlock. There will need to be subsidies. There always have been national subsidies for energy, whether for shipping coal, funding oil depletion allowances or the national highway system, to mention a few. Investing in new sources of renewable energy will take leadership and vision. And right now and for the foreseeable future, state governments are supplying these scarce political commodities.

One of the most economically significant factors of wind power development is that further offshore you go, the more the wind blows. Because the amount of power produced from wind turbines varies with the cube of wind speed, relatively small differences in velocity make huge differences in power output.

During the next few decades, the rate at which offshore wind energy develops will also be significantly influenced by whether natural gas prices stay low. Huge new deposits of natural gas that were heretofore locked in unrecoverable tight shale deposits have recently hit the market, contributing to a sharp drop in gas prices. This new technology may slow wind energy development. Energy companies are unlocking these deposits through a process called "hydro-fracking" or hydraulic fracturing, which involves injecting large volumes of chemically laden water into the ground to help release the gas, and which may or may not menace groundwater drinking supplies. No one knows who will end up on the winning side of that particular environmental argument, but wind companies will be watching closely.

In the meantime, offshore wind will likely be coming to a coast near some of us.

Foggy sunrise over the Fox Islands, with Mount Desert Island in background

Gary Comer
in Greenland and the
book he inspired,
The Fate of Greenland

(Facing) Climate
roundtable participant,
Gerry Cushman with
brother, Randy; Sea level
rise undercuts shorelines on
Pond Island and flooding
low-lying areas such as
Scarborough Marsh

Maybe not tomorrow, but it is just over the horizon for many Atlantic shorelines. Among the key questions will be whether Maine is able to develop its wind resources offshore, and if so, who will benefit and who will pay.

Climate Change

Gary Comer, the chairman and founder of the direct mail company Lands' End, became a founding member of the Island Institute, partly because he liked and respected islanders. Before migrating to Maine, one of Comer's favorite stories came from an islander who built a dock for him on Beaver Island in northern Lake Michigan. When Comer came to inspect the dock, he noticed that there was a light on a post at the end of it, but also one at the head of the dock. He asked the contractor why the light at the edge of the shore? "Well in case you want to back a vehicle down the dock," replied the islander. "Why would I want to do that?" asked Gary. "Well, in case someone told you, you couldn't." As Comer neared retirement, he built a new oceangoing vessel that would allow him to cruise the far watery reaches of the globe and invited me aboard as a naturalist for a series of cruises to the Arctic Ocean.

On a 2001 cruise up the west coast of Greenland, we witnessed the iceberg surges off the world's fastest-moving glacier at Ilulissat, which has since roughly doubled its speed. After I departed, Comer and his crew, who had crossed Baffin Bay at 80 degrees north latitude, were downloading ice reports through satellite communications and saw that the ice had retreated northward. They dashed through the legendary Northwest Passage and became the first private voyage through this ice-choked route completed in a single season without the services of a government icebreaker-and the fastest in history. They completed the crossing in sixteen days and eight hours.

Scientists have long known that the currents in the North Atlantic off Greenland flowed past the Labrador coast and ultimately entered the Gulf of Maine through a deep channel between Georges and Brown's Bank. What they did not suspect until recently is that the changes in Greenland directly influence the marine ecology of the great current gyres in the Gulf of Maine, which sweep past all the island communities southwestward to the tip of Cape Cod.

What happens if these ocean currents change course—if the boundary between the cold nutrient-rich Labrador Current waters flowing south into the Gulf of Maine and the warm northward flowing Gulf Stream shifts? Lobsters thrive in cold water and are subject to disease and death in warmer waters as a recent catastrophic collapse of lobster fishing in Long Island Sound has demonstrated.

In order to monitor how future climate change might affect islanders and fishermen, the Island Institute has been conducting a series of "roundtable" meetings with lobstermen from different regions along the coast for the past five years. The observations from these fishermen and their detailed historical knowledge of patterns in the marine environments provide a network of "front line" observations to complement research from the scientific community on the ecological health of our most valuable marine fishery—Maine lobsters.

One of the roundtable participants, Elliott Thomas who fishes in Casco Bay, describes his fishing strategy: "I have a thermometer that I keep in one of my traps, and if I see it's 47 degrees, I slam everything into the water because 48 [degrees] is when lobsters start moving." Usually bottom temperatures in the Gulf of Maine do not reach this temperature threshold until sometime during the last two weeks in April, and quite a bit later in the season farther east, where bottom temperatures are influenced by cold currents from Labrador, the northern reaches of the North Atlantic.

During the past decade, lobsters have moved inshore earlier and earlier in the spring. Tom Marr, a lobsterman from Long Island in Casco Bay, who used to have big catches starting in July after lobsters had shed their old shells, reported, "We've been catching lobsters [shedders] in June—which is wrong." He added, "The shed just started so early. A lot of gear went into the bay [Casco Bay] without buoys being painted."

Lobstermen also report that after the earlier shedding season, lobsters move off into deeper, cooler water earlier in the season than they used to. "The places I fish in August," said Jim Wotton of Friendship, "are the places we used to fish in October." Statistics collected by Maine's Department of Marine Resources shows that the peak harvests of the lobster-fishing season have moved later and later into the year. In 2000 and 2001, the peak harvests were in August. By 2003 and 2004, lobster harvests peaked in September. In 2005 and 2006, landings peaked in October.

The areas of the Maine coast with the largest harvests have also moved from the Midcoast fishing communities of Knox County farther east. In 2007, Sonny Sprague of Swan's Island said, "I do believe global warming is happening because this year Hancock County was the top dog in lobsters, and the top dog most of the time has been Spruce Head and Vinalhaven. Now it's shifted a bit eastwards. Before long they're going to be by us; they'll be in Nova Scotia."

Of course, it is not just lobstermen who are affected by the changing climate, but one of the most fundamental lessons of island history during the last century is that the surviving year-round island communities would have been swept into the dustbin of history if it had not been for the existence of the lobster fishery. Under most climate-change scenarios, the ocean will become more acidic as more carbon dioxide dissolves into the ocean to form carbonic acid,

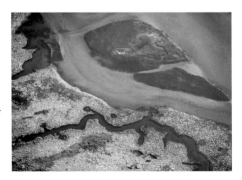

Only time will tell whether lobstermen will be able to adapt to the effects of future climate change in the Gulf of Maine.

which dissolves carbonate shells of lobsters, clam and coral. Sea level will also continue to rise, inundating low-lying properties along the coast and islands. Storms, including damaging northeasterlies and hurricanes, are predicted to increase in intensity. As the exchange of air masses from warming tropical areas migrates north in our hemisphere, the winds over places like the islands and Gulf of Maine will likely increase. That is bad news for fishermen who will lose more gear to storms, but it may be good news for those like Fox Islands Wind and other offshore wind developers whose electric production from turbines increases by the cube of wind speed. Even small increases in wind speeds over time can result in dramatic increase in economic output.

Most scientists believe we cannot now avoid significant climate change, which will

express itself differently in different regions of the country. As the level of carbon dioxide inexorably increases in the atmosphere, there will be more heat driving more evaporation, resulting in shifting precipitation patterns and more intense storms. But it is important to reflect that fishermen have had to adapt to changing weather for centuries and thus may be in the vanguard for adapting to the impending changes on the horizon. At least that is the opinion of one of our fisherman partners in our "climate of change" project. "We'll roll with the climate changes," John Drouin of Cutler said.

Here's hoping the rest of us can, too.

Afterword

No Island is an Island

In the life of each of us there is a place remote and islanded,
and given to endless regret or secret happiness.

—Sarah Orne Jewett

The strength of the island character is born of loneliness and isolation where ideas enter the mind, elsewhere too often cluttered by entertainments to penetrate deeply. The inhabited islands of Maine stand out as examples of an idea, at once simple and complex—that the special nature of islands creates a unique island culture that is shaped by its emboundedness; where nature is not tamed, but human nature is.

In the midst of ceaseless change, a handful of persistent island communities have not just survived during the past three decades, they have triumphed. Maine's 15 island communities put the lie to the belief that all efforts to preserve isolated communities will pass away, as others have before them, receding into an encroaching forest or extinguished by bad luck, human failing and the grinding economic realities of daily life.

On islands, old ways hang on longer, unlike the out-with-the-old-in-with-the-new credo of American culture. From an island it is possible to look back at the brash and swift pace of change on the mainland and recognize a little more of what's important—what is of value.

Among these islands is an underlying tautness that characterizes any remote coast. It is the tension between rootedness and impermanence; between bounty and failure; between ungiving rock and rolling stone. Here at these hard edges, any observer with an instinct for local history will find its stories etched into its ecology; here is where we experience a different pulse of time that loops both forward and backward and comes back around to offer us the sense of life's unending cycles.

Fourth of July celebration over Curtis Island, Camden

Island communities also reinforce the lesson that our fates are inescapably interconnected. None of us, nor any island, is an island, complete unto itself. It's our friends and friendships, both given and received, across oceans of different experiences, that rekindle our essential humanity. No matter who we are—fisherman, artist, shepherd, or sailor—we learn over and over again that we are truly cast together as if in a small lifeboat in a cold, dark sea, seeking refuge. When one among us falters through misfortune, sickness, or simply the luck of the draw, then a hand, an encouragement, a lifeline skillfully offered can make the difference between continuity and extinction.

A hundred years from now, just as today, Maine's island culture will give the region a distinction that no other place in America and few on the globe can replicate. And all their friends can and must do their small part to help.

Acknowledgments

The author and photographer gratefully recognize all the people whose support and behind-the-scenes work contributed to this edition of *Islands in Time*. First and foremost, our families tolerated long absences for the field-work on which this volume is based. The fieldwork was fun and wonderful for the two of us, far less so for those left behind. During the past several years there were long disappearances into the digital caves that in-house book production now enables—we might say requires—resulting in innumerable late dinners and lost weekends.

Countless island families and fishermen, with whom we have and will continue to partner, have invited us into their homes and fishing territories and extended us the trust, quite literally, to invade their space and place; for this great tolerance, we are humbled.

The board of the Island Institute, for whom and with whom we have worked, has provided us with enormous freedom and encouragement to follow the stories we record here from Maine's island and working waterfront communities. Without the board's often gutsy resolve during many a trying time, this volume would not have been possible.

Many island historical societies contributed time and images to this volume. In particular, we are grateful to Bill Chilles and his staff of volunteers at the Vinalhaven Historical Society, Lydia Webster Brown of the North Haven Historical Society, Donna Damon of the Chebeague Island Historical Society, Hugh Dwelley of the Islesford Historical Society, the volunteers at the Peaks Island Fifth Maine collection. We would also like to recognize the photographic contributions from the Monhegan Historical Society, the Swan's Island Educational Society, the Eastport Historical Society and the Penobscot Marine Museum.

The staff of the Island Institute, whose programs are now widely regarded as serving as national models for innovative ideas, is the underpinning for most all of the work described in the second half of this volume. They will provide the energy and imagination to help carry this work forward. Nancy Carter, Kristin Collins, Mary Terry, and Gillian Garratt-Reed chased down innumerable details, both substantive and technical. Bridget Leavitt was an essential and invaluable design and production partner. Kathy Allen ably assisted the compilation of sources.

To the 5,000 far-flung members of the Island Institute—on island and off—who have helped build an organization that will be a permanent presence among the islands of Maine, we are deeply appreciative of your loyal support and generosity.

To those friends of the photographer—you know who you are—who helped him get back behind a camera after a life-threatening medical odyssey, this book would not have happened without your determined support.

PHOTOGRAPHS

Many of Peter Ralston's images in this book are titled and already exist as limited edition prints. Others are reproduced here for the first time, a singular pleasure and honor. All these images are also available for purchase through the Institute's gallery, Archipelago Fine Arts (www.thearchipelago.org), or through Ralston Gallery, Rockport, Maine (www.ralstongallery.com).

All of the remaining photographs in this volume are also Peter Ralston's, with the following exceptions:

p. 24, Island Institute photographic collection, courtesy of McLane family

p. 30, 31; Island Institute photographic collection, courtesy of Charles McLane

p. 43, Island Institute photographic collection, courtesy of Lolly Cochran

p. 51 (top), 52, 53, 54 (top and middle); Vinalhaven Historical Society collections

p. 54, (top and middle), Vinalhaven Historical Society collections (bottom), Island Institute photographic collection, courtesy of Rick Perry

p. 56, Island Institute photographic collection, courtesy of Philip Conkling

p. 60, Island Institute photographic collection, courtesy of Rick Perry

p. 71, Island Institute photographic collection

p. 77, Island Institute photographic collection, courtesy of George Putz

p. 75 (top), Island Institute photographic collection

p. 78 (top), Island Institute photographic collection

p. 98 (top), Island Institute photographic collection, courtesy of Philip Conkling

p. 102, Island Institute photographic collection, courtesy of Philip Conkling

p. 117, Island Institute photographic collection, courtesy of Philip Conkling

p. 118 (bottom), Island Institute photographic collection, courtesy of Philip Conkling

p.120, Samuel K. Conkling

p. 121 (bottom), Island Institute photographic collection, courtesy of Steve Baird

p. 126, Island Institute photographic collection, courtesy of Goodridge family

p. 132, Island Institute photographic collection, courtesy of Jamien Morehouse

p. 136, Island Institute photographic collection, courtesy of Philip Conkling

p. 139 (top), Vinalhaven Historical Society collections

p. 140, Island Institute photographic collection, courtesy of Jack Morton

p. 146, Vinalhaven Historical Society collections

p. 147, Island Institute photographic collection

p. 148, 149, Monhegan Historical Society collections

p. 150, The Rooms Provencial Archives, Newfoundland

p. 150 (bottom), Vinalhaven Historical Society collections

p. 151 (top and bottom), Vinalhaven Historical Society collections

p. 152 (top), Vinalhaven Historical Society collections

p. 153 (top and bottom), Vinalhaven Historical Society collections

p. 154 (top), Island Institute photographic collection, courtesy of Eastport Historical Society

p. 154 (bottom), Penobscot Marine Museum collection

p. 159 (bottom), Island Institute photographic collection, courtesy of Philip Conkling

p. 166, Island Institute photographic collection

p. 167 (top and bottom), Island Institute photographic collection, courtesy Stanley French

p. 172 (bottom), Courtesy of Cook family

p. 173, Vinalhaven Historical Society collections

p. 174, Island Institute photographic collection, courtesy of Andree Kehn.

p. 189 (top and bottom), Island Institute photographic collection

p. 198, Island Institute photographic collection , courtesy of Swan's Island Education Society

p. 209 (bottom), Island Institute photographic collection, courtesy of George Putz

p. 211 (top), Island Institute photographic collection, courtesy North Haven Historical Society

p. 214 (top), Island Institute photographic collection, courtesy of David Platt

p. 215, Island Institute photographic collection, courtesy of Bridget Beesaw

p. 224 (bottom), Island Institute photographic collection, courtesy of Peggy Krementz

p. 239 Island Institute photographic collection, courtesy of David Tyler

p. 243, Island Institute photographic collection, courtesy of *The Working Waterfront*

p. 253, Island Institute photographic collection, courtesy of Philip Conkling

p. 257, Island Institute photographic collection, courtesy of *The Working Waterfront*

p. 260 Island Institute photographic collection, courtesy of David Tyler

p. 280, Island Institute photographic collection, courtesy of Calendar Islands Maine Lobster

p. 289, Island Institute photographic collection, courtesy of Suzanne Pude

p. 296, Island Institute photographic collection, courtesy of Gary Comer

ANNOTATED SOURCES AND RESOURCES

Acheson, James. *Lobster Gangs of Maine*. Hanover, NH: University of New England Press, 1988

This is the most insightful, carefully documented picture of how lobstering works by Maine's leading cultural anthropologist. It describes lobster community dynamics by focusing on the groups, or gangs, of lobstermen who work in complex, closely knit networks with information from scores of harbors along the Maine coast.

Albion, R. G. *Forests and Seapower*. Cambridge, Mass.: Harvard University Press, 1926.

Authoritative study of British interest in the settlement of Maine from the point of view of their drive to control the supply of masts of white pine from the coast and islands.

Albion, Robert G., William A. Baker and Benjamin W. Labaree. *New England and the Sea*. Mystic, Conn.: Mystic Seaport Museum, Inc., 1972.

A comprehensive, well written, and authoritative history of the maritime industries of New England including fishing, shipbuilding, and international and coastal trading.

Ames, Edward A. *Cod and Haddock Spawning Grounds in the Gulf of Maine*. Rockland, Maine: Island Institute. 1996.

Based on interviews with two dozen retired fishermen, it lays out the case for protecting spawning grounds, including those inside state waters, which once supported local stocks.

Anthony, Athene R. *Vinalhaven Reminiscences*. Vinalhaven, Maine: Printed by the "Wind" of the Union Church, 1978. Second Printing Island Printers. Vinalhaven, Maine. 1981.

Apollonio, Spencer. *The Gulf of Maine*. Rockland, Maine. Courier-Gazette, 1979.

This thin book was the first effort to describe what is known about the Gulf of Maine since Henry Bigelow's pioneering work of the 1920s. Apollonio served as Commissioner of Marine Resources for 12 years and as the first Executive Director of the New England Fisheries Management Council.

Atkins, C. G. *Sixth Report of the Commission of Fisheries of the State of Maine*. Augusta, Maine, 1872.

Useful for its line drawings of various types of fish weirs used at the time.

Audubon, Maria R. *Audubon and His Journals*. New York: Charles Scribner's Sons, 1897.

Audubon's letters describing his voyages to Eastport, Maine, where he fitted out for his Labrador expedition.

Babcock, Charles. *Along the Shores from Boston to Mount Desert*. 1865.

Pamphlet describing the coast of Maine from deck side, with a few descriptions of the islands.

Backus, Richard H., ed. *Georges Bank*. Cambridge, Mass.: MIT Press, 1987.

A fabulous treasure trove on Georges Bank and the Gulf of Maine. The publication is in large format and rich in maps and scientific illustrations.

Baird, John C. "Some Ecological Aspects of the White-Tailed Deer on Isle au Haut, Maine." Orono, Maine: University of Maine, Master's Thesis, 1966

Documents how island deer use intertidal seaweeds.

Barbour, M. G. et al. *Coastal Ecology*. Berkeley, Calif.: University of California Press, 1979.

Basic ecological characteristics of coastal plant habitats.

Baxter, James P., Ed. *The Trelawney Papers*. In Collections of Maine Historical Society, Second Series, Documentary, Vol. III. Portland, Maine, 1884.

The letters of Jonathan Winter, giving the best early description of island living, including accounts of fishing, farming, and lumbering on Richmond Island and Casco Bay islands, 1632-45.

Baxter, James P., Ed. *George Cleeve of Casco*. Portland, Maine, 1885

As is the rest of Baxter's work, this is a highly readable account of early Maine history that provides ecological details omitted in many accounts.

Baxter, James P., Ed. *Sir Ferdinando Gorges and His Province of Maine*. Boston, Mass.1890.

Description of the Popham Colony on Georgetown Island and references to later settlements on Damariscove and Monhegan.

Baxter, James P., Ed. *Christopher Levett of York*. Portland, Maine, 1893.

Levett's account of his voyage to the Maine coast is one of the best sources of ecological information on the pre-settlement forests. Nicely edited by Baxter.

Beacom, Seward E. *Pulpit Harbor—Two Hundred Years: A History of Pulpit Harbor at North Haven, Maine 1784-1984*. North Haven Historical Society, 1985.

A detailed study of the early local history of this fabled harbor.

Belknap, Jeremy. *History of New Hampshire*, Vol. I. 1784; Vols. II and III, later.

One of the few contemporary accounts of the white pine mast industry conducted along the coasts of Maine and New Hampshire.

Bent, Arthur C. *Life Histories of North American Petrels and Pelicans and Their Allies*. Washington, D.C.: Bulletin, Smithsonian Institution, 1922. Reprint. New York: Dover Press.

Breeding information on Leach's storm petrels on Maine islands.

Bent, Arthur C. *Life Histories of North American Wildfowl, Part II*. Washington, D.C.: Bulletin, Smithsonian Institution, 1925. Reprint. New York: Dover Press.

Information on eiders and winter ducks.

Bent, Arthur C. *Life Histories of North American Birds of Prey, Parts I and II*. Washington, D.C.: Bulletin, Smithsonian Institution, 1937 and 1938. Reprint. New York: Dover Press.

Accounts of the distribution of ospreys and eagles on Maine islands.

Beveridge, Norwood P. *The North Island: Early Times to Yesterday*. North Haven, Maine, North Haven Historical Society, 1976.

Bicentennial history with informative descriptions of North Haven farming and shipbuilding.

Bigelow, Henry B. "Physical Oceanography in the Gulf of Maine." *U.S. Bureau of Fisheries Bulletin, Vol. 40,* Part 2, 1927.

Companion piece to Bigelow's pioneering work, "Fishes of the Gulf of Maine," this volume lays out what Bigelow deduced of the gulf current and temperatures from two decades of research cruises.

Bigelow, Henry B. and William C. Schroeder. *Fishes of the Gulf of Maine*. Fishery Bulletin No. 74. Washington: United States Government Printing Office, 1953.

Still the single definitive text on the distribution, reproductive biology, and ecology of over 200 species of fish that are found in the Gulf of Maine, including life history information where this is known.

Binnewies, Esther and Muriel Davisson. *A History of Bartlett's Island: Mount Desert, Maine.* Privately printed. Peggy and David Rockefeller, 1981.

Carefully researched local history for this 2000-acre island that was farmed and fished for most of the 19th century.

Bishop, W. H. "Fish and Men in the Maine Islands." *Harper's New Monthly Magazine*, 1880. Reprint. Camden, Maine: Lillian Berliawsky Books.

Contemporaneous accounts of the cod, haddock, herring and lobster fisheries among the islands of Maine in the 1880s.

Blanchard, Peter P. III. *We Were an Island: The Maine Life of Art and Nan Kellam*. Lebanon, N.H.: University Press of New England, 2010

Sensitive account of Nan and Art Kellam based on their diaries and daily entries of their insular life alone during four decades on Placentia Island off Mount Desert.

Blunt, Edmund M. *The American Coastal Pilot, Containing Directions for the Principal Harbors, Capes and Headlands on the Coasts of North and South America.* 1800, with revised editions every few years.

  Navigational directions into several Maine harbors give detailed descriptions of the conditions of various islands, useful in reconstructing the composition of original island forests.

Bolton, Charles K. *The Real Founders of New England: The Stories of Their Life Along the Coast, 1602-1628.* Boston, Mass. 1929.

  Firsthand accounts of the techniques of mackereling, haking, longlining, salting, drying, lobstering, canning, et cetera, conducted on and around the Maine islands at the height of the fishing industry. Excellent drawings.

Bourque, Bruce. "Aboriginal Settlement and Subsistence on the Maine Coast." *Man in the Northeast.* No.6, Fall, 1973.

Bourque, Bruce. "Fishing in the Gulf of Maine: A 5,000-Year History." *Blackberry Reader.* Gary Lawless, Ed. Brunswick, Maine: Blackberry Press.

  Bourque's two articles give one of the most recent reviews of Indian use of the resources of the islands of Maine. Much of the information is based on artifacts excavated from North Haven. Bourque is an archaeologist at the Maine State Museum.

Bourque, Bruce. *Diversity and Complexity in Prehistoric Maritime Societies: a Gulf of Maine Perspective.* New York: Plenum Press, 1995.

  A new work describing the state of what is known of Maine's prehistory from Maine's State Archeologist based on twenty years of digging and analysis.

Bradford, Peter Amory. *Fragile Structures: A Story of Oil Refineries, National Security, and the Coast of Maine.* New York: Harper's Magazine Press, 1975.

  A well written and lively account of the story of the failed attempt to site and build a refinery on the Maine coast during the panic stricken days of the early Arab oil embargoes and the resulting "energy crisis."

Brayley, Arthur W. *History of the Granite Industry of New England.* Boston, Mass: Authority of The National Association of Granite Industries of the United States, 1913.

  Useful tome that describes the Maine island quarries in the context of others in New England.

Bureau of Industrial and Labor Statistics of Maine. "The Granite Industry of Maine." 16th Annual Report. Augusta, Maine, 1902.

  Listing of all of the major island and inland quarries and a summary of the major projects for which each supplied stone.

Burrage, Henry S., ed. *Early English and French Voyages, Chiefly from Hakluyt, 1534-1608.* New York, 1906.

  Annotated accounts of Rosier's relation of Waymouth's exploration of the Saint George Islands in Muscongus Bay. Also, Pring's discovery of the Fox Islands and the relation of the voyage to Sagadahoc (the account of the failure of the Popham Colony).

Byrne, Deirdre and Andrew Thomas. "Remote Sensing and Hydrographic Characterization of Penobscot Bay," Penobscot Bay Marine Research Collaborative, Year One Report. Rockland, Maine: Island Institute, 1997.

Cabot, Thomas D. *Avelinda: The Legacy of a Yankee Yachtsman.* Rockland, Maine: Island Institute, 1991.

  A highly readable account of 40 years of cruising the Maine islands and coast by one of New England's legendary conservationists and industrialists.

Calderwood, Ivan E. *Days of Uncle Dave's Fish House.* Rockland, Maine: Courier-Gazette, 1969.

  Colorful stories of Vinalhaven's history told by the island's most venerable oral historian.

Carleton, W. M. "Masts and the King's Navy." *New England Quarterly,* 12, (1939): 4-18.

Carr, Benjamin F. *The Story of Bustins: A Maine Summer Island.* Yarmouth, Maine: Islandport Press, 2008

  Lively account of the history of one of Maine's oldest and largest summer island communities.

Carter, Nancy McLeod and David Tyler. Ed. *A Climate of Change: A Preliminary Assessment of Fishermen's Observations on a Dynamic Fishery*. Rockland, Maine: Island Institute, 2008

   Fishermen's observations from the "Climate Roundtables," 2007-2011.

Centennial Committee, Ed. *Brief Historical Sketch of the Town of Vinalhaven*. Rockland, Maine, 1900.

   One of the few early histories of Vinalhaven, mostly reconstructed from the town records, with a few important pieces of information.

Chadbourne, Ava H. *Maine Place Names and the Peopling of its Towns*. Freeport, Maine: Bond Wheelwright Co., 1955.

   Town-by-town summaries of the dates of incorporation, with important facts about the establishment of island communities. Reissued in 1970 by counties.

Chapman, Carleton A. *Geology of Acadia National Park*. Greenwich, Connecticut: Chatham Press, 1970.

   Best single source of technical information on Maine coast geology, emphasizing the granite belt and written for a non-technical audience. Also includes self-guided tours of Mount Desert and Schoodic Islands. Self-guided tours are the best way to teach yourself geology.

Clark, Charles E. *The Eastern Frontier: The Settlement of Northern New England, 1610 - 1763*. Hanover, N.H.: University Press of New England, 1983.

   Excellent history of the real frontier along the Maine New Hampshire coastal and interior wilderness during the 17th and 18th centuries.

Clifford, Harold B. *Charlie York: Maine Coast Fisherman*. Camden, Maine: International Marine Publishing Company, 1974.

   Colorful history and narrative of an old fashioned fishermen who fished in small boats and larger ones from Bailey's Island to Bristol.

Clifford, Harold. *The Boothbay Harbor Region 1906-1960*. Freeport, Maine: Bond Wheelwright Co., 1960.

   Some interesting details of the fishing industry at the beginning of 1900 and hard times in the industry.

Clifford, J. Candace and Mary Louise Clifford. *Maine Lighthouses: Documentation of Their Past*. Alexandria, Virginia: Cypress Communications, 2005.

   Valuable historical research on all 67 of Maine's lighthouses based on primary sources, including extensive records in the lighthouse collections of the National Archives.

Colby, A. H. *Colby's Atlas*. Portland, Maine, 1881.

   Shows the numbers of dwellings and commercial establishments on islands, particularly around Vinalhaven, Deer Isle, and Mount Desert.

Collins, J. W. and Rathbun. "The Mackerel Fishery" Section V, Part II of "The Fisheries and Fishery Industries of the United States," George Brown Goode, Ed. Washington, D.C.: Government Printing Office, 1887.

   Excellent description of the mackerel fishery, including the Gulf of Maine, at the height of the industry before the collapse.

Conkling, Philip W. Ed. *From Cape Cod to the Bay of Fundy: An Environmental Atlas of the Gulf of Maine*. Cambridge, Mass: MIT Press, 1995.

   Satellite pictures and ecological relationships along the coast, islands, waters and watersheds of the Gulf of Maine.

Conkling, Philip W. *A Natural History Guide to the Coastal Islands of Maine*. Rockland, Maine: Hurricane Island Outward Bound School, 1979.

   Detailed ecological descriptions of 200 islands used by the Hurricane Island Outward Bound program.

Conkling, Philip W. *Green Islands Green Sea, A Guide to Foraging on the Islands of Maine*. Rockland, Maine: Hurricane Island Outward Bound School, 1980.

An illustrated foraging guide to common plants, berries and intertidal creatures along the shores and islands of Maine.

Conkling, Philip. "Fish or Foul?" *Maine Policy Review,* Vol. 9. No. 2, pp.12-19. Orono, Maine, Margaret Chase Smith Center for Public Policy, 2000.

Overview of the factors behind the rise and decline of Maine's salmon aquaculture industry.

Conkling, Philip W. and David D. Platt. Eds. *Holding Ground: The Best of Island Journal 1984-2004*. Rockland, ME: Island Institute, 2004.

A compendium of the best stories, essays, poetry, art and photography, celebrating the art and science of island life from 20 years of Island Journals.

Conkling, Philip, W., W.H. Drury, and R.E. Leonard. *People and Islands: Resource Management Issues for Islands in the Gulf of Maine*. Rockland, Maine: Island Institute, 1984.

Studies of the impacts of fire, sheep, logging and recreation on soils, vegetation and wildlife on a series of islands in Muscongus, Penobscot, Jericho Bays.

Cook, Melville Bradford. *Records of Meduncook Plantation and Friendship, Maine 1762-1899*. Rockland, Maine: Shore Village Historical Society, 1985.

Good for information on Friendship Long and Morse Islands off Friendship.

Cook, Sherwood. Interview with Jayne Lello. Tenants Harbor, Maine. March 1972 (typed transcript). Northeast Archives of Folklore and Oral History, Department of Anthropology, University of Maine at Orono.

Excellent observations from a veteran island lobsterman on islands' territorial boundaries.

Crowell, Kenneth L. "Experimental zoogeography; introductions of mice to small islands." *American Naturalist*, Vol. 107, No. 956, 1973.

Describes Crowell's experiments with mice on Maine islands for the technical audience.

Crowell, Kenneth L. "Downeast Mice." *Natural History*, October 1975.

Same information for nontechnical readers.

Crowley, John S. *Sustainable Design for Two Maine Islands: A Study conducted by the Institute for Energy Conscious Design*. Boston, Mass: the Boston Architectural Center, 1985.

An early visionary design "charrette" focusing on incorporating sustainable building and community design challenges for Peaks Island and Vinalhaven.

Daughters of Liberty. *Historical Researches of Gouldsboro, Maine*. Bar Harbor, Maine, 1904.

A few bits of information on Stave and Ironbound Islands in Frenchman Bay.

Davis, Deborah, Ed. *Keeping the Light: A Handbook for Adaptive Re-Use of Island Lighthouse Stations*. Rockland, Maine: Island Institute, 1986.

A practical guide for local non-profits who lease or own island lighthouse properties.

Davis, H. A. *An International Community on the St. Croix (1604-1930)*. Orono, Maine: University of Maine, 1974.

A good local history of this important area straddling the border between Maine and New Brunswick.

Davis, Ronald B. "Spruce-Fir Forests of the Coast of Maine." *Ecological Monographs*, Vol. 36, Spring 1966.

Best technical introduction to the vascular flora of coastal spruce forests.

Day, Clarence A. *A History of Maine Agriculture 1604-1865*. Orono, Maine: University of Maine Study Series No. 68, 1954.

Comprehensive account of farming methods from the earliest settlement to the Civil War, with a surprising amount of interesting ecological detail.

Day, Clarence A. *Farming in Maine 1860-1940.* Orono, Maine: University of Maine Study Series No. 78, 1963.

Good description of island sheep farms.

Deer Isle Granite Industry. Stone Slabs and Iron Men. Stonington, Maine: Deer Isle Granite Museum, 1997

A beautifully produced small volume celebrating the dozen or so large and small quarries established on the islands and waterfront of Stonington, with an emphasis on the history of Crotch island.

Diamond Island Association. *Great Diamond Island.* Portland, Maine, 1972.

Mostly late-nineteenth- and twentieth-century history of this Casco Bay island.

Dorr, George B. *The Story of Acadia National Park.* Bar Harbor, Maine: Acadia Publishing Company, 1997

A special edition reprint of the memoir originally written by George Dorr, the individual who spent 47 years of his life helping to acquire the properties that became Acadia National Park.

Dow, Robert L. "The Need for a Technological Revolution in the Methods of Catching Marine Fish and Shellfish." *Marine Technology Society Journal*, December 1979-January 1980.

Useful summary of the recent history of commercial fishing in the Gulf of Maine, with some summaries of landings for the 1960s.

Drury, William H. Jr. *Chance and Change, Ecology for Conservationists.* Berkeley and Los Angeles: University of California Press, 1998.

Excellent discussion of evolutionary biology with many examples of Drury's decades of Maine island research.

Drury, William H. "Rare Species." *Biological Conservation*, Vol. 6, pp. 162-68.

Theoretical discussion of the importance of islands for maintaining sources of genetic diversity.

Drury, William H. "Population Changes in New England Seabirds." *Bird Banding,* vol. 44, pp. 267-313, and Vol. 45, pp. 1-15, 1973-74.

Definitive study of the breeding ecology of the major species of seabirds nesting on the New England coast, and an account of how their numbers fluctuate over time.

Duncan, Roger F. *Coastal Maine, A Maritime History.* NY: W.W. Norton & Company, 1992.

The single best history of the coast of Maine written in a lively narrative style by one of the coast's great sailors and co-author of an equally definitive cruising guide.

Earll, R. Edward. "The Herring Fishery and the Sardine Industry," Section V, Part VI of *The Fisheries and Fishery Industries of the United States,* George Brown Goode, Ed. Washington, D.C.: Government Printing Office, 1887.

Important details of the structure of the herring industry and fishing practices, particularly centered on Eastport and Lubec.

Eastman, Joel W. *A History of Sears Island, Searsport, Maine.* Searsport Historical Society, 1976.

Well-researched history of this north Penobscot Bay island, gleaned mostly from the Knox Papers. The study was financed by Central Maine Power Company, which proposed in recent years to build either a nuclear or a coal-fired power plant on this island.

Eaton, Cyrus L. *Annals of the Town of Warren, etc.* Hallowell, Maine, 1872.

Good details of early shipbuilding along the upper reaches of the Saint George River.

Eaton, Cyrus L. *History of Thomaston, Rockland and South Thomaston, Maine, from their first exploration, A.D. 1605.* Hallowell, Maine: Masters, Smith, 1865.

Includes family genealogies.

Eckert, Allan W. *Great Auk.* Boston: Little, Brown, 1963.

Story of the extinction of this giant seabird, told from the point of view of the auk with a great deal of ecological detail.

Eckstrom, Fannie Hardy. *Indian Place Names of the Penobscot Valley and Maine Coast.* Orono, Maine: University of Maine Study Series No.

55, 1941

Compendium of definitive information and carefully documented research on the meaning of Indian place names.

Eliot, Charles W. *John Gilley, Maine Farmer and Fisherman.* Boston: Beacon Press, 1899.

Admiring portrait of the paterfamilias of Baker Island by one of Mount Desert Island's early summer people, who was, incidentally, president of Harvard College.

Enk, John C. *A Family Island in Penobscot: The Story of Eagle Island.* Rockland, Maine: Courier-Gazette, 1953.

Mostly the recollections of Captain Erland Quinn of the four generations of Quinns who inhabited Eagle Island and the various occupations they pursued.

Fairburn, William A. *Merchant Sail.* 6 vols. Center Lovell, Maine: Fairburn Marine Educational Foundation, 1945.

Unique work of everything anyone will ever want to know about the days of merchant sail. The section on Maine boats is as comprehensive as that of any other work in print.

Farrow, John P. *History of Islesborough, Maine.* Bangor, Maine, 1893.

Mostly genealogies of the early settlers, some of whom settled on the smaller surrounding islands. The written descriptions of original lots on the island give a surprisingly detailed look at the composition of the original forest.

Farrow, John P. *The Romantic Story of David Robertson Among the Islands, Off and On the Coast of Maine.* Belfast, Maine, 1898.

This story might not be as interesting if it hadn't been written by a historian. With great attention to detail, the author describes the life of the original settler of Lime Island in Penobscot Bay.

Faulkner, A., and G.F. Faulkner. *The French at Pentagoet, 1635-1674, An Archaeological Portrait of the Acadian Frontier.* Maine Historic Preservation Commission, Augusta, Maine, 1987.

The complex archeological history and role played by the French at Castine in the thirty-one years covered.

Fillmore, Robert B. *Gems of the Ocean.* Privately published, 1914.

Various facts about turn-of-the-century life on Matinicus and Ragged Islands and Matinicus Rock. Available from the Maine State Library.

Fisher, Jeff Ed. *Maine Speaks: An Anthology of Maine Literature.* Maine Writers and Publisher's Alliance. Brunswick, ME: Maine Literature Project 1989.

Excellent anthology of Maine writing and literature from earliest times to the present.

Formisano, Ron. *The Great Lobster War.* Amherst, MA: University of Massachusetts Press, 1997

The story of the famous "tie-up" and strike that shut down the Maine lobster fishery during the summer of 1957, and the ensuing court case that charged the Maine Lobstermen's Association with unconstitutional restraint of trade.

George, Carl J. "Remarks on the More Conspicuous Vascular Plants of Appledore Island Isles of Shoals, Maine." Schenectady, NY: Union College, 1980.

A good description of island flora around a seabird colony.

Goldburg, Rebecca and Tracy Triplett. *Murky Waters: Environmental Effects of Aquaculture in the United States.* Washington, D.C.: Environmental Defense Fund, 1997.

Includes case studies on New England and New Brunswick, Canada, including a section on Maine aquaculture practices by Anne Hayden and Philip Conkling.

Goode, George Brown. *Fishery Industries of the United States.* U.S. 47th Congress, 1st Session (1881-1882), Miscellaneous Documents, Vol. 7, Section II, 1882.

Valuable source of information on American fishing near its height; compiled by regions.

Goode, George Brown, et al. *The Fisheries and Fishery Industries of the United States Section V: History and Methods of the Fisheries.* 3

Vols. Washington, D.C. Government Printing Office, 1887.

The definitive work on America's fisheries during the 18th and 19th centuries, including port by port descriptions of what fisheries are pursued, by how many fishermen, in what kinds of boats, using which methods. Very detailed descriptions of the cod, haddock, herring and lobster fisheries of Maine with detailed statistics and with excellent local detail provided by individual fishermen.

Goold, Nathan. *A History of Peaks Island and Its People*. Portland, Maine, 1897.

Smattering of useful historical details.

Graham, Frank. *Gulls—A Social History*. New York: Random House, 1975.

Complete history of the relationship of gulls and men from the mid-nineteenth century through the present. The majority of it focuses on Maine nesting islands. Also, lovely photography by Chris Ayres.

Grant, W. L. *Voyages of Samuel de Champlain, 1604-1618*. New York: Charles Scribner's Sons, 1907.

Descriptions of Champlain's two voyages along the Maine coast, reconstructed and annotated from Champlain's detailed notebooks.

Greene, Francis B. *History of Boothbay, Southport and Boothbay Harbor, Maine, 1623-1905*. Portland, Maine, 1906.

Standard and comprehensive history.

Greenleaf, Moses. *A Survey of the State of Maine (in Reference to its Geographic Features, Statistics and Political Economy)*. Portland, Maine, 1829.

Greenleaf was the man hired to survey the publicly owned islands after Maine because a state. Lots of original hard data.

Griffin, Carl R. III, and Alaric Faulkner. *Coming of Age on Damariscove Island, Maine*. Orono, Maine: The Northeast Folklore Society, 1981.

Essentially the story of Alberta Poole, who with her family, were the last year round residents of this ancient fishing-island fishing harbor.

Grindle, Roger. *Quarry and Kiln, The Story of Maine's Lime Industry*. Rockland, Maine: Courier-Gazette, 1971.

Grindle, who grew up in Rockland, provides a look at the lime industry mostly gleaned through old newspaper accounts.

Grindle, Roger. *Tombstones and Paving Blocks, The History of the Maine Granite Industry*. Rockland, Maine: Courier-Gazette, 1972.

Useful background information on the operations on Vinalhaven, Hurricane Island, Clark Island and Dix Island.

Gross, A. O. "The Present Status of the Double-Crested Cormorant on the Coast of Maine." *Auk*, Vol. 62, pp. 513-97.

Valuable historical review of the fortunes of the cormorant.

Gross, A. O. "The Present Status of the Great Black-Backed Gull on the Coast of Maine." *Auk*, Vol. 62, pp.241-56.

Describes the range extension of this Arctic species.

Gross, Clayton H. *Steel Over Eggemoggin: A History of the Deer Isle-Sedgwick Bridge*. Stonington, ME: Penobscot Books, 1989.

A thorough local history over the epic bridge building project written by a resident..

Grossfield, Stan. *Nantucket: The Other Season*. Chester, Conn: The Globe Pequot Press, 1982.

A compelling pictorial portrait of this island community in winter with a good, sparse narrative.

Halle, Louis J. *The Storm Petrel and the Owl of Athena*. Princeton, New Jersey: Princeton University Press, 1970.

Delightful series of essays about pelagic seabirds written by a gifted amateur naturalist.

Hardin, Garrett. *The Tragedy of the Commons. American Association for the Advancement of Science,* 1968.

The definitive intellectual analysis of why people fail to conserve local natural resources even as they are being depleted before their eyes which became a mantra for environmentalists after Earth Day.

Hayden, Anne. "Eelgrass and Fisheries in the Gulf of Maine." Rockland, Maine: Island Institute, 1996. Sixteen pages.

The relationship between eelgrass and fisheries.

Herrick, George G. A Season on Roque Island. Ipswich, Mass: The Ipswich Press, 1996.

Journal entries from several seasons on this legendary island downeast.

Herrick, George Gardner. *Ten Years on Roque Island 1988-1997*. Chevy Chase, Maryland: Posterity Press, Inc., 2000

A lively personal account of one of Roque Island's "citizens."

Hill, A. F. "The Vegettion of the Penobscot Bay Region, Maine." *Proceedings of the Portland Society of Natural History,* Vol. 3, (1923), pp. 305-438.

Comprehensive and useful description of island vegetation in Penobscot Bay; written by a botanist of the old school (that is, someone who went out and identified plants in the field and arranged them according to habitat).

Hosmer, George L. *An Historical Sketch of the Town of Deer Isle, Maine: with Notices of its Settlers and Early Inhabitants.* Boston, 1886.

Definitive history of Deer Isle that contains a great deal of interesting detail about this island and the smaller ones in Merchant Row.

Howard, Jean G. *Bound by the Sea: A Summer Diary.* Portsmouth, N.H.: The Tidal Press, 1986

Hoyt, Edwin P. *Nantucket: The Life of an Island.* Brattleboro, Vermont: The Stephen Greene Press, 1978.

A good, relatively recent narrative history of this island community.

Images of America: *Vinalhaven Island.* Dover, N.H.: Arcadia Publishing, 1997.

Excellent pictorial history of this community, which relies heavily on the archives of the Vinalhaven Historical Society.

Incze, Lewis Lajos. *Once Upon a Maine Island, Hell and Heaven at Sea, A Saga in Island Life.* 1983.

An interesting account of a Casco Bay island personal and family history.

Island Institute. *Exploring Limits: Making Decisions About the Use & Development of Maine's Islands.* Rockland, Maine: Island Institute, 1994

An examination of the ecological factors that have influenced island land use decisions during the past quarter of a century.

Island Institute, Ed. *Island Journal.* v. 1-26, 1984-2010. Rockland, Maine: Island Institute.

The annual publication of the Island Institute, which celebrates island life, culture, history and letters of the Maine archipelago.

Island Institute, Ed. *Sustaining Island Communities: The Story of the economy and life of Maine's year-round islands.* Rockland, Maine: Island Institute, 1997.

Descriptions of what it takes for Maine's fifteen year-round island communities to sustain themselves

Jenness, John. *Isles of Shoals, An Historical Sketch.* 1873.

Comprehensive island history, which is useful for understanding island's early 17th century history and how it became an early summer community.

Jenney, Charles F. *The Fortunate Island of Monhegan, A Historical Monograph.* Proceedings of the American Antiquarian Society, Vol. 31.

Summary of Monhegan's history compiled from secondary sources.

Jewett, Sarah Orne. *The Country of the Pointed Firs.* New York: Houghton Mifflin Co., 1910.

Sketches of coastal life and the inhabitants of a small fishing village. Includes one or two island characters.

Johnson, Douglas. *The New England-Acadian Shoreline*. N.Y.: Hafner Publishing Company, 1967.

Definitive description of the major landforms of the coast of Maine.

Johnston, John. *A History of Bristol and Bremen*. Albany, New York, 1873.

Good descriptions of the various Indian tribes that influenced the early history of Maine.

Jones, Herbert G. *The Isles of Casco Bay in Fact and Fancy*. Portland, Maine, 1946.

Mostly fancy.

Josselyn, John. *An Account of Two Voyages to New England*. William Veazie, ed. Boston, Mass. 1865.

Excellent source of contemporary descriptions of everything from fishing and fishermen to black flies, Indians, lobsters, and wolves around his brother's plantation in Saco during the 1630s and 1640s.

Josselyn, John. *New England Rarities Discovered*. Edward Tuckerman, ed. Boston, Mass. 1865

Josselyn's second volume from his recollections of his stay in the New World is a source of descriptions of native grasses and wildflowers. His species accounts of New England wildlife, although entertaining, are sometimes fantastic and at other times misleading.

Joy, Barbara E. *Historical Notes on Mount Desert Island*. Bar Harbor, Maine, 1975.

Compendium of historical facts that provide some interesting details not available in the standard histories of the area.

Katona, Steven K., Valerie Rough and David T. Richardson. *A Field Guide to the Whales Porpoises and Seals of the Gulf of Maine and Eastern Canada: Cape Cod to Newfoundland*. N.Y.: Charles Scribner's Sons, 1983.

Definitive field guide with brief narrative on the habits of marine mammals in the Gulf of Maine.

Kelley, J. T., D. F. Belknap, 1989. Geomorphology and Sedimentary Framework of Penobscot Bay and Adjacent Inner Continental Shelf. Maine Geological Survey, Report #89-3.

Kingsbury, John M. *The Rocky Shore*. Greenwich, Connecticut: Chatham Press, 1970.

One of the best introductions available to the life found in the rocky intertidal zone, by the former director of the Isles of Shoals Marine Laboratory. Fine drawings by Marcia and Edward Norman allow it to be used as a field guide.

Kleinhans, John. *An Image of Monhegan*. West Hurley, New York: Precipice Publications, 1997

Black and white platinum prints of the iconic cottages and vistas of Monhegan.

Kobbe, Gustow. "Heroism in the Lighthouse Service: A description of life on Matinicus Rock." *Century Magazine*, 1897.

A few useful tidbits.

Kohl, J. G. *History of the Discovery of Maine*. Collections of the Maine Historical Society, Portland, Maine, 1869.

Good introduction to the geography of the coast and the waters of the Gulf of Maine by an authoritative German geographer.

Korschgan, Carl E. *Coastal Waterbird Colonies: Maine*. U.S. Fish and Wildlife Service, Biological Services Program, 1979.

Listing of the number and distribution of the various waterbirds that breed on the Maine coast. Also includes a useful summary of historical changes and a good bibliography.

Kress, Stephen W. "The History and Future of North Atlantic Seabird Populations."

Unpublished pamphlet, available from the National Audubon Society.

Kurlansky, Mark. *Cod: A Biography of the Fish that Changed the World*. N.Y.: Walker and Company, 1997.

A wonderful book written by a journalist who contributes to both environmental and gourmet magazines which combines lively history and ecology with 500 years of recipes for this most ancient species of fish.

Leighton, Oscar. *Ninety Years at the Isles of Shoals*. Boston, Mass.: Beacon Press, 1930.

Isles of Shoals around the turn of the century.

Lewis, J. R. *The Ecology of Rocky Shores*. London: Hodder and Stoughton, 1964.

British text that gives the most comprehensive account of the dominant plant and animal communities of rocky shores.

Locke, Marie and Nancy Montgomery. *Memories of a Maine Island: turn-of-the-century tales & photographs*. University of Maine, Orono, Maine: Maine Folklore Center, 1998

Lockely, R. M. *Gray Seal, Common Seal*. New York: October House, 1968.

Detailed species accounts of these two seals common to Maine waters. Written in informative, nontechnical language.

Long, Charles A. E. *Matinicus Isle: Its Story and Its People*. Lewiston Journal Printshop, Reprinted by Higginson Book Company, Salem, Mass., 1926

A thorough and careful history for this most isolated island community in the Gulf of Maine.

Loomis, Alfred F. *Ranging the Maine Coast*. New York: Norton, 1939.

Classic account by one of Yachting magazine's excellent writers. Lots of interesting historical information woven into the narrative of his voyages aboard the hotspur.

Lunt, Dean Lawrence. *Hauling by Hand. Frenchboro, Maine*: Islandport Press, Inc., Yarmouth, Maine, 1999.

Thorough account of the history of Frenchboro by writer-journalist-publisher, Dean Lunt, a native of the island.

Lunt, Vivian. Frenchboro: *Long Island Plantation: The First Hundred Years*. Penobscot, Maine: Downeast Graphics, 1980.

Pictorial history of Maine's smallest, and arguably most threatened year round island community by the island's official and unofficial keeper of the flame.

MacGinitie, G. E., and Nettie MacGinitie. *Natural History of Marine Animals*. New York: McGraw-Hill, 1968.

Husband-and-wife team who obviously spend their spare time together collecting creatures from California's rocky intertidal zone. This volume was most useful for its introductory chapters on marine food webs.

Maclean, Charles. *Island on the Edge of the World: The Story of St. Kilda*. N.Y.: Taplinger Publishing Company, 1972.

The amazing, but cautionary story of the most isolated Hebridean Island community, 110 miles off mainland Scotland, that collapsed in the 1930s after a millenium of settlement.

Maine DMR. 1976. *Maine Landings: 1955-1976*. U.S. Dept of Commerce, Washington, D.C.

Fish landings compiled by the Maine Department of Marine Resources for a twenty-year period.

Manley, Sean, and Robert Manley. *Islands: Their Lives, Legends and Lore*. Philadelphia: Chilton, 1970.

For hard-core island buffs.

Manville, Richard H. "The Vertebrate Fauna of Isle au Haut." *American Midland Naturalist*, Vol. 72, 1964.

One of the few accurate accounts of mammalian species found on an offshore island of Maine.

Martin, Kenneth R. and Nathan R. Lipfert. *Lobstering and the Maine Coast*. Bath, Maine: Maine Maritime Museum, 1985.

A wonderfully interesting account of the history of this most vital of coastal fisheries from carefully researched documentary evidence that accompanies a substantial display at this museum.

Marvel, Lucilla Fuller. *Bear Island Centennial Book 1904-2004*. Privately printed.

A wonderful set of accounts and recollections of this island that was the summer home of among other luminaries, Buckminster Fuller.

May, R. M. "Island Biogeography and the Design of Wildlife Preserves." *Nature*, Vol. 254, pp. 177-78

Interesting theoretical discussion that bears on the preservation issues confronting Maine islands.

McLane, Charles B. and Carol Evarts McLane. *Islands of the Mid-Maine Coast: Penobscot Bay, Volume 1*. Revised edition. Gardiner and Rockland, Maine. Tilbury House and Island Institute, 1997.

A revision of the 1982 edition of the McLane's life-long work. It contains definitive accounts of islanders and their islands from town records, deeds and early written accounts of the mid coast islands with lovely black and white archival photography.

McLane, Charles B. *Islands of the Mid-Maine Coast, Mount Desert to Machias Bay, Volume II*. Falmouth, ME: The Kennebec River Press, Inc. 1989.

Covering the histories of islands from the Cranberries off Mount Desert all the way downeast to Cutler.

McLane, Charles B. *Islands of the Mid-Maine Coast, Muscongus Bay and Monhegan Island, Volume III*. Rockland, ME: The Island Institute & Tilbury House, 1992.

Very good review of the early history of Monhegan with arresting portraits of the collapse of island communities throughout the rest of Muscongus Bay.

McLane, Charles B. *Islands of the Mid-Maine Coast , Pemaquid Point to the Kennebec River, Volume IV*. Rockland, Maine: The Island Institute & Tilbury House, 1994

Covering the early history of Damariscove Island, the Boothbay Islands and the islands of the Kennebec including Georgetown and Arrowsic.

Mendall, H. L. "The Home-Life and Economic Status of the Double-Crested Cormorant, Phalacrocorax auritus auritus. Orono, Maine: University of Maine Study Series (2nd Series) No. 38, 1936.

Detailed history and biology of the cormorant.

Mendall, H. L "Eider Ducks, Islands and People." *Maine Fish and Wildlife*, Vol. 18, 1976, No. 2, 4-7.

Author's hypotheses on the disturbance to nesting eiders posed by human visitation to islands.

Merrill, John, and Suzanne Merrill, Eds. *Squirrel Island, Maine, the First Hundred Years*. Freeport, Maine: Bond Wheelwright Co., 1973.

Story of the island's summer colony.

Miller, S. *Bibliography of Penobscot Bay Scientific Research*. Rockland, Maine. Island Institute, 1995.

Comprehensive listing by subject, author, title of published research covering Penobscot Bay.

Monks, John Peabody. *History of Roque Island, Maine*. Boston, Mass.: The Colonial Society of Massachusetts, 1967.

Definitive history of this family-owned island during the first hundred and fifty years of habitation.

Moore, Ruth. *Cold as a Dog and the Wind Northeast*. Camden, Maine: Gordon Bok, 1973

Rollicking and humorous ballads from a native of Great Gott Island, who was also an accomplished novel writer.

Morison, Samuel E. *The Story of Mount Desert Island, Maine*. Boston, Mass.: Little, Brown, 1960.

A colorful and amusing history by one of Mount Desert's most respected summer residents.

Morison, Samuel E. *The European Discovery of America: The Northern Voyages*. Boston, Mass.: Little, Brown, 1971.

What makes Morison such an excellent naval historian is that he has cruised much of the same area as the original explorers. Also, few other historians have such a graceful prose style.

Morison, Samuel E. *Samuel de Champlain: Father of New France*. Boston, Mass.: Little, Brown, 1972.

Morison on Morison's favorite explorer. Includes a good description of Champlain's two expeditions along Maine's coast.

Morse, Ivan. *Friendship Long Island.* Middletown, New York: Whitlock Press, 1974.

The recollections of one of the island's oldest residents, whose memory stretches back to before the turn of this century. A good oral history.

Moulton, John K. *An Informal History of Four Islands: Cushing, House, Little Diamond, Great Diamond.* n.p., n.p., ca. 1991.

A manuscript of some of what is known of the history of these four islands in Casco Bay.

Nash, Anne C. *Pond Island Heritage: The Families and History of a Maine Island.* Brattleboro, Vermont: Ann Nash Publications, 1992.

Good family history of this summer community downeast off Milbridge.

Norton, Arthur H. "Some Noteworthy Plants from the Islands and Coast of Maine." *Rhodora*, vol. 15, No. 176, 1913.

Norton was the backbone of the Portland Museum of Natural History for almost three decades and traveled extensively along the Maine coast visiting nesting islands and collecting plants.

O'Leary, Wayne M. *Maine Sea Fisheries: The Rise and Fall of a Native Industry, 1830-1890.* Boston, Mass.: Northeastern University Press, 1996.

A real classic of historical research that paints a vivid picture of the fishing industry, from the perspective of its glory years of the mid 19th century

Palmer, Ralph S. *Maine Birds.* Bulletin of the Museum of Comparative Zoology. Cambridge, Mass.: Harvard College, 1949.

Palmer graciously acknowledges that this volume is "based largely on data gathered by Arthur Herbert Norton." It provides a unique look at the breeding colonies of the Maine islands with many notes on the condition of the vegetation.

Platt, David. Ed. *Island Indicators: A Report by the Island Institute.* Rockland, Maine: Island Institute, 2007

One of a series of publications that tracks demographics, economics and civic indicators of the sustainability of Maine's island communities.

Platt, David. Ed. *One Land-Two Worlds: Maine-Mawooshen 1605-2005. the 400th Anniversary of George Waymouth's Voyage to New England.* Rockland, Maine: Island Institute. 2005.

A series of essays on the history, culture, politics and ecology of the Maine coast and islands upon the 400th anniversary of Waymouth's voyage and two-month encampment on Allen Island.

Platt, David D. Ed. *Penobscot: The Forest, River and Bay.* Rockland, Maine: Island Institute, 1996.

An account of the history, geography and economics of thirty towns that line Maine's largest bay, including descriptions of five island towns.

Platt, David D., Ed. *Rim of the Gulf, Restoring Estuaries in the Gulf of Maine.* Rockland, Maine: Island Institute, 1998.

This book, with its maps, photographs, and narration, chronicles the estuaries of the Gulf of Maine. It highlights the need for action, research, and public education.

Platt, David. Ed. *Saving Working Waterfronts: Mapping the Maine Coast's Economic Future.* Rockland, Maine: Island Institute, 2005.

A report on the mehtodology of mapping Maine's working waterfronts and preliminary findings.

Platt, David. Ed. *The System in the Sea; Applying Ecosystems Principles to Marine Fisheries.* The Island Institute Conference at Harvard University, June 16-18 1992. Volume 2: Conference Proceedings. Ed. by David D. Platt, Rockland, ME: Island Institute, 1993.

Proceedings of an ecosystem conference on the ecological structure of marine systems.

Platt, David, Ed. *The Last 20 Miles: Mapping Maine's Working Waterfronts.* Rockland, Maine: Island Institute

The report that paved the way for amending Maine's constitution to provide property tax breaks to commercial fisheries properties along the Maine coast.

Pratt, Charles. *Here on The Island: Being an Account of a Way of Life Several Miles off the Coast of Maine.* N.Y.: Harper & Row, 1974.

A compelling written and pictorial account of several years of living the island life on Isle au Haut in the 1970s.

Porter, Eliot. *Summer Island.* Sierra Club.

A lovely book about a Penobscot Bay island, written by the man who nearly invented color nature photography.

Proper, Sedgwick Ida. *Monhegan, The Cradle of New England.* Portland, Maine: The Southworth Press, 1930

Valuable historical references.

Raisz, Edwin J. "The Scenery of Mount Desert Island, Its Origin and Development." *New York Academy of Sciences,* Vol. 31, 1929.

Good description of the glacial epoch and its effects in shaping landscapes.

Reed, Roger G. *Summering on the Thoroughfare: The Architecture of North Haven, 1885-1945.* Portland, Maine: Maine Citizens for Historic Preservation, 1993

Descriptions of the great cottages and restored farmhouse and properties of North Haven and the north end of Vinalhaven by an architectural historian.

Rhodes, Janet. *Beach Island: A Light History of Penobscot Bay to 1800 and Then of Her Center Island.* Rockland, Maine: Coastwise Press, 1992

Richardson, David T. "Final Report, Assessment of Harbor and Gray Seal Populations in Maine." Augusta, Maine: Department of Marine Resources, 1975

Thoroughly researched.

Richardson, David. "Final Report, Feeding Habits and Population Studies of Maine's Harbor and Gray Seals." Augusta, Maine: Department of Sea and Shore Fisheries, 1973.

The only original research on the feeding habits of seals on the Maine coast. Richardson, E. M. Hurricane Island: The Town That Disappeared. Rockland, ME: Island Institute, 1989, reprinted 1997.

Richardson, Eleanor Motley. *Hurricane Island, The Town That Disappeared.* Rockland, Maine. Island Institute. 1987.

A minor classic of this great quarry island that existed for 47 years at the end of the 19th and beginning of the 20th century in outer Penobscot Bay.

Richardson, Eleanor Motley. *North Haven Summers: An Oral History.* n.p., Catharine Little Motley, 1992.

The story of North Haven's summer community.

Robbins, Sarah Fraser and Clarice M. Yentsch. *The Sea Is All About Us.* MA: The Peabody Museum of Salem and The Cape Ann Society for Marine Science, Inc., 1973.

Rogers, Donna K. *Tales of Matinicus Island: History Lore and Legend.* n.p., Offshore Publishing, 1990.

Tales and accounts from offshore.

Rogers, Orville F. *Grandma's Island and Grandma's Ocean.* 1970.

Rolde, Neil. *An Illustrated History of Maine.* Augusta, Maine: Friends of the Maine State Museum, 1995

A beautifully produced volume of Maine history by one of Maine's noted authors and politicians.

Rowe, William H. *Shipbuilding Days on Casco Bay.* Portland, Maine, 1946.

Accounts of forest cutting for shipbuilding.

Rowe, William H. *The Maritime History of Maine: Three Centuries of Shipbuilding and Seafaring.* Freeport, Maine: Bond Wheelwright Co., 1948

Sequel to the volume described above.

Russell, Howard, S. *A Long Deep Furrow: Three Centuries of Farming in New England*. Hanover, N.H.: University Press of New England, 1976.

   One-of-a-kind book that is both an encyclopedic historical reference and a good treatment of the ecology of farming.

Russell, Howard S. *Indian New England Before the Mayflower*. Hanover, N.H.: University Press of New England, 1980.

   An informative account of how Indians used and altered the landscape before the arrival of the Europeans.

St. Pierre, James A. "Maine's Coastal Islands: Recreation and Conservation." August, Maine: Bureau of Parks and Recreation, 1978.

   Listing of the significant resources attached to Maine islands. Also a comprehensive bibliography.

Sanger, David. *Discovering Maine's Archaeological Heritage*. Augusta, Maine: Maine Historic Preservation Commission, 1979.

   An older classic, now somewhat dated.

Sauer, Carl O. *Northern Mists*. San Francisco: Turtle Island Foundation, 1968.

   One of the only serious histories of European exploration of the New World to research the question of whether early unrecorded fishing voyages visited the New England coast.

Schemnitz, Sanford D. "Marine Island-Mainland Movements of White-Tailed Deer." *Journal of Mammalogy,* Vol. 56, 1975.

   Documents the swimming abilities and migratory habits of white-tailed deer.

Shain, Charles and Samuela.*The Maine Reader: The Down East Experience 1614 to the Present*. Boston, MA: Houghton Mifflin Company, 1991.

   A thoroughgoing and generally delightful compilation of the best writings of natives and visitors throughout Maine's history.

Shettleworth, Earle G. Jr. *The Summer Cottages of Isleboro: 1890-1930*. Islesboro, Maine: Islesboro Historical Society, 1989.

   Definitive account of the design and architectural influences of Islesboro's great summer "cottages."

Simmons, M. H. "Report on Island Titles Along the Coast of Maine, under the Resolve of 1913, Chapter 180." Reports of the Maine Forest Commissioner. Augusta, Maine, 1914.

   Listing of the islands that were found to be in the public domain in 1913.

Simpson, Dorothy. *The Maine Islands in Story and Legend*. Philadelphia: J. B. Lippincott, 1960.

   Research material compiled from the Maine Writers Research Club.

Small, H. W. *A History of Swan's Island, Maine*. Ellsworth, Maine, 1898.

   Thorough history of the island compiled by a resident and based on many firsthand recollections of the island's old people.

Smalley, Albert J. "St. George, Maine." Typewritten manuscript.

   First-rate informative history of everything from the design of tidal sawmills to a description of the methods of quarrying granite. Available from the Maine State Library.

Smith, George Otis. "Description of the Penobscot Bay Quadrangle, Maine." Geologic Atlas Folio, 149. Washington, D. C.: Government Printing Office.

   Geological maps of Penobscot Bay islands.

Smith, John (Capt.). *A Description of New England: or the Observations and Discoveries of Captain John Smith (Admiral of that Country) in the North of America in the Year of Our Lord 1614*.

   Smith's account of his voyage to the coast of Maine, which, together with Rosier's and Levett's accounts, gives us the best look at the condition of Maine's forest and fishing resources at the time.

Snow, Edward Rowe. *The Romance of Casco Bay*. New York: Dodd, Mead & Company, 1975.

Sentimental accounts of Casco Bay island stories by a popular Boston-based writer-journalist.

Snow, Wilbert. *Collected Poems*. Middletown, Conn.: Wesleyan University Press, 1963.

Snow was born on Whitehead Island in the Muscle Ridge, where his father was part of the lifesaving-station crew. His poetry reflects a great deal of the flavor of Maine island living, from fishing to quarrying to hunting.

Spiess, Arthur E. and Mark H. Hedden. *Kidder Point and Sears Island in Prehistory.* Augusta, Maine: The Maine Historic Preservation Commission, 1983. Occasional Publications in Maine Archaeology Number Three.

The official word on the rich archeological resources of this area near the head of Penobscot Bay, which has been proposed for various industrial development projects.

Stahl, Jasper J. *History of Old Broad Bay and Waldoboro: Volume One - The Colonial and Federal Periods*. Portland, Maine: The Bond Wheelwright Company, 1956.

The definitive story of the beginnings of Waldoboro from its early German roots through the great shipbuilding era.

Sterling, Robert T. *Lighthouses of the Maine Coast*. Brattleboro, Vermont: Stephen Greene Press, 1995.

Dates of the construction (and often the automation) of every lighthouse on the Maine coast, with a short anecdote from the history of each light.

Sterling, Robert Thayer. *Lighthouse of the Maine Coast and the Men Who Keep Them*. Brattleboro, Vermont: Stephen Daye Press, 1935.

A collection of great lighthouse stories during a time when these iconic structures were still inhabited by dedicated corps of lighthouse-keeping families.

Stern, William L., ed. *Adaptive Aspects of Insular Evolution*. Bellingham, Washington: Washington State University Press, 1974.

Theoretical discussion of the effect of isolation of small gene pools.

Thaxter, Celia. *An Island Garden*. Facsimile edition re-issued, 1988 of the original book. Boston, Mass: Houghton Mifflin, 1894.

An ode to the Isles of Shoals, the summer home of Celia Thaxter who maintained a salon in her home for artists and literary personages. The illustrations by Childe Hassam are considered some of his finest impressionist works.

Tilton, Tom. *Tom Tilton, Coaster and Fisherman*. Orono, ME: University of Maine, 1982. The Northeast Folklore Society Annual, Volume 23.

Excellent folklore of a Maine man who spent his most of his life at sea in small boats.

Tinbergen, Niko. *The Herring Gull's World*. A Study of the Social Behavior of Birds. New York: Harper and Row, 1960.

Classic account of the behavior of this highly social bird by the man who helped define and later won the Nobel prize for ethnology.

Townsend, David W., and Peter F. Larsen, Eds. *The Gulf of Maine*, NOAA Coastal Ocean Program Regional Synthesis Series Numbers 1. Washington, D.C.: U.S. Department of Commerce, February 1992.

An important collection of scientific papers.

Tyler, David. Ed. *A Fishery for the Future*. Rockland, ME: Island Institute, 2009.

A publication covering the establishment of the Midcoast Fishermen's Association and their effort to establish a local brand, "Port Clyde Fresh Catch."

Varney, George J. *Gazetteer of the State of Maine*. Boston, Mass.1882.

Valuable source of odd pieces of historical data for island towns.

Vinalhaven Historical Society. *Images of America: Vinalhaven Island.* Dover, New Hampshire: Arcadia Publishing, 1997.

> Important archival photographs covering quarries, early boat building, and fishing of this Penobscot Bay island.

Vincent, Ellen. *Down on the Island, Up on the Maine: A Recollected History of South Bristol, Maine.* Gardiner, Maine: Tilbury House Publishers, 2003

> South Bristol, now connected by a swing bridge, was an island community for most of its early existence and its character and characters reflects its insular geography.

Wallace, Gordon T., and Eugenia F. Braasch, Eds. *Proceedings of the Gulf of Maine Ecosystem Dynamics,* Scientific Symposium and Workshop. RARGOM Report, 97-1. Hanover, New Hampshire: Regional Association for Research on the Gulf of Maine, 1997.

> Collection of two-dozen scientific articles on fisheries, aquaculture, oceanography, and ecology in the Gulf of Maine.

Wass, Philmore. *Lighthouse in my Life.* Camden, Maine: DownEast Books, 1987.

> A warm and spirited account of growing up on the Libby Island Light Station off Machias by a man who went on to become a university professor.

Wasson, George S. *Sailing Days on the Penobscot: The Story of the River and the Bay in the Old Days.* New York: Norton, 1932.

> Description of the coasting world in the 1870s and 1880s with an interesting chapter on Isle au Haut.

Westbrook, Perry D. *Biography of an Island: The Story of a Maine Island, Its People and their Unique Way of Life.* Cranbury, N.J.: Thomas Yoseloff, Publisher, 1958.

> Interesting account of Swan's Island in the 1950s.

Wheeler, George A., and Henry W. Wheeler. *History of Brunswick, Topsham and Harpswell.* Boston, Mass.,1878.

> Dates of early settlement for the islands on this side of Casco Bay.

Whipple, J. M. *A Geographical Review of the District of Maine.* Bangor, Maine, 1816.

> Interesting listing of the timber products that were commercially valuable at the time, with notes on their distribution.

Williamson, William D. *The History of the State of Maine 1602-1820.* 2 vols. Hallowell, Maine, 1832.

> Good coverage of the Indian Wars. Volume 1 has a section on the islands.

Winship, G. P. *Sailors' Narratives of Voyages Along the New England Coast 1524-1624.* New York, 1905.

> Descriptions and accounts of little-known voyages to Maine.

Winslow, Sidney L. *Fish Scales and Stone Chips.* Portland, Maine: Machigonne Press, 1952.

> Classic account of Vinalhaven in the first half of the 20th century written by an island son.

INDEX

hernshaw 104
Heron Island 31
Heron Neck lighthouse 22, 189
herring 95, 112, 150, 155, 156, 158
  weir 106, 154, 155
herring fishermen 111, 155
herring gulls 107, 122
hickory 75
Hildreth
  Hoddy 209, 210, 232, 233, 234
  Wooly 209, 210
Hiram 70
Hog Island (Bremen) 102, 111, 116, 117
Hog Island ledges 231
hogs 95, 117, 131
Holloway, Josh and Heidi 247, 248
Holmquist, Olaf 174
Hooper Island 78
Hopkins boatyard (Vinalhaven) 208
Hopkins, Eric 268, 269
Hopkins-Davisson, Nancy 215
hornbeam 74, 78
Hosmer, George 79, 108
House Island 29
Howard, Clarence 19
Hudson River 206
Hurricane Island 2, 8, 9, 10, 11, 12, 14, 22, 26, 27, 29, 30, 31, 34, 38, 40, 48, 49, 50, 52, 53, 54, 55, 56, 58, 59, 60, 62, 64, 68, 71, 81, 88, 97, 110, 124, 126, 127, 174, 188, 208
Hurricane Island Foundation 56
Hurricane Island Granite Co. 55, 119
Hurricane Island Outward Bound 2, 8, 9, 56
hurricanes 70, 71, 298
  1635 72
  1815 72
  1938 72
  Bob 72
  Carol 72
  Edna 72

Hugo 72
Hurricane Sound 14, 19, 46, 53, 119, 124, 208
Hussey, Arthur 49
Hussey Sound 231

I

ice bridge 131
Iceland 10, 280
Incze, Lew 176
Independent Seiners Association 157
Indian Creek 17, 76, 157
Indian Island 144
Indian summer 15
Indiana, Robert 269
Inter-Island League 263, 264
Inter-Island News 201
intertidal zone 11, 95, 127, 164, 168, 174, 240
Iron Point 213
ironwood 78
Island Aquaculture Co. 191, 267
island beaches 59
island fellows 263
Island Fellows 261, 262
Island Indicators 270, 276
Island Institute v, ix, xii, 24, 50, 119, 133, 138, 161, 176, 182, 186, 188, 189, 190, 191, 192, 193, 194, 196, 199, 202, 204, 205, 209, 218, 219, 221, 223, 224, 235, 247, 259, 261, 262, 263, 264, 265, 267, 277, 281, 285, 287, 288, 289, 296, 297, 303
Island Journal ix, 20, 144, 168, 188, 190, 217, 250
Island Partner Scholarship 259
island schools 192-193, 241 258, 259, 260, 261, 262
Island Schools Conference 193, 241
island sheep 38, 82
island wool 89
Isle au Haut 90, 108, 129, 130, 155, 167, 178, 183, 190, 195, 202, 203, 204, 205, 241, 252, 258, 261, 263, 269, 270, 271, 287

Isle des Perroques 41
Islesboro vi, 33, 60, 62, 77, 78, 94, 135, 180, 193, 198, 206, 217, 218, 219, 243, 259, 270, 271
Islesford viii, 17, 36, 193, 199, 201, 202, 205, 268
Islesford Dock Restaurant 201
Islesford Neighborhood House 202
Isles of Shoals 24, 27, 44, 140, 148, 149, 160, 268,
Isles of Springs 31

J

Japanese buyers 174
Jefferson, Thomas 89
Jefferson memorial 52
Jeffrey's Ledge 147, 156
Jericho Bay 34, 139, 142
Jewell Island 231, 232
J.O. Brown and Sons Boatyard 210, 213
joiners 79
Jonesport 26, 37, 40, 41, 49, 51, 52, 58, 182, 188, 195
Jordan 238
  John 279, 280, 281
  Nancy 238, 239
Jordan Pond 48
Jordan's Delight 98
Josselyn 154
Junger 72, 73, 205
Junk o' Pork 58

K

Katrina 287, 288
kelp beds 175, 179
Kelty 56, 57
Kennebec River 30, 48, 69, 77, 118, 228
Kent Cove 144, 162
Kent, Rockwell 268
Kermish-Allen, Ruth 219, 259
Kettle Bottom 149
Kienbusch, William 269
Kilkelly, Marge 221
killick stone 58

kilnwood 78, 79
kilnwooders 80
Kimball Island 90, 131
King, Thomas 147
King Resources 233, 234
King's Pine 69
King's Woodward 77
Kinnicutt family 219
Kirk, Raymond 81
Kittery 26, 123
knees 78
Knight, Heather 259
Knox County 203, 297, 167
Knox, Henry 35
Kox Woolen Mill 89
Kraft Food 244
Kraus, Scott 141
Kress, Steve 102, 104, 105, 111, 112, 113, 117

L

Labrador 116, 296
Labrador Current 12, 297
Labrador duck 123
Ladle (Island) 58
Lairey's Island 12
Lairey's Narrows 12
Landers John 54
Landers, Thomas 54
Lands' End 296
Lane, Fitz Hugh 268
Lane, Timothy 150
Lane and Libby Co. 150
Lane's Island 120, 208, 209
Lapland 132
larch 37
Last 20 Miles 265
Laughlin, Robert 231
LAURA B 84, 85
law of the knife 183
Lazy Gut Island 35
Leadbetter Island 52
Lend-Lease Act 232
Leonard, Ray 27, 43, 64, 66, 68, 69, 72, 73, 81, 100, 109, 110, 186, 188